The Criminology and Criminal Justice Companion

Susan Robinson

Tracy Cussen

The Criminology and Criminal Justice Companion

 palgrave

First published 2017 by
PALGRAVE

Palgrave in the UK is an imprint of Macmillan Publishers Limited, registered in England, company number 785998, of 4 Crinan Street, London, N1 9XW.

Palgrave® and Macmillan® are registered trademarks in the United States, the United Kingdom, Europe and other countries.

ISBN 978–1–352–00042–9 hardback
ISBN 978–0–230–22992–1 paperback

This book is printed on paper suitable for recycling and made from fully managed and sustained forest sources. Logging, pulping and manufacturing processes are expected to conform to the environmental regulations of the country of origin.

A catalogue record for this book is available from the British Library.

A catalog record for this book is available from the Library of Congress.

With thanks to J, always

Brief Contents

Contents

List of Tables

List of Figures

Key Criminological Research Debates

Features to Aid Your Learning

Throughout the book we have included features to assist your learning. These are:

> Are people inherently governed by their feelings or their thoughts?

Reflective Questions: for you to consider, which we hope will encourage you to think critically about what you are reading. These questions will also help you to apply what you are reading to real-life situations.

Case Studies: to provide some real examples of practical areas raised within the text.

Case Study

Remand in Custody: The New Zealand Experience

In New Zealand in 2006, the Ministry of Justice reported that only 44% of 15,143 cases involving custodial remand actually resulted in sentences of imprisonment. When analysing these cases, the New Zealand Ministry of Justice discovered that while 26% of cases were convicted but received a sentence other than imprisonment, 30% were not convicted at all despite having spent significant time in custody. The average time a person was held in custody on remand in 2006 was 51.6 days. When looking more closely at these cases, it was apparent that around 32% of these alleged offenders spent only the first quarter of their case on remand and this was while their access to bail was being resolved. It was also found that 36% spent only the final part of their case on remand while they awaited sentencing. It was reported, however, that 30% of people remanded in custody during 2006 spent their entire case in custody.

Source: NZ Ministry of Justice. 2008.

Key Criminological Research Debates

Is Criminal Behaviour the Result of Nature or Nurture?

The debate surrounding whether criminal behaviour is a result of nature (inborn) or nurture (learned) has been the focus of much research over the years. These are often framed in terms of genetic or environmental explanations of criminal behaviour. While genetic or inborn causes have been found to explain criminal behaviour in a small number of specific conditions (e.g. foetal alcohol syndrome), in the whole it has been social and environmental explanations of crime that have dominated the research (Levitt 2013). Lombroso (1876/1911) is a leading theorist in biological/genetic explanations of criminal behaviour that is a seminal work in the nature argument. His research was focused on identifying inborn physical traits in criminals that could be used to identify people who were likely to become criminal. While much of Lombroso's work has been discredited, with advances in genetics there has recently been a resurgence of interest in biological explanations of criminal behaviour, particularly genetic causes of violent and antisocial behaviour (Levitt 2013). The nature/nurture debate has been called redundant by Craddock (2011) who views the debate as unhelpful and outdated. This is due to the fact that biological explanations of crime can lead to the discrimination and mistreatment of people labelled as genetically predisposed to criminal behaviour. Levitt (2013) supports the contention that the nature/nurture debate is obsolete and argues that criminal behaviour is most likely influenced to some degree by both genetics and environment.

References

Craddock N 2011 'Horses for Courses: The Need for Pragmatism and Realism as Well as Balance and Caution: A Commentary on Angel' *Social Science and Medicine* 73 636-638

Levitt M 2013 'Perceptions of nature, nurture and behaviour' *Life, Sciences, Society and Politics* 9(13) 1-11

Lombroso C 1876/1911 *Criminal Man* Fifth Edition Translated by G Ferrero New York, USA: GP Putnam

Key Criminological Research Debates: designed to get you thinking about your values and beliefs and, through this self-reflection, how the material you are learning in your course is having an impact on these beliefs and the assumptions that naturally arise from them. We also hope some of these key discussions will help you to determine your key areas of interest in the field.

Let's Consider Boxes: similarly designed to explore your thinking and values on a particular topic.

Let's Consider!

The Differences between Comte and Hume

Table 2:2 provides you with a quick reference guide as to the main differences between Comte and Hume. While they both arise from the positivist school, they differ from each other in some important ways. Hume was fundamentally a rationalist who believed humanity is contrived in individualism whereas Comte tempered his rationalism with emotion and conceived humanity as being based in collectivism. Hume rejected `religion as redundant whereas Comte embraced it. Table 2:2 provides more detail of these differences.

Tables and Figures: provide a ready visual reference to accompany the text.

⊞ Table 2:1 Differences between Beccaria and Bentham		
	Beccaria	Bentham
Human Nature	People act out of self-interest which sometimes conflicts with the social contract.	People are motivated by seeking pleasure and avoiding pain. People are rational actors with free will.
Criminal Behaviour	The seriousness of a crime is assessed according to the harm it causes to others but all crime should attract punishment in order to produce a deterrent effect	Only criminal behaviour that produces unhappiness or pain to others should be considered worthy of punishment.

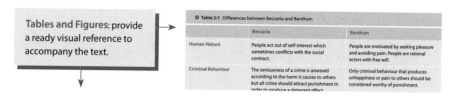

Time period	1200–1699	1700–1789	1790–1900	1900–1949	1950–present
Main influences	FEUDALISM AND RELIGION	PHILOSOPHY SOCIOLOGY	SOCIOLOGY PHILOSOPHY BIOLOGY	SOCIOLOGY PSYCHOLOGY	CONTEMPORARY CRIMINOLOGY
	SUPERSTITION	PHILOSOPHICAL NATURALISM	POSITIVISM	PSYCHOLOGICAL THEORIES	PSYCHOSOCIAL THEORIES
	Trial by ordeal	Locke	Comte	Labelling theory Social cognitive theory	Social learning theory Symbolic interactionism Differential association
	Magna Carta	Rousseau	Lombroso	Mead	Bandura Sutherland
		Kant	Spencer	Becker	Neutralisation theory
	Common law	Hume			Sykes and Matza
			TRADITIONAL CLASSICISM	NEO-CLASSICISM	CONTEMPORARY CLASSICISM
			Beccaria	Right realism	A general theory of crime
			Bentham	Hernnstein, Murray and Wilson	Gottfredson and Hirschi Rational choice theory
				Social control theory	Cornish and Clarke
				Sutherland	Routine activity theory Cohen and Felson
				SOCIOLOGICAL THEORIES	
			Durkheim	Anomie	Subcultural theory
			Functionalism	Merton	Cloward and Ohlin
			Durkheim	Strain theory	Albert Cohen
			Comte	Merton	Stanley Cohen
				Agnew	
			Critical criminology		
			Marxist criminology	Conflict theory	Left realism
			Marx	Vold	Young
				Political economy theory	Feminist criminology
				Bonger	Adler; Smart Walklate; Carlen Heidensohn Chesney-Lind

⊞ **Figure 3.1**   The development of criminological theory over time

mainly focused on the criminal justice system and its response to crime. These theorists offered guidance for how to administer punishment and developed principles for a fair and humane criminal justice system. These theories belong to the classical school of criminology. By the nineteenth century,

Emboldened Terms: terms that are defined in Chapter 8: Key Terms, Concepts and Definition are highlighted for ease of navigation.

Further Reading

Lilly, J. R., Cullen, F. T. & Ball, R. A. 2011. *Criminological Theory: Context and Consequences* (5th edition). Thousand Oaks, California: Sage Publications.
> This book provides an introduction to criminological theory and differs from most textbooks in that it does more than just describe and explain: it also engages in an analysis of theoretical perspectives. It covers both traditional and contemporary theories and is useful for developing an understanding of how criminological theory is used to shape criminal justice policy.

Newburn, T. 2016. *Criminology* (3rd edition). Basingstoke, UK: Routledge.
> This is a comprehensive textbook that covers the basics of criminology in detail. It is well illustrated and provides up-to-date examples to help the student contextualise the material. This book provides a detailed overview of criminological theory and aspects of the criminal justice system relevant to the criminology student. It draws out the key debates in the field of criminology and critically analyses them in a way that encourages the student to think more deeply about the topic or issue under discussion.

Further Reading: a list of useful readings at the end of most chapters with a short synopsis of what the book or article covers.

Biographical Synopsis

Jeremy Bentham 1748 – 1832
Jeremy Bentham was born on the 15th February 1748 in London England. Bentham was a vocal advocate of social welfare and human jurisprudence and called for the abolition of slavery, the death penalty and physical punishment. He was also known as an advocate for animal rights. He was influenced by the classical utilitarian school of thought and espoused the "greatest happiness principle" or the principle that happiness

Biographical Synopsis: related to key theorists in the field of criminology throughout the history of the discipline. This feature is restricted to Chapter 3.

Introduction

What Is *The Criminology and Criminal Justice Companion?*

The Criminology and Criminal Justice Companion is a reference book for students undertaking undergraduate studies in criminology and/ or criminal justice. It provides a user-friendly and practical introduction to, and overview of, the discipline of criminology which invariably involves the study of criminal justice and the criminal justice system. It includes a wide-ranging but brief coverage of some of the theories and issues relevant to the study of criminology and the criminal justice system. It is targeted at students who have had no prior exposure to criminology as well as those wanting a handy reference book to refer to at any point in their study journey. This companion presents some of the key criminological theories and some of the key issues that you will encounter while studying your course. It also addresses how to approach studying within the discipline of criminology and the types of careers that you can pursue with a criminology degree.

This companion usefully condenses the main theories, topics and issues and provides this information in an accessible and user-friendly format. It also provides summaries, annotations, case studies and questions to help you to apply, synthesise and remember the material you are studying. In addition to introducing some of the key theories in criminology, this book can also be used as a handy reference book to clarify concepts and terms you have trouble in understanding. *The Criminology and Criminal Justice Companion* is particularly useful in that it has an international focus which makes it relevant to students living in diverse jurisdictions.

How to Use This Book

This book is intended to be a companion to your course materials and text books. It is a quick reference guide that can help you to understand the key terms, definitions and theories presented in criminology. It should be seen as a support to your text book and study materials. It is expected that you will dip in and out of *The Criminology and Criminal Justice Companion* as you need to rather than reading it from cover to cover, although you can utilise it in this way too. You can also use it as a revision tool. The questions posed throughout the book encourage you to think more deeply about what you are reading and its application in the real world. This helps you to synthesise what you are learning. The annotated reading lists at the end of most chapters give you some ideas for further reading if you are interested in a specific topic and want to explore it in more depth.

How This Book Is Structured

This book is structured to be user friendly and to allow you to go directly to the relevant section as you need to. It is divided into seven further chapters with the information on studying at the beginning and key definitions and terms at the end. The chapters are broken up as follows:

Chapter 2 – Studying Criminology

We commence the book with a discussion of what it is to study and how you go about approaching studying in criminology. This chapter looks at the skills you need to develop to be successful in your studies and the types of criminology courses that are available around the world. It gives you an introduction to what you can expect from your criminology course and how you should approach your studies. Practical advice is given as to how you can improve your assessment outcomes and prepare for exams. Essays are a fundamental part of the assessment process in most criminology courses so we spend some time discussing how to develop your essay for the best result.

Chapter 3 – Key Theories and Theorists

In Chapter 3 we begin to get into the heart of criminology. This chapter gives you a detailed overview of the main theories relevant to the discipline and how they have evolved. Brief biographies are provided to give you some background about the key theorists themselves. We have attempted to keep the language simple for you to understand and have therefore avoided academic jargon where possible and we have used case studies to illustrate specific points. This chapter is not an exhaustive coverage of all the theories used in criminology but does provide an overview of the main theories criminologists use today.

Chapter 4 – Criminological Research

Chapter 4 is devoted to the discussion of research in criminology. It begins with a presentation of the key types of research that criminologists may undertake. Quantitative and qualitative approaches are discussed and compared and a quick reference table is provided to help you decide which would be the best approach for your project. The chapter finishes with a look at how to use existing research and the limitations of this data.

Chapter 5 – Key and Emerging Issues in Criminology

Chapter 5 provides an overview of some of the key issues and topics explored in criminology. It begins with a presentation of variables commonly linked to offending, examines victims of crime

and philosophical perspectives influencing criminological research and criminal justice practice. The chapter concludes with discussion of key areas of current and emerging interest in the criminological field.

Chapter 6 – The Criminal Justice System

Chapter 6 provides an introduction to the areas that make up the criminal justice system. It gives you an overview of the functions of this system and the key components that it comprises. Criminal justice systems have similarities and differences across jurisdictions and while we have tried to remain generic we have also pointed to some specific criminal justice examples too.

Chapter 7 – Careers in Criminology

Chapter 7 gives you a sense of what you might go on to do with your degree. It presents an overview of some of the main careers within the criminal justice system that students of criminology may be drawn to. There are a range of choices and you will need to think outside the box to ensure your chosen path matches your interests and taps into the wide variety of career options available to you. The careers presented here are not exhaustive and you are not restricted to just these areas. You will be surprised how versatile your qualification can be once you begin looking.

Chapter 8 – Key Terms, Concepts and Definitions

Chapter 8 summarises some of the key definitions, concepts and terms used in criminology and the criminal justice system. It is not exhaustive but is designed to help you refresh your understanding as you navigate this book, your course and the multitude of reference materials you will come across in your studies. Throughout the book you will find bolded and coloured words or phrases. You will find the definitions of these terms in this chapter.

Summary

This chapter has introduced you to the purpose and structure of *The Criminology and Criminal Justice Companion*. A companion book is intended to be a support tool to your textbook and the study materials provided by your lecturer. It does not provide a comprehensive coverage of theory and issues, but rather highlights and gives an overview of these. You have chosen to study an immensely interesting topic and we hope you will find it rewarding and enjoyable. We think you will find this book to be an invaluable companion, assisting you throughout your studies and beyond.

Studying Criminology

Welcome to the study of criminology. Before delving into a more detailed discussion of theory and practice in criminology it is useful for us to consider what it is you are studying. It may appear to be an obvious statement but when considering criminological study we must first give some thought to what we understand when we refer to crime. The study of crime captures the imaginations of many people because it delves into areas of human behaviour that are considered deviant or taboo. The criminal justice system may be mysterious and in some ways frightening for people who have little to do with it. The study of criminology encapsulates a range of subject areas related to crime and criminal justice including: criminal offending, the dynamics of crime, theories to explain crime, crime prevention, crime scene analysis, criminal justice careers, prisons, supervising offenders in the community and victimology. This chapter will introduce you to the study of criminology and will cover some of the basic issues involved in criminological study including the skills you will need to study at degree level.

What Is Criminology?

Criminology is a dynamic discipline that is greatly influenced by other fields such as sociology, law, psychology, philosophy, anthropology and biology. What sets criminology apart from these fields is covered in the next section, but first it is useful to know that many of these fields have a specific branch that deals with the study of crime. For example, sociology has a branch referred to as the 'sociology of deviance'; psychology has 'forensic psychology' and 'criminal profiling' and biology has 'forensic biology'.

It can be seen from this that criminology is a diverse and interesting topic and the focus of the criminologist can differ depending upon the academic discipline that has had the greatest influence on them. All of these differing approaches have one thing in common and that is the intention to understand and address crime. Put simply, then, criminology is the study of crime, the individuals who commit crime and the victims of crime as well as the study of the systems and processes in society that deal with crime.

What Sets Criminology Apart?

Criminology offers a distinctive way of looking at the world. Criminology does not just borrow from other fields, it synthesises them into a rich tapestry of scholarly knowledge that informs the understanding of crime and victimisation in society. Another thing that sets criminology apart from other academic fields is its relative youth. Although the word criminology itself was first used in the late nineteenth century, criminology was academically considered to be a sub-discipline of sociology, anthropology or psychology, while the first UK criminology department (at Cambridge) grew out of the faculty of law. It is only since the mid-twentieth century that criminology has been a degree course and the number of universities offering courses is rising. Now, out from under the shadow of sociology, criminology is growing up and maturing as theorists begin to question some of the traditional theories upon which it was built. This is not in the sense of rejecting the traditional theories but instead building on and refining them and to gain fresh insights and perspectives on crime. A criminologist will investigate an issue by using empirical research and scholarly sources and also by utilising tools such as government reports and statistics. The criminologist will consider effects on individuals, society and the system and bring all of these sources and perspectives together when enquiring into an issue. This is another way in which criminology is set apart from other disciplines which tend to favour enquiry that is restricted to sources and approaches within their own discipline. By synthesising knowledge from other disciplines the criminologist has a unique and holistic vantage point from which to view the problem of crime.

What Is Crime?

Crime is a term that is generally applied to any behaviour, by act or omission, which breaches the criminal law of a nation-state. Deviant behaviour, or that behaviour which breaches the norms of a society, may be upsetting and may even be dangerous, but unless it breaches an enacted law it is not considered to be criminal. Criminal law is generally divided into the types of crime that it relates to which usually fall into property crimes, crimes related to people, or crimes related to both. Crimes against property may include arson, burglary, vandalism and motor vehicle theft. Crimes against the person may include homicide, assault and sexual offences. Some crimes, such as armed robbery, involve both property and persons. Some crimes are related to other issues that do not fall into these three categories such as animal cruelty. There are different perspectives as to what constitutes crime (see Table 2.1) and these perspectives cover the areas of legal, moral, social, humanist and socially constructed.

You will be able to see how these different perspectives influence the thinking of key theorists in criminology in Chapter 3 where we discuss criminological theory. However, firstly, we need to consider crime in context. As you will discover, crime is contextual and the time, place and audience all have a role in how crime is perceived and responded to.

Crime in Context

When considering context the first thing to keep in mind is that crime is best understood in relation to the historical time frame and the culture and society in which it occurs. Historically we have several examples of laws that have been enacted to address a perceived problem and later repealed. Crime is also contextual in relation to the religious and moral norms of the time. For example, prior to 1967 the practice of homosexual behaviour was illegal in England, Wales and Scotland and people could be arrested and prosecuted for engaging in homosexual acts. Laws were amended in England, Scotland and Wales but it remained illegal in Ireland until 1982. It is no longer illegal in the United Kingdom to engage in homosexual acts and it would be frowned upon today if people were arrested because of their sexual preference. Moral panics can be created by politicians, the media and special interest groups in relation to certain social problems, behaviour or groups of people seen to behave differently to the norm. *See Chapter 3: Key Theories and Theorists.*

▣ Table 2.1 Perspectives on crime	
Legalistic	Behaviour that breaches the criminal code.
Moralistic	Behaviour that offends the generally accepted rules of right and wrong and may incur stigma, shaming or some other social punishment (it may be, but is not always, included in criminal law).
Socialistic	Behaviour that breaches social norms (and may include breaking the law).
Humanistic	Behaviour of individual people, organisations or states that impedes or denies basic human rights (may not be included in criminal law).
Socially constructed	Behaviour that is defined as criminal by the powerful who control the law-making and law-enforcement functions in society.

Why Study Criminology?

The study of criminology is important if we are to understand why people engage in criminal behaviour and what can be done to reduce crime or mitigate its impact. Law and order is important in any society as it helps to keep social order which means providing a safe, organised and civilised way in which people can coexist. Without it there would be anarchy and social order would disintegrate. It is social order that allows us to live together in the same community without hurting each other or impinging on the rights of others. Criminologists undertake research and advance theories in order to better understand criminal behaviour and patterns of crime. They have adopted methods of study from other disciplines such as biological sciences but **criminological research** methods mainly derive from the social and behavioural sciences. Criminological research and the advancement of criminological theory lead to the development of competing viewpoints which is important in the study of criminology because it encourages debate about topical issues related to the nature, extent, causes and prevention of crime.

What to Expect From Your Criminology/Criminal Justice Course

You may find that there are differences in criminology courses across universities but while the units, modules and subjects may differ, most will share common aspects in the type of areas that are studied. In your first year you will likely undertake several foundation courses that will introduce you to the theories underpinning criminology before you examine the systems, specific offences or people involved. The following are some modules and subject areas that you may encounter in a criminology and criminal justice course.

Criminological Theory

All criminology courses will have at least one module that covers criminological theory. This is an important component of the criminology course and in most cases will take the student through a journey that begins with the classical theorists and ends with the modern theorists. The degree to which the theory is studied will depend upon the level of the course and the year in which it is applied. For example, first year undergraduate modules will simply introduce the theory, whereas third year undergraduate modules will deal with the theory in a more in-depth and advanced way. Criminological theory provides the student with a way in which to understand and conceptualise crime and the formalised responses to it. By studying criminological theory, the student will be exposed to new ways of thinking and will gain a better understanding of different perspectives. This exposure allows students to develop a balanced approach that leads to increased respect and tolerance of different viewpoints related to crime and crime control. *See **Chapter 3: Key Theories and Theorists**.*

Sociology of Deviance

The sociology of deviance underpins criminology. This type of module brings students to an understanding of the broader sociological concepts that are the foundations for criminological theory. The concepts of deviance, conformity and control constitute a trilogy of the main abstract concepts that lead criminologists to the development of theory. This subject is the starting point for developing the thought process required to be an effective criminologist. It begins with the question: 'What is it that makes people conform to society's rules?' It is just as important to understand what makes people obey the rules as it is to understand what makes them likely to deviate from them. Inherent in this is an examination of social control and who makes and benefits from the rules and the context in which the rules are made and enforced.

Criminological Research Methods

All criminology undergraduate courses will have a module related to research as this is an important topic for the student to cover. Developing research skills is not only an advantage for a criminologist; it is essential. These skills include doing research, and the module will usually involve some sort of research project. They also include being able to interpret existing research and officially collected statistics. Criminologists rely on many sources of statistical data, not just those they collect themselves. It is therefore important that criminology students learn how to read official statistics and understand the limitations inherent in their collation and in regard to the definitions used. Issues such as research ethics will be covered in this module. See *Chapter 4: Criminological Research*.

The Criminal Justice System

Most criminology courses will include a study of the criminal justice system. Such a module will include a study of the police, adult prisons, adult community corrections, the courts and juvenile justice. This subject may vary according to the jurisdiction in which the course is studied as the administration of justice differs from country to country. The study of the criminal justice system covers the administrative processes involved in the operation of the justice system and the people who work within it. Some courses will focus specifically on aspects of sectors within the criminal justice system such as policing, penology and punishment. See *Chapter 6: The Criminal Justice System*.

Social Policy and Legislation

In many criminology and criminal justice courses there will be a subject that covers how the government works, and how legislation and public policy are developed. The processes involved in these areas are of interest to criminology but so is the end product, which is the implementation of legislation and public policy that directly influences the criminal justice system. Privatisation of the criminal justice system is something that is being seen more frequently around the world, but most of the responsibility for the criminal justice system lies with the government. It is therefore important for the criminology student to understand the workings of government and the political influences that impact on the criminal justice

system. It is also important to understand how legislation works together in the criminal justice system because there are many laws that must be considered in unison in order for the system to work effectively. See *Privatisation (Chapter 6); Policy Development Officer (Chapter 7)*.

Crime Prevention

In any criminology course, there will be one or more modules that cover the nature of crime and approaches to crime prevention. Such a topic provides the student with a holistic understanding of crime types and the various approaches to crime prevention. In most cases, this module will encourage the student to apply the criminological theory to practice situations. Such a subject intellectually prepares the criminology student for working in the criminal justice system by demonstrating how the theories are applied. Differences associated with gender, age and culture are usually explored in a module such as this but can also be studied in a separate, specially designed module. See *Situational Crime Prevention (Chapter 3); Gender and Crime (Chapter 5); Race and Crime (Chapter 5)*.

Specialist Elective Options

Sometimes criminology courses will have set programmes of study, but most large universities will offer elective options that allow the student to be able to tailor their degree to suit the area in which they intend to work. Examples of specialist electives within criminology might include: victimology; violent crime; youth justice; and international or global crimes. Students are able to choose electives that interest them or which they need in order to get into a specialist area when they are ready to seek employment. See *Victims and the Justice System (Chapter 5); Violent Crime* (Chapter 5*); Juvenile Justice (Chapter 6)*.

Studying Criminology

Studying criminology is much the same as studying any academic subject at degree level. It requires commitment, patience and determination

Table 2.2 What skills do I need?		
Organisation	**Research**	**Academic**
Time management Study schedules	Getting the most from the library Using the internet Data literacy	Reading skills Writing skills Referencing Critical thinking
Memory	**Presentations**	**Computer**
Note-taking Retention Revision Recall – examinations	Preparation Public speaking	Word processing Spreadsheet Presentation software Online meetings

and a range of skills such as critical thinking, written communication, organisation and time management. Table 2.2 summarises some of the key skills you need for studying at this level.

There are also a range of additional factors that will assist you in studying in this discipline including knowing how to reference your work correctly and how to use the library to maximise the effectiveness of your research time, all of which we discuss in this chapter. We have also included references to several study guides at the end of this chapter that you might find useful for more in-depth coverage of these topics.

At the university level you are expected to be an independent learner. This means being ready to learn, setting your own goals and actively engaging in the learning process. Being an independent learner does not, however, mean that you are on your own. In addition to the material you review in this book and any materials your lecturer may provide, you should seek out information from librarians at your university. Most universities have study guide aids to help you navigate the expectations of your institution and online e-learning activities to help you reinforce the knowledge and practise the skills. In this chapter we start out with the most important skill you will develop – critical thinking. We then describe some of the basic skills that will help you succeed such as time management, reading and note-taking, lectures, seminar discussions and presentations, and some general research skills. Finally we provide some information on

two of the key assessments you'll be exposed to: academic writing and exams.

Critical Thinking

Critical thinking is a process which is essentially just thinking carefully and methodically when interpreting information. You need to apply a fair amount of scepticism to everything you read and hear and keep asking yourself: 'How do I know?' Before we get into more specifics it is a good idea to know why critical thinking is so important. Basically, if we do not teach ourselves the habit of thinking critically we will be more likely to make decisions or form arguments that are biased, uninformed or simply wrong. When we refer to an 'argument' we do not mean a fight. We mean giving reasons for an opinion or conclusion or justifying claims. What we want is to improve our thinking, ensuring it is based on good information that we have questioned so that when we write a paper or give a presentation or just present an idea it is well thought out, persuasive and stands up to the scrutiny of others. In this section we want to identify some of the key aspects of critical thinking that you should be aware of which include: being aware of bias, ways to improve your thinking, and how to apply critical thinking. A very thorough guide to critical thinking is *Critical Thinking Skills: Developing Effective Analysis and Argument* by Stella Cottrell (2011) and if you only read one book on the topic, this should be it.

Being Aware of Bias

When thinking critically one of the key things to avoid is bias. It is important to be aware of our own biases and those of others. Human beings have a tendency to accept things when spoken from authority so you need to be aware of that. Your lecturers are the authority in the classroom and, as knowledgeable as they are, they expect you to verify what they are telling you and think for yourself. Two other biases to be aware of are what are referred to as the familiarity bias (or availability heuristic) and confirmation bias. The familiarity bias essentially is an assumption that if we can think of an example of something, then that thing must be common or representative. It also gives weight to events that are recent, personal and emotional. So, for example we might read in the newspaper about a number of burglaries and think the crime rate is increasing or become worried and afraid.

Confirmation bias is when we accept information and events that support our beliefs and interpret them positively. We all do it and more often than we like to admit. But you need to be aware of it so that when you read a study and it concludes something you believe you remember to ask yourself: 'But what evidence does that have?' For example, you might think that drug and alcohol misuse is a leading cause of crime. You might read some media reports about a case that describe the offender as intoxicated at the time of the offence. Confirmation bias may lead you to think the intoxication was the reason the crime was committed. But unless we look further into the facts of the case we really can't know.

Ways to Improve Thinking

Making effort to improve your thinking is necessary to develop critical thinking skills. In this section we highlight three areas to concentrate on to improve your thinking – being reflective, alert and inquisitive.

Be Reflective

One of the key ways we improve our thinking is reflecting on how we think which includes not only considering our own biases but also the influences on our thinking. All of us have a world view. This is influenced by upbringing, the views of parents, siblings, friends and the culture in which we live. It is also constantly being influenced by our adult experiences and the events that occur in the world around us. Your world view may be strengthened by studying criminology but it may also be challenged by exposure to viewing things from a different perspective. This is good. As a criminologist you need to be able to consider different perspectives and be willing to change your own assumptions if the evidence is telling you your assumptions are not correct. You might start by considering what influences your own thinking.

Be Alert

As critical thinkers we also need to be alert to vague thinking and language. Vague thinking and language are found where the meaning isn't clear. One thing you can do to be more alert to your own vague thinking is to improve your attention and concentration by focusing on one thing at a time. When you are ready to make your points, verbally or in writing, provide examples so that your audience has a good understanding of what you mean. Vague thinking is also often reflected in the use of vague or ambiguous language. Often it is important for an author to qualify his or her statements in some way so as not to mislead the reader. Just remember to watch out for the use of words that might suggest the author is not sure or that a claim doesn't have sufficient evidence or has been accepted without question.

Be Inquisitive

It is important to be inquisitive and to question how we conceptualise or understand things to be. In order to avoid making assumptions we need to ask questions and constantly clarify our position and that of others. Each of us has limited knowledge and a limited perspective. In fact both our knowledge and perspective may be limited in ways we are not aware of. We simply don't know what we don't know. It is important therefore to be curious and test our thinking with others. In this way we might be introduced to, or seek out, new reading material and additional perspectives that we would not normally have chosen to read but which will allow us to more broadly understand issues and make better and more persuasive arguments, both written and orally. It's okay to be uncertain and it's also okay to change our minds.

Applying Critical Thinking

At degree level you are expected to critically consider the information you are learning and reading rather than just accepting it at face value. As we said at the beginning of this section, critical thinking is a process so once you have identified what you are reading, writing or meant to be thinking about it is a good idea to examine your own assumptions. Once you have established what you think about a topic you can begin to consider the opinions of others and make judgements about the claims they are making. Again, it is not easy but with time and practice you will improve. In Figure 2.1 we have compiled, based on information gained from a range of sources, a summary of the steps you need to take to improve your critical thinking.

Exercising critical thinking	
Step 1:	Define the topic
Step 2:	List what you already know about the topic
Step 3:	Recognise the opinions and biases you already have about the topic
Step 4:	Identify the resources available to you for researching the topic
Step 5:	Gather evidence
Step 6:	Use the facts to accept or reject the opinions presented in source materials and those based on your own beliefs

◻ **Figure 2.1** Steps to critical thinking

Time Management and Organisational Skills

Besides critical thinking skills, time management and organisational skills are very important when you are studying. As we have already mentioned, studying at degree level means self-directed study. Ultimately you are responsible for your own time management so it pays to consciously develop skills in this area. Most students think they use their time effectively but this is not always the case. In fact Alan Clarke points out, 'there is often a considerable difference between how you think you use your time and how you actually do' (Clarke 2008:176). Your lecturers will give you assignments with deadlines and you may find that your course timetable leaves you with free time between classes. It will be up to you to keep on top of what you need to do and where you need to be. Attention to how you organise your time can really help you get on the front foot for your studies and stay there. There are lots of resources out there to help you. A good place to start is at your university library or the university's online resources. These will give you a perspective on time management directly related to studying. But don't forget that time management is an important skill in everyday life. Blogs such as Time Management Ninja (https://timemanagementninja.com) offer valuable advice to get you motivated about being effective with your time. In the remainder of this section we will identify the importance of planning and prioritisation and your study environment.

Planning and Prioritisation

One key to effective time management is good planning that allows you to prioritise everything you need to do. There are a lot of different ways to approach this and it will be up to you to figure out what works best for you. Something that will help you get organised is spending some time thinking about your behaviour. Ask yourself how you spend your time every day. What commitments do you have (for example work, family and recreational activities)? You will want to have some balance in your life but ultimately you also need to make sure you have time to study and complete assignments. When you commence your course you need to find out what the deadlines are and ensure you record these in a diary or electronic calendar so you don't forget. Count out the weeks leading up to when an assignment is due and plan your study schedule to ensure you can fit the commitments in. You will also need to set aside blocks of time when you can review material and study. The duration of these blocks of time may differ depending on how difficult you are finding the course content, whether you are reviewing for an exam or whether you are reading assigned material. Criminology is a subject that will challenge your normal way of thinking. It covers many theorists that you have probably not had exposure to prior to studying this course, so you need to allow time to become familiar with the theories and concepts that are important to criminological thought.

Many students find it really useful to have multiple plans – plans that cover daily tasks as well as plans that cover medium- and long-term priorities (see examples in Table 2.3). You might want to develop a term or semester plan that lists all assignments and tests, including their due dates, as well as any other commitments you have over the time period. From there you may

Table 2.3 Example study plans

Short-term plan	Long-term plan
Purpose: revision for exam 1, criminological theory.	**Purpose:** semester study schedule, course 001, criminological theory.
Goal: identify your personal objective, for example the grade you would like to achieve.	**Goal:** identify your personal objective, for example submission of all assignments on time.
Key dates: record exam date and time.	**Key dates:** record all exam and assignment dates as well as dates and times of classes and/or tutorials.
Daily plan: record material to review each day in preparation for the exam as well as other personal obligations.	**Weekly plan:** record key tasks for the duration of the semester including key personal obligations and any conflicts with other courses (for example, exams for two courses on the same day).
Establish time frames: record the length of time you plan to devote to each activity in your plan.	**Establish time frames:** record the length of time you plan to devote to each activity in your plan.
Prioritise activities under your plan: number each activity in order of importance.	**Prioritise activities under your plan:** number each activity in order of importance, be prepared to amend this over time – some tasks will be more difficult than others so you may need to start them earlier or leave time for additional help.
Activities not completed, by day: update your plan daily noting anything you were unable to complete from a previous day.	**Activities not completed, by week:** update your plan weekly noting anything you were unable to complete from a previous week and any new tasks/activities that have emerged.
Results and achievements: did you achieve what you set out to achieve? Why/why not? Record what you achieved against your purpose and goal and use this to help you in future short-term planning.	**Results and achievements:** did you achieve what you set out to achieve? Why/why not? Record what you achieve on a weekly basis to help you stay on track and make modifications to your plan as necessary. At the end of the semester record your overall results against your purpose and goal and use this to help you in future planning.

develop a weekly schedule that records each class you have to attend and any assignments due or exams to take as well as when you plan to study. A daily schedule will focus your attention on immediate priorities and give you a sense of accomplishment as you complete the tasks. Just remember to carry over any tasks you didn't complete to the next day's plan. Part of planning your study schedule may include working out what tasks might be difficult and which are more easily achieved. This, along with knowing the deadlines will help you to prioritise what you need to do. It is usually a good idea to work on the difficult stuff first. Not only will you need more time to complete difficult tasks but you might also find that you are more focused. It can, however, sometimes be good to do smaller tasks to get a sense of achievement early. The important thing is to have a clear plan and to be mindful of the deadlines.

Your Study Environment

Another key aspect of making effective use of your time is paying attention to your study environment. Again, this is a personal choice but something that is well worth considering.

Your study environment includes all the conditions that assist you to do your best work. You will want to create an environment that is free from distractions so that you can concentrate. You may find that you are more attentive in the mornings, or at night. You may require regular breaks or exercise to keep your focus. You may find that you write best in your own room, while you find reading is best done in the library. You may require silence when reading but find background music is helpful when you write. The important thing is to be flexible and find the circumstances or conditions that work well for you. Importantly, developing good time management and organisational skills takes time. Try not to stress about it. You may have the best intentions of completing your assignments early and a good plan in place to achieve that but sometimes it just won't be feasible. The important thing

is to learn from what went wrong so you can avoid similar issues or mistakes in the future. And give yourself a break. Studying is hard and making it a success takes a lot of work. Make sure you acknowledge your accomplishments along the way.

Reading and Note-Taking

When we are studying we tend to focus on the assessment items – the exams and essays we need to complete. The day-to-day attendance at lectures and the review of course materials and readings can be taken for granted. Learning to effectively read and take notes will help you to get the most from those activities and to achieve good results in your assessments. In addition to online reference materials available from your university you might want to purchase a book on reading and note-taking such as Jeanne Godfrey's *Reading and Making Notes* (2014). This is a handy pocket book reference source that can act as a quick reference to reinforce the development of good habits.

Reading

University courses involve a lot of reading. You will be expected to read material to prepare for lectures or tutorials and your assignments will require you to conduct research. Most courses will have a reading list. Some of these readings will be required and you should read them all as they will likely contain necessary background information or key concepts you need to become familiar with. You may also be tested on your comprehension of these materials. Other readings may be recommended and while the more you read the more you will know, in order to effectively manage your time you may need to be selective about which of these recommended readings you actually complete.

At university you need to read with a purpose in mind. This helps you to make use of your time but also focusses your attention on the task. It's a good idea to ask yourself what you are trying to get from the reading. Are you trying to understand concepts and ideas, looking for specific information or familiarising yourself with a particular topic? Having the purpose in mind will target your attention to selecting what you need to read as well as how much of it. If your purpose, for example, is to identify what happened on a specific date and who was involved you may only need to read enough to answer those questions. If you are trying to understand concepts you may need to read more widely, from a number of sources, to understand different perspectives. Regardless of your purpose you are likely to need to take some notes (see the next section on note-taking).

Reading is an area where you will apply your critical thinking skills so it is a good idea to think about what you already know before you start reading. If you are reading to understand something you may want to record your assumptions and make a list of questions you want to answer from your reading. If the material is difficult it's important to be prepared to read it twice or to first break the reading down into manageable portions, moving on only when you feel comfortable that you have understood the content.

Note-Taking

(From lectures, online subject sites and books)

Note-taking is a useful skill to develop as it will greatly assist your comprehension and retention of the material you are studying. As previously mentioned, in a course such as criminology, you are likely to come across to a lot of information that you have never had exposure to before including new terms, concepts and theories. In addition to this you will be encouraged to think differently about day-to-day experiences and social systems you had once taken for granted. Only exceptional people can retain all that new knowledge without some help. Note-taking provides you with a means of keeping track of the new knowledge you are acquiring and gives you a method of being able to find the information quickly when you need it for essay writing or when engaged in discussions such as in tutorial workshops. Good notes will also help you when it is time to revise for exams.

There are many methods of taking notes. You might want to try different methods and see what works best for you. For example, you might want to use an electronic recorder to record lectures and just jot down key points using pen and paper. Always get permission from the speaker before you make a recording. You might prefer to take all your notes using pen and paper or directly onto a tablet, laptop or electronic notebook. It is useful to have some method of being able to retrieve the information you write down, such as having separate notebooks for different subjects or separate folders on your electronic drive. If using electronic tools backing up your work is important.

Whatever system you use there are some key ideas that will help support effective note-taking. Keep in mind that note-taking during a lecture is going to be different from note-taking while reading. In a lecture information is coming at you and you cannot pause. Make sure you ask clarifying questions if something is confusing or unclear so that your notes do not reflect incorrect information. When making notes from written material it is usually best to read the material first before taking notes. This allows you to focus on understanding the material and generally means you only record the most relevant information. Whether you are taking notes from lectures or from written material it is important to summarise the information in some fashion. You will want to record the topic, main issues presented, any conclusions reached and the evidence presented that supports or detracts from the conclusions. You'll also want to record your own thoughts.

Importantly you should always try to use your own words or paraphrase what has been said or is on the written page. If you are making notes from written material you'll need to record the bibliographical information (*see **Referencing***). If you decide to note a direct quotation make sure you use quotation marks and note the page number. If you rely on your notes later when drafting an essay you will need these references to ensure you avoid plagiarism and can readily reference the source. It is really hard to go back through a book to try to find a page number for a quotation unless you were using an e-book with a quick search function. Although it is a good idea to review your notes regularly you may find that, with the passage of time, you don't remember everything. Be careful to use abbreviations that you understand and that you will recall later. Your notes need to be able to be understood so that you can make use of them.

Seminar Discussions and Presentations

As a university student you will sometimes be asked to prepare and present a seminar or tutorial to your peers. This allows you to research a particular topic and test out your understanding, viewpoint and arguments in a peer review environment. These seminars and tutorial discussions are designed to provide you with confidence in public speaking and feedback on your work. They also allow you to test your views in an academic environment. Some of these seminars and tutorial presentations will be assessed and others will be held just for the purpose of developing the skills in critically discussing issues and presenting information to an audience. In such an environment it is important to be respectful of other people's opinions and to be open to receiving alternative views on your work. Not everyone will agree with you and some people may have quite interesting and alternative perspectives on your topic. By treating this as a learning process you will strengthen your own work because you can use the feedback from seminars and discussions when writing your essays to develop the counter arguments which you need to include when critically analysing the topic.

Group and Team Work

Some universities use group work and team work as methods of learning. Group work and team work skills are important skills for criminal justice students to learn because collaboration between different departments, sectors, states, provinces and/or council areas are important

to the successful functioning of the criminal justice system. Criminologists will often work as part of a multidisciplinary team and will from time to time be called upon to speak to the media, at a conference or at a public gathering. Public speaking skills will also be useful as a criminologist when you need to advocate for research funding or for practical outcomes in the community.

Throughout your studies you may be asked to participate in group or team work in a number of ways, including group discussions in lectures or tutorials, or more formally as part of a project or to prepare a report. Working in groups has a number of strengths but can also present challenges. Some of the strengths of group work include being exposed to multiple points of view on a topic. Group work might also mean that you have responsibility for just one part of a project which could give you additional time for other aspects of your studies.

Working in groups can also be difficult, particularly if everyone doesn't contribute equally. It's important to set clear expectations on group behaviour right at the beginning. These expectations may include: defining the role and responsibilities of each member of the group; setting deadlines for tasks; establishing progress review points; and keeping records of meetings and agreed actions. Your university internet site will likely have some advice on how to get the most from group activities (see, for example, study advice from the University of Reading: www.reading.ac.uk/internal/studyadvice/ StudyResources/Seminars/sta-groupwork.aspx).

Research Skills

Research skills are very important to university-level study and developing good research skills will make writing your essays and preparing for oral presentations much easier. Broad research that seeks to discover the varied perspectives on a topic provides a good foundation for developing critical thinking and being able to critically analyse specific issues and theoretical works. We discuss criminological research in more depth in Chapter 4. In this chapter we highlight three general research skills (using the library, using the internet and building data literacy) to get you started.

Using the Library

As we have established, research skills are important to every student and using the library to enhance studying is a skill set that every student needs to have. Most university libraries will offer tours and information sessions. It is important that you take the time to let the information specialists show you their world so that you can understand all of the resources available to you. Most libraries today also have an online presence, which means that they can be accessed via the internet. Library catalogues can therefore be found via an internal computer system at the library or online via a public internet portal or the university's library 'intranet' system where students can log on using designated user IDs and passwords. See Figure 2.2 for information on the library catalogue system.

The library will provide you with access to peer-reviewed books and journal articles. Peer review means that these sources have been examined, usually by at least two, and sometimes more, 'experts' on the topic before they are published. Books will provide in-depth coverage of the topic, while journal articles may only go into detail about a specific aspect of the topic. It is useful, when researching books and journal articles in the library, to read the abstract of journal articles or the contents page of books to establish if they cover the topics that you are

1. Look at the **contents page** – does it cover the areas you are interested in?
2. If the book has an **index** review it – how well does it cover your topic?
3. Look at the **publication date** – is it a recent publication? (You don't want books that are too old unless your topic requires you to consider established or classical theorists).
4. Look at **the author** – is he or she on your course reading list? Is the author well known in the field? If not, does the author present a new or different perspective on the issue?

▣ Figure 2.3   Choosing a book

interested in researching. Titles can sometimes be deceiving in regard to what is actually included in the content of the book or article. Doing this will save you a lot of time later on (see Figure 2.3).

 What is the benefit to you of reading the abstracts of journal articles or the contents page of a book?

The library will also hold non-peer-reviewed material or 'grey literature' such as government reports. Just because these reports are not peer reviewed doesn't mean the information isn't credible. Grey literature can be very valuable in understanding the operations of a system, such as how police conduct their work, and provide useful up-to-date statistics, for example the current crime rate in a specific jurisdiction. Making good use of the library and all of its resources will help you to obtain the information you need to support your studies and give you access to the range of perspectives on a topic to help your critical thinking.

Using the Internet

E-learning is the use of information technologies such as the internet, podcasts, blogs and other computer-based technologies for educational purposes. Many people today utilise information technologies for social networking and computer-based education is an extended usage of an already

Online or hard copy catalogue searches will allow the student to search using one or more of the following fields:

- author
- title
- ISBN or ISSN
- subject
- keywords

▣ Figure 2.2   Library catalogue searches

□ Table 2.4 Characteristics of successful e-learners

Successful e-learners tend to have the following characteristics:	
Confidence	They have confidence in themselves as independent learners.
Competency	They are competent with computer technology.
Positivity	They have a positive attitude to learning.
Motivation	They are self-motivated to study.
Communication	They have effective communication skills.
Inquisitiveness	They ask questions when they need to.
Self-discipline	They are self-disciplined towards their studies.

accepted and widely used forum. Table 2.4 brings together the key characteristics that are associated with successful e-learning. The internet provides access to a range of information and sources of research that criminology students can use to enhance their study.

Many publishers of criminology and criminal justice text books offer their books in hard copy and electronic copy formats. If you are required to purchase a textbook for your course, it is worth checking the publisher's website to see if you can obtain an electronic copy if you are unable to find a hard copy to purchase or if you prefer to have it in that format. With so much information at your fingertips on the internet, it may be tempting to ignore hard copy academic sources of information when researching such as books or rely on Google Scholar to assist you in finding journal articles rather than your library's databases. Keep in mind, however, that only your library's database will have more comprehensive sources of academic texts so you should always check the library as well. Although you always need to think about the credibility of any source, use of the internet presents some additional challenges.

The reason for additional caution when using the internet is that you are accessing a much broader range of information from various sources and in a very short space of time. When researching on the internet you may discover unreliable non-academic websites and blogs. Some of these sites can be interesting but are not reliable in terms of the accuracy of the information contained on them and may not be considered suitable sources in terms of academic scholarship. It is important that the criminology student is discriminating about the sites that they rely on for academic purposes. As a general rule you would not use unreliable websites as sources of information, especially for the purposes of referencing in your essays. In addition to evaluating the reliability of websites you should also check the requirements of your university, school and in particular your lecturer.

 Why should you avoid using unreliable websites as reference sources in your essays?

Building Data Literacy

Building your data literacy is an important skill to develop early in your criminology studies. Data literacy is important because criminology draws heavily on the presentation of both qualitative and quantitative data, including statistics (see *Chapter 4: Criminological Research*). As a result, the sooner you are able to read data, and be discerning about what it means, the better. In addition, using visual graphics of data in presentations and assignments can be a good way to present complex information. There are a number of web-based videos available to help you understand and evaluate number-based claims in the media and in written material as well as understand basic statements and claims being made involving rates and percentages. One good site is www.gapminder.org which has several videos by Professor Hans Rosling, a Swedish statistician and public speaker, who provides insight into the power of understanding statistics.

Key Criminological Research Debates

Is there a case for not using internet sources in academia?

The internet has revolutionised the way in which students study and do research but is it okay to rely on the internet for academic information? The internet is fast and efficient and provides a readily accessible array of information. The question is, how does a student know if they can trust this information? Unreliable websites may be popular but are not well received in academia because the information they contain is either not objective or it cannot be verified. Unreliable sites include those sites where authorship is uncertain, that do not have publication dates or that have unsupported opinions about the topic. In criminology that includes unsupported opinions about crime and the criminal justice system. The Yale Center for Teaching and Learning (2015) suggests that scholarly sources are 'those that have been approved by a group with recognised expertise in the field under discussion' and these can include internet-sourced information. Tertiary education requires that students develop sound academic or scholarly skills and this includes being able to discern the reliability of sources used in academic writing. This doesn't, however, mean that all non-academic sources are forbidden; to the contrary, government reports, newspaper articles and reliable internet websites can be used but they must be able to be locatable by a person who reads an essay and they must be reliable. The nature of the assignment and the requirements of the discipline and institution will tell the student if non-academic sources are appropriate to be used in their course (Monash University 2016). As with most universities, the University of Illinois (2016) allows the use of reliable internet sources but advises that students evaluate the reliability of an internet source by asking the following questions:

How did you find the page?
What is the site domain?
What is the authority of the page?
Is the information accurate and objective?
Is the page current?

The answers to these questions should guide the student to determine whether or not a particular internet source is sufficiently reliable to use in their academic work.

Academic Writing

At some point you will be required to write a report or essay, usually based on topics selected by your lecturer, that are relevant to the course you are studying. This can be a bit daunting, especially if you haven't done it before or if it has been a while since you last studied. Essay writing gives you the chance to demonstrate in-depth knowledge about a topic and it lets you express your thoughts in a logical detailed way. It will also test your time management skills. There are three stages in the process of preparing an essay: planning, gathering and using information, and writing. We'll walk you through each of these stages and signpost reference materials you can explore to help you with your assignments.

Planning

The first step in preparing your assignment is planning. Before commencing an essay you need to organise your thoughts and plan how you will approach the paper. This means looking at the requirements, including the essay question, word length and due date, so that you can be realistic about what you will need to do to complete and submit the assignment on time. First you need to consider the essay question carefully. What does it mean and what are you being asked to do? Each word in the question is important. It will not only reveal to you the topic but also give you some instruction and may also contain limitations on the scope. Take, for example, the differences in the following tasks:

(1) <u>Describe</u> the influence of criminological theory on the criminal justice system;
(2) <u>Assess</u> the influence of criminological theory on the criminal justice system; or
(3) 'Criminological theory has had considerable influence on the criminal justice system': <u>Analyse and discuss</u> this statement.

 Why is it important to be organised and to plan ahead for your essay?

Analysing the Question

The topic generally looks the same for each of these essay questions – criminological theory and its influence on the criminal justice system – but each has different instructions that require you to approach the essay in different ways. In question 1 you are being asked to provide a description only, which might mean that you select some of the key areas where theory influences the system. In question 2 you are being asked to assess that influence, which will require an argument – does theory influence the system? In what ways? You'll need to apply your critical thinking skills to develop your opinions and conclusion. In question 3 you are being told what the position is and asked to discuss it. This question is actually somewhat similar to question 2, as you will need an argument either agreeing or disagreeing with the statement and then backing up your point of view with your evidence. But, because the question is asking you to discuss the position you will need to cover more material from both sides of the argument. Hopefully you can see why carefully examining the question is important. If you fail to do so you might gather the wrong information for

your purpose. You may come across other essay questions that ask you to 'analyse', 'evaluate' or 'debate', 'comment on' or 'consider' a topic. If you are to evaluate or analyse a topic you will need to have much more evidence to support your argument than if you are simply commenting on or discussing it (Peck and Coyle 2005). Other essay questions may simply ask how, what, where or when without specifying how you should approach the writing of the essay. The important thing to remember is to read the question carefully so you can extract all of the elements. There are lots of useful websites that can help. For example, www.learnhigher.ac.uk/writing-for-university has a lot of useful material to help you plan and organise your essay writing.

During your planning you will have identified what you are being asked to do and you can start to organise your thoughts, including what you know already and what you need to find out. Take, for example, the assignment: '*Assess the importance of drug and alcohol treatment to the rehabilitation of female offenders in the United States*'. The topic in this question is drug and alcohol treatment. Your instruction is to assess its importance and you are being asked to limit your scope to female offenders in the US only. We will come back to this example in the information gathering and writing sections that follow. It is really important that you start with your own ideas. If you write them down you will be aware of them as you read and research to clarify if others agree with you, and more importantly why they do not.

Information Gathering

When you gather information, just like when you read, it should be for a purpose and it should be relevant. You need to identify the key bits of information you need to know in order to answer the research question. Selecting the information you need is not only about answering the question. You also need to pay some attention to the source of the material. You will mostly use books and journal articles, but there may also be statistics or specific procedural information in government reports. It is a good idea to look at primary source material when it is available. Primary source material is the original piece of work, whether that is a book or a journal article. Academics are always referencing other work but when they do they are using it for their own purposes and unless you check the original source you won't know whether this secondary source interpretation is accurate.

Let's look at our essay question from the last section, '*Assess the importance of drug and alcohol treatment to the rehabilitation of female offenders in the United States*', and identify some of the information that might need to be gathered and some sources for that information. In the first instance you will want to identify the extent of the problem so you might try looking for available statistics on the prevalence of alcohol and drug use in offending by women in the US. Are the offences women are committing directly linked to substances such as selling, manufacturing or trafficking in drugs, or are they related, for example, to committing assaults while intoxicated? You might also want to examine whether women in the US are more or less likely than women in other jurisdictions to be found guilty of offences linked to substance misuse so you can determine whether you think treatment is particularly important to your subject population. To answer these questions you'll want to look for recent statistics, often from government websites or recent journal articles.

Next you might want to examine some theory and identify what, if any, programmes and treatments are available to women offenders either in prison or in the community. Have there been any evaluations of these programmes? Have they been shown to work for this population?

Writing

The third step in crafting your essay is the actual writing. If you have planned well and gathered relevant material you will be in a good position to write. Writing is difficult so it is important to allow yourself plenty of time to draft and revise your essay. Your lecturer will have given you a word limit and it is important that you stick to it because you may be penalised if your paper is either too

short or too long. The word limit lets you know how much content your lecturer thinks is required to examine the question. Some lecturers are strict in terms of adhering to the word limit and others are more flexible. It is best to check this with your own lecturer prior to commencing the essay. Once you are underway with your writing, the first thing you will need to do is structure your essay and develop an outline as to how you will include what where.

The Essay Structure

Generally an essay will have an introduction where you set out your main idea and purpose, several paragraphs (the body) each representing the evidence for one idea, a conclusion and a reference list or bibliography (see Figure 2.4). Sometimes it is the convention to commence the paper with the conclusion (as is the case in many psychology and hard science courses) so you should review the standards at your university or just ask your lecturer before you start to write.

Using the structural elements of the essay you will need to develop an outline which will document the main points you want to make in each section of your essay and in an order that will develop a logical flow to your discussion. The *introduction* is usually about 5% of the length of the essay. In the introduction you should provide the background and context of the topic under discussion and should describe the purpose for writing the essay. You will need to tell the reader how you intend to answer the question and define any terms that are difficult or could be interpreted in multiple ways. It is best to write the

---

The structure of an essay is very important and should follow a logical design. For example, an essay should always contain the following elements:

- Title
- Introduction
- Body – made up of several paragraphs
- Conclusion
- References/bibliography

▪ **Figure 2.4**   How do I structure my essay?

introduction last or at least revise it at the end, because as you write you may refine the direction of your essay and the conclusions.

The *body* makes up about 90% of your paper. The purpose of the body is to present the information that supports your argument. It is made up of several paragraphs, each of which is made up of several sentences. Each *paragraph* should deal with one main idea or issue related to the main topic. You will need to introduce the idea, present your argument, provide evidence (and references for that evidence) and discuss the evidence, making a concluding point that reflects your position. This you will repeat until all of the evidence is presented. It is important, when crafting your outline, that you try to arrange issues and evidence in a logical manner so that your reader can follow what you are saying and you can be seen to be building a strong case. When you write, there should be critical analysis of the points made by other authors and you should not be afraid to critique their views and/or their work. This will make the discussion in your essay more interesting and stronger in terms of the conclusions and viewpoints you have presented. The *conclusion* summarises the main points and arguments raised in the essay. There should be no new information introduced into the conclusion. The conclusion needs to demonstrate that you have answered the question. The *reference list* is an alphabetical list of all the books and journal articles referred to throughout the essay (*see Referencing* in the next section). A *bibliography* is a list of the books, reports, articles and other sources you have consulted for your writing. You may not have cited these items directly as with the reference list.

Let's again look at our essay question from the previous sections, '*Assess the importance of drug and alcohol treatment to the rehabilitation of female offenders in the United States*' and what an outline might look like (Figure 2.5).

Critical Analysis

As with most academic disciplines, in criminology critical analysis is very important and most lecturers will expect to see some critique of the literature, including the theories under discussion. Try not to accept the views of authors, including traditional theorists, without question. Ask yourself whether you agree with them and if so, why? If you disagree with the author, why do you disagree? Has the author provided evidence for

---

Title: *Assess the importance of drug and alcohol treatment to the rehabilitation of female offenders in the United States*

Essay length: 2,000 words (excluding references)

Introduction: 250 words

1. Provide the background and context and briefly outline the argument.

Argument: Treatment is essential for improving rehabilitation outcomes for female offenders in the US.

Body: 1,500 words

2. Identify the proportion of offending committed by women in the US over the last ten years that has been directly related to drug and alcohol misuse and describe the offences.
3. Discuss whether this profile of offending is different from male offending in the US and from that of women in other jurisdictions.
4. Discuss rehabilitation programmes available to women offenders.
5. Analyse the outcomes of participation in these programmes by women (both positive and negative).
6. Assess the impacts on reoffending.

Conclusion: 250 words

7. Summarise the discussion and restate the argument and the conclusions reached.

References

◪ **Figure 2.5**   Sample essay outline

their theory or opinion and if so, is the evidence sound? What do other writers think? These are the types of questions that will assist you in critically analysing the source material that you use. When it comes to including critical analysis in your essay, it is good for you to remember that your opinion about the topic becomes 'your argument' and while it is necessary for you to express your argument it should be supported by evidence. This evidence is found in the research that you do, which should include articles, books and other sources of information that provide support for your argument and which also disagree with your argument. You must present all perspectives in your essay, even the argument against your viewpoint. If you present sufficient evidence to support your argument, however, you will be able to conclude at the end of your essay that your argument is the most likely position to take based on the evidence presented.

Literature Reviews

It is also common in criminology to write literature reviews. A literature review is an in-depth look at all of the relevant literature about a topic; for example, you might be asked to write a review examining what is the current understanding about the relationship between drugs and crime. A literature review requires you to present as much of the literature you can find for and against particular perspectives relevant to the topic. The approach to writing these is a bit different from your standard essay and you should review university guides on how to write this type of review to ensure you are using the preferred format of your institution. Regardless of what you are writing you will need to craft your piece according to the style used at your institution, including complying with the rules of grammar.

Referencing

Once of the most confusing areas students must navigate and become skilled in is avoiding plagiarism. What is plagiarism? Plagiarism is the act of using somebody else's work and

passing it off as your own or not appropriately acknowledging them as the source. In a technical sense it involves using the same words used by someone else in roughly the same sequence as they have used them. It can also involve using other people's ideas and theories without acknowledging them. It is essential that you ALWAYS acknowledge someone when you refer to their work. This is called referencing and it is as important to criminology courses as it is to other courses. All universities have reference guidelines which your university will provide to you when you enrol in your course. These may differ between institutions so it is important that you become familiar with the referencing method used at your university. Reference information (or citation) is included throughout the text, whenever you refer to someone else's argument, idea or theory. This usually involves putting the author's name, year of publication and, if a direct quote, a page number.

The Reference List

At the end of your essay you will include a reference list which will follow a specific structure depending on the method of referencing you are using. The reference list must include the full information for all the citations included in the text of your essay, including the title of the book or article and the details of the publisher. A bibliography differs from a reference list. It is a list of all the books, articles and other reference material read or considered in the writing of your essay, whether cited in text or not. Bibliographies are generally not included in academic essay writing unless asked for by the lecturer but are often included at the end of government reports and in some books.

 Why is plagiarism considered to be so serious in university study?

Revision and Exams

Most courses require you to sit for exams. If your university course has an exam as an assessment item you will need to prepare for it. Part of preparing for your exam will be revising the material presented in lectures, tutorials and from assigned readings. Developing and applying good revision skills early and throughout your course will help you to be successful at exam time. In this section we describe some of the key things to keep in mind as you prepare for your exams. Most universities have good detailed online resource materials to help you at this critical and often stressful stage of your studies. See, for example, the University of Leicester Student Learning Development pages at www.le.ac.uk/succeedinyourstudies which are a good example of the study support provided by universities. Seek out the support that is available for you through your own university.

Revision

When it is time to revise for exams you will need to review the material presented in lectures and obtained from your independent reading. The notes you took will likely be invaluable (see *Reading and Note-taking*). If possible, talk to lecturers and past students to find out what the exam covers, and ensure you focus on that material. You might even be able to obtain an old exam paper to use as a revision guide. It is important that if you find it necessary to miss any lectures you make sure you get hold of the information from the lecturer or another student and take the time to read it later. If you have any doubts about your comprehension of the material, see your lecturer. It is good to ask questions early to clarify anything you are unsure about. Prior to the exam, develop a study process that involves revision. This can include forming a study group with other students so you can help each other to remember the material. Revision is about checking your understanding and making links between different aspects of the topic. It is also about testing your memory and identifying gaps in your knowledge. Table 2.5 provides some tips on recalling information. Sometimes it is useful to take notes you have previously written and summarise them again, or put them into a new format such as Table 2.5 suggests.

Table 2.5 Tips for recalling information for exams	
Some useful techniques for improving the memory for exams include:	
Rote learning	Learning some information such as definitions and terms off by heart.
Using acronyms	The use of acronyms and ditties are useful to prompt the memory on larger chunks of information.
Using links	Link key information with familiar objects or names (keywords) so recalling that keyword triggers the linked information.
Everyone is unique in how they learn and recall information and it is important for you to experiment to find the best ways that work for you.	

Mind Maps

Mind maps or concept maps can be a great way to structure key points from your readings or notes because they allow you to see the relationship between the ideas or simply allow you to visualise content. For example, see the start of a mind map identifying key theories in criminology in Figure 2.6.

You can expand on this by adding in sub-theories and/or theorists (see Figure 2.7).

Figure 2.7 demonstrates a further developed mind map that was commenced in Figure 2.6; however it still requires more work in terms of identifying the points of critique. This could lead to a new linked mind map as the analysis progresses. You can expand these conceptual

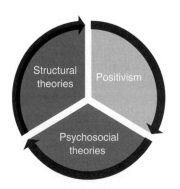

🔲 **Figure 2.6**   Basic mind map

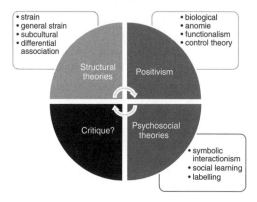

🔲 **Figure 2.7**   A further developed mind map

maps over time, incorporating and adjusting the content as required. The important thing is to find study methods that work for you and that you can become engaged with. Although it's a good idea to revise throughout your course on a regular basis, this isn't always feasible. You may find yourself needing to cram at the last minute. If you have to cram you'll need to be selective and skim books and other resources for the main points only. Study groups are sometimes useful for aiding with last-minute cramming.

Sitting the Exam

Taking exams can be very stressful, even when you are feeling prepared. It's important to get rest and eat properly in the lead up to the exam so that you can be at your best. Make sure you know where and when the exam will be held and give yourself

plenty of time to get there. You do not want to be flustered just prior to the exam. There are different types of exams; for example, open-book exams, essay exams, multiple choice, and exams with short answers as well as essay questions. It's a good idea to find out the format for the exam in advance so your preparation is appropriately directed. When you are given the exam paper you will need to read the instructions. Use this time wisely and read the instructions carefully. If you are not sure about anything ask the exam invigilator to explain it to you. Try to answer all the questions in the paper. At the beginning you will be told how much time you have. Go through the paper and find out how many questions you need to answer in that time and this will give you an idea of how quickly you need to be moving through the exam. Remember to allow more time for essay questions. If you are caught out and do not have enough time to complete short answers or essay questions then get down as many bullet points as you can in the time left. At least this will give you some points rather than no points. Once you have finished your exam, use the remaining time to go back over the paper to make sure you have answered everything. Again the best place to get exam advice is your university because every institution does things a bit differently and it's important to understand the approach used locally.

How Should I Approach My Criminology Course?

By enrolling to study criminology you have chosen one of the most interesting and challenging courses that will be offered at university. When studying criminology as an entire course, or as a subject within a criminal justice course, you will be asked to think more deeply and more broadly about many issues that you have previously taken for granted. What was once black and white will suddenly have many areas of grey. For example, you may have thought that people who steal should always be sent to prison but your studies may expose you to the impacts that poverty, age, intergenerational offending and/or environmental design have on this crime. Exposure to these new perspectives may change the way in which you view crime and the people who commit crime. Criminologists are social scientists who seek to understand the way things are from the various perspectives in which they can be viewed, rather than relying on their own preconceived ideas. Enter the study of criminology with an open but inquisitive mind and you will get the most from your course.

 Why do you need an open and inquisitive mind to study criminology?

Summary

This chapter has covered the basics of what you can expect from your criminology course, including the skills that you need to study at a university level. Criminology is an interesting subject and you can expect to be challenged by new ways of looking at things throughout your course. It is hoped that you will enter the study of criminology with an open and enquiring mind, seeking to acquire not only new knowledge but also a different way of viewing the world at large. Criminology is a rewarding course of study that can lead you into varied and interesting careers in the criminal justice system and beyond.

Further Reading

Cottrell, S: 2017. *Critical Thinking Skills: Effective Analysis, Argument and Reflection* (3rd edition). London, UK: Palgrave.
Critical thinking skills are important in most tertiary education courses and this book provides a comprehensive look at what is meant by critical thinking and in particular how to apply critical thinking skills to developing a sound argument.

Cottrell, S. 2013. *Study Skills Handbook* (4th edition). Basingstoke, UK: Palgrave Macmillan.
This book is developed for students who are committed to succeeding in their studies. It covers all the basics essential to being successful as a student, including the core skills necessary for success. The author uses an easy-to-follow approach which makes the book interesting and user friendly.

Greetham, B: 2013. *How to Write Better Essays* (3rd edition). Basingstoke, UK: Palgrave Macmillan.
This book presents useful tips for students who want to develop academic writing skills. It is particularly useful for students who have never studied before or who have been out of the education system for some time and want to refresh their knowledge. It is a simple and readable guide for students wanting to develop skills in writing an essay.

Peck, J. & Coyle, M. 2012. *The Student's Guide to Writing, Spelling, Punctuation and Grammar* (3rd edition). Basingstoke, UK: Palgrave Macmillan.
This book is written for students who want to improve their writing skills. It breaks down the writing process into its component parts and teaches the student how to construct a sentence, how to develop a paragraph and how to structure an essay. It also covers the writing basics such as punctuation, grammar and spelling.

Key Theories and Theorists

Criminological Theory in Context

The word 'theory' originates from the Greek word *thorós* which means 'spectator'. A theory is a system of ideas, assumptions or propositions that attempt to explain observed phenomena that in some cases may be abstract in nature. It is a rational way of thinking about a topic so as to link cause and effect and is arguably an attempt to make the intangible tangible. Some definitions of theory, usually scientific, define a theory as being a hypothesis that is backed up by evidence. Theories are mental maps or conceptualisations to explain perceived reality. In criminology, theories seek to explain the occurrence and prevention of crime, why some people commit crime, why some people fall victim to crime and how criminals and victims are processed by the criminal justice system. It is worthwhile to briefly expand on the role of theory in a criminological context and why theories are important in criminological study.

Why Is Criminological Theory Important?

Criminological theories can guide the student's search to understand why people do or do not commit crime; help identify what information is needed to design an effective intervention strategy to apprehend offenders; and provide insight into how to design a programme so it is successful in reducing offending. Theories and models help to explain behaviour as well as suggesting how to develop more effective ways to influence and change it. There are two broad types of theory – *explanatory theory* and *change theory* – which may have different emphases but are complementary to each other. For example, understanding why a person steals is one step towards preventing

offending, but even the best explanations won't be enough by themselves. Some type of change model will also be needed to complement the theoretical explanation of causation. Theories that gain recognition in a discipline shape the field, help define the scope of practice, and influence the training and socialisation of its professionals. Today, no single theory or conceptual framework dominates research or practice in criminology and the discipline continues to pull together conceptual understanding and practice wisdom from a range of theoretical backgrounds.

 Why is theory important to criminology?

How Has Criminological Theory Developed?

Criminological theory is influenced by the various schools of thought that have been instrumental in the development of criminology and you will be able to see these influences underpinning the theoretical perspectives we will discuss in this chapter. The chapter provides basic information about some of the key theorists in the discipline of criminology and the theories they have contributed. It is true that criminology first originated from within the disciplines of philosophy and sociology, but it has gained ground as an established field of study in its own right over the past two centuries and especially in the modern era. To some extent, the advancing technologies and expansion of knowledge associated with modern society promoted the advancement of criminology and helped it to become the accepted and respected field of study it is today. Criminology has not developed sequentially but has rather seen the development of several branches of study that have evolved simultaneously. Each of these branches presents a different perspective on the issues of crime causation, prevention and response. Refer to Figure 3.1 for an overview of the development of criminology. You can see from this illustration that criminal justice in the middle ages was very punitive with harsh punishments for lawbreakers. By the eighteenth century, criminal justice was being influenced by philosophy, and several theorists such as Kant, Locke and Rousseau appeared with theories about the nature of man and society. By the late nineteenth century the field of sociology was providing a greater influence with theorists such as Durkheim, Lombroso and Marx providing theories that sought to explain why people engage in crime. Many of these theorists leaned towards social and structural explanations that argued that criminals are created by the environment in which they live rather than being born criminal. Lombroso, on the other hand, was focused on developing a biological explanation for crime which argued that people are born criminal and, what's more, there are physical markers in their skull and face that identify them as criminals. Other theorists at this time, such as Bentham and Beccaria, mainly focused on the criminal justice system and its response to crime. These theorists offered guidance on how to administer punishment and developed principles for a fair and humane criminal justice system. These theories belong to the classical school of criminology. By the nineteenth century, the fields of philosophy and sociology were strongly influencing criminology; this can be seen in the development of the positivist and classical schools of thought. In the twentieth century, a range of theorists redeveloped classical theory and became known as the neo-classical school, and today has led to the school of thought known as contemporary classicism. In the twentieth century, the discipline of psychology began to become influential in criminology and contributed to the psychosocial theories of crime. In addition, feminism gained ground and made significant contributions to criminology, especially to the study of women and crime.

Exploring Theories of Crime

In this section we will attempt to categorise some of the main theories relevant to the study of criminology. It is difficult to categorise these theories in a single way because there are so many cross overs between them and different authors will have their own preference as to how they should be presented. It is therefore likely you will see these theories grouped a little differently in different books you might read. We have chosen to group them under headings that bring together the theories that have similar influences and theoretical bases, beginning with the theoretical influence of philosophy.

Philosophical Theory

In the sixteenth, seventeenth and eighteenth centuries, before criminology was a recognised academic discipline, and when sociology was in the earliest stages of development, it was philosophers who sought to explain deviance and in particular law breaking. The field of philosophy provided the early explanations for crime and how to understand and respond to it. These theories tended to focus on the nature of man within society and the natural world, as well on as the nature of man.

Philosophical Naturalism

Philosophical naturalism was one of these early philosophical theories. Philosophy is the study of knowledge formation, existential matters and ethical considerations. Naturalism is the reliance on natural explanations of phenomena and the belief that the scientific method can explain all things. This theory expounds the idea that only natural laws and forces operate in the world. It doesn't seek to prove this is the case, it just accepts it is so based on the absence of belief in anything beyond the natural. This was a controversial concept in the Middle Ages, as the belief in supernatural forces and spiritual laws were widespread and the dominant socio-political movement of the time.

Time period	1200–1699	1700–1789	1790–1900	1900–1949	1950–present
Main influences	**FEUDALISM AND RELIGION**	**PHILOSOPHY SOCIOLOGY**	**SOCIOLOGY PHILOSOPHY BIOLOGY**	**SOCIOLOGY PSYCHOLOGY**	**CONTEMPORARY CRIMINOLOGY**
THEORISTS AND THEORETICAL DEVELOPMENT	SUPERSTITION Trial by ordeal Magna Carta Common law	PHILOSOPHICAL NATURALISM Locke Rousseau Kant Hume	POSITIVISM Comte Lombroso Spencer TRADITIONAL CLASSICISM Beccaria Bentham Durkheim **Functionalism** Durkheim Comte CRITICAL CRIMINOLOGY Marxist criminology Marx	PSYCHOLOGICAL THEORIES Labelling theory Social cognitive theory Mead Becker NEO-CLASSICISM Right realism Herrnstein, Murray and Wilson Social control theory Sutherland SOCIOLOGICAL THEORIES **Anomie** Merton Strain theory Merton Agnew Conflict theory Vold Political economy theory Bonger	PSYCHOSOCIAL THEORIES Social learning theory Symbolic interactionism Differential association Bandura Sutherland Neutralisation theory Sykes and Matza CONTEMPORARY CLASSICISM A general theory of crime Gottfredson and Hirschi Rational choice theory Cornish and Clarke Routine activity theory Cohen and Felson Subcultural theory Cloward and Ohlin Albert Cohen Stanley Cohen Left realism Young **Feminist criminology** Adler; Smart Walklate; Carlen Heidensohn Chesney-Lind

Figure 3.1 The development of criminological theory over time

David Hume

One philosopher in the eighteenth century who grappled with concepts of good and bad and the inconsistencies of human nature in his book the *Treatise of Human Nature* was David Hume (1739/1958). The treatise consisted of three separate documents and it was in this early work by Hume that he first attempted to apply a scientific approach to the study of man. He referred to this as the 'experimental method of reasoning' (Stroud 1977:4). In referring to the experimental method of reasoning, Hume was in fact simply arguing that social scientists must draw conclusions only from sources that are supported by experience. In this way, Hume distinguished between knowledge based on related ideas and knowledge based on fact. He argued that ideas come and go in the mind and these ideas connect with inherent character traits, propensities and dispositions in human beings that influence and cause human behaviour (Stroud 1977). It is feeling and not reason that is responsible for people's thoughts and behaviour, according to Hume. This view was considered to be revolutionary in the eighteenth century because it completely reversed the traditional belief about human nature from being divinely given and external to the self to being inherently embedded in the self. At around the same time that philosophical naturalism was being developed as a way of understanding human deviance, the classical school of criminology was also finding its feet with theorists such as Beccaria and Bentham.

 Are people inherently governed by their feelings or their thoughts?

Synthetic Philosophy

Synthetic philosophy is in effect the theory of natural law and evolution in social development. It is sometimes referred to as 'social Darwinism'. It is concerned with what are seen as the natural processes of social evolution as opposed to the man-made and influenced processes involved in social development.

Biographical Synopsis

David Hume 1711–1776
David Hume was a Scottish philosopher who lived in Edinburgh in the eighteenth century. He was an important figure in Western philosophy and his teachings greatly influenced the disciplines of sociology and economics. Hume is credited with introducing the concept of the social contract which espouses that in any society individuals have consented to surrender some of their rights and freedoms to the will of the governing body in exchange for the protection of other rights and freedoms they may possess. He outlines differences between natural rights and legal rights both of which, it is argued, are essential to the maintenance of political and social order. Hume also posited a moral philosophy that suggested people are unwitting products of their passions rather than reason. Thomas Hobbes, John Locke and Jean Jacques Rousseau also supported the conceptual idea of the social contract posited by David Hume.

Herbert Spencer

Herbert Spencer introduced the theory of evolution to social development. His theories were influenced by the theories of Charles Darwin and Cesare Lombroso. He believed in the universality of natural law and sought to discover one universal law that could be applied to the social experience. He called this law the principle of evolution, with his work eventually becoming known as synthetic philosophy. Herbert Spencer (1857) believed that the universe was governed by natural laws and the first principle of synthetic philosophy held that these laws applied to everything, without exception, including the social world. The second principle of this theoretical position held that these laws naturally led to progress. Spencer theorised that everything in the universe developed as a simple differentiated entity that progressed in development to become more complex. He also believed in natural selection and the inheritability of traits and characteristics. *See Positivism*.

Classicism

Classicism and classical criminology arose out of the positivist school of thought and were popular in the late eighteenth century at a time when Europe was expanding and the intellectual pursuit of knowledge was rapidly advancing. At the same time, the governing authorities were concerned that the lower-class population was rapidly growing and a fear about sustaining social stability began to develop. According to Hume, people are slaves of their passions and rationality and logic has no agency of its own but simply serves and obeys a person's passions. Classical criminology on the other hand presumes that human beings have a normal tendency towards criminal behaviour and rather than being simply a slave to their passions, they are capable and willing actors in their own crimes, with the freedom of choice to opt for alternative courses of action.

Cesare Beccaria

In 1764 Cesare Beccaria wrote *An Essay on Crimes and Punishments* in which he establishes the fundamental principles of jurisprudence that are largely followed in the modern criminal justice system. These principles included the view that the law should be as least restrictive on the individual as possible and must guarantee the rights of the accused throughout the criminal justice process. When considering punishment, Beccaria believed that punishment is only justified because the offender has infringed the rights of others or has disturbed the common good of society and the seriousness of the crime is therefore determined by the harm it causes to others (Beccaria 1764/1819). He considered that penalties should be proportionate to the crime and should be no more than is necessary to deter the offender and others from committing future crimes. Excessive punishment was thought to be ineffective and inefficient.

> ◉ Should the punishment of offenders give more weight to the rights and needs of the offender or to the common good?

Beccaria was adamant that the written law should clearly spell out what behaviour is deemed unlawful and what sanctions will be imposed for breaching the law. He argued that punishment should be received swiftly so there would be a close association between the crime and the punishment and that the inflicting of punishment should be free from prejudice and corruption. While not considered to be a criminologist, Cesare Beccaria is one of the most influential theorists in early criminology. In addition to punishment, his work focused on the nature of law and the governmental changes he considered to be necessary to prevent crime. He believed that people possess free will and rationality and that they are able to be manipulated (they can change). The utilitarian principles Beccaria posited were groundbreaking for the time and can be seen to remain relevant today. In addition to the swiftness of punishment, he also argued that punishment should be proportionate to the crime; that all laws must be clear and simple and there must be a certainty of punishment for committing crime; and, finally, that there should be a reward for virtuous conduct. These principles can be seen to influence the criminal justice system today in countries such as the United States, Australia, New Zealand, Canada and the United Kingdom. These countries administer their criminal justice system according to established principles based on Beccaria's principles of jurisprudence, such as the right to a fair trial; the right to have legal representation; the right to a speedy trial; and the right to early parole for good behaviour. Remand in custody is one area of criminal justice processing that may cause dilemmas in regard to Beccaria's principles of jurisprudence. Curtailing the freedom of liberty of people who have not yet been found guilty is sometimes necessary but causes moral dilemmas. Such a person may lose their job, have their children placed

Case Study

Remand in Custody: The New Zealand Experience

In New Zealand in 2006, the Ministry of Justice reported that only 44% of 15,143 cases involving custodial remand actually resulted in sentences of imprisonment. When analysing these cases, the New Zealand Ministry of Justice discovered that while 26% of cases were convicted but received a sentence other than imprisonment, 30% were not convicted at all despite having spent significant time in custody. The average time a person was held in custody on remand in 2006 was 51.6 days. When looking more closely at these cases, it was apparent that around 32% of these alleged offenders spent only the first quarter of their case on remand and this was while their access to bail was being resolved. It was also found that 36% spent only the final part of their case on remand while they awaited sentencing. It was reported, however, that 30% of people remanded in custody during 2006 spent their entire case in custody.

Source: NZ Ministry of Justice. 2008.

in foster care and have their relationships put under enormous pressure. Losing employment can have long-term financial implications but so can having employment interrupted while on remand. The remanded person may not be able to pay their rent or mortgage and therefore lose their housing. If they are subsequently found not guilty in court, the negative effects on their lives can be devastating and difficult to overcome. Unfortunately, swiftness of punishment remains an ideal that is frequently hampered by long delays in processing court cases, leaving too many people in remand prisons awaiting trial (see case study).

Beccaria believed the primary purpose of punishment was to prevent crime and in regard to crime prevention he postulated that preventing crime comes down to three fundamental elements, which are:

- Certainty: how likely an individual is to receive punishment;
- Celerity: how quickly punishment is received; and
- Severity: how severe the punishment is (i.e. how much pain is inflicted).

It can be seen from the New Zealand example provided in the case study that the remand in custody experience for accused people does not meet at least one of these principles, namely the speed at which the punishment is administered following the criminal act.

Biographical Synopsis

Cesare Beccaria 1738–1794

Cesare Beccaria was born on 15 March 1738 in Milan, Italy. In the early 1760s Beccaria was instrumental in the formation of a society known as the 'academy of fists', which was focused on political, economic, administrative and social reform. In relation to addressing criminal behaviour, he was considered to be a utilitarian who thought that punishment should serve a practical social purpose and should therefore be justified in terms of the greater good. Beccaria introduced classical jurisprudence and outlined utilitarian principles for law enforcement and punishment. Many of these principles still influence criminal justice policy today.

Jeremy Bentham

In addition to Cesare Beccaria, another influential classical theorist of the eighteenth century was Jeremy Bentham and he followed the classical utilitarian school that also influenced Beccaria. He believed that people are, on a basic level, motivated by a pleasure and pain dichotomy: in particular, that people will seek pleasure and will try to avoid pain. According to Bentham, when people engage in criminal behaviour they are trying to maximise pleasure and excitement and the challenge for the criminal justice system is to ensure that any pleasure derived from engaging in criminal behaviour is outweighed by the pain of punishment (Bentham 1789/1982). Bentham defines 'good' as being whatever produces the most amount of happiness and 'evil' whatever produces the most amount of pain. Critics of Bentham argue that his conception of justice lacks fairness in that they believe he would argue that it is justified to inflict pain (such as torture) on one person if it results in greater happiness for the majority. His theory is tempered by the principle of distributive justice, which would, however, preclude such outcomes, as it shows that Bentham was not in favour of the sacrificing of the few for the benefit of the majority.

> Can you think of any crime types where offenders will endure pain in order to achieve their desired end?

Bentham spent much of his life attempting to reinvent the prison system by introducing a radical new prison design he called the 'panopticon'. He tried to convince the authorities that this architectural design, based on a circular building arranged around a central point at which every cell could be visible, provided continuous surveillance. In addition to the architectural design, Bentham also suggested changes to operational management of the prison by suggesting that prison managers should employ the labour of inmates. According to Bentham, this process would include the proviso that the manager should be on a contract whereby they would share in the income generated by this labour, but would be financially liable if the inmate reoffended on release from the prison or if too many prisoners died while in prison. Prisons should be transparent and accountable and open to inspection by external bodies. Bentham thought that this architectural design and operational approach would provide an answer to the human problems of incarceration including idleness, mental instability and poverty (Bentham 1789/1982). While there were two prisons built in the nineteenth century according to the theoretical propositions advocated by Bentham – Millbank and Pentonville Prison in London – and the Statesville Correctional Centre in the US in the early twentieth century (see case study), a panopticon was never built during Bentham's lifetime and his theories have largely remained unimplemented by modern correctional organisations. There have been suggestions that in addition to the above institutions, his principles have influenced the design of prisons in France, Cuba, Canada, Hungary, Spain and Ireland due to their similarity in design to the panopticon but there is no overt association with Bentham's design in these jurisdictions.

Bentham opposed the death penalty in all crimes except murder because he believed the negative effects of this punishment cancelled out any positive effects it may have. In fact, he believed punishment to be overwhelmingly negative in effect and therefore that it should be strictly limited, advocating instead for prison as an effective alternative. See *The Role of Punishment (Chapter 6).*

Case Study

Illinois, US: Statesville Correctional Center

A modern-day example of a panopticon was the Statesville Correctional Center's F House in Crest Hill, Illinois. The Statesville Correctional Center F House was built as a maximum security adult male prison which originally had the capacity to hold 1,500 inmates. This prison was purpose built to meet the panopticon design and it was opened in March 1925 and closed in 2016 as it was thought to be archaic. The Statesville Correctional Center is now a modern facility that holds around 4,105 inmates. It is primarily a maximum security prison holding men and women but now has other sections such as a large reception unit, program units and a minimum security section that is separate from the main prison.

Source: Illinois Department of Corrections. 2014. 'Statesville Correctional Center Illinois' Accessed online on 3 November 2016 at: https://www.illinois.gov/idoc/news/2016/Pages/StatesvilleCorrectionalCenter'sFHouseofficiallyclosed.aspx.

Jeremy Bentham 1748–1832
Jeremy Bentham was born on 15 February 1748 in London, England. Bentham was a vocal advocate of social welfare and human jurisprudence and called for the abolition of slavery, the death penalty and physical punishment. He was also known as an advocate for animal rights. He was influenced by the classical utilitarian school of thought and espoused the 'greatest happiness principle' or the principle that happiness should dominate over pain.

Bentham wanted his body to be preserved, and his mummified head and skeleton are held at University College London (UCL) where they have been since 1850. An artificial body with the mummified head attached is displayed in a wood and glass case at the university.

While Cesare Beccaria and Jeremy Bentham share many similarities in their approaches to understanding and responding to crime, there are some key differences that are worth considering. Table 3.1 explores the differences between these two theorists.

┌─ **Let's Consider!** ─

The Differences Between Beccaria and Bentham
Table 3.1 provides you with a quick reference guide as to the main differences between Beccaria and Bentham. While they are both classical theorists who share the utilitarian approach to punishment, they differ from each other in some important ways. Beccaria expanded on the concept of the social contract (arguing the government existed to serve the people) and punishment for criminality was only justified if it furthered the social contract. Bentham believed that social action should be aimed at increasing the happiness of the majority. Table 3.1 provides more detail of the differences between these two classical theorists.

Positivism

Positivism is also known as the 'scientific approach' and differs from classical criminology (classicism) in that positivism assumes that criminals are inherently different to non-criminals whereas classicism assumes that everyone has the propensity to commit crime. Positivism can be separated into three distinct branches: biological, psychological and social. The underlying focus and aim of positivism within criminology is to categorise and treat offenders and also to build knowledge. The building of knowledge within positivism revolves around describing a phenomenon rather than trying to explain it or to question if it exists or not. The main assumptions of positivism are that the methods of the natural sciences can and should be applied to the social world; that the foundation of our knowledge of the world is derived from observation (referred to as our epistemology); that the basis of scientific knowledge is the data objectively collected by the researcher; that facts have to be distinguished from values; and that the core method of obtaining new knowledge involves the collection of data and the development and testing of hypotheses (referred to as deductive reasoning). The combination of natural scientific method and deductive reasoning led to a preference for quantitative over qualitative data.

Auguste Comte

Auguste Comte is credited with having introduced positivism to the study of sociology. His major works included *Discourse on the Positive Spirit* (1844), *A General View of Positivism* (1848) and *Religion of Humanity* (1856). He claimed that human culture develops in three stages: theological, metaphysical and scientific. The presumptions that underlie these three stages are: the theological is a stage where human beings rely on divine explanations of the world; the metaphysical stage is where people attribute effects and events to abstract and poorly understood causes such as the occult; and the scientific, which is the most advanced stage where human beings understand that scientific laws control the world. He promoted applying the scientific method to the study of

◘ Table 3.1 Comparing Beccaria and Bentham

	Beccaria	Bentham
Human nature	People act out of self-interest which sometimes conflicts with the social contract.	People are motivated by seeking pleasure and avoiding pain. People are rational actors with free will.
Criminal behaviour	The seriousness of a crime is assessed according to the harm it causes to others, but all crime should attract punishment in order to produce a deterrent effect.	Only criminal behaviour that produces unhappiness or pain to others should be considered worthy of punishment.
Main focus	Utilitarian: utility in regard to the social contract. That which is necessary to advance the social contract. The social contract prevents chaos.	Utilitarian calculus: the greater good principle.
Crime and society	There is a contractual relationship between people and the state. Crime has a normative role to play in society. It reinforces the boundaries of acceptable behaviour and censures behaviour that is rule breaking or against the social norms.	The good of society is measured by the happiness of the individuals in it. Social action should be guided by the greatest good for the greatest number of people.
Punishment	Punishment should be justified by achieving a greater good and advancement of the social contract. Proportionality: Punishment should fit the crime. Excessive punishment is ineffective and is likely to increase crime rather than deter it. Capital punishment is ineffective.	Punishment should be restricted to that which is necessary to achieve the desired outcome. The severity of punishment should increase with the severity of the crime. Capital punishment is justified in crimes such as murder.
Policy positions	Proportionality in sentencing. Deterrence. Rule of law.	Prison reform. Deterrence. Human rights and due process.

social phenomena to increase the reliability of findings. Auguste Comte viewed positivism as being more than a theoretical framework and more like a religion, which he referred to as the 'religion of humanity'. Comte is also hailed by some as having created the social sciences due to the introduction of the scientific method into the study of society and social processes. While there are commonalities in the empiricist thinking of Comte and Hume there are also some significant differences. For example, while Hume thought that human nature was basically unchanging and society stable, Comte believed society passed through three developmental phases of intellectual development as outlined above (see Table 3.2 for more detail about the differences between Hume and Comte). Auguste Comte

Biographical Synopsis

Auguste Comte 1798–1857
Auguste Comte was born in Montpellier in France on 19 January 1798. He is acclaimed as the founder of sociology and is the original theorist responsible for the positivist approach. His positivist theory emphasised the important relationship that exists between theory, practice and human understanding of the world. Influenced by David Hume, Comte argued that theory must derive from observable facts. In fact the invention of the word 'positivism' in sociology (and hence criminology) is attributed to Comte.

was a major influence on nineteenth-century sociological thought across disciplines such as sociology, philosophy and anthropology.

Let's Consider!

The Differences Between Comte and Hume

Table 3.2 provides you with a quick reference guide as to the main differences between Comte and Hume. While they both arise from the positivist school, they differ from each other in some important ways. Hume was fundamentally a rationalist who believed humanity is contrived in individualism whereas Comte tempered his rationalism with emotion and conceived humanity as being based in collectivism. Hume rejected religion as redundant whereas Comte embraced it. Table 3.2 provides more detail of these differences.

Biological Positivism

Biological positivism assumes that the disposition for criminal behaviour is inherent and present from birth. This has led to theories that aim to identify the physical characteristics that can identify criminals and personality traits that are common to certain types of criminals. It leads to heredity and evolutionary arguments for explaining criminal behaviour and to the nature or nurture debate. Are criminals predisposed to criminally offending due to an inborn genetic flaw or are they influenced by their environment to become criminal? This debate has plagued criminologists for ages. Criminology largely moved away from biological explanations of crime following Lombroso's work, but with advances in genetic studies and DNA profiling it has recently gained more interest from criminologists and from geneticists (see Key Criminological Research Debate, p. 37).

Cesare Lombroso

Moving away from the assumption that criminal behaviour was an unavoidable part of human nature and an accepted fact of life, Cesare Lombroso was the first to suggest that criminals physically differed from non-criminals and that crime and criminal behaviour could be scientifically examined and studied (Lombroso 1876/1911). The central theme of Lombroso's work was the concept of the 'born criminal'. He believed that criminals were born to be criminals and that this was a recessive evolutionary throwback to a

---

□ Table 3.2 Comparing Comte and Hume

	Comte	Hume
Human nature	Humanity is based on collectivism.	Humanity is based on individualism.
Criminal behaviour	Evidence of failure of society to maintain social cohesiveness.	Humans are a slave to their passions.
Main focus	The family unit and the community.	The individual.
Causation of criminal behaviour	Society has failed to bind the individual to the collective.	The individual is responsible for their own choices, not society. Intention is the main criteria of concern, not causation.
Punishment	Language, religion and employment are the modes that reform deviance.	Punishment should be proportional to the intention.
Underlying assumptions	Nothing is absolute, everything is relative.	Reason overrides passion but reason alone cannot determine moral conduct.

Key Criminological Research Debates

Is criminal behaviour the result of nature or nurture?
The debate surrounding whether criminal behaviour is a result of nature (inborn) or nurture (learned) has been the focus of much research over the years. This is often framed in terms of genetic or environmental explanations of criminal behaviour. While genetic or inborn causes have been found to explain criminal behaviour in a small number of specific conditions (e.g. foetal alcohol syndrome), on the whole it has been social and environmental explanations of crime that have dominated the research (Levitt 2013). Lombroso (1876/1911) is a leading theorist in biological/genetic explanations of criminal behaviour that are seminal in the nature argument. His research was focused on identifying inborn physical traits in criminals that could be used to identify people who were likely to become criminal. While much of Lombroso's work has been discredited, with advances in genetics there has recently been a resurgence of interest in biological explanations of criminal behaviour, particularly genetic causes of violent and antisocial behaviour (Levitt 2013). The nature/nurture debate has been called redundant by Craddock (2011) who views the debate as unhelpful and outdated. This is due to the fact that biological explanations of crime can lead to the discrimination and mistreatment of people labelled as genetically predisposed to criminal behaviour. Levitt (2013) supports the contention that the nature/nurture debate is obsolete and argues that criminal behaviour is most likely influenced to some degree by both genetics and environment.

more primitive human condition. In addition to his views about biological determinism, Lombroso was also interested in psychiatric explanations of crime. In the first edition of his book, *Criminal Man*, first published in 1876, Lombroso studied 290 criminals looking for signs of mental illness and physical afflictions of the brain but found only 7.2% of the sample he studied that could be placed in these categories (Lombroso 1876/1911). This finding did not support his thesis but did not deter him from seeking biological explanations of crime. Lombroso categorised criminals into three groups: the born criminal (physical differences set them apart); the insane criminal (controlled by insanity, dementia, imbecility and epilepsy) and criminaloids (habitual criminals). Lombroso coined the term 'moral insanity' to describe criminals who lack a sense of morality and the ability to distinguish good from bad. Lombroso differentiates between people who are morally insane and those who are criminal; however, he goes on to link moral insanity with the born criminal, suggesting the link is inevitable due to the similarities between the two conditions.

In the fifth edition of his book *Criminal Man*, Lombroso (1876/1911) examined 100 photographs of criminals who were diagnosed

Biographical Synopsis

Cesare Lombroso 1835–1909
Italian-born Cesare Lombroso was the founder of the Italian School of Positivist Criminology having rejected the classical criminological assumption that criminal behaviour was a part of human nature and instead holding that the tendency towards criminal behaviour was inherited. He worked within the disciplines of medicine and criminology to develop his theory that criminals could be identified by physical features, a theory which fell into the realm of anthropological criminology (combining the study of humans with the study of criminality). He is credited with the controversial theory of atavism which argues that criminals are distinguishable from non-criminals due to physical traits and characteristics. He thought that criminals were throwbacks to Neanderthal ancestors and suggested that all criminals had shared physical characteristics. Lombroso's theories have been disproven by subsequent criminologists and criminal researchers.

as being insane prior to committing any crime in an effort to prove that there were inherent physical characteristics that identify them as criminal. He determined that 44% of the criminals whose photographs he examined possessed the characteristics of the full criminal type. This consisted of: 'jug ears', enlarged sinuses, large jaw and cheekbone, sullen or crossed eyes and thin upper lips. He concluded that the existence of these features was higher than for the population in general. He suggested that criminality was a manifestation of 'atavism', which is a biological throwback to lower evolutionary forms. The focus on analysing physical, behavioural and psychological traits is a branch of criminology known as anthropological criminology and has developed from the early work of Lombroso.

 Are people born to be criminals or are they encouraged to become criminal by their environment?

Lombroso and Female Offending

Cesare Lombroso and Guglielmo Ferrero produced a book in Italian, which in English is translated as *The Female Offender* (Lombroso and Ferrero 1895) and which offered more pessimistic conclusions about women's proclivity to criminally offend than Lombroso's earlier work (Lombroso 1876/1911). Lombroso refused to accept the legitimacy of official statistics that showed women to be less criminal than men and argued that their crimes are hidden in the domestic sphere and are therefore less visible and less likely to be noticed by law enforcement officials. Lombroso and Ferrero (1895), however, formed the opinion that women were biologically incapable of criminal behaviour. This was not a compliment to women, as their view in this regard was that women were morally immature and less evolved than men with less scope for degenerating further. They argued that if women are to fall into criminal behaviour it is more likely to be in prostitution than in any other crime. To explain women who were involved in general criminal behaviour they suggested that these women were mentally and physically more masculine than feminine and therefore biologically prone to be criminal. Lombroso (1876/1911) argued that while fewer women than men are born criminals, female criminals are much more

---

Case Study

United States: Stanford Prison Experiment

An American psychologist, Professor Philip Zimbardo, undertook a controversial experiment in the US in the early 1970s. It became known as the Stanford Prison experiment. The aim of the experiment was to determine to what extent people would ignore morality and the law to follow authoritarian orders. It also provides an insight into the debate as to whether criminal behaviour is inborn or learned. Zimbardo and his research team established a mock prison in the basement of the School of Psychology in Stanford University in 1971. The research team selected 24 undergraduate students from a larger group of 70 volunteers and randomly assigned half to the role of prisoner and half to the role of prison guard. The 'prisoners' were placed in realistic-looking cells and there was an isolation cell available to the 'guards'. These guards were given eight-hour shifts but prisoners had to remain in the cells for 24 hours a day for the duration of the experiment. It was planned that the experiment was to extend over 14 days but it had to be stopped after six days due to the extreme aggression and abusive behaviour of the prison guards. Zimbardo, who acted as the prison warden, overlooked the abuse until the ethics of continuing was questioned by one of the students. He declared: 'Only a few people were able to resist the situational temptations to yield to power and dominance whilst maintaining some semblance of morality and democracy, obviously I was not among the noble class'.

Source: Zimbardo, P. 2007. *The Lucifer Effect: Understanding How Good People Turn Evil.* New York: Random House.

ferocious. He cites the crimes of women as being mainly abortion, bigamy, infanticide, prostitution and child abuse. Lombroso was among one of the first criminologists to focus attention on female offenders and he studied female offenders extensively, initially concluding that they rarely exhibit the signs of criminality or moral insanity seen in men. *See Feminist Criminology*.

> ❯ Why are women significantly under-represented in official criminal offending statistics at all points in history including today?

Avshalom Caspi and Colleagues

Caspi et al. (2005) undertook longitudinal studies with maltreated males and identified a genotype that was negatively correlated to antisocial and delinquent behaviour. They argued that this genotype, when present in the genetic coding of individuals, modified the effects of maltreatment in childhood, making these individuals resistant to antisocial and delinquent behaviour. In addition, Caspi et al. (2005) point to other studies that, while inconclusive, have identified specific genotypes on the X chromosome which may be linked to antisocial and aggressive behaviour in men.

The Theory of Anomie

Robert Merton and Émile Durkheim are the key theorists behind the sociological theory of anomie, although the meanings the two theorists give to anomie are slightly different. In his work *The Division of Labour in Society*, Durkheim (1893/1964)) argues that anomie results from a failure of society to properly regulate and control deviance. Anomie develops when a society emphasises culturally acceptable goals and achievements, but fails to emphasise the culturally approved means of achieving them. The underlying premise in Durkheim's theory is that capitalism emphasises individualism and self-interest rather than the collective good and

this provides a foundation for anomie to occur. Durkheim also believed that the aspirations of criminals differed from the aspirations of the non-criminal members of society. In addition to this, capitalism forces individuals into a division of labour that results in an economic hierarchy where their class position is determined at birth and not freely chosen by the individual. He argues that this results in resentment and the estrangement of individuals and causes many to aspire to social positions that are closed off to them. Durkheim further argued that human aspirations need to be regulated and channelled into socially acceptable means. He advocates for increased levels of social control as the means to control crime.

Robert Merton

In his article 'Social Structure and Anomie' (1938) and his book *Social Theory and Social Structure* (1957), Robert Merton describes anomie as being a state of being where individuals have loose bonds to society that result from not having the legitimate means available to them to meet the social and populist goals of that society. According to Merton (1957), disadvantaged people in society strive to meet the socially accepted goals but are prevented by social inequality and structural limitations from meeting those goals. This in turn causes frustration and despondence and a rejection of the social norms. In such conditions, the individual could resort to deviant behaviour such as criminal offending in order to fulfil these social goals that would otherwise be out of their reach. Merton used the theory of anomie as the basis for developing strain theory which has been criticised for failing to explain why so many poor people do not engage in unlawful or deviant behaviour even though they are limited by structural barriers all their lives. *See Strain Theory*.

> ❯ If poverty causes criminal behaviour, why aren't all poor people involved in crime?

Biographical Synopsis

Robert Merton 1910–2003
Robert Merton was an American
sociologist who was born in Philadelphia,
Pennsylvania. He studied sociology at
Temple University and spent much of his
career teaching at Columbia University. He
is acclaimed for his theory of anomie and
strain and is noted for his contributions to
sociology of concepts such as 'unintended
consequences', 'role model' and 'role strain'.
He is also credited with creating the term
'self-fulfilling prophecy' which refers to the
process by which an individual may adopt
others' expectations and beliefs which then
determine or influence the behaviour of the
individual and ultimately the outcome of an
event or series of events.

Functionalism

Functionalism argues that society is made up
of various parts that all work together to give
meaning and stability to the whole. Structural
functionalists believe that by studying the various
parts of society (norms, customs, traditions
and institutions), the social scientist can gain a
better understanding of the whole. Functionalists
believe there are four basic needs that are essential
for maintaining social order and these are: food,
shelter, money and clothing. Functionalism does
not advocate for active social change because it
assumes that the whole will naturally find ways
to adapt and compensate for any problems that
arise.

Émile Durkheim

Durkheim believed that criminal behaviour is a
normal adaptation to living within a society that is
highly structured and which is based on a division
of labour and societal values of competitiveness
and individualism (Durkheim 1893). According
to Durkheim, crime has important functions
within highly organised societies. These functions
include:

— *Adaptive function*: new ideas and ways of
doing things are introduced to society;
— *Boundary maintenance function*: crime
reinforces society's rules and norms through
the collective reaction against deviance.

He did, however, consider that too much crime
was bad for society and crime should therefore be
controlled with appropriate sanctions. Durkheim
also believed that institutions within society have
important functions. For example, educational
institutions have the function of transmitting
society's norms, rules and values with the aim
of creating and maintaining homogeneity and
ultimately changing an individual being into a
social being (Filloux 1993). This socialisation leads
to the development of a 'collective conscience' and
conveys the society's norms as to what is right and
wrong. Durkheim used the term 'social solidarity'
to distinguish different types of society which he
referred to as organic and mechanical.

Mechanical solidarity: is applied to less
advanced societies and refers predominantly
to territorial and tribal bonds. Durkheim saw
this type of society as being punitive and highly
regulated by informal but repressive social

Biographical Synopsis

Émile Durkheim 1858–1917
Émile Durkheim was a French sociologist
whose fields of expertise included
sociology, philosophy, anthropology
and religious studies. He was primarily
a positivist theorist who was a major
proponent of structural functionalism. He
saw societies as being either mechanical
or organic in nature and coined the term
'solidarity' when distinguishing them.
Durkheim was credited with making
sociology accepted as a science and was
therefore one of the first social scientists.
He is also credited with developing the
academic discipline of sociology and
is often acclaimed as the architect of
contemporary social sciences.

sanctions. Mechanical societies are highly religious and value the needs of the whole over the needs of the individual.

Organic solidarity: applies to more advanced societies and is based on the division of labour and in particular the interdependence that originates from the specialisation of work. This type of society is highly organised with an emphasis on restitution rather than punishment. It is secular rather than religious and the needs of the individual are more important than the needs of the group (dignity, equality, work ethic and social justice). *See The Theory of Anomie.*

Let's Consider!

The Differences Between Positivism and Classicism

Table 3.3 provides you with a quick reference guide to the main differences between positivism and classicism. The underlying premise associated with positivism is that people are born criminal and their behaviour is therefore predetermined. It is thought they are mostly unable to control or to change their behaviour but can in some circumstances do so if they are given the right help. The underlying premise with classicism is that people will naturally tend to seek rewards and avoid negative consequences (pain). They have free will and make rational choices after weighing up the risks involved. They can change their behaviour by being encouraged to make better choices by increasing the severity of punishments as a deterrence and increasing the possibility that criminals will be caught. *Refer to* Table 3.3 *for more detail.*

Psychosocial Theories of Crime

In addition to sociological theories of crime, which tend to take a broad social perspective, criminologists have also used psychosocial

and psychological theories of criminality. Psychosocial theories consider crime from the perspective of the individual acting from within the social context and include theories such as symbolic interactionism, social cognitive learning and labelling theories. The disciplines of sociology and philosophy have most greatly influenced the theories of criminology but from the 1960s onwards psychology began to play a much more prominent role. Psychological theories focus mainly on the individual and the internal factors that influence behaviour and include theories such as cognitive theory, behavioural theory and cognitive-behavioural theory to explain criminal behaviour.

Symbolic Interactionism

Symbolic interactionism is another psychosocial theory that derives from the group of theories known as learning theories and is greatly influential in many areas of criminology. The theory of symbolic interactionism assumes that individuals do not develop their personality or their self-concept in isolation but as a result of interacting with others in the social environment. The major contributors to the theory of symbolic interactionism are George Herbert Mead (1934) and his student Herbert Blumer (1969).

George Mead

Mead (1934) observed that humans use symbols in all their interactions. Language, particularly written language, is also made up of symbols and people use these symbols to convey ideas and to signify specific activities or to denote institutions (e.g. logos). So long as the meanings attached to these symbols are shared then it contributes to the predictability and orderliness of society. Mead believed the nature of reality is governed by symbols and the meaning attached to interactions based on these symbols which may or may not be hidden. This leads to the assumption made by Mead that if a situation is defined as real then it becomes real. According to Mead (1934) social life and effective communication between people are only possible when a common language is used and understood. He made a distinction

Table 3.3 Comparing classicism and positivism

	Classical approach	Positivist approach
Human nature	People naturally seek pleasure and avoid pain.	People's behaviour is determined at birth but they can change their behaviour if given the right help.
Criminal behaviour	Everyone has the propensity to engage in criminal behaviour. People possess rational choice and free will.	People are born criminal due to genetic defects. Criminal behaviour is determined. People cannot control the urge to criminally offend without help. Environment also influences behaviour.
Response to crime	Crime prevention through deterrence. Proportional punishment.	Individualised treatment programmes. Rehabilitation.
Main focus	Focus on the crime not the criminal.	Focus on the criminal not the crime.
Causation of crime	Pleasure and pain (the rewards outweigh the risks and consequences).	Multiple factors cause crime. Genetic and biological defects.
Punishment	Punishment should be severe but proportional, swift and focused on deterrence.	Reformation rather than punishment.
Underlying assumptions	Crime is a rational act that violates the values and beliefs of society.	Crime is an act that emanates from internal and external forces that the individual cannot control without help.
Political response	Get tough on crime policies influenced by the dual goals of punishing the offender and deterring future crime. Human rights and due process.	Welfare-based policies influenced by the goal of modifying the motivation of the individual to criminally offend.

between the 'I' (as observer) and the 'me' (the observed) to illustrate that self-concept cannot exist except in interaction with others. He argues that people lack a strong sense of self (i.e. who they are and what they are capable of doing) without feedback from others. Therefore deviance only becomes deviance when the language and symbols of social interaction make it so. Mead advanced the theory of 'pragmatism' which held that true reality is created as people interact with the social world; that people base their knowledge of the world on what they have found useful and alter those elements that no longer work; that people define social and physical objects according to the use they have for them; and that to understand people you must look at their behaviour. Mead considered social control to be an internal process linked to the meanings people give to acting and being

rather than external forces. Linguistic and visual symbolism is important to this interactive negotiation of meaning.

Herbert Blumer

Based on the works of Mead, Blumer (1969) stated that the core principles of symbolic interactionism are divided into three elements: meaning, language and thought or 'minding' (see Figure 3.2).

1. *Meaning*: refers to a process by which human beings assign meanings to objects and to the interactions they have and observe with other people, especially the family and the community. Symbols are a part of this process of social interaction and what is important are the meanings that people attach to these symbols. These meanings are modified

◘ Figure 3.2   The three core principles of symbolic interactionism

through an interpretive process as an individual has experiences with other people.

2. *Language*: gives humans the ability to convey meaning and also refers to the tendency that human beings have to name things: by naming things, humans give meaning to those things.

3. *Thought*: refers to the innate ability that humans have to be able to think about things rather than mindlessly reacting to situations. The thought process also modifies the interpretation each individual gives to symbols. The concept of self is not developed at birth, but develops through social interaction with others (Blumer 1969).

Symbolic interactionism suggests that people will take on the role and/or socially ascribed labels that are assigned to them by the important social groups to which they belong such as the family and community. If these roles are negative (such as 'this adolescent is a delinquent'), even if the assigned roles are not accurate, the individual will attempt to meet the expectations of their social group because this is the meaning that is given to the individual and is the self-concept that the individual has developed as a result.

Edwin Schur

Schur viewed the labelling of criminal behaviour as a social construction created by professionals from within the criminal justice system, the media and the general public. He was particularly concerned with the labelling of crime in regard to victimless crimes, and viewed these labels as contextual and attributable to the meanings society placed upon the labelled behaviour rather than upon the significance of the behaviour itself. The victimless crimes Edwin Schur cited are no longer considered crimes in many countries. These include homosexuality, adultery and the possession of marijuana. Schur (1971) expanded upon Mead and Blumer's theory of social interactionism by suggesting that if individuals who are labelled as criminal or deviant could group together and thereby gain political power, they could eventually change the prevailing views of the society as was seen with the prohibition of alcohol in America (see case study). *See Labelling Theory*.

Social Learning Theory

Social learning theory is an example of the movement towards more psychologically based theoretical explanations of crime and Albert Bandura is a leading theorist in this field; however, this theory is also closely linked to the sociological process of socialisation that can be seen to occur in all groups and societies and is at the basis of the criminal justice attempts to rehabilitate offenders. Socialisation is one process that results in social learning but other processes are also involved in the development of social behaviour. According to social learning theory, human behaviour is determined by three main factors: cognitive, environmental and personal. Cognitive factors include attitudes, expectations, beliefs and knowledge. Environmental factors include social norms, rules, laws and expectations, pressures from the social network, peer pressure, access to community supports and family influence. Personal factors include skills, traditions, practices, self-esteem, self-efficacy. These elements interact together to reinforce positive social behaviour or to conversely reinforce negative social behaviours. The illustration in Figure 3.3 shows the factors that are involved in the development of human behaviour according to the social learning theory.

United States: The Prohibition of Alcohol in America

From 1920 through to 1933, the American government banned the possession, transportation, production and consumption of alcohol. This was done in an effort to reduce crime and domestic violence and was in response to lobbying by health reformers and the Temperance movement. It was the 'noble experiment' that failed, according to Mark Thornton in his analysis of the effect that this policy had on the country. An analysis of the criminal, social and economic effects of prohibition show that it failed to achieve its goals of reducing alcohol consumption, crime rates and social problems such as poverty. In fact, after an initial decrease in alcohol consumption, there was an overall increase in alcohol consumption. This increase was only addressed with the repealing of the prohibition in 1933 and the introduction of welfare programmes such as Alcoholics Anonymous. Prohibition was also intended to reduce all types of crime such as robbery, burglary, murder and assault, which all went up during the prohibition. These crime rates were reversed when prohibition was repealed. Corruption of public officials increased dramatically during prohibition and this also reduced once it was repealed.

Source: Thornton, M. 1991, 17 July. 'Alcohol Prohibition Was A Failure' *Cato Institute Policy Analysis* 157.

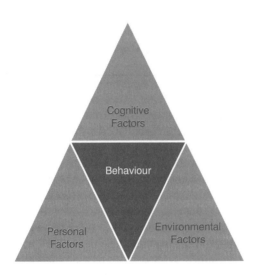

🔲 **Figure 3.3** Elements related to the development of behaviour according to the social learning theory

The social learning theory was developed by Albert Bandura, but shares common elements with differential association and control theory in respect to the importance of early socialisation in ensuring the development of positive social behaviour. *See Differential Association.*

Albert Bandura

Albert Bandura (1986) is the leading theorist in relation to social learning, which he later revised and called social cognitive theory (Bandura 2002). Social learning theory proposes that people learn from a combination of observing their social environment and positive and negative reinforcement from their social network (Bandura 1986). This theory is based in behavioural approaches to psychology, influenced by early theorists such as B. F. Skinner who espoused the theory of operant conditioning (Skinner 1963). In relation to deviant behaviour, and in particular criminal behaviour, unconscious positive and negative conditioning by family members or deviant peers reinforces the criminal behaviour. As he developed his theory further, Bandura deviated from the unconscious conditioning aspect of social learning, such as that associated with socialisation, to incorporate a more conscious cognitive component. This theoretical development by Bandura proposed that people vicariously learn from the social environment but they maintain personal agency and choice over what behaviour they replicate (Bandura 2002). According to his latest theory, Bandura postulates that human agency takes three main forms: personal agency, proxy agency and collective agency. Personal agency refers to the individual's choice to act in a certain way and their belief that by their own actions they can influence their own social environment. Proxy agency is the ability of people to get other people to act on their behalf where they are unable to give effect to a desired outcome themselves. Collective agency refers to the shared beliefs and concerted action of a group that results in collective effort to achieve a desired outcome (Bandura 2002, 2006). Collectivist cultures are said by Bandura (2002) to develop ways of constructing their environments to their own liking and develop in a way that insulates them from external pressures. The values, beliefs and styles of behaviour can be passed on to others through social modelling and experiential learning (Bandura 2002:272).

Bandura (2002) explored social forms of learned behaviour and thought in studies like the Bobo Doll experiments in which he found different forms of social learning. In the Bobo Doll experiments, modelling of aggressive behaviour in children was observed using three differing scenarios: a control group who observed no model at all; another group who watched the doll (the model) act in a subdued non-violent manner, and the third group who observed the doll acting in physically and verbally aggressive ways. In the findings of the experiment Bandura (1978) and his colleagues found that the children who observed the physical and verbal abuse showed double the level of aggressive behaviour compared to the children who observed nonaggressive behaviour or no model at all. This suggests that social learning, particularly direct observation, has a direct impact on the replication of aggressive behaviour by children.

> Can watching violent movies or playing violent video games influence children to become violent?

The Bobo Doll experiments have been criticised for failing to address threats to internal validity such as selection bias, history, maturation and ambiguous temporal sequencing (Hart and Kritsonis 2006:4). The criticisms mainly refer to the failure of Bandura (1978) to take into account the normal developmental changes that occur with age, and external variables and events that may have influenced the outcomes. These criticisms do not, however, detract from the underlying efficacy of the social cognitive theory

Biographical Synopsis

Albert Bandura 1925–
Canadian psychologist Albert Bandura has made significant contributions to the field of psychology which have also been used within criminology for better understanding criminal behaviour. The theory of social learning has been particularly influential. In his early career Bandura attracted controversy for his Bobo Doll experiments where he studied children's reactions to seeing a model behave aggressively towards a doll. There were many criticisms about the validity of the research method used.

and its contribution to understanding deviant behaviour. See *Symbolic Interactionism*.

Labelling Theory

Labelling theory has two major perspectives that explain deviant and criminal behaviour. The first suggests that the labelling of specific behaviour as deviant or criminal influences an individual's self-concept to the extent that they will conform to the expectations of others created by the label (Tannenbaum 1938; Becker 1963). An example of this is where a teenager's behaviour, which was once called 'stubborn', is now labelled as being 'aggressively oppositional'. According to this theory, this teenager is likely to develop aggressive or more overt rebelliousness due to the label that has been attached to them.

The second is where once normal and acceptable behaviour is socially constructed to be deviant (Mead 1934). An example of this is the changing social attitude to smoking tobacco (see case study).

Labelling theory considers the possibility that crime can be socially constructed (Braithwaite 2011). Labelling theorists encourage criminologists to consider that behaviour is not in itself criminal or non-criminal. They argue that behaviour is only considered criminal when

Case Study

Australia: Changing Cigarette Smoking Trends

The Australian government was concerned about the health effects of smoking on the population and introduced mandatory health warnings on all cigarette packets in 1973. Following this there was a decline in smoking among Australian men but an increase in the number of women who smoked. By 1974, 45% of men and 30% of women smoked. By 1976, in an effort to reduce the overall number of people who smoked, the government issued bans on all cigarette advertising on radio and television. In 1990 bans on advertising in newspapers and magazines were also introduced. The Australian government was still concerned about the level of smoking in the population and in 1992 increased tax on cigarettes and other nicotine products making them more expensive to buy. In 1993 the *Tobacco Advertising Prohibition Act 1992* was enacted. In 1995 nationally consistent health warnings were required on all tobacco products across Australia and this was followed in 1998 with bans on point-of-sale advertising. From 2006 graphic health warnings were required on the packaging of tobacco products. Increasing pressure was brought from anti-smoking groups such as the Cancer Council and between 1986 and 2006 phased bans on smoking in workplaces and public places were introduced. In 2010 the Australian government increased the excise on tobacco products to 25%. And in 2012 plain packaging was introduced with updated graphic health warnings. This social engineering programme by the Australian government has resulted in a drop in tobacco consumption with only 12.8% of the population now smoking tobacco products. The most significant impact has been in the numbers of youth smoking which has decreased from 25% in 1991 to 13.3% in 2013.

Source: The Australian Government Department of Health. 2015, 13 February. 'Key Facts and Figures on Tobacco Sales, Consumption and Prevalence'. Accessed online on 4 November 2016 at: www.health.gov.au/internet/main/publishing.nsf/Content/tobacco-kff.

that particular label is attached to it. In addition to this, previously acceptable behaviour can become deviant due to changes in the moral position of a society and subsequent amendment to, or introduction of, legislation that results in that behaviour being reconceptualised as deviant.

Frank Tannenbaum

Labelling theory is thought to have started with the work of Frank Tannenbaum (1938) in the publication of his book *Crime and Community*. He introduced the term 'tagging' to describe the process by which delinquent youth incorporate negative labels into their general perception of themselves and then adopt the behaviours consistent with the label. The central concept purported by Tannenbaum was that if the delinquent label is given too much attention then it will serve to increase the criminal behaviour. He argued that the only way to change this is to refuse to use negative labels to describe delinquent youth. The modern application of this theory is seen in the movement away from using terms such as 'delinquent' and 'youth offender' from the titles of departments dealing with delinquents and instead referring to them as 'juvenile justice' departments.

Howard Becker

Howard Becker, in his book *Outsiders* (1963), discusses public order crimes and refers to those who create public order rules as being 'moral entrepreneurs'. He argues that the creators of moral rules, which give way to public order crimes, operate under complete certainty that their views are right and that the breaching of these rules is evil. The 'crusaders' of these rules operate from a position of moral fervour and self-righteousness and demonise the people and institutions that they believe are responsible for the evil. Politics and political factions often influence the crusaders referred to by Becker. The second perspective explains continued deviance by pointing to the way in which the labelled individual is excluded from acceptable and conventional social structures (Bernburg and Krohn 2003). An example of this is the reintegration of prisoners into society. Once they are released from prison, offenders must try to

Howard Becker 1928–
American sociologist Howard Becker is
another scholar in a long line of American
theorists who studied at the prestigious
University of Chicago. He was the principal
theorist who introduced labelling theory to
the study of deviance and this theory has
had a significant influence on contemporary
criminology. This theory opened up the
possibility that deviant behaviour was
not always attributable to a flaw in the
individual but could be a result of changing
perceptions of the onlookers who label the
behaviour they see. Howard Becker is best
known for his book *Outsiders* (1963).

find employment and stable housing if they are to
remain free from engaging in criminal behaviour.
This is frequently difficult to do as they experience
discrimination and suspicion from others due to
their criminal past.

 How can ex-prisoners be helped to
reintegrate into the community so
that they can become constructive
and contributing members of society?

Unfortunately for ex-offenders many areas of
employment and the housing industry require
referee and police checks, and as a result these
individuals are sometimes prevented from gaining
access to the conventions within society that
would assist them to effectively reintegrate. This
process results in the labelled individual returning
to the deviant behaviours that conform to the label
they have been given and allying themselves to
deviant social groups which accept them.

John Kitsuse

John Kitsuse (1969) argued that definitions
of deviance must include how the behaviour
came to be labelled as deviant. He suggests that
deviance is a process by which a group of people,
a community or a society interprets behaviour as

deviant; defines people who so behave as a certain
kind of deviant; and accords to them the treatment
considered appropriate to such deviants (Kitsuse
1969). Following a study of people's reactions to
homosexual behaviour, Kitsuse (1969) concluded
that the broader implication for the sociological
study of deviance is the need to take into
account the variety and range of viewpoints and
understandings concerning deviant behaviour.
According to Kitsuse, it is important to determine
how the diverse views about deviance interact
together to influence the labelling of the deviant
behaviour and to be clear about the point at
which an official label is assigned. This theoretical
perspective is important to criminologists in that
official statistics are often gathered according
to assigned labels and categories and it cannot
be assumed that statistics in each jurisdiction
will measure the same thing and therefore will
be able to be compared. The ambiguity and
inconsistencies inherent in the gathering of
official statistics were analysed in detail by Kitsuse
and Cicourel in their paper entitled 'A Note on the
Uses of Official Statistics' (Kitsuse and Cicourel
1963). *See **Social Constructionist Theory**.*

Why should you be cautious when
using official statistics in criminology?

John Kitsuse 1923–2003
American sociologist John Kitsuse made
substantial theoretical contributions
to criminology. His major contribution
was in defining deviance through the
development of social constructionist
theory. Within this theoretical perspective,
he studied social problems and deviant
behaviour as social constructions. He also
made an important contribution to the
field with his work on the uses and abuse
of official statistics. John Kitsuse is credited
with bringing a new perspective to the
sociology of deviance.

Jon Gunnar Bernburg and Marvin Krohn

Building on the theory introduced by Becker (1963), Jon Gunnar Bernburg and Marvin Krohn (2003) maintain that deviant labelling can have deep negative impacts on the person's social standing and may be a vital step in building a blueprint of deviant behaviour. Often deviant groups provide support to each other for engaging in deviance and the dynamics of the group are such that deviant behaviour is accepted and even encouraged. This can be seen in motorcycle and street gangs. In addition, the deviant group may provide social shelter from those people and groups that react negatively towards the deviant behaviour (Bernburg et al. 2006).

Neutralisation Theory

Neutralisation theory is a psychosocial theory that deviates from the learning and labelling theories. It explains how criminals are able to justify their actions to themselves and to neutralise the social norms that deem the behaviour to be wrong. The main theorists to espouse the neutralisation theory are Gresham Sykes and David Matza (1957).

Gresham Sykes and David Matza

Matza and Sykes contend that people must learn how to neutralise conventional values and attitudes in order to engage in law-breaking activity. By doing this, they are able to drift backwards and forwards between law-breaking and conventional behaviours (Matza 1964). They point out that criminals, including juvenile delinquents, are not constantly engaged in criminal activity but have times of more conventional activity such as attending school, going to work, religious observance and social gatherings. The assumptions that underpin this theoretical perspective are that criminals sometimes voice guilt over their criminal activity; that they sometimes show respect and admiration for honest, law abiding citizens; they define who they can victimise; and they are not immune to the demands of social conformity. According to neutralisation theory, criminals develop a distinct set of justifications for their criminal behaviour, but in order for this to work they must first neutralise the accepted social values that would challenge these justifications. They do this by learning a set of techniques that allow them to counteract the moral dilemmas their criminal behaviour produces. These techniques are:

- *denial of responsibility*: the criminal behaviour is not their fault;
- *denial of injury*: no harm has been caused by their criminal actions;
- *denial of the victim*: blaming the victim;
- *condemnation of the condemners*: shifting the blame to people in the criminal justice system who can't be trusted and therefore have no right to point the finger;
- *appeal to higher loyalties*: the needs of the criminal gang or group take precedence.

Attempts have been made by criminological researchers to test the theory of neutralisation empirically but the results of these studies have been inconclusive. If neutralising views are held by the broader community, it is easier for criminals to find justifications for their criminal behaviour and easier for victims to be blamed for being victimised (see case study).

Social Constructionist Theory

John Kitsuse was the founder of the social constructionist approach in which he argued that deviance and social problems are socially constructed phenomena (Spector and Kitsuse 1977). Social constructionism argues that social problems are socially constructed and that the social processes involved in defining social phenomena as problematic are just as important for the criminologist to understand as are observing the problems themselves. It also considers conceptual conditions such as gender as social constructs, the meaning and process of identification of which is to be taken into consideration rather than being accepted as inevitable. It would argue that the way in which we present ourselves is influenced by the social

Survey of Attitudes to Sexual Assault in Great Britain

In a recent telephone survey conducted by ICM and commissioned by Amnesty International in Britain, it was found that a third of British people believe that a woman who acts flirtatiously is completely, or at least partially, to blame for being raped. In the same survey, more than a quarter of the population said that a woman who wears sexy or revealing clothing is at least partly responsible for being raped. One in five British people thought the woman is to blame if she has had several sexual partners in the past and more than a third thought a woman was responsible for being raped if she fails to voice the word 'no' during the attack. It was found in this survey that more men than women held these views although more women than men thought that if a woman was drunk when she was raped then she was completely to blame for it. Following the release of these findings, Amnesty International called on the British government to take action to address the high incidence of rape in Britain and to also address low conviction rates in court which it saw as being linked to a sexist blame culture in Britain.

Source: Amnesty International. 2006, 28 March. 'UK: Rape: New Government Measures Welcomed, But Much More Needed'. Press Release. Accessed online on 4 November 2016 at: www.amnesty.org.uk/press-releases/uk-rape-new-government-measures-welcomed-much-more-needed

interactions around us. Social constructionists believe that reality is not only observable but is also formed and influenced by the actors who observe it. This perspective has its origins in the early works of Durkheim, Mead and Karl Marx. Contemporary social constructionist theorists have moved into broader areas of study such as environmental design. The key elements of social constructionism are summarised in Table 3.4.

◻ Table 3.4 The key elements of social constructionism

Social construction of **crime**.	Environmental and urban design may facilitate and/or create crime.
Social construction of **self-concept**.	The concept of self is created by social interactions with others.
Social construction of **reality**.	The observer also influences what is being observed.
Social construction of **social problems**.	The processes used to define social problems and the definitions used may create the problems.

Structural Theories of Crime

Structural theories focus on social origins of crime and the way in which the processes and institutions within society might contribute to crime. These theories tend to have a macro view of the societal influences that may create pressure and tension for individuals or which may present barriers to individuals that prevent them from succeeding. Strain theory is one of the better known of this group.

Strain Theory

Strain theory has its origins in the functionalist school of thought and is the work of Robert Merton (1938), arising from his revision of Durkheim's theory of anomie. It is a theory that focuses on the socio-economic structures of society and in particular the ways in which members of the lower socio-economic groups are obstructed from successful participation in the mainstream society.

Robert Merton

Merton (1938) viewed the causation of crime as being rooted in an unjust social structure where success was determined by an accident of birth rather than by meritorious effort on the part of the individual. He argued that an irony existed in modern society whereby universal education had established expectations for success but that society lacked the universal opportunities to deliver on these expectations. Merton suggested that strain theory describes the struggles of ordinary people as they try to adapt to the tensions within a highly stratified society by using legitimate and criminal means. He also referred to the influential and broad-reaching cultural messages conveyed by mass media and advertising, which exacerbate these tensions. Merton's theory challenged the positivist conception of 'them' and 'us' and blurred the previously held distinctions between criminal and non-criminal. His main thesis was that if people were unable to achieve their goals through legitimate means, due to disadvantage or obstruction, then they would resort to finding illegitimate means to do so.

Albert Cohen

Albert Cohen (1955) was influenced by this thinking and also argued that crime emanates from the tensions created by an inability to achieve the goals of success in a society such as wealth, status and the accumulation of material possessions. His study of delinquent boys attempted to fill in the gaps he thought existed in Merton's theory. In particular he was critical of Merton's use of the word 'culture' which seemed to suggest a single homogeneous culture rather than recognising the existence of various cultures within a society. He argued that strain theory focused only on the lower class and crimes aimed at financial gain. He thought that strain theory could not be used to explain white collar crimes and crimes that were done just for the thrill such as graffiti. He used this theory as the basis for developing his subcultural theory. See *Subcultural Theory*.

 Are poor people likely to commit more crime or is it just the case that they are more likely to get caught?

Richard Cloward and Lloyd Ohlin

Cloward and Ohlin (1960) shared Albert Cohen's perspective of strain theory and also applied it to juvenile delinquency. They focused on lower working class boys who were successful at school but who encountered barriers when trying to gain employment. At the time there was a surplus of equally qualified applicants and employers resorted to looking at other criteria such as class, race and religion to select staff. Cloward and Ohlin found that these boys, having been successful in attaining the appropriate educational requirements, became aggrieved at not being able to access jobs that were commensurate to their educational level and which they had been led to expect. This then led these boys to abandon the conventional norms of society, adopting instead delinquency as a means for achieving what they could not through legitimate means. By integrating Merton's strain theory and Sutherland's subcultural theory they developed their own theory called the differential opportunity theory to explain why some boys became delinquent while others didn't. They saw the lack of an explanation for why some and not all engage in deviance as being a major flaw in Merton's strain theory. See *Subcultural Theory*.

The General Strain Theory

The general strain theory advances on the strain theory by including tensions and strains that may not necessarily be financial in nature but that lead to negative experiences and which cause similar stress for individuals. It opens the possibility that social influences and the failure of socialisation could have more of a role to play in criminal offending than economic deprivation.

Robert Agnew

Robert Agnew is a leading criminological theorist who was influential at this time and he developed the general strain theory. Agnew (1992) was influenced by Robert Merton but argued that there are several sources of strain beyond just the inability to achieve economically derived aspirational goals. This 'general strain theory' expanded on Merton's strain theory to include gender and negative external stimuli such as discrimination.

 What are some of the structural obstacles that might limit disadvantaged people from meeting the goals of society such as stable employment and home ownership?

Agnew recognised that in addition to there being variable strains on the individual, there are also multiple ways in which a person can adapt to these strains including cognitive, emotional and behavioural adaptations. Some of these adaptations can be negative, such as involvement in crime. Robert Agnew (2001) expanded on his original general strain theory by describing in greater detail the characteristics of events that cause strain. He stated that strain results in crime when it:

(a) is seen by individuals and groups as being unjust;
(b) is high in magnitude;
(c) has associated low levels of social control; and
(d) generates pressure to engage in criminal coping strategies.

Agnew claimed that while these types of strain are linked to criminal offending other types of strain are not. He claimed that the focus of researchers up until this point had been on the wrong aspects of strain. *See The Theory of Anomie; Subcultural Theory; Conflict Theory.*

Subcultural Theory

A common criticism of anomie and strain theory was that they failed to take into account the diversity that existed in society but, rather, assumed homogeneity in norms and values. Subcultural theory filled this gap. Albert Cohen (1955) and Stanley Cohen (1972) are leading theorists in subcultural theory. Criminologists do not only study individual criminal behaviour

Biographical Synopsis

Robert Agnew 1953–
Robert Agnew is an American sociologist and criminologist born on 1 December 1953 in Atlantic City. His main interests are in criminology and juvenile offending and he is credited with the development of the general strain theory to explain criminal offending. This theory expanded on the strain theory introduced by Robert Merton to include additional sources of strain such as gender and negative stimuli in the social environment. Robert Agnew has held many prestigious academic positions throughout his career.

but also collective behaviours that are defined as illicit and which are often organised, such as behaviours seen in organised crime syndicates and street gangs. Subcultures are micro-systems within society, with their own language, symbols, norms, values and behaviours, and often exert a high level of influence over their members.

Albert Cohen

Albert Cohen (1955) first introduced the theory of delinquent subcultures in his book *Delinquent Boys* which attempted to answer the questions he felt were left unanswered by Merton's strain theory and Durkheim and Merton's theory of anomie. In this book, Albert Cohen focused on cultures, arguing that if a dominant culture exists, then it implies that other cultures also exist. He termed these other cultures 'subcultures' and the tension experienced as a result of not being able to achieve goals 'status frustration'. Cohen espoused the view that delinquency in youth from lower socio-economic areas was inextricably linked to their social conditions and he viewed delinquent behaviour as a protest against the culture, norms and values of the middle class within American society. Albert Cohen studied delinquent gangs, which he identified are predominantly male, lower-class phenomena and tend to epitomise behaviour, values and goals that are the antithesis of the broader societal culture, namely short-term hedonism and irrational behaviour. He was strongly influenced by strain theory and suggested that people who experience strain in society as a result of social injustice are often not alone in their experience. He argued that if those people collectively, and at the same time, adopt a solution to their situation of social disadvantage, including their lack of access to achievement, then a deviant or criminal subculture emerges. Lower socio-economic environments and cultures are thought by Albert Cohen to socialise boys into delinquent lifestyles. Many disenfranchised youth join gangs and engage in antisocial and criminal behaviour because they are frustrated with the low class status they were born into and they can obtain higher status from within the gang. Within the gang there are opportunities for achievement and advancement although these are generally dependant on involvement in criminal activities which are normalised within the gang.

 How can lower socio-economic environments socialise boys into criminal lifestyles? Why is this less likely to occur in more affluent areas?

Biographical Synopsis

Albert Cohen 1918–2014
American criminologist Albert Cohen studied under both Robert Merton and Edwin Sutherland and his theories synthesised the theories of these great criminological thinkers. He is best known for his work on subcultural theory and delinquent gangs and in particular for his book *Delinquent Boys: The Culture of the Gang* (1955). He argued that when subgroups such as youth were thwarted in terms of being able to legitimately meet social goals, they formed their own group (gang) which created their own rules and expectations, generally by inverting the rules and expectations of society. For example, where society celebrated academic success, the gang celebrated academic underachievement.

Let's Consider!

The Differences Between Strain Theory and Subcultural Theory
Table 3.5 provides you with a quick reference guide to the main differences between strain theory and subcultural theory. The underlying premise associated with strain theory is that goals are universal and society is homogeneous in terms of the strains experienced and the goals aspired to. Subcultural theory allows for heterogeneity in society in relation to subcultures and the different goals and motivations each different group may have. *Refer to* Table 3.5 *for more detail.*

Stanley Cohen

Stanley Cohen (1972), despite sharing the same surname, is not related to Albert Cohen. Coincidentally, he also studied the role of the media and the portrayal of youth subcultures, which he wrote about in his book *Folk Devils and Moral Panics*, and took a different approach to understanding youth culture than his predecessor Albert Cohen. He suggested that the media and public officials create moral panics about the

---

Biographical Synopsis

Stanley Cohen 1942–2013
Stanley Cohen was a highly respected criminologist who was born and raised in South Africa and was indelibly influenced by the apartheid social structure in which he grew up. He contributed greatly to the sociological understanding of youth subcultures and is acclaimed for his creation of the term 'moral panics' to describe the way in which the apparent threat caused by youth behaviour is exaggerated. He was instrumental in broadening the study of crime to include the influence of social control on criminal behaviour. In 2009 he was the first person to receive an Outstanding Achievement Award from the British Society of Criminology.

◘ **Table 3.5** Comparing strain theory and subcultural theory

	Strain theory	Subcultural theory
Human nature	People are a product of their social environment and in particular their social status which is determined by their socio-economic position.	People are a product of their social environment but are also influenced by their collective experiences and the culture of the group they belong to.
Criminal behaviour	People from low socio-economic circumstances will engage in criminal behaviour because they experience strain and become frustrated. Criminal behaviour is an adaptation to the strain. Crime is committed for financial gain.	People (especially young people) will become frustrated with their circumstances but will engage in criminal behaviour for the thrill as well as for the reward.
Response to crime	Crime prevention through improving access to opportunities such as education and employment. Reduce opportunities to commit crime (e.g. increased security on homes to reduce burglary).	Preventing gang formation. Intelligence-led policing and no-association laws.
Main focus	Focus on the individual.	Focus on the collective.
Causation of crime	Social structures that obstruct individuals from reaching the desired goals of the society.	The norms and accepted behaviour of the group. Deviant subcultures that reject the mainstream norms of society.
Punishment	Punishment should reinforce the norms of society.	Punishment should act as a deterrent to others.
Underlying assumptions	Crime is inevitable in a society where there are differences in the relative wealth of its members.	Crime is a result of people adhering to deviant norms and rules operating within the culture of their group (or gang).
Political response	Welfare-based policies to improve the skills and opportunities of disadvantaged communities.	Early intervention in at-risk communities to prevent delinquent gang formation. Zero tolerance policing.

symbols of youth subcultures and the apparent danger and threat they represent to society. Stanley Cohen looked at the development of the 'rock and mod' culture in Britain and highlighted the ways in which the media created moral panics by exaggerating and distorting the amount and the degree of violence or damage caused by young people involved in altercations with the police. Stanley Cohen noted that while individuals from within the youth subcultures may be involved in delinquent acts, the media portrayed these acts as typical of the collective whole, thus generating fear and panic in the broader community.

Subcultural theory has contributed significantly to the understanding of crime causation and recidivism and is still used widely in modern criminology, especially to explain gang crime. In addition to applying this theory to criminal groups, subcultural theory can also be applied to the understanding of the dynamics involved in the development of collective behaviour seen in situations of misconduct in law enforcement organisations, such as those employing prison officers and police. This is because these occupational groups also have strong subcultures with distinctive language, symbols, norms, values and behaviours and which develop external to the prevailing societal culture; however, they do not necessarily fit the Stanley Cohen assumption of lower-class origins.

 How do gangs provide youth with the sense of belonging and a higher social status than they can achieve in broader society?

Differential Association

The theory of differential association was developed by Edwin Sutherland and is a theory of deviance that has been very influential in contemporary criminology. This theory espouses the view that criminal behaviour is learned in association with other people. This includes the learning of the skills of criminal behaviour. Associations with anti-criminal persons can be influential in steering people away from crime just as associations with antisocial persons can steer people towards a criminal career (Gaylord and Galliher 1988).

 What is intergenerational crime and how does it occur?

Edwin Sutherland

Edwin Sutherland (1939) first introduced the theory of differential association in his book *Principles of Criminology*. It was considered to be controversial because it was viewed as suggesting that criminals are made as a result of their associations, including the family. Sutherland discussed 'definitions' and suggested that if the definitions in the social influences around the person supported obedience to the law then the person was more likely to be law-abiding. If the definitions supported law breaking, and there were sufficient accumulated definitions in the social environment that all support law breaking, then the person was more likely to engage in criminal behaviour. In a broad sense, this theory would suggest that people reared in homes where criminal behaviour is considered the norm would grow up to become criminals themselves, because this is the behaviour and values they have learned (see case study).

Within an antisocial environment, criminal and antisocial behaviour is rewarded and reinforced and law-abiding, prosocial behaviour is punished. This theory is often linked with subcultural theory as it supports the conception that people who are in close association with each other, such as in a sub-group, a family or a gang, will develop their own rules and norms which may differ from those of the broader society. There are alternate theories that link criminal behaviour to genetic predisposition and lead to the question: are people are born bad or are they made bad by their environment? This debate is

---

Case Study

Georgia, US: Stephen 'Tony' Mobley

Stephen Mobley, also known as Tony, was on death row in a Georgia prison awaiting execution for his crimes until 2005. Mobley was raised in an affluent white, middle-class American family and did not fit the normal demographics that are normally associated with criminals. He was not abused or mistreated, his family did not engage in criminal behaviour and he was raised to respect the law. From an early age he showed signs of violence and this behaviour worsened as he grew older. At the age of 25 he walked into a pizza shop, robbed it and shot dead the manager in the neck. After shooting the manager he joked that he would apply for his job. He had previously committed several armed robberies of restaurants and dry cleaning shops in the area. Mobley's aunty became a witness for the defence at his trial. She gave testimony that despite outward appearances, various members of the family had been plagued by violent behaviour over the past four generations. His lawyer used this to present a defence based on genetic predisposition that should, his lawyer argued, mitigate his responsibility for the crimes he had committed. Mobley was found guilty and sentenced to death but his lawyer appealed that his family history should be taken into account.

Stephen Mobley was executed on 1 March 2005 after his appeals were rejected.

Source: Connor, Steve. 1995, 12 February. 'Do Your Genes Make You a Criminal?' *The Independent*. Accessed online on 4 November 2016 at: www.independent.co.uk/news/uk/do-your-genes-make-you-a-criminal-1572714.html.

Edwin Sutherland 1883–1950
American sociologist Edwin Sutherland was influenced by the symbolic interactionalist school of thought and is acclaimed for developing the differential association theory of crime. He was also well known for defining white collar crime which challenged previously held assumptions about upper class and aristocratic people being uninvolved in crime. His seminal work in this area, *White Collar Crime* (1949), was extremely controversial at the time and attracted threats of legal action from big corporations in America. He produced several editions of a foundational text book in criminological theory which he first produced in 1924. Differential association theory is closely associated with subcultural theory.

known as the nature versus nurture debate. *See Labelling Theory*.

Social Ecology Theory

Social ecology is a branch of criminology that focuses on how individuals relate to their social environment. It is linked to the Chicago School of sociological thought. Social ecology is influential in contemporary criminological studies of juvenile offending. It has its roots in the theory of social disorganisation which gained popularity in the 1950s and 1960s but which was rejected in favour of other theoretical approaches such as psychosocial and strain theories in the 1970s and 1980s (Brown et al. 2015). It shares theoretical similarities with strain theory but focuses on the individual responses to the social environment rather than the social processes and tensions involved. According to social ecologists crime manifests because of the breakdown in social relationships due to the impermanence of communities and the transitory nature of social life. Social ecologists see parallels between the

social organisation of humans and the adaptive processes of plants and animals.

Clifford Shaw and Henry McKay

In order to discuss contemporary social ecology, we must first look at social disorganisation theory which is where it originated. Social disorganisation and cultural transmission theory was proposed by Americans Clifford Shaw and Henry McKay (1942) to explain juvenile delinquency in Chicago. They developed spatial maps which plotted the occurrence of crime across the city and found that areas with high crime rates were characterised by high percentages of immigrants and African Americans. They also found that there were high levels of welfare dependence and low rates of home ownership in these areas. The housing tended to be low in value with low rents. In addition to this they found high rates of truancy, high infant mortality and high levels of preventable diseases. They concluded that delinquency is associated with physical and social environments and how these are structured. Their theory held that poverty led to social disorganisation because poorer areas lacked the resources to change things or to address the problems that exist in them. Informal social control declines in these areas because there are no shared values and delinquent behaviour is therefore allowed to flourish. This delinquent behaviour is handed down from one generation to the other in a process known as cultural transmission. Shaw and McKay applied their theory to practice when they developed the Chicago Area Project (CAP) which was a crime prevention programme targeting juvenile delinquents. The goal of this programme was to generate a sense of community and to encourage the development of informal social control as a means of reducing the level of juvenile delinquency. A major criticism of the Shaw and McKay research was their exclusive reliance on police data in their research. *See Strain Theory; Limitations of Publicly Available Data (Chapter 4).*

Anne Cattarello

Chicago researcher John Johnstone (1983) investigated gang behaviour and found that the poverty of the community in which the juveniles lived was linked to the formation of gangs. While the opportunity to form gangs was correlated with the poverty of the neighbourhood and the social deterioration of the area, the decision of the individual to join a gang was influenced by their attachments to others and to community institutions. Anne Cattarello (2000) introduces a contemporary approach to social ecology which links macro-level theories of crime with micro-level theories. Cattarello built upon the work of Shaw and McKay (1942) in her own empirical research to test her theoretical model. Cattarello (2000) also drew on the work of Hirschi (1969) and Akers (1985) and census data to develop an integrated theory of delinquency that involved bringing together spatial analysis of crime clusters with theories of social disaffection. The results suggested that while social disorganisation affects peer associations it does not affect social bonds. She found that bonds to family and commitment to school were not influenced by social disorganisation. She also found that the effect of delinquency is completely mediated by positive peer associations. Her integrated model proposes that at the neighbourhood level, transience and mobility impact just as strongly on social disorganisation as do poverty and racial variables and this may be a modern issue of urban/suburban life.

Critical Criminology

Critical criminology comprises structural theories that use socio-political and socio-economic structures and processes to explain crime. These theories tend to look at the big societal picture rather than just at the individual such as is the case with psychological theories. Critical criminology focuses on challenging traditional understanding and beliefs about the nature of crime and revealing where these understandings fail to adequately explain crime. It incorporates a range of theoretical positions such as radical criminology, Marxist theory, political economy theory, conflict theory and feminist criminology.

Marxism

Although this theoretical perspective is often referred to as Marxist criminology, Karl Marx did not specifically address the issue of crime in his theoretical work. Despite this, his work on political and social economies has been enormously influential in some areas of criminology. Marxist criminology became particularly popular in the 1960s and 1970s. Marxism conceptualises capitalism as having two competing and opposing groups: the rich and elite (bourgeoisie) and the poor and ordinary citizen (proletariat). Within this class struggle, the bourgeoisie are the holders and controllers of wealth, resources and power and the proletariat are the exploited and powerless underclass.

Karl Marx

In *The Communist Manifesto*, which was published as a political pamphlet in 1848, Karl Marx and his colleague Friedrich Engels argued that inequality will always exist within a capitalist economy because the owners of the means of production (the bourgeoisie) own the wealth and, through the state, rule those who contribute their labour (the proletariat) (Marx & Engels 1848/1977). Over time, tension develops between the bourgeoisie and the proletariat and Marx and Engels saw this tension as inevitable (McLellan 1977). Engels had previously published *The Condition of the Working Class in England* in 1845 in which he discussed the class struggle inherent in a capitalist economic society (Engels 1845/1969). At a later point, Marx published his work *Das Kapital*. According to Marxism, the proletariat will always strive to obtain a fair share of the wealth and resources while the bourgeoisie will always fight to keep it. It is not difficult to see why criminologists have used Marxist theory in an attempt to explain crime. For instance, a Marxist perspective of criminology locates crime within the social, political and economic structures of society, which Marx argues are determined by the wealthy and powerful elite. This theoretical perspective is also concerned with the opportunities afforded ordinary citizens to legitimately reach the goals of society in order to obtain and maintain their basic needs. Marx views agents of social control, such as the police, as agents

Biographical Synopsis

Karl Marx 1818–1883
Karl Marx was born in Germany and was a renowned sociologist, philosopher, economist and political scientist. He was considered to be a revolutionary who inspired many communist regimes around the world in the twentieth century. He introduced a unique method of social analysis and a unique conceptualisation of capitalist society based on unequal power dynamics. He raised the issue of class struggle and the systemic suffering and exploitation of the working class. He viewed feudalism and capitalism as natural progressions that all societies must pass through as they move toward the ideal of socialism.

harshly punish the poor. Bonger argued that the capitalist system emphasises financial success and individualism, which leads to the selfish pursuit of pleasure that in turn creates the preconditions and encouragement for criminal conduct. This is a similar perspective to that of Durkheim's anomie (1893), but Bonger differs from Durkheim in that he does not advocate for increased or more efficient use of social control to combat the crime problem. Instead he advocates for changes to the social structure from a capitalist system to a socialist system, arguing that crime would eventually be eliminated in a society where the interests of all are equally valued and represented. There are modern theorists who have expanded on the political economy theoretical perspective, including Box (1987) who raised concerns about the link between unemployment and crime and Chambliss (1975) who suggests that crime reduces the level of unemployment in legitimate society by providing a black economy.

 In what ways might unemployment be linked to crime?

of the elite (the bourgeoisie) that are deployed to ensure the ordinary citizens (the proletariat) are kept in their place. Marx also believed that people have an inherent need to be engaged in productive work. An absence of productive work leads to demoralisation and in a capitalist system there will always be a group of people denied the right to engage in productive work.

Political Economy Theory

Based on Marxist theory, a Dutch criminologist by the name of Willem Bonger (1916) utilised the political economy theory to explain the inequities within society and the social polarisation of the crime rates he discovered when he studied crime in Europe in the late nineteenth century. Bonger found capitalism to be a selfish and exploitative social, political and economic system wherein the exploited were forced by the circumstances of capitalism to expend their labour in helping the exploiters to become richer and more powerful. He viewed the capitalist system as unequally policing crime in that the rich and powerful engaged in criminal behaviour without fear of punishment whereas the law tends to

Conflict Theory

Conflict theorists assume that human nature is inherently amoral and that society is comprised of numerous different and opposing groups with different interests that conflict with each other. Conflict theory argues that the root causes of all crime are the social, economic and political structures and forces in a society. *See Strain Theory.*

Max Weber

Where Marx emphasised tension between social classes, conflict theorists such as Max Weber (1905/2002) saw conflict arising from multiple sources, some of which were more important and prominent than economic conflict. Additionally, where Marx viewed cultural ideas in a society as being moulded by the economic system, Weber saw a society's economic system as being moulded by the culture. Another point of difference between Marx and Weber was in the way they viewed the role of capitalism. Marx thought that inequality would exist until capitalism was destroyed and replaced with a fairer social system (socialism) whereas Weber believed that inequality would exist in all social systems, regardless of the way in which it was structured. He saw capitalism as having a functional role in bringing class-based disputes into the open for debate. Conflict theorists emphasise the role of the state in defining deviance and in establishing and policing rules. As with Marx, Weber (1905/2002) viewed the law as being the mechanism by which the ruling class controlled the masses and he saw the law as being derived from class interest with the ruling class imposing its will by criminalising acts it deems contrary to its interests. Rules are made to serve the 'elite' class in a society and deviance is defined as conduct that does not conform to the desired behaviour of the elite. This undesirable behaviour is suppressed by the use of legislation and legitimate state force (i.e. police forces). According to conflict theory, behaviour that threatens the interests of the elite and of capitalism is considered to be the most threatening and therefore receives the most severe sanctions. The basic assumptions of conflict theory are similar to those found in radical criminological theory. *See **Radical Criminology**.*

William Chambliss

William Chambliss is a conflict theorist with a strong Marxist influence. He argued that as the gap between the bourgeoisie and the proletariat grows in contemporary capitalist societies, more punitive measures of social control would increasingly be needed to maintain social order. The most important contribution William Chambliss made to criminology was his study of organised crime, which he published in *On the Take: From Petty Crooks to Presidents* (1978). He observed the existence of a nexus between powerful individuals and groups and organised crime in America. He argued that organised crime is essentially a capitalist activity, which to some extent is protected from

the intervention of law enforcement due to its links with powerful interest groups. Chambliss (1964) also produced a paper analysing the vagrancy laws in Britain and America entitled *A Sociological Analysis of the Law of Vagrancy*. In this paper he questioned the basis upon which vagrancy laws were introduced, suggesting that the real purpose of these laws was to control the movements of workers and to force people into employment, even though the wages on offer were low. By criminalising unemployment and homelessness, the authorities ensured a ready supply of cheap labour for the burgeoning industrial economy.

 How does having a ready supply of cheap labour benefit the owners of production?

Radical Criminology

Radical theory assumes that human nature is generally good but the circumstances into which people are born will shape their personality and behaviour and lead them into a lifestyle that is socially unacceptable. Radical criminology is influenced by Marxist theory and is divided into two main schools of thought: American radicalism and British radicalism. As with conflict theory, radical criminology is concerned with the structure and organisation of society and the power relationships within. The concept of criminalisation is central to radical criminology. In this conceptualisation, the criminal justice system exists to meet the needs of capitalism and any resistance by the working class is criminalised. Criminal law is therefore necessary to maintain class cooperation in a capitalist society. There are three main criticisms of radical criminology, which can be referred to under the headings of teleology, determinism and idealism. The teleological criticism of radical criminology holds that radical criminology fails to take into account the difference between arbitrary power and the rule of law. This criticism suggests that while inequities may exist in the execution of the law, the law itself is inherently based on the best interests of all people. It is therefore important that when inequities are identified they are exposed and corrected. The determinist criticism of radical criminology suggests that the class structures and social imbalances that underpin this theory do not allow for free agency and are posited as the 'only determinants' of criminal conduct. The theory also does not explain why the majority of people from lower classes choose not to engage in criminal behaviour. The idealist criticisms hold that social constructionist approaches, particularly Marxism, are unrealistically idealistic especially in their belief in a crime-free society and the way in which structural constructionist approaches make criminals into victims of the state.

American Radicalism

American radicalism emerged in the US in the 1960s and was strongly influenced by Marxist criminology and conflict theory. It gained traction in America during the great economic depression of the 1930s when, as a political movement, American radicalism presented a reform agenda with a firm social basis that argued for change from the conservatism that had preceded it. The main theorists who developed this approach in criminology are George Vold, Austin Turk, Richard Quinney and William Chambliss.

George Vold

The basic assumption of American radicalism, according to Vold, is that people naturally form groups in society and these groups have differing needs and viewpoints. The groups therefore come into conflict with each other. Vold (1958) contended that criminal activity is something that needed to be understood in the context of social inequality. He argued that criminal activity is often carried out by groups for the benefit of groups and certain types of crimes stem from conflicts between workers and the owners of industrial production. He held that the theory of group conflict applied mostly to four types of crime:

1. crimes that arise out of labour disputes;
2. crimes that arise out of political protests;
3. crimes that arise out of disputes between trade unions; and
4. crimes that arise from cultural, ethnic and racial clashes.

Vold was also concerned with the process of criminalisation, which is the assignment of the status of criminal to an individual, and the unequal way in which this occurs due to the imbalance of power in society. He believed that the process of law making and law enforcement are fundamentally linked and are influenced by class conflicts and by conflicts between particular interest groups. He claimed these conflicts represented a struggle for control of police powers, which came with the control of the legislative process. He further claimed that the group that gains control of the legislative process and police powers also dominates the policies that decide who is and who isn't a criminal. An example of clashes arising from disputes between the government and trade unions is seen in the Polish case of Lech Wałęsa and Polish Solidarity (see case study). This case highlights the tensions that develop between the working and ruling classes (as understood by radical theorists).

Austin Turk

Another major theorist in the American radicalist tradition is Austin Turk (1969) who was attracted to the radical approach by his growing perception that the existing criminological theories were unable to adequately explain the many problems and conflicts being acted out in modern America. In his book *Criminality and Legal Order* he presented an alternative view of class tensions to that presented in Marxist criminology. He argued that there were two positions in society: one of domination and the other of subjugation. He believed that class tensions that arose were not necessarily linked to wealth and property relations, as is the case in traditional Marxist theory but similarly argues that conflict between these two groups is inevitable. According to

Poland: Lech Wałęsa and Polish Solidarity

In the 1970s and 1980s, Poland was governed by a communist government during a time of rising food costs. During the 1970s the police killed a number of demonstrators who were protesting about high food prices. The demonstrations had resulted in riots involving protestors and police. In 1980, workers at the Lenin shipyards in Gdańsk went on strike in protest at the rising food costs. Being a communist system, the shipyard was owned by the government. Lech Wałęsa was appointed the leader of the strike committee and negotiated a successful outcome with management after only three days of strikes. Wałęsa was very brave in doing this as striking was illegal under the communist regime. Soon workers from factories in other areas from Gdańsk and surrounding areas sought the help of Wałęsa who formed an inter-factory strike committee. This gave the workers unprecedented power and they used it to demand political rights such as the right to strike, the right to protest and the right to form trade unions. Eventually farmers and other unions joined the movement and the original strike committee became a national federation of unions known as Solidarity. Fearful of the growing power of the people, on 13 December 1981 the Polish Government made Solidarity illegal. Wałęsa and solidarity were forced underground and Wałęsa was subjected to constant harassment. In 1988 in response to impending economic collapse, the government reluctantly entered negotiations with Solidarity which was as a result made legal again. Solidarity became a political party and Wałęsa its leader.

Source: *Encyclopaedia Britannica*. 2014.

Turk (1969) social order is maintained as the subjugated masses continually negotiate how to behave in relation to those in authority. Conflicts will arise between those in authority and the subjugated, and criminalisation of the latter's behaviour results. As with Marx, Turk (1969) also contended that social and institutional norms develop in a way that protects the interests and social status of the dominant group and he was concerned with the unequal distribution of power in modern society.

 How might definitions of crime represent the interests and needs of the rich and powerful in a society?

Richard Quinney

Richard Quinney's work is influenced by the work of Turk and Chambliss and the Frankfurt School and has become progressively more radical. His theoretical position began with conflict theory and advanced through various evolutions to eventually become what he termed 'peacemaking criminology' which contained a blend of Marxist criminological and theological influences. Quinney's early work was very much concerned with the social structure and the distribution of power in society and how the interplay of these elements constructed crime. To Quinney, criminal definitions represented the interests and needs of the powerful in capitalist society (Quinney 1970). He thought that the powerful elite enacted laws that serve their own interests rather than the interests of society. Ordinary people then accept those laws as their own and grant authority to those in power to carry out whatever actions are necessary to promote their own interests. Quinney eventually developed his theory of crime to a point that the ruling elite and the state are central. This is referred to as an instrumentalist view of the law and has its origins in Marxism and *The Communist Manifesto*. Quinney (1977) published a book entitled *Class, State and Crime* in which he provided a typology of crime. This typology of crime included crimes of domination; crimes of accommodation and resistance; and crimes of resistance. Crimes of domination include crimes of control such as crimes committed by the police, governments and financial crimes committed by large corporations. Crimes of accommodation and resistance include predatory crimes such as burglary and theft and personal crimes such as sexual assault and homicide. Crimes of resistance include political crimes and terrorism. *See **Structural Theories of Crime**.*

British Radicalism

Radical criminology emerged in Britain much later than in the US. Ralf Dahrendorf (1959) was a German-born British sociologist who was concerned with social inequality and is best known for his influential work entitled *Class and Class Conflict in Industrial Society* in which he attempts to bring together the functionalist and Marxist approaches. He was one of the founding theorists of conflict theory, which is the foundational theory underpinning radicalism.

Ralf Dahrendorf

Dahrendorf's conflict theory contended that Marxist theory was too simplistic and was not reflective of modern class conflict. Rather than describing class differences by property ownership he argued that in modern capitalist society class conflict was inherently linked to people's access to authority, which is connected to status, position and role. Austin Turk was greatly influenced by the work of Dahrendorf. Radicalism found an impetus at the *National Deviancy Conference* in Britain in the 1960s and was a response to dissatisfaction with the positivism among criminologists in the UK. British criminology was at a crossroads at this time and Jock Young was involved, with others in writing *The New Criminology*, a groundbreaking work in which they announced this new approach to criminology (Taylor et al. 1973). Around the 1960s two distinct and opposing theoretical streams emerged in Britain: radical criminology and administrative criminology. Administrative criminology, Young suggested, had a narrow, empiricist and policy-oriented focus. Radical criminology was considered to be more open and creative as it presented a view of crime causation as being rooted in class conflict and social inequality.

Realist Criminology

Realism is an example of a modern theoretical perspective that has built on earlier theories and continues to develop and evolve today. Much of this theory has been influenced by theoretical concepts such as radical criminology but has added something new to the understanding of criminal behaviour. Jock Young (1988), for example, was a radical theorist who contributed greatly to the area of radical criminology until he became a critic of the radical approach and began to advocate for a new approach that included personal responsibility. As a result he founded left realist criminology.

Left Realism

Left realism evolved not only from radical criminology but also from the growth of feminism and in particular the growing political concerns about sexual and domestic violence. A tension developed in relation to the continued theorising about class and gender struggles that erupted within radical criminology. This occurred at a time when criminal justice analysts and policy makers in Britain and the US were grappling with the rising dominance of right-wing theories of crime and crime control. Left realism rose to prominence in Britain in the 1970s and 1980s but was not really embraced to any great extent in the US. Roger Matthews and Jock Young (1986) were the main theorists to pronounce a left realist ideology.

 What do you think right-wing theorists would be suggesting in relation to crime and crime control?

Table 3.6 summarises the four important aspects that underpin left realist theory. The main theorist behind this approach is Jock Young. *See **Strain Theory; Right Realist Criminology**.*

◘ Table 3.6 The four important aspects underpinning left realist theory

Empirical	The process of developing empirical knowledge surrounding crime occurrence and the impact of crime.
Causal	The focus on explanations of causality.
Inter-relational	The exploration of relationships and associations that exist between offenders and victims and formal and informal crime controls.
Policy	The effort to develop realistic criminal justice policies aimed at reducing crime.

Jock Young

Jock Young is a British criminologist who emphasised the dualities of crime which are: offender and victim; actions and reactions; crime and control. He proposes that crime rates are generated by the social relationships between four elements: the police (the formal system), the community (the informal system), the offender and the victim. It is argued that each of these four elements interact together to either facilitate or hinder crime. Young was instrumental in introducing the left realist theoretical arm to modern criminological thinking. He suggested that left realism emerged from the evolution of criminological thought through a series of linked processes. These included the aetiological crisis, the crisis in penalty, the increased awareness of victimology and the increased public demand for efficiency and accountability in the public service. The central theme of left realist criminology is to focus on the reality of crime. This requires criminologists to reject tendencies to romanticise, pathologise, underestimate or exaggerate the nature and extent of crime. Tierney (1996) is a left realist criminologist who identifies four main aspects relevant to left realism as being: empirical, causal, inter-relational and policy.

John Lea and Jock Young (1984) published a well-known work entitled *What is To Be Done About Law and Order?* In this book they reject the Marxist portrayal of the criminal as a political revolutionary to adopt a more realistic view of criminals as predators who prey on the poor, the disadvantaged and the disenfranchised. They argued that, as a result, the poor were doubly victimised because they were firstly abused by the capitalist state and then by members of their own class system. Matthews and Young (1992) continued this movement away from Marxism and severely criticised radicalism as being left idealism that assumed that all crime that occurred in the working class was as a result of poverty, with crime being portrayed only as an attempt to redress economic inequality.

 Can all crime be seen as being linked to poverty and economic inequality? What crimes are not influenced by these structural issues?

Left idealism, it was argued, presented the view that to blame the criminal who comes from low socio-economic origins for their crimes was akin to blaming the victim, but in fact this theoretical position ignored the impact on victims and alleviated the criminal of responsibility for their criminal actions. The left realist approach has continued to develop since being introduced by Young in the 1980s with the work of Roger Matthews (2014).

Roger Matthews

Matthews (2014) criticises the domination of conservative, positivist approaches in modern criminology and answering claims that criminology has become increasingly socially and politically irrelevant. He attaches the label of 'administrative criminology' to the tendency of modern criminology to focus on situational crime prevention and theories such as rational choice and routine activity theory and argues that despite the emphasis on these particular theories, contemporary criminology is largely absent of a theoretical base. He saw instead a tendency towards categorising crime with no empirical or theoretical rigour attached. Matthews provides a fresh perspective on left realism and applies a neo-realist perspective to the uses of social control in modern society. *See Strain Theory; Labelling Theory; Positivism.*

Right Realist Criminology

The opposite of left realist criminology is right realism. Right realism emanates from conservative views about crime and criminal justice and has borrowed elements of control theory. It aims to provide the theoretical foundations of more realistic policies for crime prevention and reduction. It is a conservative approach to criminal justice that ignores socio-economic factors in understanding and responding to crime and while right realist criminology is a controversial approach to criminology among some academics it has been politically popular and influential,

particularly in America and the UK. The major proponents of right realist criminology are James Wilson, Richard Herrnstein, Charles Murray and Lawrence Mead. Right realist criminology emphasises individual responsibility but tends to ignore structural inequalities and environmental influences when dealing with issues of crime and punishment. This approach is linked to conservative responses to law enforcement including 'get tough on crime' policies. The major criticisms levelled at this approach are that it assumes rationality in human behaviour and fails to account for the interceding influence of power.

> ❯ Is getting tough on crime likely to reduce the overall crime rate in lower socio-economic areas? What crime types might respond well to this approach?

James Wilson

American scholar James Wilson adopts a positivist approach and rejects the assumption that there are underlying socio-economic causes of crime. He is known for having introduced zero tolerance policy approaches to addressing crime when employed as an advisor to the Reagan government in the US in the 1980s. Figure 3.4 summarises the main steps and conceptual processes involved in a zero tolerance crime prevention approach. This approach proved to be successful in reducing crime and has been adopted by many police departments around the world. *See Broken Windows Theory.*

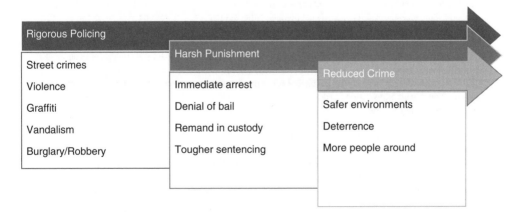

◘ **Figure 3.4** Zero tolerance approach to crime prevention

James Wilson collaborated with a colleague, Richard Herrnstein, to reconceptualise classical approaches. In their contentious book entitled *Crime and Human Nature*, James Wilson and Richard Herrnstein's (1985) characterisation of the criminal harkened back to the biological positivist theories of Lombroso and Ferrero in that they espoused a biosocial approach to understanding criminal behaviour. Their work focuses on the cognitive deficits that they assert can be found in people who engage in criminal conduct. *See **Biological Positivism**.*

 What were the theories posited by Lombroso and Ferrero?

According to the biosocial approach, the criminal has a biological predisposition to criminal behaviour and therefore forces of social conditioning and control are unable to completely eradicate crime. This work is criticised for being too narrow in scope because it focuses on more serious violent and sexual crimes rather than taking a broader focus. The tools developed by Wilson and Herrnstein to address conceptual deficits are further criticised for not being supported by scientific or empirical evidence and also for the difficulty experienced by other researchers when attempting to test their theory. Despite the criticisms, the theory as to whether there are biological markers for crime has been the subject of some research over the years (see case study).

Richard Herrnstein

An American psychologist, and colleague of James Wilson, Richard Herrnstein was an enthusiastic supporter of the right realist approach. Herrnstein and Murray made a significant, if controversial, contribution to criminology with the publication of *The Bell Curve: Intelligence and Class Structure in American Life* (Herrnstein and Murray 1994). They used data obtained from the *National Longitudinal Survey of Youth* to assert that people with low IQs were more likely to report having been involved in crime. In making this assertion, they did not take socio-economic status into account even though social class and poverty are clearly linked to criminal offending. It is also known that people of lower intelligence and low educational achievement tend to be more predominantly represented in lower socio-economic residential areas. This approach to conceptualising criminal behaviour stigmatises people from lower socio-economic areas who may not have the same opportunities for educational achievement as people from more

---

Case Study

Do Paedophiles Have Physical Differences to Non-Paedophiles?

Paedophilia was once thought to originate from social and psychological influences in childhood. More recently, experts are coming to the conclusion that it is a sexual orientation that is as inherent as heterosexuality or homosexuality. They suggest it is an inborn and deep-rooted predisposition that emerges during puberty and does not change over the course of the lifetime. It is a predisposition that appears to mainly afflict men. It is estimated that between 1% and 5% of all men are paedophiles. Paedophilia means that they have a dominant attraction to prepubescent children but not all paedophiles molest children. Not all child molesters are paedophiles either as there are different types of sex offenders, paedophiles being just one. At one time it was thought that sexual abuse in childhood was responsible for paedophilia, but this has been discounted by researchers who now point to biological causes. Studies have found that 30% of paedophiles are left handed or ambidextrous which is triple the general rate. This is suggestive of a genetic link. Researchers have also found that paedophiles are nearly an inch shorter on average than non-paedophiles and have a lower IQ which tends to be around ten points below average. In a study of MRI scans of the brain conducted on 65 paedophiles, it was found that paedophiles had less white matter than criminals with no history of sexual offences. It has been suggested that as white matter forms the connective circuitry of the brain, a process of cross-wiring could be occurring where images of children stimulate the same neural response that other men would have to images of an attractive woman.

Source: Zarembo, A. 2013, 14 January. 'Many Researchers Taking a Different View of Paedophilia' *Los Angeles Times*.

affluent areas. This is why the theory became so controversial and the controversy was made worse by Herrnstein and Murray's postulation that IQ differences are racially determined. Other studies of IQ and criminal behaviour show that IQ levels account for only minimal variations in self-reported involvement in crime.

> Why was there such a great controversy about Herrnstein and Murray's views about intelligence and in particular IQ levels? Do you agree with them?

The Bell Curve has been widely criticised for misusing statistics, omitting facts and arriving at unsupported conclusions. This book has led policy makers in the criminal justice system to emphasise the need for clear rules and consequences with punishment and deterrence being the key policy directions and little to no focus being given to the rehabilitation of offenders.

Charles Murray

Charles Murray is a British criminologist whose major contribution to right realist criminology is his 1990 work *The Emerging British Underclass*, which impacted significantly on the discussion of social class and crime. His reference to the 'underclass' and his stereotyping of poor families as 'unkempt' and prone to unemployment and juvenile delinquency caused much controversy in the debate on crime. According to Murray, the traditional family has broken down leaving young men in particular with no appropriate role models. The traditional methods of socialising the young have likewise broken down, resulting in a decline of the social solidarity within communities. This social solidarity is essential to social order and without it communities will become fragmented. The norms that develop in such communities are those that support crime.

Broken Windows Theory

In 1982, George Kelling produced and article with James Wilson that introduced the theory of broken windows. This theory suggests that if small things are ignored in a community such as broken windows it will encourage vandals to break more windows and if litter on the ground is ignored more people will litter. If small crimes are ignored then more serious crimes will occur (see case study).

The broken windows theory proposes that no crimes should be ignored and all crimes, no matter how small, should be punished. Crime prevention can be increased in a community that addresses problems such as broken windows, graffiti and vandalism quickly and punishes perpetrators swiftly (Kelling and Coles 1997). Kelling (2015), however, argues that the broken windows theory is being misused by police to excuse poor policing with police in America being criticised for targeting mainly poor black men for minor offences under the guise of addressing the small crimes in order to prevent more serious criminality. This has obvious ramifications for the over-representation of poor black people in the criminal justice system. He argues that the theory proposed by Kelling and Wilson (1982) has been largely misunderstood. Kelling (2015) suggests that the broken windows policing is highly discretionary. He argues that it was intended to convey the importance of making public spaces safe and orderly to

---

Let's Consider!

The Differences Between Left Realism and Right Realism

Table 3.7 provides you with a quick reference guide as to the main differences between left realism and right realism. The underlying premise associated with left realism is that people are made criminal by their environment. They can only change their behaviour if the inequities in the socio-economic system are addressed. The underlying premise with right realism is that people weigh up risks, consequences and rewards when considering criminal behaviour. According to this perspective, crime exists and it doesn't matter why: it must be controlled. *Refer to Table 3.7 for more detail.*

Case Study

Stanford, USA: Zimbardo Broken Windows Experiment

Philip Zimbardo is a psychologist with the Stanford University. In 1969 he undertook an experiment where he placed a car with no licence plates and the hood up idle in the Bronx, New York and another car in the same condition in Palo Alto California. The Bronx is an area that experiences a lot of vandalism and crime whereas in Palo Alto crime and vandalism are less prevalent. The car that was placed in the Bronx was stripped of everything of value within minutes of having been left there. Once everything of value had been removed, the cars windows were broken, the upholstery was ripped and children began using the car to play on. The car in Palo Alto remained untouched for over a week. At this point, Zimbardo went to the vehicle and smashed its windows with a sledge hammer. Shortly afterwards, other people joined in the destruction of the car. Zimbardo noted that the vandals involved in the destruction of the car in Palo Alto and the destruction of the car in the Bronx were well-dressed, respectable-looking citizens dispelling the myth about vandals being from poor backgrounds.

Source: Zimbardo, P. 2007. *The Lucifer Effect: Understanding How Good People Turn Evil.* New York: Random House.

☐ **Table 3.7** Comparing left realism and right realism

	Left realism	Right realism
Human nature	People are born good but circumstances can make them become bad.	People are born greedy and selfish.
Criminal behaviour	People are made into criminals by an inequitable socio-economic system. Criminal law is a social construction that benefits the ruling class and marginalises the working class. Criminal behaviour must be understood within the social context.	Some people will make rational choices to become criminals. In poorer neighbourhoods law-abiding citizens are forced out by delinquents giving way to lawlessness in these areas.
Response to crime	Short-term strategies that impact change with the victim, the offender, state agencies and the public. Increased community policing.	Crime prevention through deterrence. Increased police powers to prevent opportunities for crime. Rehabilitation.
Main focus	Focus on the social system not the criminal.	Focus on the criminal and social control not the crime.
Causation of crime	Social construction of crime. Relative deprivation and marginalisation.	A failure of social control and socialisation.
Punishment	Minimal use of prison. Community- based options.	Tough sentences as a deterrent to others and to get criminals off the streets.
Underlying assumptions	People are not responsible for their criminal behaviour; it is caused by social deprivation.	It doesn't matter why crime occurs, it exists and therefore it must be controlled.
Political response	Increase alternatives to prison and address social disadvantage and marginalisation.	Get tough on crime law and order policies.

encourage people to use them. By encouraging people to use public spaces, crime is deterred in these areas. Conversely, abandoned and run-down public spaces tend to attract crime. *See Right Realist Criminology*.

Environmental Criminology

Environmental criminology is the study of crime, criminality and criminal victimisation in a spatial context. It firstly looks at how these aspects relate to a particular place and secondly how individuals organise and manage their activities so as to be influenced by spatial factors. Environmental criminology would argue that the physical design of the environment can create crime. An example of this is the design of motorways and the frequent changes in speed limits in a particular stretch of road that may inadvertently increase road traffic offences by causing confusion in drivers. By addressing problems with the design of the roadway, traffic offences may be reduced. Environmental criminology is also concerned with utilising the design of the built environment as a means for socially engineering the behaviour of particular individuals and groups and minimising certain types of crime. This can include such things as the installation of CCTV cameras and additional lighting in urban hotspots to prevent violent crime and robberies and also to prevent break-ins at commercial and residential properties. The routine activity approach is an example of environmental theory. This perspective is not concerned with the underlying causes of crime but only with the crime itself and emphasises the significance of 'place' in generating or facilitating crime.

Routine Activity Theory

Contemporary theory has continued to develop with varied ways of looking at the issue of crime and crime prevention that differ enormously from earlier theories. The routine activity theory is a way of viewing crime within the context of time and space and has been enthusiastically embraced by local councils and domestic law enforcement agencies as it has practical and easy-to-understand applications for understanding and preventing crime.

Lawrence Cohen and Marcus Felson

Cohen and Felson (1979) introduced the concept of the routine activity approach which was a new way in which to analyse crime rate trends and cycles of crime. It postulated that in order for crime to occur there needed to be a convergence in space and time of likely motivated offenders, suitable targets (victims) and an absence of capable guardians. A motivated offender is an offender who is motivated to commit crime and who is capable at that particular point in time of committing crime. A suitable target is a person who is available at the same time and place to be targeted by the motivated offender. It is a person or an object that is attractive to the offender as a target. The absence of a capable guardian refers to the absence of a person or other entity that would deter the offender from committing the crime. A guardian can be a person who is physically present and able to intervene or can be the visible presence of police or surveillance cameras.

> ⊙ What can a potential target do to reduce their risk of becoming a victim?

The concept of guardianship has been developed further by Hollis-Peel et al. (2011) who suggest that there is a hierarchy of guardianship. Invisible guardians are the most common and are generally not visible in the public space and may not be aware of what is going on. Available guardians are present in the area and visible to would-be criminals but they may not be paying attention to what is happening in the area. Capable guardians are visible to would-be criminals and are also actively monitoring and observing the area. They are very much aware of what is happening. Intervening guardians are visible, actively monitoring and ready and

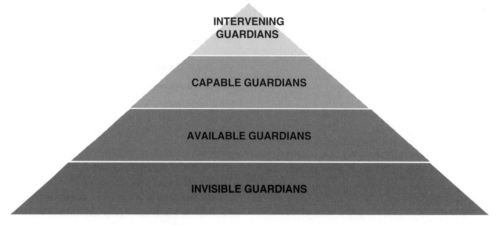

Figure 3.5   The hierarchy of guardianship

willing to take action if required. This hierarchy is depicted in Figure 3.5.

Marcus Felson

Marcus Felson (1998) elaborated on the concept of routine activity theory in his book *Crime and Everyday Life*. The underlying premise of this theoretical perspective is that, with all things being equal, criminal activity will rise according to the opportunities available to commit crime for profit. According to Felson, there will always be people motivated to commit crimes if the opportunity presents and therefore crime is a function of changing social conditions. With the development of large urban centres, the opportunities to commit crime increase because there is greater anonymity, allowing predators to hide and escape detection. Felson examines how the social environment encourages or inhibits crime in everyday routine activities such as the modern tendency for all members of the family to be absent from the home (at work or school) during the day, providing greater opportunity for would-be burglars to gain access to their home. Felson points to changes in the structure and functioning of society to explain changes in the crime rate, such as the greater availability of potential victims on the street due to people being more active outside the home.

Deviant Places Theory

Some places seem to unintentionally attract crime and some places actively promote and condone criminal activity. Deviant places theory is a theory about the ecology of crime and is a human ecology theory (Stark 1987). The ecological approach of deviant places proposes that characteristics of certain neighbourhoods will attract crime, deviance and other social problems that are not associated with poverty. Stark (1987) suggests that certain groups of people (e.g. African Americans) who congregate in areas where the crime rate is high are more likely to enter the criminal justice system themselves. When African Americans are dispersed more equally throughout suburbs and rural areas, their involvement in crime drops. Stark sees this as a result of their being able to benefit from factors that are conducive to a lower crime rate such as better housing and education. Deviant places theory has been heavily criticised for demonising and labelling poor neighbourhoods.

Vegetation and Crime Prevention

A little-known area within environmental criminology is the study of how the strategic placement of vegetation, particularly in urban settings, can increase or reduce crime (Kuo and

Sullivan 2001). Early studies have shown that densely vegetated areas significantly increase the fear of crime (Schroeder and Anderson 1984; Talbat and Kaplan 1984). This fear is in some respects well founded as later studies have shown that dense vegetation is used by criminals to hide themselves and their criminal activities (Michael and Hull 1994). The opposing perspective argues that well-placed vegetation in urban settings can deter crime (Bevilacqua 2013).

Frances Kuo and William Sullivan

The dominant theorists in the field of the study of vegetation and crime are Frances Kuo and William Sullivan. Their article 'Environment and Crime in the Inner City: Does Vegetation Reduce Crime?' provides a detailed analysis of various studies that have looked at the role of vegetation in creating or reducing crime (Kuo and Sullivan 2001). To show the long tradition the role of vegetation has played in crime prevention they refer to a decree made by King Edward I in thirteenth-century Britain, ordering the clearing of vegetation along the highways in order to remove areas where would-be criminals could conceal themselves and do harm to passing merchants (Campbell-Culver 2006). Kuo and Sullivan (2001) argue that not all vegetation contributes to crime by enabling concealment and/or blocking offenders and victims from the view of others. In fact some vegetation, such as well-kept and regularly mown lawns around entrances to buildings, do not add to crime at all and, to the contrary, can deter crime by increasing and preserving visibility and by mitigating the psychological stressors that are linked to crime (Kuo and Sullivan 2001).

Mary Wolfe and Jeremy Mennis

The perspective arguing that trees and other strategically planted vegetation can reduce crime has been studied by Mary Wolfe and

---

Key Criminological Research Debates

Does vegetation in urban areas facilitate or deter crime?
A modern criminological debate is whether vegetation in urban areas encourages crime Michael, Hull and Zahm (2001) or deters it (Wolfe and Mennis 2012). Michael et al. (2001), in a study of theft from motor vehicles, related that criminals admitted using the cover of trees and vegetation to facilitate their crimes. The main issue in regard to vegetation seems to concern its capacity to conceal criminal activity from view in addition to increasing people's fear that crime could occur in areas that are densely vegetated. Kuo and Sullivan (2001) suggest that most studies arguing that vegetation causes crime are fear-of-crime studies that seek people's perceptions of crime rather than the link between vegetation and crime. An exception to this perspective, however, are the studies conducted by Michael et al. (1994, 2001). Most studies seem to support the positive role that vegetation in urban spaces has in terms of reducing and deterring crime. Wolfe (2010) has found that there is less graffiti, vandalism and littering in urban outdoor spaces that have natural landscapes. In residential neighbourhoods, property crimes are fewer when there are trees in the 'right of way' and vegetation around houses. According to Wolfe, public housing residents with trees and natural landscape close to their public housing estates report 25% fewer domestic violence-related incidents than public housing residents that have no natural landscape close by. Troy et al. (2012) undertook a study in Baltimore and found that a 10% increase in tree canopy was associated with a 12% decrease in crime. It is argued, however, that vegetation in urban areas is only associated with deterring crime when it is well maintained. Vegetation that is allowed to get out of control and is neglected may tend to attract crime (Bevilacqua 2013).

Jeremy Mennis (2012) who argue that well-maintained urban vegetation deters crime. In contrast to this, they suggest the accumulation of rubbish and the uncontrolled growth of vegetation leads to spaces where crime can be allowed to flourish. Their study, conducted in the city of Philadelphia, found that in areas with more well-placed vegetation there were lower rates of assault, robbery and burglary. They also found that in the crimes can be facilitated by poorly placed and ill-maintained vegetation (Wolfe and Mennis 2012). Matt Bevilacqua (2013) agrees with this position and proposes that it is not sufficient just to include green spaces in urban environments and argues that these spaces need to be well maintained if they are to deter crime.

Contemporary Classicism

Contemporary classicism moves away from focusing just on the individual offender and their motivations to offend to considering the offender within the context of the criminal event itself. Well-known theorists in this field are Ronald Clarke and Derek Cornish. This perspective deals with the utility of crime and proposes that criminals commit offences because it suits them to at the time (for example it is the quickest and easiest way to get what they want). One of the leading theories of contemporary classicism is rational choice theory.

Rational Choice Theory

The theory of rational choice has its origins in classical criminology and proposes that offenders are rational beings who will weigh up the rewards and consequences with the risk of being caught before deciding to commit an offence. Crimes are therefore deliberate and rational acts that aim to benefit the offender in some way. The offender decision-making processes will differ slightly depending on the type of offence that is committed but according to rational choice theory they will always engage in some sort of cognitive decision-making process.

Derek Cornish and Ronald Clarke

Rational choice theory was proposed by Cornish and Clarke (1986) who built on rational choice theory in economics and applied it to criminology. They emphasised the need to focus on the rationality of offenders in the commission of crime in order to develop more effective crime prevention strategies. In addition to proposing that offenders are rational actors they also took into account situational factors, including the opportunities for crime. Rational choice theory formed the basis of opportunity theory and situational crime prevention theory and these theories are widely used by police departments worldwide. The criticism of this theory suggests that it does not address impulsive crimes such as assault, domestic violence and homicides committed out of passion. Felson and Clarke (1998) argue that even seemingly impulsive crimes such as assault require a decision-making process.

Opportunity Theory

Opportunity theory has its origins in rational choice theory (Cornish and Clarke 1986) and routine activity theory (Cohen and Felson 1979). Where rational choice theory argues that offenders go through a rational decision-making process before they commit crime, and routine activity theory argues that three elements must converge in time and space for crime to occur, opportunity theory suggests that it is simply the existence of opportunity that causes crime. It presupposes that people are generally motivated to offend if the opportunity to do so presents itself.

Marcus Felson and Ronald Clarke

Felson and Clarke (1998) have been credited with identifying opportunity theory. Opportunity theory proposes that opportunities for crime exist in everyday life and are concentrated in time and space. These opportunities are dependent on the day-to-day activities and movements of people and one crime may produce opportunities for other crimes. Felson and Clarke argue that where previous explanations do not explain all crime, opportunity theory does. They argue that all crime involves opportunities and therefore opportunity must play a role in causing crime. According to Felson and Clarke, this theory explains all types of crime, from street muggings to white collar fraud. They further argue that by reducing the opportunity for crime, then crime can be prevented. *See Routine Activity Theory*.

Situational Crime Prevention

The theory of situational crime prevention has its origins in rational choice theory (Cornish and Clarke 1986) and environmental theories such as routine activity theory (Cohen and Felson 1979). Situational crime prevention provides policing departments with simple, common-sense and easy-to-apply principles and steps, which is why it is so popular with policing agencies around the world.

Ronald Clarke

Ronald Clarke (2011) describes situational crime prevention as a theory about reducing the opportunities to commit crime. It is a theory that proposes that situational factors must be taken into account when considering crime and how to prevent it. This theory is focused more towards the prevention of crime than understanding why crime occurs and it therefore ignores the theories of biological, social, psychological and intergenerational causes of crime. Clarke (2011) argues that while the theories that look to explain the root causes of crime are useful, it is the disposition of the criminal to offend, converging with the opportunity and temptation to offend, that results in crime. The focus of law enforcement should therefore be on the situational factors that provide opportunities for crime rather than on the individual. He reasons that there will always be individuals in society with a disposition to offend. Situational crime prevention incorporates a range of other theories to explain the occurrence and prevention of crime such as routine activity theory (Cohen and Felson 1979), crime pattern theory (Brantingham and Brantingham 1993) and rational choice

theory (Cornish and Clarke 1986). This theory operates at three levels, with routine activity theory explaining societal changes that influence opportunities to commit crime at the meso level. The crime pattern theory operates at the meso level and explains how offenders come across opportunities to offend in their own neighbourhood when they are just going about their day-to-day activities. The rational choice theory explains opportunities to commit crime at the micro (individual) level and the decision-making factors that intervene in that process. Situational crime prevention is not concerned with the causation of crime motivation but rather preventing the opportunities that allow crime to occur. *See Classicism; Routine Activity Theory*.

Republican Criminology

Republican criminologists are committed to social systems that enhance political and economic equality; in particular, ways in which the criminal justice system can be encouraged to promote human rights values. Braithwaite and Pettit are the major theorists of this perspective.

John Braithwaite and Philip Pettit

John Braithwaite and Philip Pettit (1994) are Australian republican criminologists who posited republican theory in the 1990s. This theoretical approach is aimed at simplifying the theoretical perspective underpinning the criminal justice system in order to promote human rights and justice within the system. They argue that if the criminal justice system focuses on just one goal, that of dominion, then all the other values of human rights will also be taken into account. In their book *Not Just Deserts: A Republican Theory of Criminal Justice*, they argue that dominion is the absence of any arbitrary power of interference in a person's life (Braithwaite and Pettit 1990). A further underlying presumption of republican theory is that the institutions and policies of the criminal justice system should be constructed in a way that promotes more, rather than less, dominion. Dominion is the absence of arbitrary power and the absence of the evil intent by another. According to Braithwaite and Pettit the criminal justice system should be open and transparent and should be designed to take into account all aspects of the system when planning for the promotion of dominion. The promotion of dominion requires the courts to acknowledge that the crime has harmed the dominion of the victim and provide a sentence that rectifies the harms that have been caused to the victim's dominion. In addition to this, it should also set right the harms caused to the community in general. Braithwaite and Pettit (1990) also advocate for public shaming as a means of curtailing crime. They argue that shaming is more effective than other criminal justice sanctions such as imprisonment. Republican criminology provides the principles upon which restorative justice was founded. *See Restorative Justice (Chapter 6).*

 Are there any disadvantages of public shaming?

Feminist Criminology

Feminist criminology had a shaky start with the study of women and crime being mainly undertaken by men. Otto Pollak published *The Criminality of Women* in 1950 in which he claims that women commit just as much crime as men but due to the chivalrous nature of police, prosecutors, judges and juries (almost all of whom were men in those days) women are treated more leniently in the criminal justice system. He argued that police were reluctant to arrest women and the court system was reluctant to prosecute and convict them. In his assessment of chivalry in the criminal justice system, Pollak fails to address the treatment of women who are arrested for prostitution and there is some evidence that women, particularly teenagers, are readily arrested by the police and treated more harshly in the criminal justice system at all levels (Carrington 1993; Chesney-Lind 1997). Pollak also viewed women as being instigators of crime rather than being directly involved themselves. He argued that the nature of women is inherently deceitful and this is based on their biology and is socially sanctioned. Echoing the biological determinist theories of Lombroso, he argued that the menstrual cycle caused women to behave irrationally and undermined their inhibitions (Pollak 1950) (see case study).

In relation to women's involvement in crimes such as shoplifting, Pollak dismissed this behaviour as due to a mental illness, kleptomania. Pollak emphasises the sexual nature of female crime and views women as entrapping men into

---

Case Study

The Role of PMS in Criminal Behaviour

Virginia, US

A 42-year-old female orthopaedic surgeon in Virginia was caught driving erratically by a State Trooper. She had her three children in the car and was under the influence of alcohol. When stopped by the police officer, the doctor began to use abusive language and tried to kick the officer in the groin. She was arrested and charged with dangerous driving and driving under the influence of alcohol. In court she presented a defence that she was not responsible for her actions because of premenstrual stress (PMS). The defence was upheld and she was acquitted of all charges. This case and similar cases that have used the PMS defence in court have caused anguish for feminists who are concerned that these cases will herald a return to draconian views, about women behaving irrationally once a month, that will hinder their involvement in employment and other domains of public life.

Source: Newsday. 1991, 16 June. 'Successful PMS Defence in Virginia Case Revives Debate' Accessed online on 5 November 2016 at: http://articles.baltimoresun.com/1991-06-16/news/1991167033_1_pms-richter-defense.

promiscuous behaviour through prostitution and extra-marital relations. In this analysis, Pollak fails to provide evidence for his claims and fails to take into account the social and economic reasons for women engaging in prostitution. He also removes the responsibility from men for their own sexual behaviour and ignores the fact that men profit from sexually exploiting women. Pollak's views on the criminality of women angered some feminist groups, but until this time there were few women providing scholarship to the area of criminology. The outrage from women as a result of this male-dominated perspective on women's criminality did not really find a voice until the 1970s and 1980s but did give rise to a wave of female criminologists who came to the fore from the 1970s onwards, focusing a new perspective on women's issues.

Liberation Theory

Liberation theory is a controversial theory that was espoused by a group of early feminist criminologists who argued that feminism and the women's liberation movement would lead to an increase in female crime rates.

Freda Adler

Freda Adler presented the controversial view in the mid-1970s that women's offending behaviour would increase as a result of the success of the feminist movement (Adler 1975). This theoretical perspective contended that women had previously possessed the same aspirations as men but lacked the power to fulfil those aspirations. As women become more emancipated and move into areas of employment traditionally reserved for men, they also go into competition with men for jobs and aspirational fulfilment. This theory holds that it is logical that women will also move into areas of criminal behaviour that were traditionally the reserve of men and compete with men for their own niche in the criminal subculture. Adler went further, to suggest that women would become more aggressive as a result of feminism. Adler (1975) referred to this as the 'darker side' of the feminist movement.

> **Biographical Synopsis**
>
> **Freda Adler 1934–**
> American criminologist Freda Adler was one of the first women to enter into the male-dominated field of criminology but her early work is not held in high regard by feminists. Undertaken in the early 1970s, this work espoused the view that female criminality would rise as a result of the feminist movement and the inevitable increase in female aggression that would follow. Freda Adler has continued to write about women and crime, becoming a respected feminist criminologist. She has also published general textbooks in criminology.

 Has feminism caused women to become more aggressive? Are women more or less likely to be involved in violent crime than men?

Rita Simon

Rita Simon (1975) proposed similar views to Adler, but her theory focused on the opportunities that feminism provided to women rather than seeing an increase in female crime as due to inherent changes that occurred within the women themselves (such as increased aggression). Simon asserted that female criminality was best explained by sociological factors rather than biological or psychiatric factors. Simon believed that as women gain greater access to education, employment and the marketplace, they will become more greatly involved in the same type of crimes that men engage in. While it is true that female crime, particularly in some crime types such as assault, have increased since the 1960s, there has not been the huge increases in female involvement in crime that was predicted by these early theorists. In fact, female crime rates are consistently much lower than male crime rates and this is true around the world. *See Gender and Crime (Chapter 5).*

Why does Rita Simon suggest that
female criminality is best explained
by sociological factors?

Socialist Feminist Perspective

According to socialist feminist theory, patriarchy
and the conflict created by gender inequality in
economic and social structures within capitalist
society locates women as victims of crime and also
victims of a male-dominated legal and criminal
justice system.

James Messerschmidt

Messerschmidt (1993) presents what he calls a
'socialist feminist' approach to criminology in
which he suggests that criminality is found in
both the powerful and the powerless in society
and both are influenced by capitalism and
patriarchy. He also argues that from a socialist
feminist perspective, gender and class power
relations are central to understanding serious
crime. Socialist feminists would argue that
the powerlessness experienced by women in a
patriarchal, capitalist society is seen in crimes
such as domestic violence and sexual assault.
Women do not engage in criminal behaviour as
frequently as men and in his book, *Capitalism,
Patriarchy, and Crime*, James Messerschmidt
(1986) explains this as being due to the
'double marginality' experienced by women
which renders them under the control of the
capitalist state and also under the control of
men. Owing to women being isolated in the
domestic arena and, more specifically, within
the home, women are not presented with the
opportunities to commit crime to the same
degree as men.

Contemporary Feminist Criminologists

In contemporary society female criminologists
are advancing feminist criminology across the
Western world. They are influenced by the range
of criminological theories that exist. A theorist

influenced by biological positivism was Katherine
Dalton.

Katherine Dalton

Dalton (1961) was one of the first female
criminologists to emerge in the 1960s but
her work echoed the determinist approach of
Pollak with her study about menstruation and
women's offending behaviour. She interviewed
156 new inmates at a British women's prison and
found that 49% of their crimes were committed
within the eight-day paramenstruum period
(four days either side of the onset of menses).
She also interviewed women who were reported
to the prison management for behavioural
breaches and discovered that 54% of them
had been paramenstruum at the time of their
misbehaviour. While the study by Dalton
provided some interesting results, it did little to
advance the broader understanding of women
in the criminal justice system or women's
criminality.

Carol Smart

It was not until the 1970s that a British
criminologist, Carol Smart, heralded a new
approach to analysing female criminal behaviour
while challenging the sexist assumptions of early
theorists in a rational and logical way. She made
one of the most significant contributions to
feminist criminology at a time when there was still
little interest or scholarship in women as victims or
as offenders (Smart 1976). In her groundbreaking
book, *Women, Crime and Criminology: A Feminist
Critique*, she argued that women are invisible in a
male-dominated criminal justice system and she
advocated for the study of crime, criminal justice
processes and victimisation to become more than
male-centric studies. She took a feminist approach
to the study of female criminality and stressed the
importance of female criminality being analysed
within a broader context that took into account
the impact of prevailing social, moral, political,
economic and sexual interests. She made the
link between female victimisation and female
offending and this is a link that has broadened in

Biographical Synopsis

Carol Smart 1948–

British feminist criminologist Carol Smart made groundbreaking contributions to criminology that have broadened the understanding of female offending and women's issues in the criminal justice system. She is a highly respected and noted feminist criminologist who is acclaimed for her work on gender and crime, particularly focused on women. She also considered the discussion of gender and crime as interlinked with historical, social, economic and political conditions and this is evident in her work in which she explores women and crime and highlights the gendered nature of criminology itself. She holds a view that criminology conceals women in the same way that women are concealed in other aspects of life. Her seminal work is a book entitled *Women, Crime and Criminology* (1976).

became a prolific scholar in the area of feminist criminology. In the 1990s she extensively reviewed crime statistics and available empirical research related to female offending and concluded that women commit fewer crimes than men and are less likely to be repeat offenders (Heidensohn 1996). Heidensohn also discovered that women are much less likely than men to be involved in serious organised and violent crimes. In her more recent work, Heidensohn (2006) has produced an edited book called *Gender and Justice* that highlights the processes by which women are exposed to harsher treatment by society and by the criminal justice system due to the phenomenon of double deviance. Double deviance results in women being exposed to greater levels of social control when they are involved in the criminal justice system, arising from paternalistic efforts to control women's behaviour. This perspective argues that women are also exposed to greater informal sanctions from family, friends and the community, which will often involve increased formal supervision of the mothering role.

contemporary criminology to be included in the study of male criminality.

Frances Heidensohn

Frances Heidensohn is a feminist criminologist from Britain who has spent many years studying the nature and extent of women's involvement in crime, including how female offenders are conceptualised in society and in the criminal justice system. Her first paper was published in 1968 and entitled 'The Deviance of Women: A Critique and an Enquiry' in which she questioned the lack of interest in sociology in women's deviance, including their low representation in criminal offending. She also critiqued the way in which criminologists had totally discredited Lombroso's work as being a legitimate explanation of male criminality but refused to challenge these same assumptions when applied to female criminality (Heidensohn 1968). Over the subsequent years, Heidensohn

Meda Chesney-Lind

Meda Chesney-Lind is a respected feminist criminologist from the US. Her publication, *The Female Offender*, provides a comprehensive look at women's criminality and their experience in the criminal justice system (Chesney-Lind 1997). In the feminist tradition, Chesney-Lind emphasises the significance of gender in an analysis of criminality and the influence of gender inequality. She contends that the interaction of gender, race and class propels women into the criminal justice system. She advocates for a movement away from the imprisonment of women towards less punitive approaches such as expanding the use of effective community-based strategies.

Joanne Belknap and Pat Carlen

Another notable American criminologist is Joanne Belknap who published *The Invisible Woman* in 2001. This publication not only addressed the issues of female criminality but also analysed women's experiences as victims and as

Key Criminological Research Debates

Women in the criminal justice system: Chivalry or double deviance?
Researchers have spent some time trying to determine whether gender bias exists in the criminal justice system and if it does, whether it advantages or disadvantages women. In this search for answers, the debate as to whether double deviance exists as an influence in the criminal justice system is offset by the debate as to whether women benefit from chivalry; these are known as the chivalry hypothesis and the evil woman hypothesis (Walklate 2001; Mallicoat and Ireland 2014). The 'chivalry hypothesis' was first posited by Otto Pollak (1950) and presumes that women are treated more leniently than men by the criminal justice system due to their gender. Research has shown that chivalry does exist in some parts of the criminal justice system but this is a complex situation as research also shows that women are frequently treated more harshly than men even when they are charged with the same offence (Mallicoat and Ireland 2014). The existence of lenient treatment appears to be dependent upon many factors, including the socio-economic circumstances of the woman, her occupation, her family background and the offence for which she is charged (Mallicoat and Ireland 2014). Research is inconclusive as to whether gender bias exists in the criminal justice system and whether it benefits or disadvantages women.

workers in the criminal justice system. Belknap believes that in order to address the inequities and oppressions that women face in society and in the criminal justice system, the historical evolution of the status and treatment of women and girls in society, in the workplace and in the home and how these continue to influence systems within society today, needs to be understood needs to be considered (Belknap 2001). She was particularly interested in the invisibility of women and girls in criminology and the criminal justice system. This interest in the invisibility of women in the criminal justice system is also shared by Pat Carlen (1983) who has noted several areas in which women are disadvantaged in the prison system such as:

— They tend to be imprisoned at greater distances from their home than men;
— The nature and range of operational regimes tends to be much more restrictive;
— Women suffer greater social stigma.

In contemporary society attention has also been given to the male-centric design and operation of prisons and the lack of programmes specifically designed for women (Carlen 2002). The major

contribution of feminist approaches to the field of criminology was to refocus attention away from pathologising the offender towards the impact of the criminal justice system on the social construction of crime and also the impact of social systems, including the criminal justice system, on women as offenders and victims. *See Gender and Crime (Chapter 5).*

Masculinities in Criminology

In response to the rise of feminism and the association made by feminist scholars between the problem of crime and masculinity, some criminologists such as James Messerschmidt (1993) and Richard Collier (1998) emerged with a branch of criminology known as *masculinist criminology*. As with feminist criminology, this branch of criminology views crime from a gendered perspective. It criticises the existing explanations of male involvement in crime as creating stereotypical characterisations that are hegemonic and one-dimensional.

Messerschmidt (1993) and Collier (1998) argue that there were many ways in which men become involved in criminal offending and these are strongly influenced by social aspects such as race, age and class. Messerschmidt (1993) suggested the idea that in all societies men attempt to become the 'ideal male' as presented to them by that society. In Western society, this involves emulating socially accepted male behaviour of being authoritative, combative, controlling and in charge. He believed that social roles and power structures in modern society limit men of alternate racial background and men from lower socio-economic classes from legitimately expressing their masculinity in the conventional ways that are open to the white middle class such as educational achievement, wealth creation and career success.

James Messerschmidt

According to Messerschmidt (1993, 2000), if a male is unable to adopt these roles, he is left feeling emasculated and unmanly and as a result men become involved in crime and other forms of social deviance because this is a method by which they can affirm their 'maleness'. He suggests that the process by which men strive to dominate women is a means of reaffirming their manliness, and he calls this 'doing gender'. In all-male groups, the more dominant males of the group can target the weakest member of the group with denigration and exploitation, which is behaviour that is more commonly directed at women. Messerschmidt also described differences between hegemonic masculinity and subordinated masculinities such as those experienced by homosexual or bisexual men.

Richard Collier

British criminologist Richard Collier published a book entitled *Masculinities, Crime and Criminology* in 1998 in which he argued that the concept of masculinism was a central theme that could be found in feminist criminology and which dominated scholarship in the areas of criminal law, criminology and related disciplines (Collier 1998). He argued that if feminist criminology made gender a key topic of study, then the study of masculinity was equally vital for a deeper understanding of crime to be reached. He also deconstructed the commonly held assumptions

of male criminal offending and introduced new perspectives to the discussion of men and crime, which included socially constructed masculinity. To emphasise how masculinity and criminology interconnect, Collier stated that 'crime, criminology and masculinity each emerge as historically specific, and interwoven, constructions of modernity' (Collier 1998:x). Collier located the discussion of masculinity and criminal behaviour clearly within a broader conceptualisation of postmodern society where tensions around heterosexuality, family and social disorder are dominant within the broader discussion of gender. *See **Contemporary Feminist Criminologists; Gender and Crime** (Chapter 5).*

 How can masculinity be socially constructed?

Contemporary Criminology

Criminology continues to grow and develop and there are many new fields of study opening up. Some of these new branches of criminology have developed in response to new areas of crime, or new manifestations of previously seen crime such as terrorism. Green crime has sprung from the growing interest in the environment and in crimes against the environment. Each of these new and developing fields draw from existing criminological theory and from other disciplines in order to advance theories to explain these developing areas. These innovations in criminological theory contribute to the goals of criminology which are to a) understand the crime, b) understand the criminal and c) understand the victim better and to d) formulate methods of preventing the crime. This section is an introduction to some of these new and emerging areas of criminological study. It is not an exhaustive coverage of the new criminological fields and if you have an interest in a particular field of study that you can't find here we recommend that you research online or in your library to see if a criminological branch dealing with the crime issue you are interested in has opened up.

Green Criminology

Green criminology is an emerging area of study that includes a range of initiatives and approaches within the criminal justice system that encourage a more sustainable relationship between people and the environment. Academically, green criminology is concerned with broad environmental and socio-ecological issues and the way in which these issues become criminalised. It is also concerned with crimes against the environment, including wildlife. It is distinct from environmental criminology which is concerned with the nature of crime in context with time, space and place. In addition to environmental issues, green criminology is also concerned with bio-ethical issues such as issues surrounding genetically modified food, bio-piracy, mass pollution of waterways and the personal and community harms resulting from environmental degradation (Wyatt et al. 2014). Green criminology is also concerned with breaches of environmental law, including corporate and government crimes against the environment and the impact of environmental crimes on individual victims and communities. This is sometimes referred to as environmental justice. Green criminology is a branch of criminological study that focuses on environmental crimes and is closely aligned with a branch of sociology called the sociology of the environment (Potter 2010). The sociology of the environment tends to focus greater attention on the social impacts of environmental crime and how environmental crime arises from the power structures within society. Green criminology is also concerned with studying these aspects but focuses greater attention on the crimes themselves and how environmental crime can be prevented. Environmental issues that are studied within green criminology include such things as wildlife poaching and smuggling (Banks et al. 2008); illegal dumping of toxic waste; and corporate environmental crime (Ruggierio and South 2013). The victims of environmental crime are also of interest to green criminologists as the impacts of this type of crime can be very serious not only to individuals but also to entire communities and can have devastating economic impacts for developing countries (Banks et al. 2008). *See Green Crime (Chapter 5).*

Vincenzo Ruggiero and Nigel South

Key criminologists working in the field of green criminology are Vincenzo Ruggiero and Nigel South who are based in the UK. They have attempted to link green criminology and corporate crime by looking at environmental crimes and the health harms that result (Ruggiero and South 2010). They make the point that human beings are the only organisms on the planet that produce non-reducible waste and, further than that, it is humans that are mass producing waste without any clear ability to appropriately manage it (Ruggiero and South 2010). They have also focused on the corporate environmental crimes of multinational organisations in an effort to identify effective crime prevention strategies (Ruggiero and South 2013).

Greening Justice

White and Graham (2015) introduced a branch of green criminology known as 'greening justice' which is concerned with the environmental initiatives and actions within the criminal justice system which, they argue, have resulted from greater ecological awareness in criminal justice. Initiatives which are identified by White and Graham (2015) as being environmental initiatives include British prisoners undertaking courses and training in conservation, woodwork and biodiversity to save honey bees; Australian prisoners working with native birds as part of conservation programmes; and Estonian prisoners developing a clothing label using eco-friendly and environmentally sustainable organic products. These initiatives promote a more sustainable relationship between humans and the environment. Green criminology encourages the building of small, eco-friendly prisons that utilise green technology in the use of renewable energy and eco-friendly waste management processes rather than the large sprawling prisons that have been built in the past.

Cultural Criminology

As the name suggests, cultural criminology focuses on culture within criminology and is greatly influenced by cultural studies, feminism, subcultural theory and symbolic interactionism. Cultural criminology is an emerging perspective and as a result it has attracted a lot of criticism for being theoretically ambiguous and lacking adequate substance in its core concepts (O'Brien 2005; Webber 2007). At its heart, cultural criminology is concerned with the meanings and representations of crime and the ways in which crime is socially constructed. It considers the cultural influences on crime and crime control, seeking to understand both of these aspects in context with culture. This perspective views culture and crime from two main standpoints: 'crime as culture' and 'culture as crime'. Jock Young, Jeff Ferrell, Keith Hayward and Mike Presdee are well-known cultural criminologists.

Dating back to the mid-1990s, cultural criminology is a theoretical, methodological and interventionist approach to the study of crime that seeks to understand crime in relationship with the culture in which it occurs. Criticism of this perspective tends to focus on its lack of theoretical clarity (Bevier 2015). Contemporary theorists such as O'Brien (2005) argue that cultural criminology is characterised by various confusions about the definition of culture and what is meant by culture when it is applied to deviance and criminality. Bevier (2015) refutes these arguments by pointing to the theoretical underpinnings of the perspective to explain what seem to be ambiguities. The cultural criminology perspective favours the use of a qualitative ethnographic methodology with narrative-based research methodologies or fieldwork where social phenomena can be observed in context with the culture. This emphasis on qualitative methods within cultural criminology was a reaction to what was perceived to be a push towards returning to positivist scientific approaches in the study of crime. This has brought more criticism on the perspective of cultural criminology, and in response Bevier (2015) argues that, in the main, cultural criminology does not lend itself to quantifiable methods and theory testing.

Jock Young

An important theorist in the development of cultural criminology is Jock Young (2003) who we discuss earlier in this chapter in relation to his work on left realist criminology. Jock Young diverged from the positivist position when he developed left realist theory and cultural criminology was a further evolutionary step for him to take in terms of his conceptualisation of crime and society. Cultural criminology developed out of concerns that Young and others had about the failures within the existing theoretical perspectives to explain all the pertinent aspects they saw as being involved in crime. Hayward and Young (2004) stated that cultural criminology simply places crime and crime control into the context of culture and, furthermore, that in addition to considering culture it highlights the interaction of crime and crime control and the culturally based meanings placed on these interactions. It also takes into account the role of media and how it constructs crime and its control within the cultural setting. *See Race and Crime (Chapter 5).*

Jeff Ferrell, Keith Hayward and Jock Young

Jock Young, along with Jeff Ferrell and Keith Hayward (2008) wrote the book *Cultural Criminology: An Invitation* which further defines cultural criminology as a theoretical position that seeks to understand culture which they say is the collective meaning and identity existing within it and also influenced by and emanating from it. They portray human culture as the symbolic environment that individuals and groups occupy rather than just a product of social class, religion, ethnicity and occupation. They do, however, acknowledge that culture cannot be considered in isolation from these elements but they argue that consideration of culture should not just be focused on social structure alone. This lifts the discussion of crime and crime control away from the emphasis on socio-economic structures that dominated anomie, strain theory, general strain theory and left realism. They discuss crime and how it is controlled in a broader context and criticise this previous emphasis in criminological theory on what they see as reductionist explanations of crime that seek to align crime with the lower working classes. According to Ferrell et al. (2008), cultural criminology places the study of crime and deviance in the context of a broader conceptualisation of late modern culture and therefore is able to explain a broader range of crimes. *See Subcultural Theory; Symbolic Interactionism; Labelling Theory.*

> How do theories such as strain theory give the impression that people from the lower classes are responsible for crime?

Developmental (Life-Course) Criminology

A developing area within the discipline is that of developmental and life-course criminology. It has its origins in positivist theories of crime and is focused on the onset of antisocial behaviour and the development of the criminal career throughout the lifespan. Developmental criminology uses the concept of 'trajectory' to describe the developmental sequences of a set of behaviours as it develops over time. There is significant interest in the relationship between age and criminal offending. The main focus of developmental criminology is on youth offending and the onset of delinquency but it also looks at the changing nature of offending over the life of an individual and the relationship of age to particular types of offending. A well-known theoretical position of developmental criminology is the maturation concept. This concept has influenced juvenile justice since the 1980s and assumes that as an offender ages and matures the rate of offending will naturally

decline. Available statistics on crime support this view; however, it is considered to be a simplistic explanation that does not fit all crime.

Terrie Moffitt

A leading theorist in this area is Terrie Moffit who developed the life-course-persistent/adolescence-limited theory (Moffitt 1993). Moffitt describes two distinct categories of juveniles. A small group shows antisocial behaviour in childhood and this persists into adolescence (life-course-persistent group) and a larger groups show no antisocial behaviours in childhood but suddenly displays delinquent behaviour in adolescence (adolescence-limited group). The late onset delinquents are said by Moffitt (1993) to be largely influenced by negative peer associations and only marginal disadvantage. This group are exposed to marginally effective parenting and as a result they do not develop serious deficits in adulthood. The life-course-persistent group are exposed to extremely poor parenting and serious disadvantage, leading to extreme neuro-psychological deficits early in their lives. Continuity of antisocial behaviour is the distinguishing feature of the life-course-persistent group. Moffitt (1993) argues that the same dysfunctional traits that get children into trouble in childhood continue into adulthood where they can be affected by a process she calls *cumulative continuity*. The antisocial actions of children have consequences that can persist to thwart them in adulthood, effectively trapping them in a process of cumulative continuity. Additionally, those who continue to offend in adulthood are faced with a range of negative consequences that have a compounding effect such as unemployment, debts, homelessness, violence, abandoned children and relationship breakdowns.

> What are some of the ways in which childhood behaviour, especially in the teen years, can negatively impact the lives of adults?

Robert Sampson and John Laub

Robert Sampson and John Laub revisited Hirschi's (1969) social bond theory and redeveloped it into a theory of age-graded informal social control. Sampson and Laub argue that at the micro level (the individual) informal social control, such as that exerted within a family, exists within a structural context which is shaped by macro social forces (Sampson and Laub 1993). These forces include poverty, employment, ethnicity and mobility. According to Sampson and Laub, informal social control is the most important factor but the individual differences of children, such as temperament, can impact on the way in which informal social control is delivered and received and this can affect the effectiveness. Sampson and Laub (1993) also added the concept of *social capital* to the social bond theory. Social capital is the idea that social relationships create value for society in that they contribute support and resources and create bonds. As the strength of the social bonds increase, the value of social capital rises. At a macro level this social capital saves the government a lot in financial cost that otherwise would need to be spent creating formal structures to replace this informal source of physical and emotional support. At an individual level social capital becomes too valuable for a person to lose and therefore makes committing crime too risky and leads to desistance. This increases the effectiveness of informal social control. Sampson and Laub (2005) updated their theory more than ten years later to expand the desistance component. In the updated version they suggest that the process of desistance is the result of several factors converging together.

Summary

This chapter has taken you on a journey of discovery through the development of criminological theory from the early theorists to contemporary criminological theories. Criminological theory provides a perspective for understanding the causation of crime and the appropriate response to it. Early theories are as relevant and important today as they were when they were first introduced. They are built on by modern theorists who seek to improve the relevance of the theories and to make them applicable in the modern era. It is important that you think critically about the theories you have been presented with so that you gain a deeper level of understanding of crime and the workings of the criminal justice system. We have given you a very basic introduction to these theories and you can gain more information by obtaining and reading the original texts. We have provided a reading list of more detailed textbooks.

Further Reading

Lilly, J. R., Cullen, F. T. & Ball, R. A. 2015. *Criminological Theory: Context and Consequences* (6th edition). Thousand Oaks, California: Sage Publications.
    This book provides an introduction to criminological theory and differs from most textbooks in that it does more than just describe and explain: it also engages in an analysis of theoretical perspectives. It covers both traditional and contemporary theories and is useful for developing an understanding of how criminological theory is used to shape criminal justice policy.

Newburn, T. 2016. *Criminology* (3rd edition). London, UK: Routledge.
    This is a comprehensive textbook that covers the basics of criminology in detail. It is well illustrated and provides up-to-date examples to help the student contextualise the material. This book provides a detailed overview of criminological theory and aspects of the criminal justice system relevant to the criminology student. It draws out the key debates in the field of criminology and critically analyses them in a way that encourages the student to think more deeply about the topic or issue under discussion.

Walklate, S. 2015. *Criminology: The Basics* (2nd edition). Abingdon, UK: Routledge.

In this book, Walklate provides an introduction to criminology. It is easy to read and covers the essential basics such as criminological theory, explanations of crime and criminal justice process. The book is specifically designed for students and enables them to get an overview of the key issues and concepts relevant to the discipline.

Criminological Research

This chapter looks at both the 'doing' of criminological research and the 'knowing' that comes from it. As a student in criminology your primary research task is likely to be writing essays based on analysis of the work of others, or perhaps you will sign up to be a research subject for a study being undertaken at your university. As your studies evolve, and certainly if you decide to take up postgraduate studies, you may become an active participant in the conduct of primary research. Regardless of your involvement in research at this stage of your studies, it is important to understand some of the key principles of criminological research so that you can effectively evaluate the evidence you collect to support your arguments. It is also important for you to understand the key methods criminologists use in research because you want to make sure the research you are undertaking yourself is valid and can stand up to the scrutiny of other criminologists. At the undergraduate level you are likely to undertake a research methods course either as a core requirement of your degree or as an elective (see *Chapter 2: Studying Criminology*). As such, in this chapter we are only going to provide you with an introduction to some of the concepts and ideas that underpin good research. Research, after all, can seem like a daunting process until you become familiar with the language of research and how it is done.

Why Is Research Important in Criminology?

Understanding crime and developing responses to its incidence requires an evidence base underpinned by research. Good criminological research provides evidence that promotes knowledge and understanding of critical issues across the criminal justice system; informs policy direction and development; identifies programmes and approaches that reduce crime or mitigate its impact; and examines the individual characteristics and social circumstances that contribute to crime. Criminological research is important because it tells law enforcement, criminologists and the general public where crime is more likely to occur, at what rates, and who the likely perpetrators or victims might be. It is important for planning crime prevention and policing activities. Research also informs criminologists and others studying crime about why crime occurs and what motivates the behaviour of criminal offenders and victims.

Is Criminological Research Different?

Research is an investigation undertaken to generate knowledge and is diverse in both form and function. When applying this to criminology and the criminal justice system, opportunities can be found for unique and innovative research projects which contribute useful knowledge to the various fields of criminology and for the improved functioning of the criminal justice system. Sarantankos (2012) identifies 15 types of social research commonly used across the social sciences, including the field of criminology. Broadly, these research types seek to develop a better understanding of a topic (through basic exploration, theory testing and/or development) or seek to identify or explain relationships (through classification, comparison, description and analysis of causality either at a specific point in time or over multiple occasions). They may focus attention on specific groups or programmes (to understand a population as in feminist research, or to assess effectiveness as in evaluation research) or attempt to solve problems or improve situations (through practical participatory research that incorporates change management and/or implementation as the research is being conducted).

> ❯ Which criminological theories would be amenable to social research?

Figure 4.1 provides a summary of what criminological research can consist of. What makes criminological research different is more than just the specific subject matter. There is inevitably a political element and interest in criminological research that operates on differing levels and in differing contexts. For example, the creation, collation, interpretation and reporting of official statistics in the criminal justice system is often done by public servants within the various departments who have little or no training in statistics. More frequently departments that make up the criminal justice system are employing criminologists and statisticians to undertake this work, but it is by no means a common trend. In addition to the statisticians working within government departments, criminologists may be undertaking research in policy areas to support policy development or in academia to explore the nature of criminal offending. Doing crime research, like research in any of the social

sciences, has its limitations. These limitations include poor data quality and lack of access to key persons or information. Understanding the limitations at the outset can help you to devise strategies to mitigate the impact on your research findings.

The Link Between Theory and Research

It is important to understand the relationship between theory and research because they have a complex inter-relationship. One informs the other (Merton 1957). Hypotheses are generated from theory and theories are refined and developed from the empirical findings of research. Some theories are also challenged or completely discredited on the basis of research findings. Theories are speculations about what may be occurring in a given social phenomenon and research provides empirical evidence to support or refute the theory. Over time a body of theory is built up in a particular discipline. Good research starts with existing theory and builds upon gaps in the theory or upon the theory itself to postulate a new or advanced theory that is tested through appropriate research methodology.

Researching Crime

There are many books available on the topic of criminological research and you will also find books on specific topics within the broad subject of criminological research such as data analysis and research design. When embarking on a research project it is wise to seek out books that will provide you with the information you need to successfully complete your particular project as in-depth examination of such specific texts will provide valuable information. This overview is intended to be a guide to aid your thinking as you consider the best means of approaching a project you are undertaking or how you might evaluate the work of others. As with anything, good planning is important if you are to produce good results and understanding the steps that are needed is a key place to begin.

1. Quantifying and following crime rates and trends.
2. Investigations of the root causes of crime.
3. Investigations of the relationships between crime and social reality.
4. Information about the operations of the criminal justice system and the people who work in it.
5. Observations and explorations of deviant behaviour and the people involved.
6. Studies about the impact of crime on victims and the community.
7. Studies about how victims and offenders experience the criminal justice system.

▫ **Figure 4.1**   What is criminological research?

The Research Process

The research process is the steps you need to take to answer a specific question or series of questions. It is about a quest to solve a mystery or to provide the added context to better understand a phenomenon. The researcher begins with a research question and the research is designed in a way that will answer the question. Finding the answers to interesting criminological questions begins with data and the way reliable data is obtained is by doing properly structured research. The research process has been summarised in Figure 4.2 which sets out the steps in research.

Principles of Good Research

Regardless of the type of research conducted, good research is governed by some key principles (see Figure 4.3). These principles underpin the range of research activities undertaken during the course of a project and are adhered to by researchers to ensure the quality and acceptance of the findings produced. Of key importance is the overarching *purpose* or aim of the research. The purpose should be articulated in plain English to be clearly understood by laypeople or people who do not have a background in the field. To define

1. It has a **purpose and aim.**
2. The **research design** is able to answer the research questions.
3. The research is **relevant and original.**
4. It is **ethically sound** with appropriate approvals in place.
5. It contributes **new knowledge or understanding** to the field or replicates the findings of previous studies to confirm their conclusions.

◨ **Figure 4.3**   What is good research? (Source: Caulfield and Hill 2014)

the purpose a general topic, for example alcohol and drug misuse and crime, is refined to focus on a specific aspect which may be exploring the issue in depth (for example, examining the relationship between drug and alcohol misuse and crime); developing a deeper understanding of behaviour (for example, identifying the effect of certain drug types on violence); or providing a critique of or solution to an identified problem (for example, evaluating drug law enforcement policy or the impact of liquor licensing restrictions on violence in the night-time economy).

Good research is also *relevant* and *original*. Relevance may be defined within the field but is also partially dictated, directly and indirectly, by funding providers. Given that criminology is an interdisciplinary subject, research often

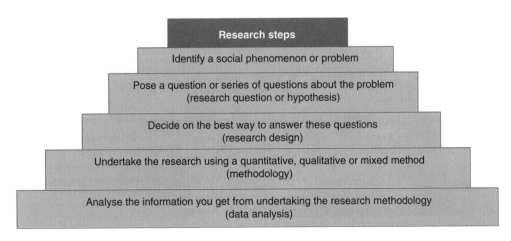

◨ **Figure 4.2**   Research steps

has relevance to a broad range of stakeholders and disciplines. In fact, whether the research is focused on systems (such as policing, courts or corrections), people (such as victims of crime, offenders and the community) or specific crime types (such as violence, human trafficking or fraud) the research findings will be of interest to a diverse audience.

> ❯ **Why do governments undertake research about crime rates and trends?**

As funding for projects is scarce and competition for these scarce funds is high, funding providers may articulate specific strategic interests or themes researchers should focus upon in order to win contracts or grants. In the academic world originality is a key consideration. Although your research may replicate earlier findings, generally each new project seeks to either cover a purely original idea or to utilise an original methodology. The capacity of your research to provide a unique or original contribution to the field may be the key to getting your results published or to being accepted into a higher degree programme such as a PhD. Originality is also important in a policy context albeit for different reasons. If your research is being undertaken for government, public funds will be used and it is therefore an important accountability consideration that unnecessary duplication of previous research is avoided. Increasingly research is a tool being used by both policy makers and practitioners to establish priority action areas and to assist in determining the allocation of resources. Researchers must ensure that what they do has relevance in these contexts but also remains *objective* and *accountable*.

The influence of policy on researchers and the research process has been described by Stout et al. (2008:26). Research may be:

— *A knowledge driver*: where researchers are supported by policy
— *A problem solver*: where researchers follow priorities set by policy

— *Interactive*: where research and policy are equally influential
— *Political*: where researchers support specific policy agendas or outcomes; or
— *Enlightened*: where research is distant from policy and affects policy development indirectly.

Regardless of the influence or role of policy in the research process, there are several ways researchers can ensure their approach and findings remain unbiased from initial concept through to presentation. Refer to Table 4.1 which provides a summary of how you can ensure your research is unbiased. Removing or mitigating the impact of research bias will help to ensure your research meets the standards of *accuracy* and *generalisability*, both of which are key to making your research valuable. These principles will be discussed further throughout this chapter as they relate to the methods you will employ to collect, analyse and/or report research findings.

▣ **Table 4.1** Ensuring findings are unbiased

Topic	Choose your topic based on an identified area of need, not solely on personal interest or the interests of others.
Literature	Review all the relevant literature, not just sources supportive of your underlying hypothesis or theme.
Research design	Choose research designs and methods that will best answer the question, not those that will just give the results you want.
Honesty	Never report data that was not collected, fabricate data or change the answers of respondents.
Reporting	Report the results accurately, including all information with a reliable assessment of its merit. Refuse to concede to external pressure to leave findings out because they may be unpalatable to some stakeholders.

Research Ethics

Research ethics is extremely important in research, particularly research that involves people. The guiding principle is that the researcher should do no harm in the process of undertaking their research. It is therefore necessary to determine what ethics approval processes need to be met prior to undertaking any research. If the researcher is attached to a university, the university will have an ethics committee and a process that the researcher must follow in order to obtain ethics approval. This process will involve meeting strict ethical guidelines in the way in which the research is conducted and the way in which data is stored and disposed of. Most government departments these days will also have their own ethics committee that considers the ethical implications of proposed research and will require all projects to be assessed by this body before approval to proceed is granted. The researcher must become familiar with all of these requirements and obtain approval from all participating stakeholders before commencing their research. Table 4.2 provides a quick reckoner to determine if your research requires ethics approval.

Human Research Ethics

Human research is research that involves human beings as research subjects and may involve direct participation or the use of data about people. Examples of human research in criminology include research where people participate in interviews, focus groups or complete surveys; undergo testing or treatment (for example, health or psychological); are observed by researchers; and/or have their information accessed by researchers (for example, individual records held by external parties such as police or health providers or personal documents). The data obtained can be identified – where you know who it is about; re-identifiable – where you or someone else can work out who it is about by linking it in some way, or non-identifiable – where all information about a specific person is removed and can't reasonably be traced back to them. The data itself does not have to be identifiable to be considered human research. Research ethics must consider not only how the data is collected but also how it is reported. Depending on the identifiability of the data and its sensitiveness it may be necessary to aggregate (group together) findings or remove them from analysis.

Table 4.2 Does your research need ethics approval?

	Yes	No
1. Does it involve people or animals?		
2. Does it involve a sensitive topic?		
3. Will your results be widely disseminated?		
4. Will the participants be able to be identified?		
5. Have the participants been coerced or deceived?		
6. Do the participants know what is involved before they give their consent?		
7. Can they withdraw their consent at any time?		
8. Are the appropriate approvals in place, including the university ethics committee?		

If you answer Yes to questions 1-5 you will need to have ethics approval. If you answer no to questions 6-8 you will have difficulty getting your application approved.

Ethical Guidelines and Codes

History shows the importance of research ethics. Following experiments conducted by Nazi scientists during the Second World War the first international code of research ethics came into being. The *Nuremburg Code 1947* outlined ten principles for the conduct of human experimentation and these principles form the basis of modern codes of ethics for the health and social sciences sectors.

> Why is it important to enforce ethical standards for the conduct of research that involves people as research subjects?

These principles include that participants must give their consent, their involvement must be voluntary and they must be told of any risks involved (see case study).

In the UK there is no single authority responsible for regulating research ethics for the social sciences. In Australia human research ethics is overseen by the National Health and Medical Research Council which has produced guidelines called the *National Statement on Ethical Conduct in Human Research*. In the United States the National Commission for the Protection of Human Subjects of Biomedical and Behavioural Research produced *The Belmont Report* which provides the ethical principles for research (US Department of Health & Human Services 1979).

In New Zealand the Health Research Council ensures all research involving humans applies ethical principles. Whether you are conducting the research for yourself or someone else, you need to check the methodology and look for signs that it was conducted ethically, otherwise the results are not reliable. This is particularly true for experimental research.

Research Design

Research design is a detailed plan that connects the different components or activities that will be undertaken during the research. The design used is determined by the nature of the problem being examined and will articulate the most appropriate methods to be used to collect and analyse data relevant to addressing or answering the research problem (Davies et al. 2011). Research designs, by necessity, vary considerably, but typically incorporate a statement of the problem and rationale for the research; a review of relevant literature; a clear research question or testable hypothesis; and a clear method describing the data necessary to answer the research questions and how it will be collected and analysed. The underlying process involved in planning and outlining the proposed research is essential. Failure to spend adequate time generating detailed research questions and thoroughly considering not only the types of evidence required but also the means necessary to obtain that information may lead to inadequate research findings that do not answer

---

Case Study

Medical Experiments in Nazi Germany

Several doctors attached to the Third Reich undertook medical experiments on adult and child prisoners who were Jews, Roma (known as Gypsies) and political prisoners. The consent of the participants was not sought and there was no care for any deleterious outcome of the experiments undertaken. As a result of these unethical experiments the *Nuremburg Code* was produced in 1947, and other international codes of ethics were later established to protect research participants. In this case the doctors were charged under the *Nuremburg Code* and convicted of crimes against humanity.

Source: 'The Nuremberg Code (1947)' in Mitscherlich A., Mielke, F. *Doctors of Infamy: The Story of The Nazi Medical Crimes*, xxiii–xxv. New York: Schuman, 1949.

the questions, fail to address the overarching problem or are weak and unconvincing.

How to Design a Research Project

Designing a research project is an important process but is not as complicated as it first appears. It is useful when embarking on your project to follow some basic steps that will ensure that your research design is sound.

Problem Identification and Topic Selection

The first step in designing your research project is to identify a problem. Selecting a topic for the research may be based on a number of factors including personal interest, funding provider need or a response to an identified problem or emerging issue.

Develop Research Questions or Hypotheses

As a researcher you need to ensure your topic is sufficiently well-defined to facilitate the generation of answerable research questions. Whether you have research questions or hypotheses will depend on whether you are doing qualitative or quantitative research. You will need to have a separate question or hypothesis for each aspect of the issue that you want to investigate. The research question(s) or hypotheses should be stated clearly, should be measurable and should be able to be investigated. Doing a literature search for similar previous studies undertaken in the particular area you are investigating will help you to formulate your own research questions and refine your own project design.

The Literature Review

A literature review is an analysis and synthesis of the available information on a topic. This review may result in a stand-alone chapter or be fully integrated into a finalised research report. In undergraduate studies, literature reviews may be separate assessment items providing students with the opportunity to examine a particular topic in depth and demonstrate analytical ability. As part of the research process, the literature review is conducted to refine research topics and inform the development of research questions and is therefore conducted near the beginning of a project. To organise the discussion of the literature logically, headings are used. These headings also guide the reader to the most important points of the discussion that you want them to be aware of.

 Why is it useful to break up your literature review by using headings?

For the purposes of designing research methodology a literature review will provide an overview of key concepts related to a topic, determine what has already been written about a topic and the challenges or limitations of previous approaches. You will find the knowledge that is referred to in the literature review from books, reports and academic journals. This knowledge assists researchers to develop project designs and methodologies that fill gaps in understanding; utilise fresh approaches or explore the issue from a different perspective; focus on specific aspects of a topic or problem; or provide a means of testing previous findings. Table 4.3 provides a list of criminology journals currently available. This is a sample of the journals available and is therefore not exhaustive.

Writing a literature review should be an inspiring process as this is when you read what various authors have said about an issue, both for and against, and when you formulate your own opinions. It is useful to have a variety of books and journal articles about the topic and related areas both for and against the main position.

Defining the Purpose and Aim

Articulating the primary aim and purpose of the research assists in translating a research topic into a research design. The aim and purpose may be determined at the outset of the project or be

▣ Table 4.3 Examples of criminology journals by type	
Subject-specific	*Violence Against Women; Crime, Media and Culture; Criminal Behaviour and Mental Health; Journal of Financial Crime*
Regional	*Asian Journal of Criminology; Journal of Scandinavian Studies in Criminology and Crime Prevention; British Journal of Criminology; Australian and New Zealand Journal of Criminology*
Practice-orientated	*Policing: a Journal of Policy and Practice; The Probation Journal; Correctional Management Quarterly; Policing Quarterly; Policing*
Methodological	*Quantitative Criminology; Journal of Forensic Document Examination; Journal of Experimental Criminology*
Theoretical	*Feminist Criminology; International Journal of Comparative Criminology; Critical Criminology*
Interdisciplinary	*Criminal Justice Ethics; Journal of Correctional Education; Journal of Police and Criminal Psychology*
General	*Criminology; Salus Journal*

developed following a comprehensive review of the literature previously published on the topic. Either way, the statement of aim and purpose will help to define all other elements of the research including the research questions, methods and analysis. Simply put, the purpose is the statement of why you are doing the research and the aim is what you expect to achieve. If the aim and purpose are not clearly stated at the design stage, there will be a risk that the research project will deviate from what you intend to do and it will not be clear to other people, especially stakeholders, why you are doing the research and what you hope to achieve.

 Why is it important to clearly state the purpose and aim of your research?

Sampling

It is often not possible to research every person in a given population. Sampling is a method of being able to research a subset of a population to represent the likely position of the broader population. This is referred to as representativeness. Randomly selecting a

sample and increasing the size of the sample are both strategies that are used to increase the representativeness of the sample.

 How does random sampling improve representativeness?

Research Methods

The research methodology specifically defines the processes and procedures that will be undertaken. These methods are typically identified as either quantitative or qualitative although most criminological research utilises a mixed methods approach.

Quantitative Research

Quantitative research is research that is numerically based and therefore quantifies the data. Quantitative research methods measure the variation in amounts of data and relationships between data which are organised into numerical categories. Statistical methods and tests are used to make sense of large data sets. Quantitative research can also be depicted as descriptive data. The strength of quantitative research lies in its ability to provide quantifiable evidence to support a researcher's hypothesis about why a certain phenomenon may be occurring.

Surveys

Surveys are a method of collecting quantitative data, although some open-ended questions included in a survey may elicit some qualitative contextual information that expands on the quantitative data obtained. Surveys generally consist of a series of questions about the topic under investigation. Demographic information is also collected. Surveys provide a practical way of being able to collect data from a large population.

Ensuring Validity and Consistency

With any research, it is important that the research is valid, in that it tests the very thing that it purports to test, that it is generalisable beyond just the subjects being studied and that it is able to be replicated by other researchers.

External Validity

External validity is a research term that is concerned with the breadth of the research findings and whether they can be generalised beyond the sample included in the study. In order to ensure the generalisability of the findings, attention must be given by the researcher to the size of the sample being studied and how the participants are selected. The representativeness of the sample is a key consideration and includes giving thought to obtaining a sample that is representative of the larger population in variables that may be relevant such as gender, age, ethnicity, socio-economic status, employment type, length of service and marital status. A random sampling technique will usually ensure the representativeness of the sample.

 What aspects do you need to consider to ensure that a sample is representative of the population?

The main question the researcher must ask is whether the findings can be generalised to a larger similar population external to the sample being studied. The second question the researcher must ask refers to cross-population generalisability. This question is concerned with whether the findings are generalisable from one group or population to a different group or population. External validity is high when the researcher can show the findings are generalisable beyond the sample studied.

Internal Validity

Internal validity is a research term that refers to the accuracy of the research design in answering the research questions and detecting causal relationships that may exist in the data. In testing internal validity for causal relationships the following standards of analysis need to be met:

Temporal order: the independent variable must precede the dependent variable in time.

Association: the independent and dependent variables must be connected and move together in some kind of patterned way.

Non-spuriousness: any and all alternative explanations of the dependent variable have been ruled out.

All three of these standards must be met before a case for causality can be made.

Measurement validity: measurement validity is a research term related to internal consistency. It refers to the extent to which the research instrument being used actually measures what it claims to measure. The instrument is the survey, questionnaire or interview guide that is used to collect data. The questions put to participants must relate to aspects of the research questions in a way that will answer the research questions when the data obtained is analysed as a whole.

Hypothesis and Null Hypothesis

When undertaking quantitative research, your research questions are usually referred to as hypotheses (the singular being hypothesis). When generating a hypothesis, the researcher begins with a theory. A theory is a possible explanation to account for the occurrence of a particular phenomenon. The researcher will consider the theory and make a prediction based on what they expect to happen when they test the theory. This prediction becomes the hypothesis. A statement of the opposite effect to that which is expected by the researcher is referred to as the null hypothesis. It is the null hypothesis that the researcher tries to disprove, nullify and reject. Some researchers overlook the use of the null hypothesis but this is poor research practice that can lead to problems with the rigour of the research. Using a null hypothesis helps the researcher to maintain objectivity and avoid bias.

Sampling

There are different methods used for contacting participants for a research study, and these are often referred to as sampling techniques. In quantitative research these methods include random sampling, representative sampling, purposive sampling and the use of existing/secondary data sources. *See Meta-analysis.*

Random and Systematic Sampling

In order for a researcher to get a spread of demographic characteristics in their sample, they can use random or systematic sampling which provide the best statistical chance of selecting such a spread by chance. Random sampling involves using a computer to generate a completely random population for the researcher to include in their study. Systematic sampling involves the researcher selecting for example every tenth person on a list. Random and systematic sampling are especially useful for selecting a smaller section of a very large population but still having a selection that represents the characteristics such as age, gender and occupation of the larger population. The researcher will try to obtain a sample that not only represents these characteristics but is also large enough for the researcher to be able to generalise their findings to the larger group.

Representative Sampling

Representative samples are rarely possible for student researchers as they involve huge populations. This type of research is usually undertaken by governments and a well-known type of representative sampling is the census. Representative sampling involves including everyone within a given population so that the findings of the research accurately represent the exact characteristics of the population.

Purposive Sampling

Purposive sampling is also known as judgemental or subjective sampling. It is a non-probability sampling technique where the researcher will purposely select a specific population to include in their study. It may be used if the researcher wishes to study a particular population such as a motorbike gang. It may also be used if the researcher wants to increase the representativeness of their sample by purposely including more women or people of a particular age or ethnic background.

Types of Quantitative Research

Quantitative research includes population studies; meta-analysis; research that includes the collection of numerical data and the testing of this data to determine relationships between variables; and studies that involve experimental design.

Population Studies

An area of research that is frequently used and accessed by criminologists is population studies. This is also a popular research approach adopted by governments who complete a census of the entire nation's population every at regular intervals. Population studies are the numerical records collected for the purpose of understanding the demographic and other quantifiable characterisations of particular populations (e.g. the census). Such records are used by genealogists and historians to map the demographic changes of particular areas. In criminology, population studies are of interest because they can tell us about the type of people who comprise a particular area, for example, the median age, gender distribution, ethnicity, socio-economic status and health status.

How could you use census data to help you understand a sudden surge in race-hate crime in a particular suburb?

Select an **experimental group**.

Select a **control group** (must be the same as the experimental group).

Randomise the selection of participants in both groups.

Pre-test, apply the stimulus then **post-test** the experimental group.

Pre-test and **post-test** the control group.

The pre-test and post-test are done on the independent variable.

☐ **Figure 4.4**   Steps in setting up an experimental research project

Crime statistics are often overlaid with this demographic information in an attempt to identify variables that might be contributing to a crime trend in a specific area. Government departments such as police services, correctional services and youth justice collect their own data from their staff and clients which provide essential quantitative information to criminologists.

Experimental Design

An experimental design is generally associated with scientific enquiry but can also be used in criminology research. Experimental design is a more formal and controlled method of research and involves the manipulation of one or more variables under controlled conditions to observe the outcome. It is generally a cause-and-effect process. When conducting an experiment, the researcher must control the research setting as well as the independent variables. A control group can be used to ensure that the changes observed are due to the manipulation of the dependent variable. Refer to Figure 4.4 which provides the steps involved in setting up an experimental design. If conducted well, an experiment allows a researcher to test for cause and effect, compare groups and explore reactions to stimuli.

Using an experimental method, researchers can investigate how people might react if placed in certain situations or given specific instructions

under controlled conditions. Experimental research is beneficial in that such observations cannot be obtained simply by self-report responses to questions but ethical considerations must be addressed prior to embarking on this type of research. To illustrate this, consider a well-known psychological experiment, the Milgram experiment, which was conducted at Yale University in the US (see case study). This experiment has important implications for criminology in that it showed that ordinary people are capable of inhumane actions under certain conditions but many of the participants experienced trauma because when they were exposed to the screams of the 'victim' they thought they were in fact hurting the 'victim'. The welfare of the participants must be a primary consideration of the researcher at all times. *See Research Ethics*.

Meta-analysis

Meta-analysis is a form of quantitative research that involves using a systematic statistical approach to test the combined results from multiple quantitative studies to increase the effect size of the results. It is used to test the statistical significance of similar results gained in different studies. It can also be used to identify the points where studies agree and disagree. A meta-analysis can provide a result that is stronger than one that can be gained just from an individual study.

Case Study

Milgram Obedience Experiment

Psychologist Stanley Milgram conducted an experiment on obedience to authority to explain the inhumane actions of so many Nazi soldiers during World War II. The experiment required participants, who were ordinary people, to give electric shocks to a person who they briefly met prior to the start of the experiment. They were given a payment for participating in the experiment but were told they could stop at any time and still keep the money. The payment was simply for turning up. Once underway a participant was selected to be the teacher and another pseudo-participant

was given the role of 'learner'. They were told to tie the learner to a chair and electrodes were placed on the learner. They were then told to give the learner electric shocks every time they made a mistake on a word pair task. They were to increase the voltage with each mistake. They were unable to see the learner but could hear them. The aim of the experiment was to see how long someone will continue to give electric shocks to another person when they are told to do so, even when they knew this could hurt them. The learner never received the shocks but the participant didn't know this.

An audio tape of them screaming was automatically triggered when the shock was given. Whenever a participant asked who is responsible the researcher said 'I am' and this seemed to reassure them to continue. It was found that even though many of the participants showed levels of discomfort, 40 were prepared to obey the instructions up to 300 volts and 25 up to 400 volts. None of the participants stopped when the learner said he had heart trouble. The experiment showed ordinary people were capable of inhumane actions when obeying authoritative directions.

Milgram, S. 1974. *Obedience to Authority: An Experimental View*. New York: Harper and Row. The Milgram Experiment

Qualitative Research

Research that relies on the depth of information obtained rather than on numerical size is qualitative. It involves in-depth interviews which are semi-structured or unstructured or observations (such as in ethnographic research). In qualitative research, the evidence can be presented in words, pictures or narratives. The strength of qualitative research lies in its ability to provide rich contextual information to further expand the understanding of the data collected. Many qualitative researchers would say that it provides the 'human' side of the phenomenon under investigation.

Identifying the Research Questions

Quantitative research projects have hypotheses and qualitative research projects have research questions. Perhaps the most important aspect of a research project is developing appropriate questions. Research questions provide direction to the project by establishing the scope of the

enquiry. These boundaries articulate what will be considered or included in the project and, importantly, what will not. Ultimately, the decisions about what data to collect, how and from whom will be determined by the underpinning research questions. It is up to the researcher to find the most direct method and most appropriate design to gather the necessary information. Research questions also serve to frame the final report, keeping the research and researcher focused, and provide an indication of the data required and the methods that can be used for data collection and analysis. For example, descriptive questions often suggest the need for administrative data. Questions may be straightforward, such as how many women are arrested by police annually, or incorporate some level of additional analysis, such as how many women are arrested annually by police for violent offences. Both of these questions are best answered by police administrative data but the first question requires only a simple count and the second question requires the categorisation of offences into violent and non-violent. If your overarching research purpose is to understand the nature and prevalence of offending by women, a nuanced question such as the second question in the example is required. If your only concern is to understand prevalence, an answer to the first question will suffice. Although this example is simplistic it underscores the importance of targeted research. Gathering additional unnecessary information is not only a burden on data providers and research subjects but may create ambiguity in the findings.

Sampling

Qualitative methodologies are not restricted to strict sampling rules as is the case with quantitative methodologies. The sampling in qualitative research can be more direct and led by the researcher, within loose guidelines.

Snowball Sampling

In qualitative research, snowball sampling is a method of recruiting participants for the purpose of doing research with them. It is often used in qualitative research and is a form of purposive sampling. The researcher will select a group of participants who are suitable to include in the study and will then utilise the social networks of these participants to recruit more. This type of sampling is good to use when the researcher believes there are potential hidden participants they would not be able to access any other way (e.g. victims of bullying in a workplace).

Purposive Sampling

The most common form of sampling in qualitative research is purposive sampling, where the researcher deliberately selects the sample based on preselected criteria (e.g. female offenders, young offenders, victims of sexual assault). The sample size is generally determined by the resources available to the researcher and the level of access the researcher has been given to a particular population. In the criminal justice system, the researcher must traverse many gateway points in order to undertake research and qualitative research

is generally looked on with some suspicion by police and prison officials who are used to dealing with statistics. Another way the sample size is limited is by the data itself. Once data stops bringing up new insights for the researcher it is an indicator to the researcher that further research is unnecessary.

Quota Sampling

Quota sampling is a purposive sampling method used in qualitative research. The researcher will select participants based on specific criteria, for example young offenders who breach their supervision orders. Demographic characteristics such as age, gender, marital status, class or ethnicity are the most common categories used to define quota sampling. The usual research rules apply: for example if the researcher is studying the effect of gender on young offenders' experience with a rehabilitation programme, the researcher will need to purposely select equal numbers of male and female participants.

Forms of Qualitative Research

There are many ways in which qualitative research can be designed and undertaken but the most common forms it takes are:

Participant observation: this method is appropriate when the researcher wants to collect data on behaviour that usually occurs in the natural setting.

In-depth interviews: this method is best when the researcher wants to collect data on a person's personal history, perspective or experiences. It is particularly useful when the topic is sensitive in nature.

Focus groups: the focus group method is effective in obtaining data on group behaviour including cultural norms, group experiences and broad overviews.

Ethnography

Ethnography is a qualitative research methodology that is designed to study cultural phenomena. It involves the researcher immersing themselves in the environment of the subjects they are studying in order to examine them in their natural context. This research methodology has its origins in anthropology where it is used to study populations and societies. It involves observation and in-depth interviews with subjects in an attempt to view the world through their eyes rather than through the perspective of the researcher (called the 'ethnographer'). Ethnographic data is holistic and comprehensive, taking into account geographical, environmental, climatic, social, cultural, linguistic, religious and historical information.

Grounded Theory

Grounded theory is a qualitative research process that begins with the data and allows the theory to emerge from the data, rather than the other way around (Glaser and Strauss 1967). Quantitative data is collected and analysed deductively, whereas grounded theory uses inductive logic and analysis. The grounded theory approach consists of a step-by-step process that scaffolds the construction of a theory to explain a phenomenon. Unlike the scientific method, grounded theorists emphasise the importance of the way in which the theory is constructed, rather than the quality of theory itself.

Narrative Analysis Approach

The narrative analysis approach utilises the stories or narratives provided by participants to obtain data about a phenomenon or issue or to just explore the experiences of a specific population. These stories can be written or oral and can be obtained from interviews. Researchers need to be skilled at encouraging participants to tell their story and need to use interviewing skills and approaches that make participants feel comfortable and which encourage participants to talk freely. Oral histories are a rich source of data for researchers seeking to understand the experiences of people over time.

 Would you use closed questions or open-ended questions to encourage someone to tell their story?

Case Study Approach

The case study approach involves the researcher concentrating on a specific case, or set of cases, to study social phenomena. It involves the researcher describing and analysing the case(s) in detail and identifying the specific themes or elements that add to the knowledge base of the field being researched. The researcher must be careful in accepting that the findings in one case can be generalised to others or to a wider population, but exploratory case studies can bring up new and interesting aspects of the issue that the researcher had not previously considered. Refer to Table 4.4 for an overview of the types of common research design.

Comparing Quantitative and Qualitative Research

Embarking on research for the first time can be a confusing experience for the criminology student. The language is new and there are so many rules you need to get to know and navigate. Take your time and read different books on the topic of undertaking research in criminology to expose yourself to different views and methods. Being knowledgeable and prepared is the best way to develop confidence in doing research. It is exciting to develop your research design for the first time but it is also challenging because you need to quickly understand these alien concepts. You may not have even heard the terms quantitative and qualitative prior to undertaking your studies and now you are being asked to choose between one and the other.

Be assured that every researcher has been in your shoes at some time in their career. It is an area that has caused anxiety in the most confident student and academic. In deciding between quantitative and qualitative methodology there is more to consider than just whether you want to end up with numerical data, as in quantitative research, or the psychosocial context of the data, as in qualitative research. It is essential that the methodology you choose is going to answer your research questions and is also a methodology that you are comfortable with using. Learning more about the differences between these two types of research will make you more comfortable with

▣ Table 4.4 Examples of common research designs

Action research	This is a research process that is undertaken along with practical participation and collaboration. Research is conducted while the community or organisation is involved in a change process. It is usually undertaken by organisations and utilises a cyclical process to produce knowledge that informs change in an integrated way to improve the organisation's functioning or a situation in the community.
	This approach is useful for researchers who need to provide data quickly to inform the actions of a change process. The disadvantage is that tension can exist between the need of the researcher to maintain research rigour and the agenda of the people who need to take action to implement the changes.
Case study design	The use of a single case or situation or a group of cases to understand the social and process elements that aid the understanding of a wider phenomenon.
	This approach allows the researcher to focus on the intimate details of what is occurring in a specific situation to better understand a larger phenomenon.
Cohort design	This is also known as event-based design. Data is collected from a specific segment of the population (a cohort) at set points in time. A cohort is defined as a group of people who share the same event, for example students in the same class, people born in a specific time period.
	This approach allows the researcher to investigate if changes over time affect a specific segment of the population differently to the general population.
Ethnographic design	Also known as ethnomethodology. This is an approach to studying cultural groups by the researcher immersing themselves in the culture and recording what they see and hear. The focus of investigation is on the rules, norms, conventions and patterns of social life.
	An advantage of this approach is that the data obtained tends to be rich with information about the group being researched. A disadvantage of this approach is that the researcher can become biased by their own close and intimate interaction with the cultural group they are researching.
Experimental design	This approach uses a rigorous and controlled environment to investigate the cause-and-effect nexus. The researcher manipulates the independent variable to observe what, if any, impact it has on the dependent variable.
	This approach has a high level of reliability, generalisability and validity but can present ethical conflicts when humans and animals are involved.
Longitudinal design	Data is collected at specific points in time to evaluate what happens over time. For example, surveying police recruits in the academy and over the first five years of their service to see if there would be any changes in their attitudes over time.
	This approach provides more information to the researcher than what can be obtained in a single-point-in-time study. A difficulty with this approach is the attrition rate of participants that occurs over the life of the study, especially when it spans over years.
Mixed method design	Mixed method designs combine both qualitative and quantitative methods together in the same study.
	The advantage of this approach is that it allows the researcher to be able to quantify certain aspects of their study while also having the detailed qualitative information to explain the data.
Population studies	This is a quantitative approach that seeks to understand the make-up (demographics) and/or the movements and activities of a population. There are two main ways in which population studies are done. The first is to build on existing data and the second is to create your own primary data.
	The advantage of this approach is that it provides broad-based data on large populations that is reasonably easy to obtain. The disadvantage is that there is no qualitative information about why observed changes have occurred.

The Differences Between Quantitative and Qualitative

Table 4.5 provides you with a quick reference guide as to the main differences between quantitative and qualitative research. Quantitative research is associated with numerical values and with attempting to prove the statistical significance of research results. Qualitative research is associated with the story behind the numbers rather than reporting just numerical values. Both research methodologies allow the researcher to design the research in many different ways. *Refer to* Table 4.5 *for more detail.*

using either and will help you make that important decision. So how do you assess whether you should go for a quantitative or a qualitative research methodology? We have provided an overview in Table 4.5 which will help you to see at a glance the differences between these two approaches. This should help you to decide which one best fits with what you want to achieve in your research project. Also see Table 4.4. for information about the different types of research you can do.

Evaluating Existing Research

Criminal justice system and research agencies like the Home Office in the UK, the Department of Justice in the US and the Australian Bureau of Statistics have centralised collections of statistics

Table 4.5 Comparing quantitative and qualitative research methods

	Quantitative	Qualitative
General approach	A more controlled style of investigating an issue or phenomenon. Tends to use structured instruments for eliciting information, for example surveys, questionnaires. Has a stated hypothesis that it wants to test.	A more flexible style of investigating an issue. Uses semi-structured methods such as interviews and focus groups. Explores an issue or phenomenon and allows the data to tell its own story.
Questions	Closed questions.	Open questions.
Analysis	Quantifies data and uses statistical testing to determine if the hypothesis is accepted or rejected. Predicts causal relationships. Describes characteristics of a population. Describes only what is evident from the immediate numerical data.	Describes and explains relationships and experiences. Uses coding to identify common themes and categories. Seeks to answer the 'what, how and why?' behind the quantitative data. Identifies and describes group norms. Infers and induces meaning from the data obtained.
Data	Numerical data. Responses to questions are given a numerical value.	Textual data. Collected from audio or video interviews and from field notes.
Research design	The research design is rigid and stable throughout. The process is predetermined so answers to questions will not influence the researcher in the direction the questions that follow will go. Researcher bias is controlled. The research process is unchanging.	Some aspects of the research design are predetermined while others remain flexible. The researcher will use participant responses to decide which questions to ask next. The research design is adjusted according to the data received.

on the criminal justice system and other areas that may be useful to a criminologist such as health data. Individual departments such as the police, courts and correctional services also have extensive collections of administrative data. This data is generally collected for agency purposes and not all data will be disseminated to the public. The data which is publicly available may not be in a format that is ideal for the research so it may be helpful to map your data collection needs in a matrix. An example of this is provided in Table 4.6.

Publicly Available Data

There is vast array of statistical information that is available to the general public on the internet and through government departments, non-government organisations and local councils. This information can be in the form of annual reports, issue-specific reports, aggregated statistics and journal articles reporting the findings of various studies. Most countries will have a government organisation that is responsible for collecting and reporting crime statistics. In Australia, statistics on populations, crime and other social issues is publicly available online at the Australian Bureau of Statistics website. Some of the reports produced

may have a nominal fee attached; however, most reports and data summaries can be downloaded for free. In the UK, the Office for National Statistics provides data on a range of crime issues. In the US, crime statistics are publicly available on the US Department of Justice website. In Canada such statistics can be found at the Statistics Canada website and in New Zealand via the Statistics New Zealand website. Most countries will have a similar website where crime statistics can be located. Figure 4.5 provides an example of the online data provided by the Australian Bureau of Statistics. In addition to websites that are dedicated to providing statistical information, there are a number of websites that will provide reports on a range of crime issues. Sites such as the Australian Institute of Criminology, the Home Office in the UK, the Federal Bureau of Investigation in the US and various police and other criminal justice organisations. Most of these sources will provide reports and other information free of charge to the general public. *See **Research Skills (Chapter 2)**.*

> ❯ What government organisation in your country is responsible for collecting and providing crime statistics to the public?

▣ **Table 4.6** Example of a data needs matrix

Research question	Data required	Source of data	Data limitations	Impact on project	Alternative data
What proportion of incidents attended by police are alcohol and drug related?	Police incident data flagged as alcohol or drug related.	Recorded police statistics.	Alcohol and drug flag may not be available.	High.	Aggregate data from police annual reports.
What impact does alcohol- and drug-related violence have on police resourcing?	Courts and police incident data flagged as alcohol or drug related and economic data.	Police personnel (operational). Recorded police statistics. Court Records. Economic mapping data.	Difficult to isolate one crime variable as being causal in increasing or decreasing funding.	High.	Aggregate data from various police annual reports over time. Bureau of statistics.

DECEMBER KEY FIGURES

PRELIMINARY DATA	Population at end Dec qtr 2014 '000	Change over previous year '000	Change over previous year %
New South Wales	7,565.5	103.0	1.4
Victoria	5,886.4	101.5	1.8
Queensland	4,750.5	64.2	1.4
South Australia	1,691.5	14.8	0.9
Western Australia	2,581.3	40.1	1.6
Tasmania	515.2	1.4	0.3
Northern Territory	244.3	0.9	0.4
Australian Capital Territory	387.6	4.3	1.1
Australia(a)	**23,625.6**	**330.2**	**1.4**

(a) Includes Other Territories comprising Jervis Bay Territory, Christmas Island and the Cocos (Keeling) Islands.

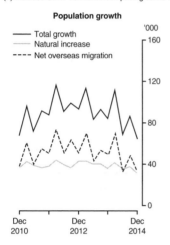

Population growth

- Total growth
- Natural increase
- Net overseas migration

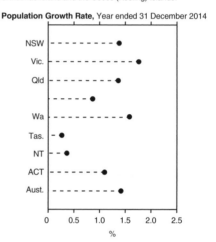

Population Growth Rate, Year ended 31 December 2014

DECEMBER KEY POINTS

ESTIMATED RESIDENT POPULATION

- The preliminary estimated resident population (ERP) of Australia at 31 December 2014 was 23,625,600 people. This reflects an increase of 330,200 people since 31 December 2013, and 64,000 people since 30 September 2014.
- The preliminary estimate of natural increase recorded for the year ended 31 December 2014 (146,100 people) was 7.8%, or 12,300 people lower than the natural increase recorded for the year ended 31 December 2013 (158,400 people).
- The preliminary estimate of net overseas migration (NOM) recorded for the year ended 31 December 2014 (184,100 people) was 14.8%, or 32,000 people lower than the net overseas migration recorded for the year ended 31 December 2013 (216,200 people).

POPULATION GROWTH RATES

- Australia's population grew by 1.4% during the year ended 31 December 2014.
- Natural increase and NOM contributed 44% and 56% respectively to total population growth for the year ended 31 December 2014.
- All states and territories recorded positive population growth in the year ended 31 December 2014.
- Victoria recorded the highest growth rate of all states and territories at 1.75%. Tasmania recorded the lowest growth rate at 0.3%.

Source: www.abs.gov.au (2015 accessed 5 November 2016).

■ **Figure 4.5**   An example of the online data provided by the Australian Bureau of Statistics

Limitations of Publicly Available Data

Publicly available data is extremely useful to criminologists conducting research as it provides readily accessible information to give context to their research. Criminologists are naturally curious beings and this trait is also useful when using publicly available data. The reason for this is that you need to question the statistics you are looking at to ensure that the official statistics are measuring the same thing as you are. For example, if you are wanting to know the total number of people who entered prison in one year, you would need to ensure that the statistics you are reviewing are measuring the first remand of each person. If all entries to prison were calculated over the year you could have the same person counted more than once (if they have been in and out of prison several times in the year). When police report on crime rate trends you need to look closely at the statistics to see if they are reporting arrests or convictions. If they are reporting arrests and using this as an indication of crime rate trends it is not a reliable indicator, because a person arrested for a crime may not be found guilty of that crime. Convictions are a more reliable indicator of crime rates. Reports of crime in a particular area are also problematic as there are many reasons why people do not report crime and therefore some crime is hidden. The definitions of crime also change over time and these definitions can also be used strategically by politicians and government departments to make their crime-fighting efforts look better. For example if the government has put additional money into fighting burglary offences in a particular area, the organisation may break down the burglary category in the annual report, specifying break and enter as a separate crime and thus reducing the number of burglary offences in the period being measured. Political interference may also impact on the collation and depiction of statistics.

> ❯ How can politicians indirectly influence the reporting of official statistics in the criminal justice system?

Non-public Data

There is a range of data that is not publicly available that may be of interest to criminologists. In the criminal justice system much of the data related to the inner workings of departments and operational processes is often considered to be too sensitive to be released to the public. This can be for perceived security reasons, it can be due to privacy concerns, or it can be a requirement of the government that certain information is not released to the public. If the data you are seeking is not publicly available you can approach a particular agency directly to request release of the data for the purpose of research. Agencies may be willing to agree to a controlled release of the data in this way so it is always worthwhile to ask. If you are unable to obtain the data in this way, you can lodge a Freedom of Information Request, which is a formal request to obtain the information under freedom of information legislation. Government departments are required by law to provide requested information unless they can show that certain exemptions are met should the information be released. Such exemptions include things such as that the release of the requested information will adversely affect victims or place a named person in jeopardy. A general exemption applies to information that is deemed to be 'classified' or 'secret'. It is not uncommon when requesting reports, for example, to have parts of the report redacted. Redacted data generally cannot be accessed. Freedom of information requests usually incur a fee that is linked to the amount of time it takes the department to locate, redact and copy the required information. These requests can also take some time to process so it is wise to allow for this when planning your research.

Summary

This chapter has introduced you to different types of research and how it is applied in criminology. It can appear daunting to embark on research when you have never done it before, but choosing your research approach is made a little easier when you assess the advantages and disadvantages of quantitative and qualitative approaches and choose the approach that will best help you to obtain the answers you are seeking. Both research approaches are used by criminologists. One of the most popular methods criminologists use to quickly assess patterns and trends is making use of existing data. As we have seen, in using existing data criminologists need to be mindful of the limitations of this data and question the source and type of data rather than assuming it measures what you are wanting it to measure.

Further Reading

Caulfield, L. & Hill, J. 2014. *Criminological Research for Beginners: A Student's Guide*. New York: Routledge.
　　This book is specifically aimed at assisting criminology students to understand the basics of how to do criminological research. It comprehensively covers the technical side of research and utilises examples to illustrate specific aspects such as designing a questionnaire.

O'Leary, Z. 2014. *The Essential Guide to Doing Your Research Project* (2nd edition). London: Sage.
　　This book provides a comprehensive overview of everything a beginning researcher will need to know to complete a research project. It takes the reader through the entire research process from planning through to implementation in an easy-to-read format with down-to-earth language.

Ruane, J. 2016. *Introducing Social Research Methods: Essentials for Getting the Edge*. Malden, MA: Blackwell Publishing.
　　Janet Ruane, the author of this book, has brought together all the essential information to give the student a basic understanding of research in a concise format. It is easy to read and understand for anyone who has not previously had experience with the language of research.

Key and Emerging Issues in Criminology

Criminology is a developing discipline and is constantly expanding to respond to the changing society that we live in. We have spent most of the time to this point discussing the criminological theories that have been influential in the past and included in that discussion are some of the issues that have impacted on the development and usage of these theories. We have also explored research principles and methods which equip you with the knowledge necessary to be able to examine the research evidence associated with the plethora of the topics that criminologists study. In addition to this, we have discussed the link between theory and research and how one informs the other. We will now spend some time discussing the current and emerging trends and issues in criminology.

This chapter investigates some of the key issues that are currently important to criminologists and emerging issues that will become increasingly important for criminologists to study and respond to, now and into the future. Key issues in criminal justice are those issues and relevant aspects that are important for criminologists to take into account. They include offender characteristics and traits and social problems that impact on criminal offending and on how the criminal justice system responds. Key issues also include aspects that are of interest to criminal justice academics and practitioners due to their close association with crime outcomes such as gender, race and mental illness. Emerging issues are also covered in this section and include new theoretical branches within criminology that have developed to address new and emerging issues such as cybercrime, terrorism and environmental criminology. While we are unable to cover every key issue and emerging trend, we think that we will provide a good overview for you in this chapter. It is definitely useful for criminology students to have such an overview of the key issues relevant to criminology and criminal justice because crime doesn't occur in a vacuum. The social context around the key issues and some of the key debates relevant to them will also be included. As with many things in criminology and criminal justice, there are crossovers and so we will signpost you to see similar discussions elsewhere in the book where we think these are relevant.

Social Aspects in Criminal Justice

This section looks at the key social aspects relevant to crime, which are important for consideration when working in or studying the criminal justice system. These issues include gender, race, mental illness and age (in particular youth offending). Some aspects such as age and mental status are dynamic and constantly changing whereas others such as gender and race are largely static, with the exception of transgender persons. As a general rule, gender and race are considered to be unchangeable aspects of a person's identity and have a significant influence in how a person experiences and interacts with the world around them. These aspects also influence, whether directly or indirectly, how the world around them views people as individuals and interacts with them. The subcategories of this section are linked by their relevance to the wellbeing of the individual in a social context and the way in which these social factors may be influential in regard to how this individual came to be in contact with the criminal justice system.

Gender and Crime

Gender is an important variable relevant to every person who comes into contact with the criminal justice system and for that reason it requires special consideration. This is true whether it is in relation to the design of prisons and rehabilitation programmes or addressing the causes and effects of crime more generally. For example, female criminality has increased in recent years but, despite this increase, men are still overwhelmingly more greatly represented in the criminal justice system, being responsible for up to 89% of all crime (Taylor 2016). When they do offend, women are more likely to be responsible for non-violent crime such as acts of theft. Interestingly, men are statistically more likely to be victims of crime, but women are more likely to be victims of violent and sexual crimes (Mallicoat and Ireland 2014). There is disagreement among criminologists as to whether women are treated more severely by the criminal justice system or whether chivalry plays a role, resulting in women being treated more leniently than men (Carlen 2002). The presumption of chivalry would assert that women are treated more leniently than men at specific and various points in the criminal justice process.

Women and Crime

It is argued by many criminological scholars that women and girls have remained virtually invisible in the criminal justice system (Chesney-Lind and Pasko 2004; Mallicoat and Ireland 2014). Prior to the twentieth century, commentators on crime tended to be exclusively male and tended to concentrate on biological determinist explanations for female criminality (Lombroso and Ferrero 1895) ignoring the social context in which female criminal offending occurred. Even when women began to enter into the field of criminology in the early twentieth century the focus remained on biological explanations for female offending (Dalton 1961).

Early Feminist Theorists

It was not until the 1970s, when feminist criminology really took hold, that a British criminologist, Carol Smart (1976), along with other feminist criminologists such as Freda Adler (1975) and Rita Simon (1975), introduced a new approach to analysing female offending. These scholars adopted a feminist criminological approach, challenging the sexist assumptions of early theorists and emphasising the need to analyse women and crime within a broader socio-political context that took into account the impact of prevailing social, moral, political, economic and sexual interests. They also made a link between female offending and victimisation, especially sexual exploitation and domestic violence.

Contemporary Feminist Theorists

As feminism gained momentum in the 1960s and 1970s women criminologists emerged who began to develop the scholarly understanding of female criminality within a social context (Walklate 2001; Carlen 2002). More recent theorists such as Stacy Mallicoat and Connie Estrada Ireland (2014) challenge the hegemonic assumptions underlying the theories of the past and consider the diversity of women's experiences. They acknowledge that feminism has made a huge contribution to the study of women and crime but they argue that to view all women as being shaped and oppressed by patriarchy is to presuppose that all women have a shared experience. They point to a 'third wave of feminism' that acknowledges the diverse gender, sexual, cultural and racial contexts within which women experience the world and influence their behaviour. See *Feminist Criminology (Chapter 3)*.

Differences in Male and Female Offending Rates

Around the world, offending rates are greater for males than females (Pritchard-Hughes 1998; Carlen 2002) and why this is the case is becoming a greater focus of criminological interest (Broidy and Agnew 2004). Adler (1975) hypothesised that female offending rates would increase as a result of feminism and the women's liberation movement; due in part to women moving from the domestic sphere into the public sphere and being exposed to more opportunities to commit crime. It has been the case that crime rates for women have risen since the 1970s but what is not clear is whether this is a result of more women engaging in criminal behaviour or a result of changes to the policing and criminal processing of women (Mallicoat and Ireland 2014). It is interesting to note that the gender difference in criminal offending is greater when violent crimes are considered and is less noticeable for property and fraud offences (Broidy and Agnew 2004). *See Violent Crime.*

Men and Crime

In response to feminist criminology highlighting an association between crime and masculinity, some criminologists such as James Messerschmidt (1993) and Richard Collier (1998) emerged with a branch of criminology known as *masculinist criminology*. Much like feminism, this branch of criminology views crime from a gendered perspective. It criticises the existing explanations of male involvement in crime as creating stereotypical characterisations that are hegemonic and one-dimensional. *See Masculinities in Criminology (Chapter 3).*

James Messerschmidt

James Messerschmidt (1993) argued that there were many ways in which men become involved in criminal offending and these are strongly influenced by social aspects such as race, age and class. He further proposed the idea that in all societies, men attempt to become the 'ideal male' as presented to them within that society. In Western society, this involves emulating male behaviour of being authoritative, combative, controlling and in charge. He believed that social roles and power structures in modern society limit men of alternate racial backgrounds and from lower socio-economic classes from legitimately expressing their masculinity in the conventional ways that are open to the white middle class, such as educational achievement, wealth creation and career success. According to Messerschmidt, if a man cannot meet the expectations of society as to what a man should be and what a man should do, he experiences role confusion and frustration which may lead to him becoming involved in crime and other forms of social deviance in order to express his manliness. He suggests that in all-male groups, the more dominant males of the group can target the weakest member of the group with denigration and exploitation, which is behaviour that is more commonly directed at women in mixed-sex groups. Messerschmidt also described differences between hegemonic masculinity and subordinated masculinities such as those experienced by homosexual or bisexual men.

Richard Collier

British criminologist Richard Collier (1998) has written widely on masculinities in crime and presenting masculinities as being as important to study as femininities in criminology. He argues that this is important if a deeper understanding of crime is to be achieved. Collier argues that the discourse around the crisis of masculinity as presented by Messerschmidt (1993) is potentially as damaging as pro-feminist criticism of all things masculine that seeks to de-gender men. He argues instead for deconstructing hegemonic associations such as the labelling of men as 'criminal men' and 'non-criminal men', suggesting that the relationship between men and crime is more complex than just the presentation of gender concepts seen to be related to masculinity. Collier (1998) sought to present a different approach to the study of masculinities and crime which placed the study of masculinities in a more central position than it had previously had, especially within criminology. He saw this as a much-needed movement away from the critical conception of men that was portrayed mainly by the Anglo-American feminist movement that did not indeed represent what he saw as the 'real' man. In particular a need for an acceptance of diversity within masculinity and a need for criminology and the criminal justice system to embrace this diversity.

Without question, men commit the largest portion of crimes and criminologists are trying to discover why this significant difference in the gender division of criminal offending exists (Broidy and Agnew 2004). Many, such as Messerschmidt and Collier, approach it from a theoretical perspective while others do so while working within the system. The main questions to be answered are: (1) Why do men become involved in criminal offending more often and (2) Why don't women become involved in criminal offending to the same level?

 What social tensions related to the changing roles of men in modern society might influence the discussion of masculinity and crime?

Gender and the Criminal Justice System

As men are more highly represented in the criminal justice system, programmes, services and building infrastructure (such as prisons) have been predominantly designed by men for men (Carlen 2002). Purpose-built prisons for women are a modern introduction to criminal justice and until recently women were housed in a separate section of the men's prison. This is still the case in many jurisdictions. In the early nineteenth century, however, women were held in conditions that were considered by welfare workers to be inhumane and that regularly exposed women to abuse and neglect (Mallicoat and Ireland 2014). A key human rights reformer in Britain, Elizabeth Fry, fought for change in London's Newgate Prison in the nineteenth century and, in doing so, influenced the women's prison reform movement in the United Kingdom (see case study).

The modern approach to incarceration is for the development of purpose-built women's prisons that are completely separate to men's prisons or for a purpose-built section within a men's prison. In addition to the physical infrastructure, women also experience the procedures within the criminal justice system differently to men. Pat Carlen (1983) has noted several areas in which women are disadvantaged in the penal system such as:

— They tend to be imprisoned at greater distances from their home than men;
— The nature and range of operational regimes tends to be much more restrictive; and
— Women suffer greater social stigma.

 Why is it more of a problem for women to be imprisoned at greater distances from their homes than it is for men?

Opinions on the treatment of women by the criminal justice system have changed considerably over time. From the claims of Otto Pollak (1950) in *The Criminality of Women* that women were treated more leniently in the criminal justice system to Belknap's (2001) belief that women are treated more harshly within prisons, the role and treatment of women in crime and the criminal justice system has been a subject of interest to criminologists. Many argue that gender equality has resulted in women being treated less chivalrously and more equally with men with many feminist criminologists arguing that for some groups of crimes women are treated more harshly (Carrington 1993; Chesney-Lind 1997; Belknap 2001). These crimes include sexual crimes, murder and child abuse and are said to attract greater public interest when the offender is female, and arguably more severe treatment by the courts. It is evident from the scholarly literature that men and women have quite different experiences with the criminal justice system. Mallicoat and Ireland (2014) suggest that girls are much more likely than boys to be charged with offences such as truancy and underage consumption of alcohol. Much work has been undertaken by feminist criminologists to identify the pathways in which women enter the criminal justice system and a history of abuse seems to be closely correlated with female criminality.

> ### Case Study
>
> **United Kingdom: London's Newgate Prison**
>
> In the nineteenth century, British human rights reformer Elizabeth Fry fought for change in the way in which women were treated in London's Newgate Prison. She was a Quaker who regularly visited prisons as a volunteer. She became concerned about the conditions in which women and children were kept at Newgate Prison.
>
> They were held in conditions that she described as unsanitary, cruel and horrific. Determined to do something about it, Elizabeth Fry encouraged middle-class women to visit the prison to educate the women outside the prison about the conditions experienced by female inmates and to enlist their help. She developed education
>
> classes for the women and established rules of conduct rather than imposed discipline. She also told people in the wider community about the conditions in prisons and used her influence with influential people to bring about change. She was the first prison reformer to focus on the needs and plight of women.
>
> Source: The Howard League for Penal Reform. 2015. Accessed online on 7 November 2016 at: www.howardleague.org.

Summary

Gender is an important focus in modern criminology and is an aspect that needs to be considered within the criminal justice system. Improvements have been made to women's experience of incarceration with the introduction of prisons designed and built specifically for women, but further improvements could be made pertaining to the criminal justice processes and greater access to programmes designed specifically for women. When seeking to better understand the processes of crime, it is important for criminologists to investigate why it is that men commit much greater levels of crime than women and their crimes tend to be more serious and violent than those of women. Is this due to gender-based psychological differences or is it due to socialisation and the gender differences in the social context of men and women? It is also just as important for criminologists to understand why it is that women largely desist from criminal offending and whether this due to rational decision-making processes or situational factors. Could it be that men simply have more opportunities to commit crime than women? These are areas for current and future research.

> Why is it important for women to have access to programmes that are specifically designed for women rather than joining in programmes that were designed for men?

Race and Crime

Making connections between race and crime has always been a problematic undertaking for criminologists and other social scientists. The problem starts with the term 'race' itself and how it is conceptualised. Most people think of race as a biological concept. Differences in skin colour between people are observed and people can be labelled on that basis – for example, people are often referred to as white, black, Hispanic, Middle Eastern or Asian based on their outward appearance. As criminologists we have had to contend with the legacy of research attempting to link offending behaviour to biological differences such as race (e.g. experiments conducted by Lombroso (1876/1911) that have since been discredited). This has led, in part, to ongoing resistance and discomfort among many criminologists to studies focused on identifying genetic differences and linking these to criminal tendency. While the pigment of our skin is certainly related to biology, the reality is that there is more genetic variation within 'races' than between them which leads most contemporary biological anthropologists and geneticists to agree that there is no biological basis for the idea of race (Jorde and Wooding 2004). In fact, much attention has been directed towards the social construction of race in recent times. *See Cesare Lombroso (Chapter 3).*

Key Criminological Research Debates

Why do men commit more crime than women?
Universally, criminologists are in agreement that men do commit more crime than women and available data supports this. Research debates therefore tend to focus on whether the gender gap in offending is stable or changing over time and whether the causes of female crime are the same or different to those of men (Steffensmeier 2003). This is important for criminal justice professionals to know so that they can better plan their services and be prepared for any expected changes in the gender ratio in prisons as this may mean the building of more women's prisons. Another ongoing area of gender research in criminology is focusing on explaining why men are much more highly represented in criminal offending than women. Research efforts such as that of Krienert (2003) have focused on trying to prove or disprove the theory of Messerschmidt (1993) that men are losing their masculine identity which is causing them to engage in criminal behaviour. Many other research studies seek to understand men's involvement in crime in relation to their biology and the increased levels of testosterone in the male body (Batrinos 2012). Early criminological research focused attention on disproving the theory that women will engage in more crime as a result of feminism. More recent research seeks to understand why women's involvement in crime is on the rise and why young teenage girls are engaging in more violent crimes.

> ❯ Why would criminologists be uncomfortable about assigning biological characteristics and physical features to criminal behaviour?

The Social Construction of Race

Social scientists have long understood race to be largely socially constructed, meaning that the labels and categories we attach to people, based on skin colour, geographic origin or cultural traditions are in the main applied by people in a social context (Hilton and MacDonald 2008) rather than being based on scientifically valid genetic differences. Our assumptions about biological differences lead us to attribute certain characteristics, either real or imagined, to various populations which are then culturally transmitted and thought of as attributable to 'race' (Sternberg et al. 2005). Furthermore, people attach certain social and economic conditions to these groups of people that have been defined by socially constructed

'race', linking these conditions to race as if they are biologically based differences. There are theorists who argue for and against biologically determined criminal tendency due to race and others that argue against the social construction of race. Machery and Faucher (2005), however, have reconceptualised these arguments and propose a theory of cultural evolution that integrates both of these positions.

Socio-economic Inequality

When a criminologist talks about race it is usually in the context of social inequality or disadvantage and the over-representation of certain racial groups in the criminal justice system. Social inequality has historically been a key area of research across the social sciences and race is used as a marker of inequality and as a descriptor in official statistics and research in criminal justice. An outcome resulting from the linking of race and social inequality has been the polarising of opinions such as seeing whites as affluent and unlikely to come into contact with the criminal justice system and non-whites as disadvantaged, over-policed and unfairly treated by the criminal justice system (Blau and Golden 1986). Neither of these polarised positions are accurate but continue to have a significant influence in criminology. Certain racial groups do appear to show higher levels of criminal offending, but it appears to be mainly against other people from within their own racial group and within the geographic area in which they live (Stolzenberg et al. 2006). At the same time certain racial groups are represented more highly in lower economic areas, have higher rates of unemployment and lower health outcomes (Australian Human Rights Commission 2016). The question is whether it is race, living in a lower socio-economic area, poverty, all of these or some other factor altogether that is the causative link with crime. In fact some of these factors, such as living in a low socio-economic area, are more greatly associated with crime than they are with race.

Over-representation in the Criminal Justice System

Official statistics reveal an over-representation of certain minorities as both offenders and victims of crime. In the US, African Americans are incarcerated at six times the rate of whites (NAACP 2016). In Australia, Aboriginal people account for around 3% of the total population but make up more than 28% of the prison population

(Creative Spirits 2016). In Canada, Aboriginal people account for around 4% of the total population and 23% of the prison population. In Canada the incarceration rate of Aboriginal people is ten times greater than that of non-Aboriginal people (Office of the Correctional Investigator 2013). Aboriginal women are also incarcerated at higher rates than Aboriginal men, a statistic not found in any other racial demographic. In New Zealand, Maori people account for about 14% of the population and 50% of the prison population (NZ Ministry of Justice 2016b). In the UK, black and Asian (Middle Eastern) people appear to be over-represented in many stages of the criminal justice process such as stop and searches and in the prison population (Merrick et al. 2012). They are also less likely than their white British counterparts to be employed, or involved in education and training. In US, tensions have been rising between African Americans and police over a number of years due to a perception that African Americans are unfairly targeted by police and that police use excessive force when dealing with African Americans (Day 2015). Further to this, that the criminal justice system does not prosecute cases involving the death of an African American at the hands of police in an impartial manner when the police officer concerned is white (see case study).

Some researchers have argued that over-representation has been reduced to a discussion

---

Case Study

United States: Black Lives Matter – the Birth of a New Civil Rights Movement

In July 2015, *The Guardian* ran a story about Black Lives Matter (BLM) which is a social movement that commenced in 2013 following the acquittal of a white man and neighbourhood watch member, George Zimmerman in the shooting death of a young unarmed black teenager, Trayvon Martin, who was walking home from a convenience store. The movement gained momentum after the 2014 death of Michael Brown in Ferguson Missouri when the Grand Jury determined that the police officer involved would not face any charges related to the death. Black Lives Matter challenges what they perceive as the regular extrajudicial killings of young black men by police and organises protests advocating for racial justice across the US. The movement uses social media and public demonstrations to draw attention to the deaths of black people killed by law enforcement officers, police brutality, racial profiling and inequality.

Source: Day, E. 2015, 19 July. '#Black Lives Matter: The Birth of a New Civil Rights Movement' *The Guardian*. Accessed online on 7 November 2016 at: www.theguardian.com/world/2015/jul/19/blacklivesmatter-birth-civil-rights-movement.

of actual elevated rates of offending by minority groups, poor statistics or apparent discrimination (see, for example, Sampson and Wilson 1995). To counter the misperceptions of increased rates of offending by minority groups that arise from the reporting of statistics and to better address underlying concerns of discriminatory treatment, Phillips and Bowling (2003) suggest that criminologists should pursue ways to increase minority perspectives in criminology. This includes how minority groups experience victimisation, criminal offending and criminal justice processing.

The Problem With Race Statistics

Researchers have identified several issues with collecting race and crime data including the unreliability of this data, lack of uniformity in how race is interpreted or measured and the possibility that the data will be used for the purposes of racial vilification. It is largely for these reasons that Canada and Australia do not routinely collect such data (except, in some cases, for Aboriginal people). To address Canadian concerns, Wortley (1999:265) identified several arguments in favour of the collection of these statistics, including:

(1) this type of information is needed to identify whether or not minorities receive differential treatment within the justice system;

(2) to challenge biological explanations of crime; and

(3) because a ban will not prevent the spread of racist ideas.

He suggested that special studies should be conducted that would include explanations of the limitations of the data. Both the US and the UK have adopted approaches to data collection and dissemination that reflect an interest in access to information. In the US the *Uniform Crime Report* data uses both race and ethnicity markers while in the UK, section 95 of the *Criminal Justice Act 1991* requires that the Home Secretary publish statistics in an effort to avoid racial discrimination in the criminal justice system. Setting aside whether this data should or should not be collected, one issue facing criminologists is how best to use it to avoid unintentionally contributing to labelling and racist sentiments.

Working With Offenders From Minority Groups

A concern for many criminologists is the cultural appropriateness of the tools and practices used across the criminal justice system. In addition to informing programme content, the risk needs responsivity (RNR) model is widely used to develop risk assessment instruments (Andrews et al. 2011). A commonly used tool for risk assessment with offenders is the level of service inventory-revised (LSI-R) – or one of its variants, including the level of service case management inventory – which was developed in Canada (Bonta and Andrews 2007). Without getting into a technical discussion of how risk assessment tools are constructed, it is important to note that they are generally based on statistical modelling drawn from the offence records and demographic data of known offenders – typically white male offenders. The question then becomes whether such instruments can validly assess the risks presented by white offenders outside of Canada, non-white offenders, and women, especially Aboriginal women (Hogg 2011). In fact, several researchers have suggested that risk assessment tools may not be appropriate for Aboriginal and culturally and linguistically diverse offenders located outside Canada (Jones et al. 2002). In response to these concerns, the LSI-R has undergone numerous validation studies in the US, Australia, the UK, Portugal and Germany and has been established as valid in these jurisdictions as well and it is therefore widely used. The tool has also been validated for use with Canadian Native offenders, including Aboriginal women. If risk assessment tools are not reflective of non-white offenders' dynamic risk factors, their needs will not be accurately identified and therefore not targeted through evidence-based treatment programmes.

Alternatively they may be subject to more intensive monitoring on the basis of misleading risk scores such as false negatives (Hogg 2011). Further, if we focus only on making the practices we have more culturally appropriate we will lose sight of the inherent problems in the system and may leave it unchallenged (Spivakovsky 2013). Either outcome could have important implications for the individual and the criminal justice system more broadly. *See Rehabilitation (Chapter 6)*.

Summary

Race and crime issues are key areas of enquiry for criminologists. There are far too many issues to explore adequately in depth here. For example we haven't touched on hate crimes or recent concerns over immigration and crime. Instead we have focused on some of the issues within the criminal justice system that we need to get right sooner rather than later so that we can increase perceptions of justice and fairness. First we need to think about the language used to ensure we can speak about discrimination and inequality in meaningful ways that do not increase marginalisation of minority groups. Second we need to improve how we collect and use data so that it is more comparable and better reflects the lived experiences of minority groups as both victims and offenders. Thirdly we need to review our practices within the criminal justice system to ensure we are not inadvertently contributing to the over-representation of specific ethnic groups by any of the methods used to research and record crime.

> ▶ Why is it that some racial groups are more highly represented in prisons than other racial groups? Do they commit more crime or is it just that they are more likely to be given a sentence of imprisonment? Where would you look to find the answers to these questions?

Mental Illness and Crime

Mental illness has had a long association with the criminal justice system both in respect to explaining criminal behaviour and also in explaining rises in incarceration rates. There are some mental disorders that are said to be more closely related to crime and studies have shown an association between some types of crime, such as homicide, and mental illness (Shaw et al. 2006). There is an alternative argument, however, that mental illness does not cause crime but that people with mental illness are more highly represented in the criminal justice system due to policies and politics. This argument holds that the closure of mental health institutions and services has resulted in people with mental illness ending up in the criminal justice system and being more highly represented in prisons (Cowell et al. 2004). For some time it has been argued that the criminal justice system is a costly and ineffective way of addressing mental health issues and that diversions from the criminal justice system are a more appropriate way of dealing with criminals who have a mental disorder.

What Is Mental Illness?

Mental illness (or mental disorder) is a term used to describe illnesses of the mind and of mental functioning that can range from minor to severe in nature. Mental illnesses are categorised according to their type, such as psychotic disorders, mood disorders and affective disorders. In the late 1800s and early 1900s, mental illness was seen to be a biological determinant and was closely linked to criminal behaviour (Maudsley 1876; Lombroso 1911). During the 1960s and 1970s a social explanation for mental disorder became popular with researchers and practitioners and resulted in mass deinstitutionalisation (Monahan and Steadman 1983). During the 1980s and 1990s, mental illness once again began to be linked with criminal behaviour (Hodgins 1992; Monahan and Steadman 1994; Torrey 1994) as more and more people with mental illness began to appear in the criminal justice system (Cowell et al. 2004).

Mental Illness in Prisons

Fazel and Danesh (2002) undertook a comprehensive review of studies of mental illness in prisoners in Western countries. There were 62 surveys involved in the studies reviewed which collectively found that there were 23,000 prisoners with serious mental disorders imprisoned in Western countries. The average age of these prisoners was 29 years with 81% of the cohort being men. The review of the findings from these studies indicated that the prevalence rate for mental illness among prisoners was estimated to be around one in seven. It also found that prisoners were significantly more likely to experience psychosis and major depression than the general population, and ten times more likely to suffer from antisocial personality disorder than the general population.

Source: Fazel, S. & Danesh, J. 2002, 16 February. 'Serious Mental Disorder in 23,000 Prisoners: A Systematic Review of 62 Surveys' *The Lancet* 359, 545–550.

The most common mental disorders in the criminal justice system are schizophrenia, depression, personality disorder and bipolar disorder (Das Gupta and Guest 2002; Fazel and Danesh 2002) (see case study).

A review of research by Fazel and Danesh (2002) found that prisoners were several times more likely to have psychosis and major depression than the wider population and ten times more likely to have antisocial personality disorder. These conditions are recognised as illnesses in the general community and are treated by the health system. This raises the question as to whether people suffering from a diagnosed mental illness at the time of offending should be treated in the health system rather than being punished in the criminal justice system, and whether this can be achieved safely for victims and for the general safety of the community (Melamed 2010). This is an ongoing debate.

The Cost and Social Impact of Mental Illness

Mental illness incurs great costs to society, which emerge as direct financial costs to the health and criminal justice systems and indirect costs such as reduced productivity (high unemployment), premature death and family breakdown. In the UK, the total financial cost of just one mental disorder, schizophrenia, was estimated to be £6.7 billion in the 2004–2005

financial year. These costs related to health and social care, private expenditures, premature mortality, provision of criminal justice services and expenditures by the social security system (Mangalore and Knapp 2007). The annual cost of bipolar disorder to the UK is estimated as being £199 million. Hospital admissions account for 35% of this figure with non-health-care-related costs accounting for £86 million (Das Gupta and Guest 2002). Indirect social costs are estimated to be £1,770 million annually. The social impacts linked to mental illness also include issues such as marginalisation, increased risk of suicide and homelessness. Additionally, the children of mentally ill parents are more frequently placed in foster care, which can result in intergenerational social disadvantage.

 What could be some of the indirect social impacts associated with mental illness that could be included in this figure?

Social policy in many countries has led to the transferring of people with mental illness from living within institutions to residing in the community (Hartwell 2004). This policy is well intentioned and aimed at empowering the mentally ill to live independently. With the availability of psychiatric medication and voluntary community-based mental health services, this policy seeks to ensure people with mental illness can remain active and productive members of the society. This policy was also expected to result in a more economic mental health system (Scheffler et al. 1998). Unfortunately it is often the case that people suffering mental illness are incapable of functioning in an organised way to consistently take their medication and to seek out these services (Hartwell 2004). Many have problems coping with the day-to-day routine of holding down a job, paying bills and shopping. When struggling to function with daily tasks such as earning an income and paying rent on time, people with mental illness frequently end up homeless and therefore more visible to law enforcement.

Coexisting Mental Illness and Substance Abuse

It is common for people with mental illness to also use substances, such as prescription and illegal drugs and alcohol, as a means of coping with their condition (Steadman and Naples

---

Key Criminological Research Debates

Is deinstitutionalisation in the mental health system displacing mentally ill people to prisons?
Throughout the mid-to-late twentieth century there was a significant shift in the understanding of, and treatment approach to, mental illness with a movement toward deinstitutionalisation (Sheth 2009). Prior to this, the favoured method of treatment involved lengthy internment in psychiatric hospitals where patients were heavily sedated and contained away from broader society. As understanding of mental illness increased, and concerns about the economic cost of institutions grew, community-based treatment options became more popular. This trend saw an increase in the number of people suffering mental illnesses such as schizophrenia and bipolar disorder becoming homeless and coming to the attention of police due to their visibility in the community, especially if experiencing a psychotic or manic episode. With reduced resources to deal with such cases in the community, the community mental health services became stretched and were forced to triage cases by degrees of seriousness, accepting only those people who were imminently at risk to themselves or others into the few available hospital beds. The result of this situation is that there has been a displacement of mentally ill people from the health system to the criminal justice system. Research conducted in the UK by Fakhoury and Priebe (2007) suggested there was a movement back toward institutionalisation in Western countries; however, this movement appears to be slow, if indeed it is occurring across all Western countries. In America, for example, more recent research has shown that there are now more people with mental illness in prison than in hospital (Fuller Torrey et al. 2010). The displacement of mentally ill people from the health system to the criminal justice system has caused much debate in criminological circles with a central argument being that prison is not the right place for people with mental illness. With no alternatives available to police, however, they continue to use arrest and criminal charging as a means of protecting this group of people and the community. In many Western countries where deinstitutionalisation has occurred, many of the physical and financial resources previously used to care for such people have been removed and the health system is left with a reduced capacity to respond to this need. The field of forensic psychiatry has developed due to a requirement for the criminal justice system to respond constructively to the needs of the mentally ill housed in prisons, and most prisons now regularly employ psychiatrists as part of the prison staff group. The numerous issues related to the displacement of people with mental health to prisons continues to be an important area of research for criminology.

2005). Alcoholism and the abuse of other substances are often found to be coexisting with mental illness (Das Gupta and Guest 2002) and criminal offending (Hartwell 2004). The dual issues of addiction to substances and mental illness can exacerbate social disadvantage and expose a person to a criminal subculture they are ill-equipped to resist. On the other hand, Healy (1998) argues that a causal link between substance abuse, mental illness and crime cannot be assumed without taking the multivariate social context into account. Healy does, however, concede that a pattern of association exists between drug addiction and criminal offending.

Mental Illness and Criminal Offending

It is estimated that mentally ill people make up between 7 and 18% of people in the criminal justice system including those arrested, remanded, sentenced and under supervision in the community (Cowell et al. 2004). This is a conservative estimate and many researchers and correctional administrators put the figure much higher. There is a great deal of evidence to suggest that mental illness leads to social disadvantage in areas of employment, education and housing and to homelessness, poor educational outcomes, unemployment and ultimately criminal offending. Draine et al. (2002) argue that this link is not as strong as is suggested in much of the literature and suggest instead that the main moderating relationship with mental illness is not crime but poverty. They argue that poverty creates loose prosocial attachments to society increasing the likelihood of crime. Draine et al. also argue that the link between social problems, crime and mental illness is complex and is not amenable to simplistic explanations. Some groups of offenders, such as those convicted of homicide, have been studied for evidence of mental illness. In one such study by Shaw et al. (2006) it was found that of the 1,594 offenders included in the study, 34% (545) had been diagnosed with a mental illness. In addition, the researchers discovered that most of the offenders with a mental illness had neglected to attend psychiatric services.

Summary

Mental illness has been associated with the criminal justice system for a long time; however, it is a complex area that cannot be understood with simple explanations. There are many variables that impact on offending behaviour, not least of which are poverty and resultant social disadvantage. As Hartwell (2004) argues, mental illness may make people more susceptible to social disadvantage and to becoming involved with alcohol and illicit substances, which further exacerbates the situation. This in turn may lead to greater involvement with the criminal justice system due to offending behaviour. It is evident that at least a pattern of association exists with illicit drug use and crime (Healy 1998) and that substance abuse and mental illness are frequently coexisting (Das Gupta and Guest 2002). Furthermore, there is evidence to suggest that a link between mental illness and crime exists (Shaw et al. 2006), although this may be more related to the social context frequently found associated with persons living with mental illness in the community rather than to the illness itself (Draine et al. 2002). The criminal justice system is still grappling with the best response to mental illness and crime with the continuing debate as to whether treatment or punishment is the best response. More research into this area is needed to ensure that whatever changes are made to the system, in an endeavour to be more humanely responsive to offenders suffering mental illness, community safety is also given equal attention.

Pathways to Youth Offending

The general public often has strong views about young offenders, which range from anger to fear. Both ends of this continuum result in cries for harsher penalties and especially for young people to be 'locked up'. The media often picks up on the community's emotions and this escalates moral panics related to out-of-control juvenile delinquents. An example of this is the James Bulger case (Paul 2003) in the UK (see case study).

United Kingdom: The James Bulger Case

In 1993 the world was shocked by the senseless and violent murder of 3-year-old James Bulger in Liverpool, England. He had been shopping with his mother at the local shopping centre when he disappeared from the butcher shop where he had been standing beside her. At first the case was simply a missing child case but it took a sinister turn when police viewed the CCTV footage and discovered that he had been lured away from his mother by two older boys, who could be seen leading him out of the shopping centre. These boys were later identified as 10 year olds Robert Thompson and Jon Venables. They had taken James to the railway and had thrown paint in his eyes, beaten, sexually assaulted and eventually killed him. They left his body on the railway track where it was subsequently hit by a train. People worldwide found it hard to believe that this toddler had been killed by two children, but as the details of the crime surfaced the public became outraged and demanded that these boys be locked up for life. They were found guilty in court and were detained at 'Her Majesty's Pleasure'. Robert Thompson was released in 2001 and Jon Venables was released in 2002 amidst a strong public outcry. Both were given new identities and their locations were kept private to protect them from vigilantes. Robert Thompson appears not to have reoffended but Jon Venables was returned to prison soon after his release due to alleged child pornography offences. He was released again but continued to be arrested for child pornography crimes and was returned to prison in 2010 after pleading guilty to downloading child pornography. He was released in 2013. Much of the outrage shown by the public has been due to the lack of remorse shown by the offenders and the extremely brutal nature of the crime they committed when just children themselves.

Source: Paul, J. 2003. *When Kids Kill*. London, UK: Virgin Books, Thames Wharf Studios. Hull, L. 2013, 5 July. 'Fury as Venables Gets Fourth New Identity as He is Set For Early Release From Child Porn Sentence' *Daily Mail*. Accessed online on 7 November 2016 at: www.dailymail.co.uk/news/article-2356231/Jon-Venables-gets-FOURTH-new-identity-set-early-release-child-porn-sentence.html.

Stories such as the Bulger case stir up outrage in the minds of the general public because such stories are newsworthy. They sell papers and attract many viewers on the television; unfortunately the stories played out in the media do little to educate the public about the reasons why young people become involved in criminal offending. The pathways to offending for young people are complex and are as greatly influenced by the structures and processes of society as by family upbringing and individual traits and characteristics. The pathways to youth offending are discussed here in regard to the societal context and the dynamics that may inadvertently but unfairly criminalise normal adolescent behaviour.

The pathways to youth offending can be categorised into three groupings that describe the level at which they operate to influence a young person: macro, meso and micro factors. These categories can be reconceptualised into more specific groupings that describe the dynamic of the grouping such as: societal, social and individual factors. There are many crossovers between these groupings that add to the complexity of understanding how these factors work to influence young people to engage in criminal offending (See Figure 5.1).

For example, child maltreatment is a well-known pathway to offending (Stewart et al. 2002; Sherman 2005; Qualtieri and Robinson 2012) that crosses over into all three levels of influence. Homelessness (Prichard and Payne 2005) operates mainly at the societal and social levels (such as breakdown of family environment) whereas alienation from education has crossovers at all three levels (Corby 1997). Other factors that can lead to involvement with the criminal justice systems are: substance abuse, poverty, peer group influence, social exclusion, bullying, intergenerational influence and young people leaving government care.

Child Maltreatment

Possibly the most important factor to take into account when trying to understand youth offending is child maltreatment, because while

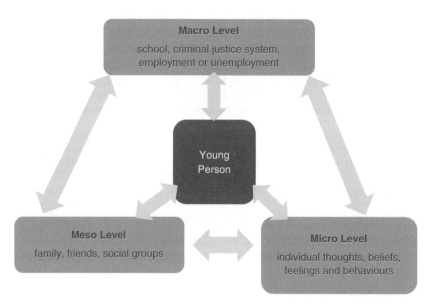

Figure 5.1 Levels of social influence on youth

not all young offenders have been maltreated it remains one of the most common pathways to offending for children and young people (Stewart et al. 2002; Sherman 2005; Qualtieri and Robinson 2012). The connection between child maltreatment and involvement with the juvenile, and later the adult, criminal justice systems is well established (see case study).

Child maltreatment accelerates entry into the criminal justice system with children who are maltreated at a younger age being more likely to commence offending at a younger than average age (Stewart et al. 2002). It is also known that children who commence offending at a younger age commit more crimes than children who begin offending later in childhood (Gonzales et al. 2005). Child maltreatment includes emotional, physical and sexual abuse and neglect (Qualtieri and Robinson 2012). Such abuse has been found to be associated with relationship problems, homelessness, poor mental health, intellectual deficits, poor school performance, eating disorders and substance abuse. Physical maltreatment can result in long-term physical disability such as visual or auditory impairment and brain damage (Richardson 2005). Sexual

Case Study

'The Sexual Abuse to Prison Pipeline: The Girls' Story'

In the US, it is reported by Saar, Epstein, Rosenthal and Vafa (2015) that up to 80% of girls in some of the state juvenile detention facilities have been sexually or physically abused in childhood. They released this finding in a report entitled *The Sexual Abuse to Prison Pipeline: The Girls' Story* which was supported by the Human Rights Project for Girls, the Ms. Foundation and the Georgetown University Law Center. This report acknowledges that the child welfare system is a pathway to juvenile justice and argues that girls are more greatly impacted by this than boys. They found that 31% of girls in detention in the US had been sexually abused compared with 7% of boys and concluded that in many cases the childhood trauma experienced by girls who have been sexually abused drives them into the juvenile justice system.

Source: Saar, M. S., Epstein, R., Rosenthal, L., Vafa, Y. 2015. *The Sexual Abuse to Prison Pipeline: The Girls' Story*. Washington DC: Georgetown University Law Center.

abuse can result in long-term psychological problems such as post-traumatic stress disorder, problems forming and sustaining relationships, fertility issues and mental illness. Emotional abuse affects the emotional wellbeing and stability of the child, resulting in poor self-esteem, a lack of confidence, inability to form relationships or to trust people and mental illness. Neglect affects all aspects of a child's development including physical, emotional, psychological and sexual development (Qualtieri and Robinson 2012). Developmental delays and the incomplete achievement of developmental milestones are common features of children who have been neglected. In all forms of neglect and abuse, children can fail to learn healthy social boundaries and may then have a tendency to develop resentment, anger and fear of authority figures, leading them to rebel against society's rules and have no respect for the agents of social control in society such as youth workers and police.

 Why do you think abused and neglected children fail to reach developmental milestones?

Comorbid Social Issues

It is common for children and young people with a history of maltreatment to have also been exposed to other family risk factors such as domestic violence, alcoholism, drug addiction and parental mental illness (Kenny et al. 1999; Qualtieri and Robinson 2012) and such circumstances make it difficult for them to obtain guidance and support at home. As a result, young people who have been abused and/or neglected at home tend to seek support and a sense of belonging from people outside the family. If child welfare authorities, such as social services, become involved, they can end up being placed in foster care and that can result in several disruptions to their home environment over a period of time. With uncertain and weak family connections, children and young people are more open to the influences of peers and are more vulnerable to further exploitation and abuse by people outside the family.

Youth Homelessness

The Australian Institute of Criminology reported that 8% of juveniles in detention in Australia were living alone or on the streets prior to entering detention (Prichard and Payne 2005). The reasons for this are varied but in a UK study of youth homelessness, family conflict, child abuse and substance abuse by the parents were cited as the main causes of youth homelessness (Wincup et al. 2003). Youth homelessness is a risk factor for contact with the juvenile justice system and is causally linked to some well-recognised risk factors that also seem to be independently related with entry into the youth justice system. For example, children and young people who are victims of child maltreatment and children living in alternative care arrangements such as foster care are more vulnerable to homelessness than other children (Stewart et al. 2002). In fact children and young people living in foster care are at significantly greater risk of homelessness than other youth (Wincup et al. 2003) and homelessness is a known pathway into the juvenile justice system (see case study).

Alternative care is also associated with higher levels of youth detention. Kerry Carrington (1993) conducted a comprehensive study of offending girls in Australia and found that many of them were fast tracked from foster care into detention due to paternalistic attitudes of police and youth workers. Her finding demonstrated the risk of juvenile detention being used as a protective welfare measure where alternatives such as youth shelters are unavailable. This is particularly likely with homeless girls due to their perceived vulnerability to sexual exploitation (Carrington 1993). Indigenous children and young people are also at higher risk of having their living arrangements break down due to alcoholism and poverty, resulting in homelessness (Day and Wanganeen 2003). In addition, there is a higher risk that official decision-making processes within the welfare and youth justice systems result in children and young people of Aboriginal or Torres Strait Islander descent being more likely to be taken into care or placed in youth detention than

Homelessness and Juvenile Offending: Hendrick's Story

Hendrick is a 19-year-old young offender. He grew up in foster care and for various reasons ended up homeless during his teens. He had several offences for shop theft as a juvenile which he states was due to him 'trying to survive'. He stole clothes, food and sometimes saleable items which he sold to get money. When Hendrick turned 18, he got a job in sales. This job was important to him as it allowed him to be independent and to support himself. He had been working for about three months when his boss asked him to provide a criminal record check, which was part of the requirement of his employment. When the police check came back it revealed his past criminal record and he was fired from his job. Hendrick no longer has a source of income and is now homeless again and at risk of reoffending to survive.

Source: Smart Justice for Young People. 2015. *Youth Diversion Makes Sense*. Melbourne: Smart Justice for Young People. Accessed online on 7 November 2016 at: www.smartjustice.org.au

non-Indigenous children and young people (Cunneen 2002). This is also true of other minority racial and cultural groups.

Substance Abuse

Substance abuse has been associated with homelessness and youth offending and occurs at all socio-economic levels (Prichard and Payne 2005). Most studies have found that the onset of drug use occurs prior to the onset of criminal behaviour, with only a small number of studies showing that criminal offending preceded drug use (Bennet and Holloway 2005). Recreation substance abuse appears to be a common practice with most juvenile offenders. The most frequently used substances are alcohol (97%); cannabis (94%); amphetamines (50%); inhalants (37%) and ecstasy (33%). An Australian study of 371 children and young people in detention between the ages of 11 and 17 found that almost all juveniles in detention had used two or more of these substances prior to entering detention (Prichard and Payne 2005). This compares with 35% substance use by the general adolescent population (Fransham and Johnston 2003). According to Prichard and Payne (2005), when compared with young people of the same age, young offenders in detention tend to:

- use drugs more often;
- start using drugs at an earlier age;
- have a family history of drug use; and
- have a history of sexual abuse.

Drug use and addiction is only one aspect of the substance abuse problem, with drug offences such as trafficking and illegal growing and manufacturing on the rise around the world (Bennet and Holloway 2005).

Interrupted Education

Children and young people engaged in the youth justice system are more likely to have difficulty in mainstream education and are more likely to have missed a significant amount of classroom time due to suspensions and exclusions than other youth (Ashmore 2005; Stephenson 2005). In the UK, the average reading age for a 17 year old entering custody is below that of an 11-year-old (Stephenson 2005). The factors that can lead to interrupted schooling include family conflict, substance abuse, maltreatment and neglect. Multiple foster placements for children in care can result in disjointed, interrupted and failed school achievement (Blyth et al. 2004). Interruption to schooling has severe consequences for children, often resulting in a vicious cycle of alienation, underachievement, poor behaviour and exclusion (Corby 1997). Once young people are alienated from the educational system, they have too much unstructured, unsupervised time in which to engage in antisocial activities and this increases their risk of offending.

Peer Group Influence

Interactions between children and young people who have a tendency towards offending is thought to encourage and even escalate their involvement in crime (Gonzales et al. 2005). Studies have shown that offending behaviour is correlated with negative peer associations such as peers who criminally offend or use drugs. Gang membership has a strong association with criminal behaviour (Roush 1996). Peer group influence is highly associated with certain types of offending such as motor vehicle theft and gang violence. It is also a major element influencing recidivism rates among young offenders (Korn 2004). It is often the case that children and young people in detention will return to the same social and peer groups upon their release and will confront the same peer pressures that may have been instrumental in the original offending, especially if no viable alternatives exist for them to avoid this.

Youth Gangs

The formation of groups is a common phenomenon among youth and most are not harmful. The term 'youth gang' generally refers to a group of young people who are collectively associated with criminal activities. A group of youth becomes a 'youth gang' when it sees itself as a 'gang' and is perceived by others as being a 'gang' primarily because of its involvement in criminal activities (White 2002). Co-offending can occur within youth gangs, but not all co-offenders are necessarily associated with a gang. In fact, co-offending is an aspect of youth crime that may distort official statistics that aggregate the numbers of offenders rather than the numbers of crime events. It has been identified that inexperienced offenders tend to co-offend, with a US study finding that 40% of first-time offenders committed their offence with an accomplice regardless of their age at the time of their first arrest (Gonzales et al. 2005). It was also been found in this study that recidivism is higher among youth who co-offend, with co-offenders being responsible for 50% more crimes than youth who offend alone.

Social Exclusion

The risk of social exclusion is highest for children and young people who experience multiple social disadvantages. It is reported in the UK that only 15% of youth from lower socio-economic backgrounds will begin higher education by the age of 21 years compared with 79% of young people from middle class or professional backgrounds (UK Social Exclusion Unit 2004). Social exclusion is mainly seen with lower socio-economic populations where poor diets, lack of exercise, high rates of smoking and drug use are more prevalent. It is evidenced by poor educational attainment, higher unemployment, poor literacy and numeracy skills, poor health outcomes, higher levels of domestic violence, child abuse and crime exposure (UK Social Exclusion Unit 2004). All these factors can lead to geographical mobility (involuntary and constant moves), homelessness and substance abuse, which further exacerbate social isolation. As was seen in the discussion on homelessness, unsettled and disrupted home environments can be an important factor in the development of a youth offending career (Korn 2004).

Let's Consider!

The Differences Between Youth and Adult Corrections

Table 5.1 provides you with a quick reference guide to the main differences between the youth justice system and adult corrections. The biggest point to make here is in regard to the assumption that underpins youth justice, which is that young people are still maturing and if given the right guidance and support can be diverted from a criminal lifestyle. The adult system still has the role of rehabilitation within its objectives, but it is not focused on a welfare model of operations in the same way that the youth system is. *Refer to Table 5.1 for more detail.*

◘ Table 5.1 Comparing youth and adult detention

	Youth justice	Adult corrections
Model	Welfare model	Criminal justice model
Criminal behaviour	Children are still maturing and learning boundaries. Criminal offending is part of the normal adolescent maturation process.	Adults must be accountable for their own criminal behaviour. They are rational actors who are influenced by external factors but who ultimately choose to engage in criminal behaviour.
Response to crime	Contact with the youth justice system is an opportunity to get children re-engaged in education which is the main mode of diverting them from a criminal lifestyle. It is also an opportunity to work with the child and their family to guide them towards prosocial choices.	Contact with the prison system is an opportunity to engage adults in education, employment and programmes to meet their criminogenic needs. Contact with the community system is an opportunity to monitor them in their own environment and to guide them towards prosocial choices.
Main focus	Rehabilitation	Deterrence, rehabilitation
Punishment	Deprivation of liberty is a punishment but also provides an opportunity to intervene.	Deprivation of liberty is the punishment, it is not the role of prisons to further punish an inmate.
Underlying assumptions	Children are still developing their moral reasoning and social behaviour and this can be influenced positively with positive role models, firm but fair boundaries and patient guidance.	Adults can be fixed in their moral reasoning and social behaviours, but with education they can learn alternative ways of interacting in the world.
Political role	The state has a duty of care to children in detention, but it has more responsibility for the care and protection of youth, especially if they are wards of the state.	The state has a duty of care for the safety of adults in prison but it is limited by the wilful actions of the adults themselves.

Summary

The pathways to youth offending are multiple and complex and are influenced by the structures and processes of society and by family upbringing, social pressures and individual traits and characteristics. The juvenile justice system sees youth offending as a product of childhood experiences and also as a stage of maturation. It therefore supports diversionary programmes that seek to inhibit the development of a criminal career, allowing teenagers to mature into making more reasoned choices. Addressing the welfare needs of children and teens and diverting them from criminal offending provides the best course of action in dealing with youth offending.

Victims and the Justice System

Just as criminologists are interested in why offenders commit crime, they are equally concerned with the support of victims and also with why some people become victims of crime and others don't. The term 'victim of crime' refers to a person who has suffered hardship, loss or injury as a result of crime (Marsh et al. 2011). Community perceptions about crime and who is likely to become a victim are not always aligned with the reality of who is most likely to become a victim. Additionally, the way in which victims experience the criminal justice system is just as important to the criminologist as the experience of offenders. In 1985, the United Nations established the *Declaration of Basic Principles of*

Case Study

United Nations Declaration of Basic Principles of Justice for Victims of Crime and Abuse of Power

The United Nations made a declaration on 29 November 1985 that the following principles would be applied to the victims of crime and abuse of power (summarised):

1. A definition of victim;

2. Access to justice and fair treatment;

3. Offenders responsible to pay restitution;

4. If adequate compensation is not available from the offender, States should provide it;

5. Victims are entitled to receive information and support.

This declaration was ratified by the General Assembly at the 96th meeting of member nations.

Source: United Nations. 1985. *Declaration of Basic Principles of Justice for Victims of Crime and Abuse of Power*. Accessed online on 7 November 2016 at: www.un.org/documents/ga/res/40/a40r034.htm.

Justice for Victims of Crime and Abuse of Power (see case study). This Declaration provides a comprehensive definition of 'victims' in Annex A 1 and 2 (United Nations 1985).

Criminologists are constantly seeking to reduce the number of victims of crime by improving their knowledge of criminal offending with a view to preventing or at least reducing crime rates. The criminological study of victims has improved the understanding of criminal offending including the ability to predict when, where and how crime is likely to occur. This study has become a branch of criminology known as victimology (Kostic 2010). Victimology as a sub-discipline of criminology dates to the early twentieth century. Following World War II it emerged as an important academic area of study and in recent years there has been considerable effort made to establish victimology as a discipline in its own right (Marsh et al. 2011). The study of victim characteristics and behaviour is considered just as important in aiding criminologists in understanding the behaviour of offenders as the study of offender characteristics and behaviour. It is also important for criminologists to study patterns of victimisation to understand why some people may be more likely than others to become victims of crime (Kostic 2010). In addition to the study of victim characteristics and behaviour, victimology is also concerned with investigating victim resilience and how the way in which victims perceive themselves to be victims impacts on their wellbeing and recovery.

Who Is Most Likely to Be a Victim of Crime?

Fear of crime is something that is generated in the community at various times, either as a result of personal experience of crime, certain crimes (such as sex crimes) getting media attention, generalised increases in crime rates in certain neighbourhoods or moral panics created by specific political or media campaigns. Elderly people and women tend to express the greatest levels of fear of being victimised, but in actuality these groups register the lowest in victimisation rates. In fact it is 15 to 25-year-old males who are most likely to be victims of crime (Roach Anleu 1995). The British Crime Survey shows that men are more likely to be victims of violent crime, but women are more likely to worry about being victims of violent crime (Jansson 2006). Victimology has tended to divide victims of crime into two groups: conventional victims and corporate victims. Victims of conventional crime are more easily identified as victims of crime, whereas victims of corporate crime may be hidden and not readily identifiable, such as the shareholders of a multinational corporation or financial organisation (Marsh et al. 2011). Conventional crime covers broad areas of criminal offending such as robbery, vandalism, arson, violence, child abuse, domestic violence, sexual assault and homicide.

Many self-funded retirees rely on
share dividends for their pension.
How might corporate fraud impact on
them?

Teen and Young Adult Victims

Teens are most at risk of becoming victims simply because they tend to be mobile in the public arena at night and engage in risky behaviours such as drug and alcohol use. Male teens and young adults in particular are at risk of falling victim to violence, especially if they become involved in street gangs. In Northern Ireland, for example, young males between the ages of 16 and 24 years are three times more likely to be victims of crime than young females (McCready, Harland and Beattie 2006).

 Why are teenage boys more likely to
become victims of crime?

An American study has found that teenagers generally are more likely than adults to be victims of all categories of crime. This includes violent crime, sexual assault and property crimes (Wordes and Nunez 2002). It is possible that inadvertently the teenager's lifestyle and risk-taking behaviour may place them at greater risk of becoming a victim of crime although a high percentage of victimisation of teens occurs in the home (25% of substantiated abuse cases are teenagers) or at school (10% of the student population report being victims of violence at school) (Wordes and Nunez 2002). *See Pathways to Youth Offending.*

Child Victims

Children are among the most vulnerable in our society and may become victims of child abuse, abduction, homicide and domestic violence. Owing to the fact that very young children are completely dependent upon adults for their basic needs and are powerless to protect themselves, they are the most vulnerable. The Canadian government has identified that children are more at risk of being

the victims of physical and sexual assault crimes than adults (Canadian Government 2009). In the UK in 2012, there were 50,573 children on child protection registers or subject to a child protection plan (NSPCC 2013). Famous cases of child abuse in Britain include Victoria Climbié (Lord Laming 2003); and Baby Peter and Amy Howson (Lovell-Hancox 2013). Children who have fallen victim to abduction and homicide in the UK include cases such as April Jones, James Bulger, and Holly Wells and Jessica Chapman (Davies et al. 2007). According to the Crime Survey of England and Wales 2011/12, children under one year of age were most likely to be the victim of homicide with a rate of 21 homicides per million population and 8% of children aged 10 to 15 years were the victim of violent crime (Home Office 2013a). *See Pathways to Youth Offending.*

Elderly Victims

The British Crime Survey shows that people over 65 years of age are the least likely to be victims of crime (Jansson 2006) but they continue to experience a greater fear of crime than other age groups (House of Commons 2001). This perception of vulnerability can be attributed to the fact that as people age, they are less able to do the things they were able to do when they were younger. Older people can become dependent upon others for their basic needs, and for support to continue to live independently, which makes them vulnerable to exploitation and abuse (Lindesay 1996). The abuse of the elderly is an increasing issue for welfare agencies to deal with. Elder abuse can take the form of financial exploitation, sexual assault and physical violence. It can also include neglect to provide the basic necessities of life.

 Why might older people be fearful of
becoming victims of crime?

Women as Victims

While women can be victims of all types of crime, they are most frequently the victims of domestic violence and sexual assault (Mallicoat and Ireland

2014). Women tend to have a greater fear of crime than men due to their differential vulnerability and socialisation but this fear is not supported by the crime figures (Van Wormer and Walker 2013). The Home Office has reported that two-thirds of homicide victims in the UK in 2011–2012 were men. Women, however, are more likely than men to have experienced domestic or sexual violence. For example, based on the Crime Survey of England and Wales 2011/12, 3% of women had experienced some form of sexual assault (including attempts) in the last year, compared with 0.3% of men. Women are more likely to be the victims of violence in the home than in public spaces. This survey also showed that women aged between 16 and 34 were more likely than any of the other age groups considered (male or female) to be victims in the previous year of sexual assaults; non-sexual partner abuse; stalking; or overall domestic violence (Home Office 2013). *See Domestic Violence; Feminist Criminology (Chapter 3).*

> ❯❯ Why is the victimisation of women more likely to occur in the domestic arena?

Theories of Victimisation

Victimology has increased the knowledge base surrounding victimisation, resulting in the development of four theories of victimisation: victim precipitation theory; lifestyle theory; deviant place theory and routine activity theory.

Victim Precipitation Theory

The victim precipitation theory holds that victims may, through activity or passivity, initiate crime. With active precipitation, the victim attracts violence and other forms of criminal offending due to his or her overt threatening or provocative actions. Passive precipitation on the other hand results from the unconscious behaviour of the victim that may instigate or attract a criminal offence such as an assault (Siegel 2006).

Lifestyle Theory

The lifestyle theory proposes that people make themselves a target for victimisation due to their lifestyle choices. According to this theory, the lifestyle of certain people may expose them to areas and situations where crime is more likely to occur and/or to criminals (Siegel 2006). The types of lifestyle factors that have been indicated are promiscuity, drug taking, gang membership, or living in 'bad' neighbourhoods. *See Lawrence Cohen and Marcus Felson (Chapter 3).*

Deviant Place Theory

The deviant place theory suggests that while the victim does not actively or passively precipitate crime, they are more at risk of being victimised if they frequent high-crime areas (Stark 1987; Siegel 2006). This can also be specific places where they are more likely to be at risk of being a victim of crime such as neighbourhoods, pubs and clubs where certain types of crime such as robbery and assault are commonplace. *See Environmental Criminology (Chapter 3).*

Routine Activity Theory

The routine activity theory is proposed by Cohen and Felson (1979) and expanded further by Marcus Felson (1998) and suggests that the presence of one or more preconditions for crime results in a higher risk for crime victimisation. These preconditions are: the availability of suitable targets; the absence of capable guardians; and the presence of a motivated offender. According to this theory, the victim does not have to be present to be victimised. For example, if someone goes away on holiday, their home becomes an available suitable target for burglars because there is an absence of a capable guardian to prevent a burglary from occurring. If there is a motivated individual in the area who has the intention of committing a burglary, their house suddenly becomes at high risk of being burgled. *See Routine Activity Theory (Chapter 3).*

Victim Culpability and Victim Blaming

Early victimology introduced a dialogue to criminology that centred on the culpability of victims. In particular the focus of this dialogue was on assessing the relative degree of innocence or blame each participant involved in the criminal act had (that is, the perpetrator and the victim). This approach is considered to be victim blaming, which is a phenomenon that occurs in the criminal justice system, in the media and in broader society. Academic blaming of the victim began with Benjamin Mendelsohn who first introduced the theory of victim precipitation, which he suggested was the degree to which the victim is to blame for the crime (Mendelsohn 1956). Victim blaming takes many forms, such as suggestions that women who dress a certain way or who walk alone at night are somehow to blame for being victimised by a rapist. It can be aspersions cast upon a victim of burglary who did not have window locks or questions about what a victim of assault was doing in the place where they got assaulted. Such dialogue puts the focus of responsibility for criminality on the victim rather than on the criminal offender and has the effect of further traumatising the victim. Women in particular have reported a feeling of being on trial when giving evidence in court as they are made to defend their sexuality, behaviour and life choices (Van Wormer and Walker 2013). Such experiences have led to improved criminal justice responses to victims.

Victim Support Services

Secondary victimisation is a process that occurs whereby the victim has experienced trauma as a result of being a victim of crime but then experiences additional trauma through the process of navigating the criminal justice system (Mallicoat and Ireland 2014). Victim support services have been developed to ensure that victims receive attention and support when dealing with the various aspects of the criminal justice process. In the UK, the main organisation that provides support to victims is called Victim Support. This organisation has a website at www.victimsupport.org.uk and has offices across England and Wales. It relies heavily on volunteers who are specially trained in how to provide services and support to victims. The main areas of support provided are emotional support, information and practical assistance (Victim Support 2013). Australia, Canada and New Zealand all have similar victim support services available.

Summary

Victims are an extremely important group of people to consider in the criminal justice system, but often report feeling that they get overlooked by the constant focus on the offenders of crime. In addition to this they frequently feel as though they are victimised again by the criminal justice system which has an adversarial court process that can treat victims as if they are to blame for the crime. With the introduction of fields of study such as victimology and the establishment of victim support services, victims of crime are receiving more attention and are having their voices heard in the criminal justice system.

Types of Crime

We have briefly covered some of the key social factors that impact on crime and the criminal justice system. We will now take some time to consider a range of crime types, including the factors that are involved in the criminal offending which is often different with each crime type being studied. Criminology covers crime from many different aspects and by looking at specific crime types we can discover what particular offender traits, characteristics and behaviours may contribute to the crime. The dynamics differ between crimes too and it is useful to know about the dynamics that operate in each type of crime. We will also consider how law enforcement and the criminal justice system generally manages these different crime types.

Violent Crime

Violent crime occurs when the offender intends to cause physical harm or death to a victim and acts on that intention (Bricknell 2008). It is a category of crime that evokes the most outrage and fear within the community as it is often violent crime that is reported in the media. These crimes both intrigue and horrify the average person, who struggles to understand how people can deliberately set out to inflict pain on another person. The term 'violent crime' covers a broad spectrum of crimes ranging from unpremeditated assault to sadistic homicide (Hsieh and Pugh 1993). These crimes sometimes contain a sexual component but not always. Criminologists study violent offenders in an attempt to understand their motivations and criminal behaviour and try to find ways in which this behaviour can be effectively rehabilitated. Domestic violence, while being a violent crime category, deserves its own essay and is therefore dealt with separately. *See Domestic Violence.*

What Is Violence and What Causes It?

Violence can also be referred to as aggression. Bandura (1978) defines aggression as intentional behaviour that causes another person to be harmed or results in property being destroyed. In the criminal justice system, violence refers to a range of actions resulting in physical harm to another person. Violent emotions such as anger, rage and fear can lead to such behaviour and these

emotions are controlled by areas of the brain known as the amygdala and the hippocampus. If these areas of the brain are damaged (e.g. in a fall or through some other physical or chemical trauma) it can lead to a person being unable to control these emotions (Marsh 2011). There has been a suggestion that exposure to violence in the mass media is causally related to the development of aggression (Huesmann and Miller 1994) and further, that it is causally linked to violent crime (Donnerstein and Linz 1995). This has been disputed by Savage (2004) who claims there is a lack of empirical evidence to support this view. There is a widespread belief that mental illness and substance abuse cause individuals to behave in a violent manner and owing to the prominence of these beliefs these factors will be discussed separately. *See Social Learning Theory (Chapter 3) and Albert Bandura (Chapter 3).*

 Can violent videos and video games cause violent crime?

Types of Violent Crime

The category of crime known as 'violent crime' covers a broad spectrum of crimes (see Figure 5.2). On the minor offending end of the spectrum are crimes such as common assault and on the more serious end of the spectrum is sadistic homicide.

In the UK, the Home Office collates statistics on various crime types and defines violent crime

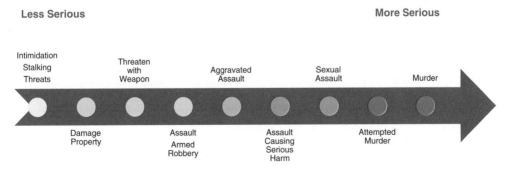

Figure 5.2   Spectrum of violent crime

as including harassment, common assault, sexual offences, robbery, snatch theft, wounding and homicide (Smith and Allen 2004). The Australian Bureau of Statistics includes murder, assault, sexual assault, robbery and kidnapping in its violent crime categories used for the purposes of collecting statistics (Australian Institute of Criminology 2007). Homicide/murder is a category of violent crime that cannot be used as an indicator of the level of crime in a particular area because it so rarely occurs (Felson 2009). It is a category of crime, however, that seems to attract a lot of media and public attention which can give a misleading perception of frequency (see case study).

Most violent crime is committed by people acting alone. According to the UK Home Office, two-thirds of violent incidents are perpetrated by a lone offender (Smith and Allen 2004) and much of this type of crime is domestic in nature with the victim being known to the offender. This is, however, different to the crime type known as domestic violence. Domestic violence is certainly a violent crime but due to the special factors relevant only to domestic and family violence and the recognition of domestic violence as a crime category in its own right by most criminal justice jurisdictions, we have dealt with domestic violence separately. *See* **Domestic Violence**.

Incidence Rates and Trends

Homicide rates tend to be used as a measuring stick to assess the level of violence within a society but, as already pointed out, this is not a good indicator of prevalence of violent crime. In addition, criminal justice processes can affect official rates of crime. For example, higher levels of reporting, such as occurs immediately following an education campaign, can account for some increases in reported incidence rates in these areas (Bricknell 2008). Furthermore, the true prevalence rates of some violent crimes such as rape are difficult to establish as these crimes are notoriously under-reported to police. The UK Peace Index is produced by the Institute for Economics and Peace (IEP) and reports that in 2013, violent crime in the UK had significantly decreased over the past ten years. The index measures comprehensively the levels of 'peacefulness' in the UK where 'peace' is defined as: 'the absence of violence or the absence of the fear of violence' (IEP 2013:5). This index reports that in the UK, homicide rates have decreased from 1.99 per 100,000 in 2003 to 1 per 100,000 in 2013. The rate of violent crime generally has reduced from 1,018 to 833 per 100,000 in this same time period and this downward trend in homicide and violent crime is replicated across Europe (IEP 2013). The downward trend in

---

Case Study

Is Violent Crime Increasing?

The *Daily Mail*, a daily tabloid newspaper in the UK, reported a story on 12 July 2015 entitled: 'Cities across the Country Report a "Scary" Rise in Violent Crime: Shootings Rise by up to 18 Per Cent After Months of Anti-Cop Anger'.

It was stated in this story that police departments across the US had been reporting decreasing crime statistics for years but had

recently reported significant spikes in homicides in Houston, St Louis, New Orleans and Baltimore in 2015. It was further reported that other cities such as New York and Chicago were also seeing sharp increases in homicides. Defying this new trend was Los Angeles, where the number of homicides had dropped slightly, however the rate of shootings had jumped by around 18%. This article went on

to describe the rate of homicide for Milwaukee had risen to 84 for the year to date which was only two less than all the homicides recorded for the entire year in 2014. Authorities have stated that it is too soon to be able to tell if this will be a permanent trend or simply a passing spike. It is also too soon to be able to tell what may have caused the sudden rise in violent crime.

Source: Daily Mail. 2015, 12 July. 'Cities Across the Country Report a "Scary" Rise in Violent Crime: Shootings Rise by up to 18 Per Cent After Months of Anti-Cop Anger' Accessed online on 7 November 2016 at: www.dailymail.co.uk/news/article-3158139/Cities-country-report-scary-rise-violent-crime-Shootings-rise-18-cent-months-anti-cop-anger.html.

homicide and violent crime in the UK has been attributed to:

- changes in police practices and technological improvements;
- ageing population;
- decreasing alcohol consumption; and
- rising real wages due to the introduction of the minimum wage (IEP 2013:9).

This trend has also been seen in the US where the homicide rate has decreased by 3.78% since 2011 and violent crime has fallen by 6.03% in this same period (IEP 2012). Unlike the UK, where the decrease in homicide and violent crime has been sustained over time, it is still not evident if the decrease seen in the US will likewise be sustained. In Canada the homicide and violent crime rates have reduced by 6% and are at the lowest levels since the early 1970s (Brennan 2011). As with the UK, the US, Canada and Europe, Australia has seen the incidence rate of homicide decrease since the early 1990s. In Australia, however, other violent crimes have defied this downward trend. Assault is the most common form of violent crime in Australia and has increased by 47% between 1995 and 2006. The most notable increase in assault rates in Australia over the past 20 years has been in the incidence of female offenders being charged with assault (Bricknell 2008). It could be that after years of declining rates, the rate of violent crime is beginning to increase again. In recent media reports, there appears to be a trend towards rates of violent crime increasing in the US also (Daily Mail 2015).

> How can the mass media manipulate their reporting of statistics to give an exaggerated impression of rising crime rates and why would they do this?

Violent Offenders

Violent offenders tend to be predominantly male but female violent offenders are increasing at an alarming rate (Smith and Allen 2004). Most violent offenders fall into the teenage

and young adult age groups (16–24) but some categories of violent offender, such as domestic violence offenders, fall into the older age groups. With some violent crime categories, such as serial rapists and sadistic serial murderers, the offenders take time to develop their offending career which usually progresses from less serious crimes such as destroying property, voyeurism, arson, exhibitionism and injuring animals, to more serious expressions of violence, sadism and homicide (Kessler, Burgess and Douglas 1992). The crimes themselves also progress and become more refined, usually having a signature about the way in which they are enacted that is unique to the offender (Berry-Dee 2003). This is not to say that sadistic murderers will not be found among teenagers and young adults, but criminal profiling suggests they are often past 25 years of age by the time they have progressed to this level.

Mental Illness and Violent Crime

It needs to be remembered that both serious mental illness and serious violent crime are rare occurrences. The exact nature of the relationship between mental illness and violence is still unclear (Stuart 2003); however, there is a great deal of literature to support the contention that mental illness is not linked to violent crime (Mouzos 1999; Fazel and Grann 2006; Ramesh 2010). In fact, a Swedish study conducted by Fazel and Grann (2006) discovered the average level of recorded violent crime that could be attributed to a person with a mental illness was only 5%. This is a long way from what most people would assume to be the case. Surprisingly, in relation to violent crime, it appears that people who have a serious mental illness are much more likely to be victims of violence than perpetrators (MacPhail and Verdun-Jones 2013). It is estimated that around 18% of people with mental illness experience violent victimisation and those suffering from psychosis are most at risk (Walsh et al. 2003). While mental illness is not predictive of violent crime there are some forms of mental illness that are more closely associated with violent crime than others. Schizophrenia, for example, has been associated with an increased risk of violent crime (Stuart 2003; Fazel et al. 2009). While psychopathy is often linked to sadistic forms of violent crime such as cruelty to animals and crimes involving the torture of victims (Kessler et al. 1992), not all psychopaths are criminals and in fact some psychopaths are extremely successful by the general standards of Western society. For example, a study in America found that approximately 3% of managers are psychopaths, which is 2% higher than the general population. Prison populations tend to only have around 15% of inmates who are psychopathic (Lipman 2013). *See Mental Illness and Crime.*

Substance Abuse and Violent Crime

Substance abuse is more closely associated with violent crime than is mental illness; and comorbid substance abuse and mental illness places people at significantly higher risk of committing violent crime (Fazel et al. 2009; Ramesh 2010). In England and Wales, victims have reported that almost half (44%) of violent perpetrators were under the influence of alcohol and 20% were under the influence of drugs (Smith and Allen 2004). The US Department of Justice reports that 61% of domestic violence offenders have substance abuse issues (Collins and Spencer 2002). In addition to substance abuse leading people to behave violently, the production and distribution of illicit substances can lead to a culture of violence that includes the perpetration of systemic violent crime as the day-to-day experience for people caught up in it (Boles and Miotto 2003).

Theoretical Explanations of Violent Crime

There are many theories expounded to explain violent crime and unfortunately there is insufficient space here to do justice to all of them. The main approaches that will be touched on are the rational choice approach, routine activity theory and social learning theory. The rational choice approach is used by some criminologists to explain violent crime. This perspective suggests that aggression is either expressive or instrumental. Expressive aggression occurs as a reaction to uncomfortable or threatening stimuli. People will lash out to hurt others in response to being hurt themselves, especially if the risk of negative consequences is low. Pain, frustration, fear and rejection can all be interpreted as suffering by such a person who is biologically attuned to be violent. When it is too costly to hit out at the person who has caused the hurt they may displace their aggression onto an innocent third party (Felson 2009). Routine activity theory (Felson and Cohen 1979) suggests that people commit crime because they are motivated to do so and there is an available and accessible target with no capable guardian present to intervene to stop the crime. This theory can be applied to many types of violent crime. For example, domestic violence or rapes are crimes that are unlikely to occur if a capable guardian is present to intervene or there is an absence of an accessible victim. It is logical that there must be a motivated offender in order for violent crime to occur. In the 1970s Albert Bandura (1978) introduced social learning theory to explain aggression. According to this theory, people acquire aggressive behaviours in the same way that they learn other social behaviours, from observation and modelling. Such behaviours are then reinforced during childhood. *See Social Learning Theory (Chapter 3).*

Summary

Violent crime is much less common than people assume but because it is attractive to the media it tends to get most of the attention. This then creates a false perception that violent crime occurs more often than it in fact does. There is also a public perception that mental illness and crime are closely linked, but this is not supported by studies which have shown that rather than being the perpetrators of violence, people with mental illness are more likely to be victims. Violent crimes such as homicides are rare but seem to get most of the attention from the media, causing moral panics within the general community. The fear of the community that results from such media attention is not supported by the crime statistics which are showing a global trend towards a reduction in the incidence of violent crime.

Domestic Violence

Domestic violence, also known as family violence, is a violent crime with different aspects and considerations from other types of violent crimes. It is a continuing problem in most developed and developing countries. According to the World Health Organization, one in three women around the world have experienced physical and/or sexual intimate partner violence or non-partner sexual violence in their lifetime (United Nations 2015; WHO 2016). Furthermore, 38% of murders of women worldwide are committed by their intimate partner (WHO 2016). The United Nations defines domestic violence as gender-based violence against women that is likely to result in physical, sexual or psychological suffering and harm (United Nations 1993). Domestic violence can involve males as victims and females as perpetrators, but globally men are overwhelmingly the perpetrators and women are the victims of domestic violence (University of Melbourne, 2016). A more recent phenomenon in this area is the growing recognition of violence within homosexual relationships that can be man-on-man or woman-on-woman violence (Australian Institute of Criminology 2009). Due to domestic violence being a mostly gendered issue with men as the perpetrators and women as the victims, this is the usual assumption made by the general public and by many professionals responding to the problem.

> ❯ Why would it be a problem for police to assume that all domestic violence victims are female and all abusers are male?

What Is Domestic Violence?

Domestic violence is also known as relationship violence, family violence and intimate partner violence (Australian Institute of Criminology

2009; Canberra Domestic Violence Crisis Service 2016) and involves the physical, sexual, psychological and/or financial abuse of a woman by her intimate male partner and can also include intimidation, threats and the deprivation of liberty (United Nations 1993). Domestic violence can occur within marriages or de facto relationships and what is often not acknowledged is that it can also occur within dating relationships and also when couples are separated (Australian Institute of Criminology 2009). Most countries, states, territories and provinces will have specific legislation to deal with domestic violence that is different from the legislation that deals with other violent crime.

Prevalence Country by Country

The definitions of domestic violence change from country to country and consequently what is included within the realm of domestic violence may differ also. Some countries restrict their definition to a strict gender-based conception that only includes man-on-woman violence within a cohabiting intimate relationship, while others include all types of violence that occur within domestic intimate relationships. In Canada, a broad definition to intimate partner violence is applied. It is reported that one-third of women in Canada have experienced intimate partner violence (Wathen 2012) and figures in Australia are similar. According to an Australian Personal Safety Survey one in five women in Australia have experienced violence by a current or previous intimate partner (Australian Institute of Criminology 2009). A slight but modest improvement in this figure is seen in 2015 when it was reported by the Business Insider (Colgan 2015) that one in six women in Australia have experienced domestic violence. In the US, the domestic violence rates are measured by the National Crime Victimization Survey. According to this survey, in the year 2000 one in every 200 households experienced domestic violence and there had been no significant difference in this rate over the preceding six years (Bragg 2003). Between 2003 and 2012, domestic violence accounted for over 20% of all violent crimes in the

US (Leins 2015). The National Statistics Surveys in the UK showed a decline in domestic violence reports in 2004–2005 and a levelling out of reports in 2008–2009. Currently almost 30% of women and almost 15% of men aged 16 to 59 report experiencing incidents of domestic violence in the UK (Travis 2015). While there are differences between countries, the rate of domestic violence appears to remain at consistently concerning levels around the world.

Dynamics of Domestic Violence

Domestic violence is best understood as an issue arising from the unequal distribution of power. The prevailing conceptual analysis of domestic violence views it as a learned and/or chosen pattern of behaviour that is about one person exerting and maintaining power over another in the intimate relationship, frequently erupting in violence. This process is often cyclical with observable phases. The cycle of violence is said by the Domestic Abuse Project to have three distinct phases.

1. *Tension building (tension-building phase)*: the time when stress and tension rises. Small outbursts can occur and victims feel as if they are 'walking on eggshells' trying not to upset their partner. Psychological abuse is common.
2. *Acute battering incident (explosive phase)*: the abusive partner becomes physically violent.
3. *Relief period/Buyback (honeymoon phase)*: relative calm in the relationship. The abusive partner tries to convince the victim the violence will not happen again. They will promise anything to get the victim to return (if the victim has left the abuser).

    (Domestic Abuse Project 2016; Bune 2007).

Victims of domestic violence suffer abuse over a long period of time and a process known as learned helplessness can develop. In addition to this, the abuser will often control the finances of the victim and will ensure the victim is isolated from family and friends who could step in to help. In a typical male-female domestic violence situation, the male will sometimes establish himself as the 'master' and intimidate his partner into adopting the role of a subservient 'slave' (Bune 2007). This may start with the male emphasising traditional male-female household roles but developing into more extreme interpretations of these roles. If the victim cries or expresses unhappiness with the situation the perpetrator may deny any abuse or place the blame for the abuse on the victim. He may express extreme gendered beliefs such as men are superior to women in order to justify his actions. Such denial of reality and lack of empathy for the suffering of the victim adds to the feelings of helplessness and despair in the victim.

 How does learned helplessness work to prevent the victim of domestic violence from leaving the situation?

Victims often report that the most dangerous time for them is when they leave their violent partner and he realises that his efforts to re-establish the relationship have failed. An example of this was seen in the Rosie Batty case in Australia (see case study).

Non-typical Intimate Partner Violence

Domestic violence typically involves a male perpetrator and a female victim and without question this is overwhelmingly the case. In some cases involving male victims the perpetrator is also a male but in the few cases where the perpetrator is a woman and the victim is a man it is often more difficult for the male victim to speak up and report the abuse. In Australia, it is claimed that one in three victims of domestic violence are male (One in Three 2015) but this is disputed by mainstream domestic violence groups which suggest that this figure is reported by men's rights groups and is exaggerated and based on faulty statistics. It is suggested the true figure is closer to one in five (Gilmore 2015). In the UK, there has been a 25% increase in the number of men seeking help from the domestic

Case Study

Australia: Rosie Batty Case

The Rosie Batty case highlights the dangers victims of domestic violence face when they try to leave an abusive relationship. Rosie Batty began to experience violence from her six-foot-tall partner Greg Anderson almost immediately after they got together. Shortly after their son Luke was born in 2002 the violence worsened. Rosie left the relationship soon after Luke's birth but the violence continued and the police became involved. The violence abated for a five-year period when she was involved in another relationship, but once that relationship ended the violence and abuse increased dramatically. Throughout 2012 the case was in and out of court as a result of the police responding to numerous calls for help from Rosie and Luke. Around 2013 Greg began to threaten Rosie's life. It was around this time that Greg showed Luke a knife when they were sitting alone in a car and said 'it could all end with this'. Rosie decided it was too dangerous for Luke to be alone with his father. At this time the court banned Greg from seeing Luke, but throughout 2013 he continued to breach these orders by turning up at Luke's sporting events, scouts and school. He was frequently arrested and jailed for these breaches of court orders, but this did not stop him. Eventually the court allowed him limited access to Luke when he was at public events such as sports. On 12 February 2014 Greg Anderson turned up at Tyabb Oval where Luke was at cricket training. There were plenty of people around, but Greg managed to isolate Luke at the cricket nets where he battered him over the head with a bat and then stabbed him to death. Greg was shot dead by police at the scene. An inquest found there was no way that anyone could predict what occurred, but highlighted many failures of the system to adequately protect Rosie and Luke. Rosie Batty was named Australian of the Year in 2015 and is now a campaigner for increased support for victims of domestic violence and is an active public speaker who is raising awareness of the issues involved in intimate partner violence.

Sources: Silmalis, L. 2014, 15 February. 'How Luke Batty's Father Descended into a Deadly Madness' *Herald Sun*. Accessed online on 7 November 2016 at: www.heraldsun.com.au/news/law-order/how-luke-battys-father-descended-into-a-deadly-madness/story-fni0ffnk-1226828297392.

Davey, M. 2014, 2 November. 'Luke Batty: Killed by a Father No-one Truly Knew' *The Guardian*. Accessed online on 7 November 2016 at: https://www.theguardian.com/australia-news/2014/nov/02/-sp-luke-batty-killed-by-a-father-no-one-truly-knew

violence helpline service (Hoyle 2013). This could be due to men feeling more comfortable with seeking help for this problem rather than an actual rise in the number of domestic violence cases involving men as victims. Many of the effects of domestic violence on male victims is the same as for women but they find it more difficult to speak out and to be believed when they do. Police are so used to the typical scenario that the male victim can end up being arrested themselves when they contact police for help (Hoyle 2013). Sometimes partners may make false accusations against them which, they say, makes it more likely they will be arrested because it fits the profile of abuse that police are most familiar with (Evans 2016). Attitudes are changing and police and the general public are becoming more knowledgeable about the diversity within domestic violence cases so this is less likely to be a continuing problem.

Legislation is also catching up, with many domestic violence laws now being expanded to include a range of relationship types (Rollings and Taylor 2008). Other areas are still catching up as support services and refuges for male victims are not as commonly provided as they are for female victims. In fact, it may be that a different service response is needed for men, but this is not known as yet because this is still an emerging area within the field of domestic violence research and service delivery.

> How difficult would it be to know when someone is making false accusations of assault against another person? What should the police do if it is not clear who is the victim and who is the perpetrator?

Law Enforcement Response

Domestic violence reports take up a considerable amount of police time (Crime and Misconduct Commission 2005). The police response to domestic violence is largely determined by legislation, with most Western countries having rigorous domestic violence laws in place. These laws usually require police to arrest the alleged perpetrator and remove them from the scene to protect the victim from any further immediate abuse. Ongoing protection is issued by the court in the form of a protection order. Unfortunately many perpetrators ignore these orders to stay away from the victim and further abuse can occur before police have a chance to respond. Some police are reluctant to process domestic violence complaints due to a belief that the victim will withdraw the complaint before it gets to court (Saraga 2011). Even though there are problems with the protection orders they do at least give the police greater powers to intervene when violence has not yet occurred but tensions are escalating or past history tells the police violence is likely to occur. In Australia, national legislation broadens police powers and allows the sharing of information across state borders (Rollings and Taylor 2008).

Summary

Domestic violence is an important issue in criminology and one that involves many areas of the criminal justice system including the police, the correctional services system, victim support services and the courts. It is also an issue that attracts a lot of attention from researchers. Although most cases involve men as perpetrators and women as victims, knowledge is emerging about the diversity of relationships in which violence occurs. Domestic violence can involve male or female perpetrators and male or female victims. Cases can also include same-sex relationships where there is male-on-male or female-on-female violence. Legislation is beginning to reflect the diversity of relationships that exist in the community. No type of relationship is immune from domestic violence

but victims in non-typical relationships can find it difficult to report abuse from their partner. As the community gains more knowledge about domestic violence and professionals such as the police are trained in the diversity of victims and perpetrators, the victims of domestic violence in non-typical relationships will feel more comfortable about reporting the abuse. *See Victims and the Justice System*.

> ❯ Why might it be difficult for a victim of domestic violence in a same-sex relationship find it hard to report the abuse?

Let's Consider!

Comparing Domestic Violence and Violent Crime

Table 5.2 provides you with a quick reference guide to the main differences between domestic violence and violent crime. It is important to remember that domestic violence, while being also a violent crime, is not categorised as such because it is dealt with as a separate crime type. This has been a strategic move by jurisdictions to ensure that domestic violence is understood within the context of the domestic and power relationships that underpin it. Domestic violence is not just about violence in the usual sense of a violent crime, it is about the subjugation of another person in a domestic relationship and the use of violence to achieve total control. This is not normally a feature in violent crime that is absent of domestic violence. *Refer to* Table 5.2 *for more detail.*

Sexual Assault

Sexual assault is an extremely sensitive type of crime because it involves a victim sharing intimately personal details with police and other

	Violent crime	Domestic violence
Nature of the crime	Physical violence generally contained within a single event.	Physical, psychological, sexual or financial violence. Can be a single event but usually occurring regularly over a period of time.
Underlying dynamic	Impulsiveness, revenge, robbery.	Gender-based power and control.
Criminal behaviour	Violence, generally a singular event.	Serial violence, often increasing in seriousness over time.
Main focus	The violence is directed to a stranger or to someone known to the offender.	Usually directed at the spouse but can be any person in a domestic relationship with the offender.
Legislation	Covered within a generic Crimes Act in most jurisdictions.	Domestic violence has its own separate legislation in most jurisdictions.
Causation of crime	Substance abuse, youth immaturity, gang related.	Disrespect of women. Patriarchal social systems.
Response to crime	Responded to in usual policing strategies.	Each police department has a special unit to deal with domestic violence.
Victim	Does not usually live with the victim and has a choice not to see the offender again.	Frequently lives with the offender and continues to do so even after a violent event. May not have a choice about whether or not they see the offender again.
Ongoing safety of the victim	The violent event is usually the end of the violent incident. The safest time for the victim is when he/she leaves the situation.	The offender may continue to harass the victim and threaten the victim, especially if they leave the family home. The most dangerous time for the victim is when she/he leaves the situation.
Focus of intervention	Violent crime is addressed by focusing on the individual criminogenic factors that led to the crime.	Domestic violence is addressed by working with the offender and the victim and all other members of the family to break the violent dynamics and to empower the victim.

Table 5.2 Comparing domestic violence and violent crime

criminal justice and medical personnel. Many victims describe a sexual assault as an invasion of their spirit as well as their body because of the nature of the crime. In the past sexual assault was seen as a property offence because women were considered to be the property of their husbands (Fileborn 2011). Men were not considered to be capable of being the victims of sexual crimes, and were seen only as the perpetrators. Nowadays women are no longer seen to be the property of their husbands and have agency in terms of their own place in the world. Just as attitudes to the role and place of women has changed, so too have attitudes to the role of men with an acceptance that men too can be victims of sexual assault and women can be perpetrators.

Defining Sexual Assault

Sexual assault is defined differently according to the legal definitions that apply in each jurisdiction. According to the Australian Centre for the Study of Sexual Assault, every state and territory within Australia has its own definition and legislation that covers sexual assault (Fileborn 2011). While there is no universally accepted definition of sexual assault, there are some common elements between the various legal definitions that apply throughout Australia and elsewhere. These are: actus reus; mens rea; voluntariness; and temporal coincidence, and it is these aspects that will need to be proven in court. We will address each of these aspects separately.

Actus Reus

Actus reus is the physical act and in legal terms is classified as the criminal act. This means that sexual assault must contain a physical sexual act that is carried out without the consent of the other party.

Mens Rea

The element of *mens rea* refers to the state of mind and the intention of the accused person. Did the accused person know the other party was not consenting to the sexual act or were they recklessly indifferent as to whether or not the other party consented?

Voluntariness

The accused person must be consciously aware of their actions, and their actions need to be voluntary, in order for them to be considered legally guilty of the sexual offence. Actions carried out when in an altered state such as hypnosis or sleep walking, and reflex actions, are considered to be involuntary actions.

Temporal Coincidence

In order for a sexual assault to occur under law, the *actus reus* and *mens rea* need to occur at the same time. This means that it needs to be shown that the accused person sexually assaulted another party while conscious that he/she was not consenting to the act or being indifferent as to whether consent was given.

Prevalence

It is difficult to get a clear indication of the real prevalence of sexual assault as in almost all countries it is under-reported and in some countries reports of sexual assault are not likely to be recorded even when reported to police (Laccino 2014). According to the *International Business Times*, which based their report on United Nations statistics, the African country of Lesotho had the highest rate of reported sexual assault with a rate of 88.6 rape cases per 100,000 people. This was said to be due to entrenched cultural beliefs about the entitlement of men and the unequal status of women in this country. South Africa was reported as having a very high rate of

sexual assault, but also a high degree of fear among victims who do not report these crimes to police. The *International Business Times* reports, however, that between 28 and 37% of adult men admit to having raped and 7–9% have raped in unison with other offenders. In Europe, the country of Sweden has the highest level of reported sexual assault with 69 cases per 100,000 people. The reported rapes in Sweden have quadrupled in the past 20 years (Laccino 2014). In the Caribbean, St Vincent and Grenadines has the third largest number of reported rapes in the world with a rate of just over per 51.21 per 100,000 persons. Other Caribbean countries were figured in the statistics with the Bahamas at 30.8 per 100,000 and Jamaica at 29.6 per 100,000. New Zealand has a surprisingly high level of sexual assault with 30 per 100,000 and Belgium was seventh highest country with 28.1 per 100,000 (see Table 5.3).

While the countries listed in Table 5.3 have the highest levels of sexual assault, other countries cannot be complacent, for many other countries have alarmingly high rates of sexual assault too. According to the Centre for Innovative Justice (2014), in Australia 17% of all women and 4% of all men over 18 years of age have been the victims of sexual assault. In addition to this, approximately 12% of women and 4.5% of this group were abused before the age of 15. In the Crime Survey for England and Wales the figures for 2011–2012 show that on average 2.5% of females and 0.4% of males reported that they had been sexually assaulted (including attempts) in the previous 12 months.

▣ **Table 5.3** Countries with the highest level of reported sexual assault in 2011

Country	Rate per 100,000
Lesotho	88.6
Sweden	69.0
St Vincent and Grenadines (SVG)	51.21
The Bahamas	30.8
Jamaica	29.6
New Zealand	30.0
Belgium	28.1

This figure has been stable for the previous three surveys (Home Office 2013). In the US a woman is raped every two minutes. A national survey in the US found that 29–32% of women and 5–10% of men report being the victim of sexual assault in childhood (WCSAP 2016).

Child Sexual Abuse

Child sexual abuse is a specific subcategory of assault. It is a group of sexual assaults where the victim is below the legal age of consent. Child sexual abuse is a very serious crime because it causes a high level of trauma to children that has lasting effects into adulthood. In addition, the perpetrators of sexual abuse on children are mostly people within the family or in caring roles and who the child should normally be able to trust to protect them. 84% of child sexual abuse occurs in the child's home or in the home of the perpetrator (Ronken and Johnston 2012). It is also the case that children who experience child sexual abuse are more likely to have also experienced another type of abuse or neglect. It is a misconception that child sexual assaults are mostly carried out by strangers as most perpetrators (95%) know the victim. In nearly all cases, a process called 'grooming' is initiated by the perpetrator. This means that the perpetrator engages in a series of behaviours that are targeted at luring or coaxing the victim into a situation where they can be abused.

Paedophilia

Serial child sex offenders are known as paedophiles, which means that they have a dominant sexual attraction to pre-pubescent children. The American Psychological Association (2000) issue a *Diagnostic and Statistical Manual* (DSM IV) at regular intervals which defines various psychiatric conditions. Paedophilia is listed in the manual as sexual paraphilia. In order for an offender to be considered a paedophile, the victim must be 13 years of age or younger and the offender must be at least 16 years of age. There must be more than five years separating the victim and offender. The World Health Organization (2007a) defines

paedophilia as a sexual preference for children resulting from a mental and behavioural disorder. Paedophiles face intense public hostility as a result of their crimes and can also face abuse from other inmates when imprisoned. For this reason they are kept separately from the mainstream prison population. Most jurisdictions have a sex offender register which restricts them from living close to schools and from getting jobs that involve working with children.

Female Sex Offenders

While most sexual abuse of children is carried out by men, women also sexually abuse children (Robinson 1998). It is difficult to establish the exact rate of sex offending by females because it is a type of sexual offence that is grossly under-reported and because many offenders tend to be diverted from the criminal justice system (Vandiver and Walker 2002). The most recent figures show that around 5% of all sexual offences are committed by women (Stathopoulos 2014). It is thought that approximately 5% of female and 20% of male victims are abused by a woman (Ronken and Johnson 2012). Research is showing that unlike men, recidivism rates in female sex offenders tends to be low, being less than 3% of offenders (Cortoni et al. 2010). This research has implications for the use of risk assessment tools in the criminal justice system, which tend to be designed for male offenders, as they are likely to indicate that female sex offenders pose a higher risk of reoffending than they actually do.

Child Pornography

Section 163.1 of the *Canadian Criminal Code 1985* defines child pornography as photographic, video, film or other visual representation of a person under the age of 18 years engaged in explicit sexual activity. This legislation is similar in other jurisdictions and includes written and audio representations too. The legislation also makes it an offence to produce, publish, photocopy, possess and disseminate such material. Accessing child pornography on the internet or via another channel, such as hard copy photographs and videos, is also an offence. The reason why

Key Criminological Research Debates

The age of consent: When are children not treated as children?
An area of debate related to the age of consent for sexual activity concerns the sexual abuse by children of other children. It is a difficult subject because many adults have trouble comprehending and accepting that children can sexually abuse other children and also because it is difficult to separate abuse from normal childhood curiosity. It is normal for children to experiment sexually with children their own age, but where there is a large age gap with the child initiating activity being much older than the child receiving the sexual advances, or where there is coercion, force or violence used, the activity moves out of the realm of normal and is considered to be abuse (Safer Society 2007). The dilemma for the criminal justice system occurs when a child, under the age of consent, is charged with a sexual offence. In Australia, a 12-year-old boy was charged with the attempted rape of an 11-year-old girl behind a shopping centre (Daily Mail 2016). In most Australian states and territories, the age of consent to sexual activity is 16 years. In the UK, a 5-year-old boy is being investigated for rape (Finan 2016) when he is clearly too young to understand this behaviour. One side of the debate asks, how can a 5-year-old or 12-year-old child be considered legally responsible for sexual activity they are not legally able to consent to; and how can they be held criminally responsible for that behaviour? Another side of the debate argues that if a child commits an adult offence, they should be charged with that offence just as an adult would be charged and not to do so would be to encourage the behaviour, leading to adult sex offending. The problem behind this debate, however, is determining at what point a child is able to understand that their behaviour is illegal and whether they have sufficient understanding of their own and others' sexual behaviour to be able to be held legally responsible. On the one hand the law says they are not and on the other hand children are prosecuted under the law. A further complicating factor is whether the child being accused of sexual assault has in turn been sexually abused. In which case they may not have appropriate boundaries regarding sexuality and may have been precociously sexualised at an age that most children are not yet active. The question then is whether a criminal justice response the best way to deal with these cases.

legislation around child pornography is so strict and the penalties are so severe is because children are sexually abused and harmed in the production and distribution of the material.

Summary

Sexual assault is an interesting area of criminology and is generally considered to be a field of expertise where criminologists will focus most of their time and attention. So much long-term harm is caused by sexual assault, especially child sexual abuse that law enforcement direct special effort aimed at reducing this type of crime. Child pornography may appear on the surface to be a harmless activity but once the victims are considered and the impact on them in the present and future is taken into account, the true nature of this crime can be seen. Many victims of child pornography can never fully move past the abuse because they are aware that their image is being constantly circulated on the internet. Sexual assault covers a range of subcategories and we have covered only a small sample here. *See Feminist Criminology*.

White Collar Crime

White collar crime costs the global economy more than $US2 trillion annually (Elliyatt 2013). The term 'white collar crime' was introduced by

Edwin Sutherland (1940) in his article 'White Collar Criminality'. White collar crime is a group of crimes that are committed by seemingly respectable people of middle class and higher social status who generally have positions of trust in financial and corporate organisations (Price and Norris 2009). A comprehensive definition of white collar crime is provided by Herbert Edelhertz (1970:3) who defines it as: 'an illegal act or series of illegal acts committed by nonphysical means and by concealment or guile, to obtain money or property, to avoid the payment or loss of money or property, or to obtain business or personal advantage'. Crimes labelled as 'white collar crime' include fraud, extortion, intellectual property theft, embezzlement and money laundering within a corporate context and are generally on a larger scale than the individual criminality usually referred to by criminal justice professionals and academics.

A Victimless Crime?

Some white collar criminals do not believe they have done anything wrong as they perceive their crimes to be 'victimless', meaning that no one is hurt by their actions. In a study of prisoners who had committed white collar crime, most believed there had been no one hurt by their actions and organisations are not victims (Dhami 2007). Justifications for why organisations are not victims include the view that large companies have a lot of wealth to back them up and most companies are insured against financial loss anyway. This of course does not take into account the shareholders of companies, many of whom are pensioners and mum and dad investors, trying to build a nest egg for their retirement. In addition to this, there are macro-economic effects that have an impact on society and which trickle down to consumers (Price and Norris 2009). These are felt by individuals as rises in insurance premiums, increases in the costs of loans and a general depression in the overall economic health of the society. As with all crime, there are definitely victims resulting from white collar crime.

 Who are the victims of white collar crime?

Causations of White Collar Crime

White collar criminals are usually quite different demographically from the common criminal. They are generally from more affluent backgrounds, are well educated, intelligent, they do not have previous convictions (Bagaric and Alexander 2014). One of the theories put forward to explain why relatively affluent, intelligent and respectable individuals engage in white collar crime is opportunity, but beyond that greed and sometimes misguided altruistic motives have been found (Bucy et al. 2012). White collar criminals can be divided into leaders and followers according to Bucy et al. (2012) who conducted research with defence lawyers and prosecutors experienced in dealing with these crimes. The leaders are more likely to be motivated by greed and the followers by altruism, or they may just be weak-willed individuals who are unable to resist the influence of the leader. The legal responses to this crime type generally recognises the difference between offenders who are leaders and those who are followers which includes aiding and abetting. These crimes often include a breach of trust or a violation of a moral code that will cause immense shame to the offender once they are caught (Bagaric and Alexander 2014). Sentences received by white collar criminals are often low range and it is suggested that this may be due to their crimes being seen not so much as criminal actions but as lapses in judgement (Morreale 2015).

Technology and White Collar Crime

While robberies, burglaries, homicide and assault are decreasing, white collar crime is increasing in the US (Cliff and Desilets 2014; Lincenberg and Neuman 2016). This could be linked to a rise in the use of computer technology. When people are employed in types of employment such as banking and investment they are given access to other people's money or the organisation's financial accounts. They are daily faced with many opportunities to commit embezzlement and fraud and these opportunities are increased further by the use of computer technology which allows them to quickly and easily transfer funds between accounts. The rewards involved have increased while the risk of detection has decreased. While advances in technology are aiding white collar criminals it is at the same time helping the police to investigate, gather evidence and charge these criminals (Friedrichs 2010). It is in the use of technology that there may be a crossover with cybercrime but not all white collar crime involves the use of computers and not all techno crime/cybercrime is white collar crime. See **Cybercrime**.

 How can technology be used to help police to investigate white collar crime?

Law Enforcement Responses

Police will use both reactive and proactive strategies to address white collar crime (Payne 2012) and most Western jurisdictions have specific targeted police responses to it. In the UK a special police taskforce known as the Serious Fraud Office (SFO) has been established to investigate white collar crime. In the US, investigations of white collar crime offences can be conducted by local, state or federal agencies. The Federal Bureau of Investigation (FBI) investigates white collar crime and related offences at the federal level and state police departments investigate them at the state level. Local police often do not have the resources to investigate white collar crime as it is not a priority when taken into account with the immediacy of other crime types they have to deal with (Payne 2012). There are also a number of private companies, usually associated with the banking sector, that investigate financial crimes. The Australian Federal Police are responsible for investigating crimes of fraud against the Commonwealth and state police

services have special units that deal with white collar crime within the state. There have been recent accusations that Australia is a haven for white collar criminals because of its apparently weak laws in this area (Mitchell 2014). The Royal Canadian Mounted Police have a Commercial Crime Program that is responsible for responding to commercial crime, counterfeiting and major fraud in Canada.

Summary

White collar crime generally involves respectable, well-educated and intelligent offenders and this is sometimes pointed to as a reason why they are treated more leniently by the criminal justice system. The crimes they commit are as devastating to victims as crimes committed by other criminals but the victims are often not as visible. Victims are not just the wealthy owners of a company but also include shareholders who for example may be retired pensioners relying on the dividends they receive to support their day-to-day living in retirement. Law enforcement responses are varied across jurisdictions but at the local level resources are limited and tend to be focused on the more immediate crimes such as domestic violence, assault and residential burglary.

Emerging Issues

The world is constantly changing and the nature of crimes is changing too. Criminals are becoming more creative and resourceful and are using technology in ways that could not have been conceived of when criminology was first developed. In addition to adapting to new crime types and new ways of engaging in crime, criminology is also adapting to the changing nature of society and with globalisation. Crimes are frequently being carried out on the global arena, crossing borders and causing jurisdictional dilemmas for law enforcement. Many crimes in the modern era are conducted in cyberspace, where international law has not yet been developed to respond to it. Socio-political

Key Criminological Research Debates

Are courts more lenient on white collar criminals than welfare cheats?
In New Zealand, welfare fraud costs the taxpayer around $22 million in 2010 but tax fraud costs around $7.4 billion. Despite tax fraud depriving the society of much more, the sentences handed down to tax evaders tend to be much more lenient than for welfare cheats (Marriott 2016). Dr Lisa Marriott conducted research into the court outcomes for these offences and found that between 2008 and 2011 only 22% of people found guilty of tax offences received a custodial sentence whereas 60% of people found guilty of welfare benefit fraud were sentenced to imprisonment. Similar sentencing outcomes are found in Australia where it is also the case that people found guilty of defrauding Centrelink (welfare benefits) usually have to pay back the money defrauded but those found guilty of white collar crimes generally do not, even though the amounts are usually much higher (Nedim 2014). Gruner (2005) argues that it is too difficult to prosecute white collar crime because these crimes are so complex. He states that when reviewing prosecution rates in the US, 34% of white collar crimes are closed without charges and 10% receive alternative non-criminal sanctions. He claims high prosecution rates for government regulatory offences (82%), theft of government property (59%) and interstate theft (55%) although prosecution results differed between states. In the UK fraud prosecutions significantly dropped in 2013 while the number of white collar crimes increased (Thornberry 2014). In many cases the criminals are allowed to keep the proceeds of their crimes with only about 10% of lost monies recovered. The prosecution of welfare cheats is unclear. Ledwith (2013) refutes the view that welfare cheats are treated harshly and reports that two-thirds of welfare cheats evade prosecution and few receive prison terms. It is claimed that in 2012 in the UK, 35,196 benefit fraud cases were identified but only 9,836 were prosecuted. In Australia, only the most serious fraud cases are prosecuted and then only the strongest are pursued (Prenzler 2011). The evidence to support these arguments is complicated and disputable. A research debate therefore exists as to whether it is in fact the case that white collar criminals are treated more favourably within the criminal justice system and whether an inequity exists in terms of the sentencing and the requirement to repay stolen money, especially when compared with other criminals such as welfare cheats.

contexts are being intertwined with organised crime as never before, and new branches of criminology, such as terrorism criminology, are emerging to respond to this. In this section of the chapter we will look at a sample of these emerging areas within criminology.

Cybercrime

The information age and emerging technologies has given the world a new form of crime: Cypbercrime. Many people incorrectly believe that 'cybercrime' is crime that occurs in 'cyberspace' when in fact it occurs in physical locations that can

vary from a large corporate building to someone's bedroom. Electronic computer equipment is mobile and flexible, allowing criminals an array of opportunities for breaking the law, exploiting people and attacking individuals and organisations. The Commission of the European Communities (2007) identified three categories of criminal activities covered by the broad term cybercrime. The first category covers traditional forms of crime such as fraud, child grooming, stalking or theft; crimes McGuire and Dowling (2013) refer to as 'cyber enabled'. The second category covers the publication of illegal content such as pornography or material inciting racial hatred. The third category is 'cyber dependent' and covers crimes that attack electronic networks, such as hacking. These categories are useful to researchers, lawmakers and policy developers seeking to understand the nature of this varied offence and target specific response or prevention measures.

The Language of Cybercrime

The absence of clear and consistent definitions of cybercrime between and within jurisdictions as well as across the numerous academic disciplines that examine aspects of this form of crime simply means that getting a grasp on the language can be a bit daunting. Cybercrime might be referred to as computer-related crime (or computer crime), high-tech crime, electronic crime (e-crime) or by any number of types of criminal or antisocial behaviour with the prefix cyber attached, such as cyberterrorism or cyberbullying. You can see that there is a specific language for discussing cybercrime but in addition there are terms used that refer to various attacks on computer systems or fraudulent scams directed at system users. This is what we refer to as the language of cybercrime and is depicted in Figure 5.3.

Across the criminological literature on cybercrime, Wall's (2001) categorisations are more commonly discussed (see Figure 5.4).

Cyber trespass	Cyber deceptions and thefts
Hacking	Fraud
Computer viruses	Scams
Attacks on ICT systems	Piracy
Spyware	
Cyber pornography	**Cyber violence**
Receipt, transmission and sharing of sexually explicit material	Stalking
	Bullying
	Grooming
child pornography	Racial vilification
	Death threats
	Terrorism

Figure 5.4   Categorisations of cybercrime

Wall (2001) constructed categories which differentiate cybercrime by the nature of the offence and with consideration of the interaction between victims and offenders which are: cyber trespass, cyber deceptions and thefts, cyber pornography and cyber violence. Many researchers of cybercrime tend to specialise in one of these categories. The Center for Cybercrime Studies at the John Jay College of Criminal Justice (US) and the Centre for Cybercrime and Computer Security at Newcastle University (UK) are two examples of research entities focused on cyber trespass. At John Jay research focuses on detecting

The Language of Cybercrime	
How many of the terms listed below can you define?	
Spam	Phishing
Spoofing	Pharming
Trojan horse	Worms
Malware	Spyware
Botnets	Viruses
Bitcoin	Dark Web
Denial of service attacks	

Figure 5.3   The language of cybercrime

and deterring cybercrime while at Newcastle, in addition to cyber security research, the centre provides education on internet safety to families, businesses and community organisations. Several research organisations, government agencies and policy frameworks target deception and fraud. The Australian Institute of Criminology, for example, annually conducts a public survey on behalf of the Australasian Consumer Fraud Taskforce to identify the extent to which consumers are exposed to and/or are victims of various scam types as well as identifying whether individuals reported the scams, to whom, and overall perceptions of whether the scams constitute a crime.

More recently, considerable research effort has gone into exploring the direct and indirect criminal behaviours associated with cyber pornography and cyber violence. In particular, research into the online use and distribution of child exploitation material has been undertaken as well as investigations of the use of social media for online child grooming and bullying. This work undertaken by organisations such as the Child Exploitation and Online Protection Command (CEOPC) and the National Society for the Prevention of Cruelty to Children (NSPCC), a British-based organisation that not only disseminates research information on these issues but also actively engages in prevention measures (NSPCC 2016). The CEOPC is a unit of the UK Police. It works with child protection partners across the UK to identify and organise coordinated responses to any threats to children with a particular focus on online threats (CEOPC 2015).

Quantifying the Problem

Accurate estimates of the incidence and prevalence rates of a range of cybercrimes is unknown and difficult to quantify (McGuire 2012). Many of these crimes are regarded as remaining unreported or under-reported and added to this are the very real problems associated with collecting data across borders. Efforts have, however, been made to improve data collection including implementing the Australian Cybercrime Online Reporting Network (which relies on reports from affected individuals) and the National Incident-Based Reporting System which holds a collection of

incident-level data from matters identified across the US. The costs of cybercrime to companies and the gains to criminals have been estimated by US firm McAfee. The annual costs to companies globally have been put at around US $445 billion and this figure also represents the gains to the criminals (McAfee 2014).

Providing an Effective Response

As a criminologist, researcher, investigator or policy maker in the cybercrime space, the problem is ensuring your role is having the desired effect of providing a meaningful response to cybercrime. Getting the balance right between full access and constraints on access is tricky (McGuire 2012). On the one hand having access to a wealth of information via social media and the internet keeps people connected and informed. On the other hand, that access may connect us to the wrong people and lead us to accept false, disingenuous information or offers. Such access can also be used by law enforcement to investigate crime or to monitor potential criminal activity. Most people are aware nowadays that as technology grows and improves we become vulnerable to having our personal information shared against our express wishes, or worse, our identities stolen (Edwards 2015). What is less known and understood is that our online activity and persona remains online forever and can be accessed in the future by employers or future partners. How then do you respond to cybercrime? There are several challenges associated with responding to cybercrime. Some of these include the globalisation of cybercrime, the difficulty in quantifying this type of crime, difficulty in identifying offenders and the lack of knowledge of this type of crime in the general public.

 How might your Facebook pictures and comments made now affect your job prospects in the future?

Responses to cybercrime need to involve international cooperation, criminal law, administrative or procedural law and

Case Study

Responding to Cybercrime

The European Convention on Cybercrime (The Budapest Convention WTS no. 185)

The first binding international instrument to address cybercrime, the European Union Budapest Convention, opened for signature on 23 November 2001 and entered into force on 1 July 2004. By May 2015 the convention had received 46 ratifications/accessions from 39 member states of the Council of Europe (including Azerbaijan, France, Hungary and the Czech Republic) and seven non-members of the Council of Europe (including Australia, Mauritius and the US). The preamble of the instrument identifies that its main purpose is to pursue a common criminal policy relating to cybercrime through appropriate legislation and international cooperation. Articles of the convention cover substantive offences such as breaches of confidentiality; integrity and availability of computer data and systems; computer-related offences such as hacking; and content-related offences such as internet child pornography. It also covers procedural laws covering the search and seizure of stored computer data and interception of content data, among other things. In essence, nations supporting the convention agree to have criminal laws within their own jurisdictions to combat and respond to cybercrime and provide support at an international level to identify its incidence and engage in prevention wherever practicable.

Source: Council of Europe. 2015. 'Responding to Cybercrime' CET 185 Treaties Office. Accessed online on 8 November 2016 at: http://conventions.coe.int/Treaty/EN/Treaties/html/185.htm

inter-jurisdictional cooperation. These elements are included in the Budapest Convention which is an international agreement organised by the European Council (see case study).

Global Reach

Cybercrime can be a local crime or can be a global/transnational offence. Offenders and victims may be located next door or opposite sides of the world. There may be more than one offender, each located in different cities or countries where laws, the administration of justice and/or access to support or other services for victims differ (McGuire and Dowling 2013). The location of offenders can be thousands of kilometres away from their victims and they are virtually anonymous while online. This poses problems in terms of identifying, arresting and prosecuting the offenders because of the differences in legislation in each of these jurisdictions. Penalties likewise differ, and are according to the legislation in place in the location where the offence occurred (as opposed to where the victim is located).

Identifying Offenders

Identifying offenders and/or their motivations is problematic. The anonymity of the internet encourages people to do and say things they wouldn't normally say or do. This can be a good thing when someone who is shy is trying to broaden their social circle, but anonymity on the internet also gives offenders the courage to be more brazen in their criminal activity. The perceived risk of getting caught is low. Not only can some offenders 'hide' using their technical skills, but they may have different false personas and various motivations, making profiling the offenders very difficult. For example they may be motivated by profit, curiosity, the challenge or a host of other factors (McGuire and Dowling 2013). This makes finding them more difficult and may make targeting crime prevention measures more difficult too.

Public Education

Public education about the nature of cybercrime may be lacking as a large portion of the population, especially among the older generations, who are unfamiliar with the way in which the internet and other computer-based services work. This may lead to victimisation or exacerbate under-reporting. In addition, some cyber activities such as stealing a person's ID may not be perceived as criminal by the public and may therefore not be reported to police. Certain types of scams such as hijacking the email account of an unsuspecting victim are unwanted and even irritating to consumers but if they are not perceived by them as criminal they are less likely to be reported.

Identity Theft: More Than 770,000 Australian Victims in Past Year

The Australian Broadcasting Corporation (ABC) has reported that in the year to April 2015, there were 770,000 victims of identity theft, costing each victim approximately $4,000 each. This information was provided by the Credit Bureau Veda. The ABC went on to say that globally billions of dollars are lost to cybercrime.

Rhonda is a victim of cybercrime and this is her story:

When thieves broke into Rhonda's email account she thought nothing of it but five months later her bank rang her asking her to confirm that she had changed her telephone number. She *immediately* rang the bank then went to an ATM only

to discover that $6,000 had been stolen, leaving her with $1 in her account. The thieves were able to obtain sufficient information from the email account and then social media to access her bank account to change the personal and security information. Once that was done they could take her money.

Source: Edwards, M. 2015, 14 April. 'Identity Theft: More than 770,000 Australian Victims in Past Year' ABC News. Accessed online on 8 November 2016 at: http://abc.net.au/news/2015-04-14/identity-theft-hits-australians-veda/6390570.

 What groups in the population are most vulnerable to cybercrime?

Such unwanted accessing of email accounts can lead onto more serious crimes such as identity theft (see case study). Educating the public about how identity theft occurs is an important tool in the reduction of cybercrime and is used by financial institutions to inform consumers and to minimise risk to the organisation (Marron 2008).

Emerging Technology

Keeping pace with emerging technology perhaps presents the greatest challenge. As technology increases and improves, the capacity for victimisation also increases and the group of

potential victims broadens. At the same time the technology available to law enforcement also increases, allowing it greater ability to identify, track and capture offenders (Rogers et al. 2011). As new and improved technology emerges, legislation and policing practices must also change and adapt in order to keep up with it. New technology may result in the creation of new crimes that have not previously existed. When this occurs, ethical considerations and moral, human rights or privacy issues need to be debated. As new technology emerges the law may not adequately manage or provide suitable authority to law enforcement for an appropriate response to be undertaken. Sometimes people can inadvertently commit an offence by using modern technology in a way that is considered to be criminal under the law (see case study).

(Innocent) 'Sexting' Gone Awry?

In 2009 an 18-year-old Florida man was convicted of sending child pornography via his mobile phone, sentenced to five years' probation and required by Florida law to register as a sex offender. The man had received nude photos of his 16-year-old girlfriend, which she sent to him, on his mobile phone

and, after an argument, sent these photos on to some of his friends.

- Does the punishment fit the crime?
- What if he had only received the images and not passed them on? Is that a crime?
- What expectations of privacy should the young woman have?

- What are the legal privacy provisions in your country?
- What have you shared through telecommunications or social media websites with the people you trust?
- Do you know your rights?

Key Criminological Research Debates

Is it ethical for police to access metadata without a warrant?
In Australia new laws have been introduced that provide police with the power to access telephone and internet metadata without a warrant (Wroe 2015). These laws will require the metadata of all customers to be retained for this purpose. No specific definition of metadata exists but the Australian Parliament has defined it in legislation as: 'data created when online tasks are undertaken and other forms of electronic communication are made' (Grubb and Massola 2014). This does not include the sites visited on the internet because a warrant is required for the police to obtain specific information such as the web browsing history. The debate in criminology centres around the needs of the police to have access to greater powers to respond to cybercrime and the potential for a breach of privacy of individuals who are not engaged in criminal activity. There is also the potential for the legal rights of the criminal to be breached if more specific data is inadvertently obtained in the process of collecting metadata. A legal dilemma then arises as to whether such information can be used and/or to what extent it is used by police during the investigation. Similar legislation is being sought in the UK, the US, New Zealand and other countries, so it is a topical area of debate.

Summary

Cybercrime is a complex and constantly changing criminal area. Existing and emerging technology aids criminals to engage in ever-more sophisticated crimes while remaining anonymous and, for the main part, out of the reach of law enforcement. As technology improves, however, new and emerging tools are being developed for law enforcement to aid it to investigate and solve cybercrime. It is a constant battle for law enforcement to stay ahead of the criminals in a rapidly evolving technological world.

Terrorism

On 11 September 2001 a series of terrorist attacks on American soil killed citizens of 78 countries, resulting not only in global condemnation of the perpetrators but the belief that the world had fundamentally changed and that we were encountering a new threat from a 'different enemy than we have ever faced' (Bush, 20 September 2001) (G.W. Bush address to Congress 2001). Prior to these attacks terrorism was almost solely researched and commented upon within the realms of international studies, political science and legal studies but it is now a topic of specialisation within many academic disciplines including criminology and sociology. Terrorism, and how to address the radicalisation of Western young people, is a growing area of interest in criminology and in sectors of the criminal justice system such as policing. Many police departments now have specialist units trained and equipped to deal with terrorism and to amass intelligence on terrorist activities in their area.

Conceptualising and Defining Terrorism

The concept of terrorism is largely subjective and conjures up for some people images of gun-wielding jihadis and suicide bombers. In academia the term is used to describe a complex set of behaviours that some researchers suggest has little meaning outside a political context. Recent acts of terrorism around the world have been linked to specific religions but previous acts of terrorism have been linked to specific political factions or ideological viewpoints. Most terrorists would not conceptualise their actions as terrorism, but as justified activities according to the specific ideology or belief system they adhere to. Acts of terrorism can appear to be like other criminal acts such as shooting and stabbing, but they differ in terms of the scale, the motive and the links with organised

---

Terrorism Act 2000 s 1 (UK)

(1) In this Act 'terrorism' means the use or threat of action where –

   a) the action falls within subsection (2),

   b) the use or threat is designed to influence the government [or an international governmental organisation] to intimidate the public or a section of the public, and

   c) the use or threat is made for the purpose of advancing a political, religious, racial or ideological cause.

(2) Action falls within this subsection if it –

   a) involves serious violence against a person,

   b) involves serious damage to property,

   c) endangers a person's life, other than that of the person committing the action,

   d) creates a serious risk to the health or safety of the public or a section of the public, or

   e) is designed seriously to interfere with or seriously to disrupt an electronic system.

(3) The use or threat of action falling within subsection (2) which involves the use of firearms or explosives is terrorism whether or not subsection (1) (b) is satisfied.

Figure 5.5   Excerpt from the UK terrorism act

groups purporting to condone, encourage and/or initiate these acts. Traditional acts of crime are typically defined as 'terrorism' if they are ideologically based and designed to influence or intimidate en masse and result in injury and/or death or instil a fear of imminent injury or death. Terrorism is generally defined in legislation (see Figure 5.5).

According to Wilkinson (2006) terrorism can be distinguished from other forms of violent crimes by the following criteria:

1. It is premeditated;

2. It is designed to cause maximum fear, death, harm and destruction;

3. It is directed at a broader target group than just the immediate victims;

4. It involves attacks on random and/or symbolic victims, including civilians;

5. It is considered to be out of the ordinary within the target community;

6. It violates any rules, laws and norms associated with protest and dissent;

7. It is used primarily to influence the political behaviour of governments or as a means to express a political or religious ideological position.

This definition separates terrorism from other violent criminal acts by the motivation for the actions and the scale of the activities. According to the Australian Attorney General's Office, terrorism is defined as:

》 an act, or threat to commit an act, that is done with the intention to coerce or influence the public or any government by intimidation to advance a political, religious or ideological cause, and the act causes:

  ▬ Death, serious harm or endangers a person

  ▬ Serious damage to property

  ▬ A serious risk to the health or safety of the public; or

  ▬ Seriously interferes with, disrupts or destroys critical infrastructure such as a telecommunications or electricity network.

(Attorney General's Office 2016:5).

This is a broad definition that could easily be taken out of context to suppress the freedom of speech and political protest, but the Australian Attorney General's Office has taken care to stipulate that this definition does not apply to lawful protests and political dissent that is expressed in a respectful and lawful way.

What Does Criminology Contribute to Terrorism Studies?

We acknowledged at the outset of this chapter, and elsewhere in this book, that criminology is a relatively young discipline and the advent of interest in terrorism from within this field is also a relatively new movement within criminology. This means that there is little 'pure' criminological research in this space to date to but this is a fast-changing picture. Much of the preliminary research has focused on the contribution criminology can make with authors from other disciplines (see, for example, LaFree and Dugan 2004; Rosenfeld 2004) advocating for the application of criminological theories and data collection methods to strengthen the evidence base of the causes and consequences of terrorism. LaFree and Dugan (2004) note the similarities between criminal events and terrorism events. Both events are measurable and exhibit patterns over time which LaFree and Dugan suggest makes terrorism events amenable to data collection and analytical methods well entrenched within criminology. The examination of incident scenes will employ or benefit from similar forensic techniques. Finally, LaFree et al. (2015) suggest that both events are mainly domestic in nature and have offenders, targets and situational characteristics, which are aspects that have been long studied by criminologists. Another important consideration relevant to the contribution criminology can make

to terrorism research is the interdisciplinary nature of criminology. As we identified in *Chapter 2: Studying Criminology*, criminology draws from several disciplines including law, psychology and sociology and much of the research and evidence is based on how crimes, and deviant or otherwise antisocial actions are defined and how responses are constructed. This in-depth understanding of social control and its application to prevention makes criminological knowledge a natural contribution to terrorism studies.

Radicalisation

Radicalisation, or the process by which an individual or group comes to adopt extreme political, social or religious views that may lead to terrorism or what is more widely termed violent extremism, is an area of interest to criminologists. Of concern historically has been how this process manifests in institutional settings such as prisons, hence the role of the criminologist in providing insights. Since the New York twin tower attacks on 11 September 2001, commonly referred to as 9/11, the focus has been largely on Islamic radicalisation and the manifestation of modern-day jihadi individuals or groups. A recent example

---

Case Study

The Rise of Daesh (ISIS)

The origins of Daesh (also known as Islamic State, ISIS and ISIL) can be traced back to 2004 in Camp Bucca in Iraq. This was a US internment camp for Islamic jihadists and other militants. It was in the confines of this camp that the leader of Daesh, Abu Bakr al-Baghdadi, established his position. The group known as Islamic State was established as an alternative to al-Qaeda in

2006 in Iraq (Stern and Berger 2015). Daesh is an extreme Islamic terrorist group that imposes a strict version of sharia law in the Middle Eastern regions which it has invaded and now controls. These are predominantly in Syria and Iraq but this group is constantly seeking to expand into other regions. The successful expansion of Daesh has been in part put down to its ability to

recruit members from all over the world. It uses social media to radicalise young people with promises of excitement and rewards to lure them to Syria to fight on its behalf. It also uses fear and terror tactics such as public executions to keep its members from leaving the group. Daesh incites terrorist attacks all over the world from its base in Syria.

Sources: Chulov, M. 2014, 11 December. Isis: The Inside Story' *The Guardian*. Accessed online on 8 November 2016 at: www.theguardian.com/world/2014/dec/11/-sp-isis-the-inside-story.

Stern, J. & Berger, J. M. 2015. *ISIS: The State of Terror*. London, UK: William Collins.

is Daesh, in the Middle East, also referred to as Islamic State, ISIL and ISIS (see case study) which has organised, directed and influenced terrorist attacks in America, the UK, Australia, France, Belgium and elsewhere.

Since 9/11 there has been a growing awareness of the emergence of terrorist networks around the world and following this event a large amount of funding has been directed towards understanding how Western people, particularly the youth, are radicalised and recruited into these groups. In addition to gaining a better understanding of the social, psychological and situational contexts in which violent extremism thrives, criminologists are also interested in the prevention of radicalisation and terrorism. Prevention studies examine diverse areas such as ways to integrate Muslim people into Western society, ways to build resilient communities, social and therapeutic interventions for people exhibiting extremist ideologies and behaviours, and the exercise of power by law enforcement and other security-based professionals to arrest people suspected of terrorist activities.

How Criminologists are Involved in Responding to Terrorism

Criminologists are also finding their expertise is being valued in the field of terrorism in respect to identifying the support needs of communities

---

Key Criminological Research Debates

Anti-terrorism legislation and civil liberties: Is the balance right?
Since the September 2001 terrorist attacks in the US there has been a proliferation of anti-terrorism legislation globally. Although everyone agrees that laws are required for national security and personal protection, the extent to which new legislation curtails fundamental human rights and civil liberties is an ongoing debate. The pro argument suggests that civil liberties and human rights are political conveniences that should not curtail government in times of emergency (Michaelsen 2006). The contra argument points to the necessity to preserve and maintain the legitimacy of these rights, particularly in times of crisis, to ensure they do not lose their effect. The United Nations High Commissioner for Human Rights suggests that when 'rushing through legislative and practical measures, [nations] have created negative consequences for civil liberties and fundamental human rights' (Office of the United Nations High Commissioner for Human Rights, n.d.). Anti-terrorism legislation threatens several human rights, including: the right to a fair trial; the right to freedom from arbitrary detention and arrest; the right to privacy; the right to freedom of association and expression; and the right to non-discrimination. Newly created detention laws, new powers to detain and question people, powers to ban terrorist organisations and the act of profiling each can threaten human rights. One of the most contested powers is control orders. These orders take many forms and generally restrict personal liberty, usually via limitations on movement and association. For these orders to have legitimacy they need to be proportionate to the identified problem and non-discriminatory. However, nations that have ratified the United Nations International Covenant on Civil and Political Rights are not equally engaged with these issues at a national level. As Conte (2010) notes, many nations do not have entrenched human rights provisions. Canada has a human rights charter entrenched in its constitution, Australia has no federal instrument, New Zealand has a bill of rights that is not entrenched and the UK links protection of human rights with the European Convention on Human Rights. The capacity of these four nations to legislate limitations on rights therefore differs significantly.

affected by terrorism and best practices in the provision of that support. Criminology provides useful theoretical frameworks for understanding radicalisation and terrorist activity and sound processes for strengthening community safety. Criminologists are being sought as consultants to assist governments in the formulation of new legislation to combat terrorism. Increasingly the close connection between serious and organised crime and terrorism (Stern and Berger 2015) is being examined and in particular the broad usage of criminal activities such as human trafficking and extortion by terrorist groups to fund their terrorist activities. While currently a relatively new branch of criminology, in the future it is likely to become more mainstream and these research areas are likely to become normative enquiries within criminological research and studies.

Summary

Terrorism has been around for a long time but it is a relatively new and emerging field of study within criminology. There are many aspects of terrorism investigation and response that have similarities with crime investigation and response and it therefore makes sense for criminologists to become interested in this emerging field. Terrorism raises high levels of fear within communities and there is increasing pressure on governments to identify causes of radicalisation and provide effective responses to combat it. In addition, there is also an expectation in the community that governments will increase the effectiveness of terrorist prevention strategies, including providing harsher penalties for offenders. All of these areas provide criminologists with opportunities to contribute to this growing field of study.

 How have laws changed in your country as a result of the increasing terrorist threat? Is this a good or a bad trend?

Human Trafficking

It is estimated that human trafficking across the world affects more than 12 million people and makes more than $43.3 billion profit for the perpetrators. Women and children are mostly affected but men are also victims. Human trafficking is the forced abduction and enslavement of another person against their will. The purpose for trafficking humans is mainly for sexual slavery and also for forced labour (Hepburn and Simon 2013). This is a growing area of interest for criminologists who are involved in working with both sides of the criminal equation: with the offenders and with the victims.

Nature of Human Trafficking

There are many ways in which children and adults become victims of human trafficking. Abduction is a common method of forced enslavement but traffickers will also use deception. They may tell parents from impoverished countries that they are taking their children to another country so that they can be better educated as a means to entice parents into agreeing for their children to be taken away. Sometimes they advertise overseas jobs and once the person is abroad they keep their passports and force them into prostitution or other forced labour in order to pay off exorbitant bogus 'debts' that have purportedly accrued. The victims become commodities to be bought, sold and used by their captors who will frequently apply physical violence and enforce drug use to keep them under control (Hepburn and Simon 2013). Their health and other needs are rarely met while they are held captive (see case study). In the Middle East and Northern Africa, human trafficking is occurring in the context of terrorist activity with women and children sold into sexual servitude and young males forced into military service to support the terrorist cause.

Where Does Human Trafficking Occur?

Human trafficking occurs in almost every country but some countries are more likely to be countries of origin and other countries are more likely to be

Human Trafficking: How a Charity is Rescuing the Victims the Authorities Knew Nothing About

A newspaper article in Britain on 29 October 2015 presented the case of a middle-aged Polish man who turned up to a soup kitchen. He was nervous, spoke no English and had no possessions. It was initially thought that the man was suffering from a mental illness, but through a translator they discovered he had been brought to Britain by Polish Roma. Suspecting human trafficking, the staff at the centre called on a Christian charity called Hope for Justice which had previously distributed posters detailing how to recognise a victim of trafficking. The Hope for Justice charity is situated in the UK's West Midlands and had rescued 82 people so far in 2015. Many of these victims were unknown to the police. Very few cases of modern slavery get through to the criminal justice system, with only 130 cases involving human trafficking successfully prosecuted in Britain in 2014–2015.

Source: Peachy, P. 2015, 29 October. 'Human Trafficking: How a Charity is Rescuing the Victims the Authorities Knew Nothing About' *The Independent* Accessed online on 25 November 2016 at: www.independent.co.uk/news/uk/home-news/human-trafficking-how-a-charity-is-rescuing-the-victims-the-authorities-knew-nothing-about-a6712661.html.

destination countries. It is probably not surprising that underdeveloped and impoverished countries such as Cambodia, Vietnam and Thailand are the main countries of origin for victims with impoverished areas of wealthier countries such as Russia and China also targeted by human traffickers. The destination countries for human trafficking tend to be wealthier developed countries such as Britain, the US, Canada, Australia and Japan (Hepburn and Simon 2013). The target countries for human trafficking can also be less stable politically with poor records for the treatment of women and children. This is being seen more frequently in the Middle East since the rise of ISIS (Chulov 2014). The target countries for people smuggling usually have relatively stable economic and political systems and a democratic government because the people being smuggled are seeking a better life.

People Smuggling

People smuggling is a different criminal issue to human trafficking. Both crimes involve the illegal movement of people across borders, but in people smuggling the people being moved are doing so voluntarily whereas in human trafficking the people being moved have no choice. There is a difference in how the criminals involved in these crimes view the people involved. In people smuggling, the people being moved are viewed as being clients who pay for a service whereas in human trafficking the people are viewed as commodities with no rights (Australian Institute of Criminology 2008). People smuggling is about gaining monetary reward from a business transaction with the people being smuggled across national borders. In human trafficking, the profits are made from the selling and exploitation of the victims themselves and it does not necessarily need to involve the crossing of international borders. Laczko (2002:1) defined people smuggling as:

>> The procurement, in order to obtain, directly or indirectly a financial or other material benefit; of the illegal entry of a person into a State Party of which the person is not a national or permanent resident.

This definition distinguishes people smugglers, whose main occupation is to transport humans voluntarily but illegally across international borders, from human traffickers who move people within and between countries against their will or through the use of coercion, bribery, force or deception for the purpose of exploitation.

The Legal Response

Due to cross-jurisdictional issues, tracking and prosecuting offenders of human trafficking is extremely difficult. In 2000 the United Nations

Protocol to Prevent, Suppress and Punish Trafficking in Persons was ratified. Since that time a number of countries have enacted their own legislation to prohibit human trafficking. Under the United Nations protocol, adults are trafficked if they are recruited, moved, harboured or received through the use of force, threats, coercion, abduction, fraud, deception or abuse of power or due to their vulnerability for the purpose of exploitation (United Nations 2000). Law enforcement in several countries have resources dedicated to investigating and prosecuting these crimes.

Summary

Human trafficking is a growing problem with enormous negative impacts for the victims. Most governments around the world are trying to prevent and respond to this problem but it is a very organised and lucrative business. The fact that victims are taken across borders also complicates the law enforcement response because laws and the legal process often prosecute victims who have violated immigration and prostitution laws rather than offenders who are very clever at covering their tracks. Victims are often afraid to give evidence against perpetrators which makes prosecutions of these crimes very difficult. In addition to assisting law enforcement and victims' groups, criminologists have a role to play in tracking trends, researching the prevalence and impact of this crime, and formulating effective responses for victims and offenders.

Green Crime

Around the world, interest is growing in environmental protection and with it a parallel interest in environmental crime or green crime and how to prevent this type of crime. Green criminology is the branch of criminology that has sprung up to focus on this area of criminality. Potter (2010) sees the rise of green criminology as being as direct result of increases in environment-related criminal activity and a corresponding increase in the development of environmental laws to combat these crimes. Green criminology is as much concerned about the power relationships between corporations and the people who are at the end point of environmental harm as it is about the crime itself. It has also been suggested that green criminology covers not only environmental harm that is illegal but also environmental harm such as deforestation and mining that is actually legal (Potter 2010). Such a view places green criminology into the realm of critical and radical criminology where criminologists may challenge the currently held paradigm of right and wrong in reference to environmental issues. *See Green Criminology (Chapter 3).*

What Is Green Crime?

Providing a single definition of green crime is problematic because green crime covers a range of different types of crime. These crimes include activities such as contaminating water and food sources; wildlife crimes; deforestation; smuggling; illegal logging; illegally processing industrial waste, illegal fishing; and the illegal dumping of rubbish. The thing that links all of the crimes that fall under the umbrella of green crime is that these are all crimes that are not directly targeted at people but are targeted against the environment. Many humans and animals are the victims of these crimes, however, and the harm caused to individuals, communities and wildlife by environmental crime cannot be discounted (Ruggerio and South 2013). Green crime occurs at the individual, community, national and global levels and is frequently seen as a crime of the powerful corporate giants against powerless and poverty-stricken families and communities. Potter (2010) suggests that green crime generally incorporates human rights abuses of the poorest people in the world and that human victims frequently lose their means of income, their homes, farms and societies. In addition to this, the wealthy corporations that are responsible for the environmental harm frequently avoid any legal accountability.

Victimology of Green Crime

The victims of environmental crimes can be animals, people and the environment (White 2007). It is the case, however, that many victims are not identified as victims of crime because the activities that have caused the environmental harm have not yet been classified as criminal (Potter 2010). Such victims have no legal recourse and may not even be entitled to fair compensation for their losses. Furthermore, the perpetrators of the environmental harm are not classified as criminals because the activities they are engaged in are not deemed to be illegal. The victims, therefore, are unable to obtain justice through the criminal justice system. Environmental crime can generate a substantial amount of money for organised criminals and legal corporations but it is rarely re-invested into the communities which have been plundered for their wood, natural resources and wildlife (Banks et al. 2008). A report on illegal logging in countries such as Indonesia and Papua New Guinea, for example, found that while the wood was retailed in the UK and America for $US 2288.00/M^3, the local community in Papua New Guinea received only $US 11.00/M^3 (Banks et al. 2008). *See Victims and the Justice System.*

Law Enforcement Response

Environmental crime is generally given a low priority by law enforcement agencies (Banks et al. 2008). The law enforcement response to environmental crime is generally a combined effort with other agencies such as joint operations between the police and border protection agencies. Due to the complexities involved in policing environmental crime it is necessary to have a range of approaches available. Banks et al. (2008:22) have highlighted the successful enforcement models as being:

- Regional cooperation;
- National coordination;
- Political will;
- Specialised intelligence units; and
- Local partnerships.

Regional cooperation involves the gathering and sharing of intelligence between regional jurisdictions and countries in order to intercept illegal shipments such as toxic substances and waste. National coordination involves multi-agency cooperation to investigate, track and intercept illegal smuggling. Political will refers to decisive measures being taken by the government of target countries to enact environmental protection laws and prosecute perpetrators of environmental crime. Specialised intelligence units are specially trained task force teams that operate from a strategic enforcement approach to police specific environmental crimes such as wildlife poaching. Local partnerships are specially formed local groups that work with law enforcement agencies to support the fight against specific environmental crimes such as the illicit wildlife trade (e.g. ivory poaching).

Prevention of Green Crime

Preventing environmental crime is an expansive area because it covers such a broad range of crimes. These crimes include intentional acts and omissions and cover human and non-human victims (White 2007). A comprehensive analysis of green crime prevention is undertaken by Rob White (2008) and it is an analysis that attempts to deal with all the complexities of environmental crime. His approach is simple in that he uses standard crime prevention strategies and applies them to green crime. He claims that the objectives of green crime prevention are intrinsically entwined with eco-philosophy. In saying that, he means that in trying to prevent environmental crime, the criminologist must be aware that prevention is linked to how human interests are perceived, the needs and wants of specific societies and also to the rights of animals (White 2008). These considerations are incorporated into the crime prevention strategies so that a good crime prevention framework includes the interests of humans, animals and the environment.

Summary

Green crime covers a vast range of activities, all of which cause harm to the environment or wildlife. This is an area that has received little attention from criminologists and law enforcement in the past, but it is gaining momentum in current times. While some people consider green crime to be victimless it is clear that there are in fact victims and that the victims can be individuals, families, communities and entire countries. The inequitable power that exists between perpetrators and victims is an area that green criminologists study in order to develop effective crime prevention strategies. Reducing environmental harm from green crime is the main focus of criminologists who operate within this field.

Summary

Criminology and the criminal justice system provide the avid student with many and varied topics of interest. We have presented a small selection of such topics in this chapter ranging from social issues of race and gender to emerging issues of terrorism and cybercrime. In addition to this we have tried to cover the main areas of importance within each topic and we have signposted the key debates and emerging issues relevant to these areas. We hope that this chapter has given you a taste of the vast array and scope of the topical areas, beyond the theoretical, that make up the enormously interesting field of criminology.

The Criminal Justice System

The organisations and processes that control law and order, administer justice, prevent and detect crime and issue official punishments are collectively referred to as the 'criminal justice system'. This is made up of a range of sectors such as the police, corrections, courts, lawyers, restorative justice programmes and victim support services and also the peripheral services and functional areas that support the main sectors that make up the criminal justice system. It also incorporates the juvenile justice system in some jurisdictions, although many countries place juvenile justice within child welfare departments. The criminal justice system is a huge bureaucracy that is funded by taxpayers through the government. Across the United Kingdom, for example, the criminal justice system employs more than 500,000 people (Pepper 2011). In Australia, there are eight states and territories, each with its own criminal justice system and criminal legislation. There is also a national system under the auspices of federal legislation. In the United States there are local, state and federal levels of law and criminal justice spanning 50 states. When you consider that each state has its own criminal justice system, including police, courts, corrections and law, the enormity of the system begins to become clear.

In this chapter we provide an overview of the functions of the criminal justice system, highlight events that occur as part of the criminal justice process, describe roles across the key components of the system – the police, the courts and corrections, and conclude with a brief overview of three perspectives that continue to influence the operation of the system – punishment, rehabilitation and restorative justice. At the end of the chapter you'll find a list of further readings which may assist you to develop a deeper understanding of the criminal justice system. We also suggest you try to find resources that describe the system where you live.

The Function of the Criminal Justice System

A civilised society requires a government to develop laws for its citizens to be able to live in collective harmony and a government requires various systems (or departments) that can enact and administer these laws. The criminal justice system serves a very important function within society which is to maintain law and order so that the community is safe from the people within it who would seek to do harm to others. Its primary objectives are to prevent crime, mitigate the impact of crime and sanction offenders. To do this the criminal justice system provides the means by which people who break the law are apprehended and ensures that those people who are accused of a crime are processed in a fair, just and equitable manner. It also provides the means by which people can be punished for breaking the law and the interventions that are designed to help them to change their behaviour so they can become productive members of society.

In 1968 Herbert Packer characterised two values representing models of criminal justice – due process and crime control. Due process emphasises the rights of defendants and the presumption of innocence, and focuses on procedural fairness. The crime control model places greater emphasis on apprehending and convicting the guilty, exercising state power and creating efficiency across the system. Both models describe, to an extent, the criminal justice system across English-speaking countries and the values that underpin many of the principles that guide the operations of the criminal justice process. Both models of criminal justice are necessary and can operate together to ensure offenders receive fair treatment and at the same time the community is kept safe. See Table 6.1 for a comparison of these models.

Let's Consider!

Comparing Due Process and Crime Control Models

Table 6.1 shows the differences between the due process and the crime control models of criminal justice. The due process model is considered to be a liberal approach to criminal justice and is guided by civil and human rights. It presumes that people are innocent until proven guilty and all people are entitled to receive a fair process that supports them to legally defend themselves against criminal allegations. The crime control model is a conservative approach that advocates removing unnecessary barriers to swift punishment. *Refer to* Table 6.1 *for more detail.*

Perspectives on Criminal Justice

Our social and legal responses to crime stem from a number of principles and values. These principles and values shape the nature and administration of criminal justice. From punishment to the rights of the victim, the theoretical leanings, ethical principles and personal values held by the key players in the criminal justice system will determine how criminal justice is dispensed. In the final section of the chapter we discuss punishment, rehabilitation and restorative justice which are all key perspectives that are essential to understand when studying the criminal justice system.

The Role of Punishment

Many criminologists have advanced theories about the role of punishment in encouraging conformity to society's norms. The punishment

---

◻ Table 6.1 Comparing the due process and control models

	Due process model	Crime control model
Central theme	Civil and human rights.	Community safety.
Underlying principle	Everyone is entitled to a process of legal procedural fairness.	Human rights must be put aside in favour of protecting the community.
Criminal behaviour	People are innocent until proven guilty in a court of law.	People would not be arrested if they were innocent.
Main focus	Protecting the human and civil rights of persons processed by the criminal justice system.	Controlling crime and maintaining social order.
Purpose	To reduce the number of innocent people being wrongly convicted.	To reduce the number of criminals on the street.
Response to the criminal	Favours rehabilitation.	Favours punishment.
Use of power	Restrictions on police powers. Increases police accountability and transparency.	Increases and broadens police powers.
Criminal justice system	Allow people to access legal supports to be able to defend themselves in court. Appeal processes.	Remove bureaucracy and move people quickly through the system.
Political approach	Liberal approach.	Conservative approach.

of individuals who break society's rules has passed through various methodological and philosophical approaches throughout history. As an example, let us consider the Middle Ages in Europe and Britain (see case study). Barbaric forms of torture were commonly used to punish people accused of breaking the law (Marsh 2004). Being wealthy helped many accused to avoid punishment but for people who were poor or who were seen to be politically opposed to the ruling elite, trials were often perverted due to bias or design and many people were prevented from receiving a fair hearing. Trials and executions were commonly held in public so as to be a deterrent to others, but were also used for public entertainment (Foucault 1975).

Punishment in Modern Western Society

Towards the nineteenth century more humane approaches to punishment were becoming popular in Western countries. Cesare Lombroso (1876/1911) claimed that the punishment of criminals should not be about inflicting pain but about making restitution to the victim and enhancing the wellbeing of society. He placed criminals into categories, which indicated whether they could or could not be reformed: 'born criminal', 'incorrigible' and 'habitual criminal' and suggested that the sentencing response should suit the category of the offender (Rafter 2009). Jeremy Bentham (1789/1982), who approached punishment from the classical criminological perspective, held the view that criminals should be judged moral or immoral based on the effect their actions had on the community and the punishment should be proportional to the crime. Punishment in modern society has the primary functions of incapacitation, deterrence, retribution, restitution or reformation. See *Classicism* (Chapter 3).

The Penal System

Michel Foucault was one of the most influential social theorists of the twentieth century and contributed enormously to the theoretical understanding of punishment and the rise of penology. In his book, *Discipline and Punish: The Birth of the Prison*, Foucault analyses the use of social control by the state and the development of prisons. Foucault (1975) discusses the historical development of punishment from torture

---

Case Study

Punishment in the Middle Ages in Europe and Britain

In medieval times, the Manorial Court dealt with almost all crimes and issues of deviance except the most serious of crimes. It was held several times a year by the Feudal Lords and all the villagers were expected to go. If someone failed to go they had to pay a fine. To ensure full attendance men were placed into groups of ten which were called tithings. Each tithing had to ensure that the other members of the group did not break the law. If someone did break the law, the other members of their tithing had to ensure the lawbreaker went to court. These courts had a jury that were made up of 12 men chosen by the villagers and one man, called the Lord's Steward, who was in charge of the proceedings. Serious crimes were tried in the King's Court. In this court, the accused person had to face a trial by ordeal which had the purpose of deciding whether the person was guilty or innocent. Trial by ordeal usually involved one of three types: ordeal by fire, ordeal by water or ordeal by combat. Ordeal by fire involved the accused person being burned with a red hot iron bar. If the wound had begun to heal in three days they were innocent, but if the wound had not begun to heal they were found guilty. Ordeal by water involved tying the hands and feet of the accused person and throwing them into a river or other water source. If they floated they were guilty but if they sank they were innocent. Ordeal by combat involved the accused person fighting to the death with their accuser, the victor being the one in the right.

Source: History on the Net. 2014. 'Medieval Life – Crime and Punishment' Accessed online on 8 November 2016 at: http://www.historyonthenet.com/medieval_life/crimeandpunishment.htm.

and deprivation of liberty to contemporary approaches which have the aim of changing the behaviour of the individual by changing them on the inside (i.e. touching their soul). He compares prisons, hospitals and schools, suggesting that the organisation of each is such that they all seek to control the behaviour of the individual to ensure that the individual conforms to the regimen of the organisation (Foucault 1975). Prisons allow the authorities to have systematic control over the time, space and behaviour of individuals who are confined to imprisonment. Prisons are categorised by maximum, medium and minimum security. There are also remand centres which hold people who are awaiting trial and pre-release centres that prepare inmates for release into the community. Prisons have a broader role than simply containing people: they also have a role in the rehabilitation of offenders and deterring others in the community. Depriving people of their liberty is the foremost role of the prison, however, and this role has the explicit intention of punishing the offender. In doing so, it also keeps the community safe from further criminal offending by that person (Wright 2008).

> 'Deprivation of liberty is the punishment and it is not the role of the prison to hand out further punishment'. What is meant by this statement? Do you agree?

Labour has a long history in prisons; however, in the past it was often simply hard manual labour with little skill acquisition and used only to keep inmates busy or to ensure the prison and grounds were maintained. The Howard League for Penal Reform was instrumental in introducing more meaningful work into prisons and linking its purpose to providing inmates with a constructive day and the opportunity to receive training for future employment. In addition it allowed them to earn some money to purchase toiletries, snacks and other limited items while inside. In addition to this, work was linked with education and training, giving inmates the chance to develop employable skills and obtain qualifications that

increase their chances of gaining employment on release (The Howard League 2011).

> Why do you think a constructive day for inmates would be important for the safety of the prison?

This was an important step for the management and rehabilitation of prisoners as it relieved boredom and gave the inmates a structure to their day. It also addressed two of the most common criminogenic factors: low educational achievement and unemployment. There is a continuing debate within criminal justice circles as to whether prison is a good option for all but the most serious criminal offenders and whether in fact rehabilitation can be successful in a prison environment (see case study). The use of prisons as a broad-based sentencing option is likely to continue despite these concerns and despite it being the costliest option. *See Correctional Services.*

Punishment in the Community

Sentencing options outside of prison are generally referred to as community-based sanctions. These include bail, probation and parole, community work, home detention, fines and programme orders. Some community-based sanctions have the added influence of public shaming which some theorists, such as Braithwaite and Pettit (1990), believe is conducive to reducing reoffending rates. Community-based sanctions are attractive to many governments as they are generally less costly than prison. There are detractors, however, who see them as a 'soft option' or an option that is poorly resourced and doomed to fail (Walshe 2012). Some victims and sections of the general public are sceptical about whether offenders take community-based sentences seriously and whether in fact these options hold the offender to account for their criminal behaviour (Victim Support 2012). Perceptions of effectiveness are important to the criminal justice system which needs public support and funding to exist. There

Effects of Prison Sentences on Recidivism

Many criminologists, such as McGuire (2000), support the efficacy of rehabilitation treatment programmes for offenders and dispute the view that punishment alone is a deterrent to offending as some conservative elements have argued. Two such studies are provided below. The findings of a research study undertaken by Lloyd, Mair and Hough (1994) in the UK supports the perspective that harsher punishment does not result in reduced offending. This study compared the offending rates, after two years, of offenders who had received differing sentence types. No difference in reoffending rates was found between sentence types, challenging the assumption that the harsher the penalty, the more effective it will be in eliminating offending behaviour (Lloyd et al. 1994). Another study that was conducted in Canada by Gendreau, Goggin and Cullen (1999) reviewed the relationship between lengths of prison sentences and recidivism. They found that rather than harsh penalties having a deterrent effect, a 2–3% increase in recidivism was found with offenders who served the longer sentences. A follow-up study in 2001–2002 supported these findings.

Sources: Gendreau, P., Goggin, C. & Cullen, F. 1999. *The Effects of Prison Sentences on Recidivism: Report to the Corrections Research and Development and Aboriginal Policy Branch*. Ottawa: Solicitor General of Canada.

Lloyd, C., Mair, C. & Hough, M. 1994. *Explaining Reconviction Rates: A Critical Analysis*. Home Office Research Study. London: HMSO

appears to be general support from victim groups and the public for community-based sanctions to be used for low-level offenders where the offences are not serious, but less support for community sanctions for recidivist offenders and where the offences are of a serious nature. *See Community-based Corrections.*

Summary

Modern punishment in Western countries is more humane than the punishment issued to those accused of crimes in the Middle Ages. Punishment is not the only objective of sentencing but it is a necessary part of the criminal justice system and it has an important role in reforming the behaviour of offenders. Punishment makes the offender accountable for their actions and is a negative consequence of their behaviour. It deters the offender from reoffending and may also have a deterrent effect on others who are witness to the punishment. Having a range of sentencing options available to the courts provides judges with the opportunity to make the sentence fit the crime while limiting the negative social impact of sentencing on the offender and their family. The ongoing debate around the efficacy of

community-based corrections for rehabilitating offenders compared with prisons continues to attract research interest.

Rehabilitation

Modern correctional departments do not just want to carry out a sentence of punishment but aim to also rehabilitate the offender so as to reduce or eliminate the criminal offending behaviour. By doing this, community safety is improved through a reduction in crime rates. Rehabilitation is described as being the result of a correctional process that combines addressing the offending behaviour with enhancing human development and promoting social responsibility (Mutingh 2005). The process of rehabilitation is supported by evidence-based research into what works in reducing offending behaviour (Harper and Chitty 2005). While the rehabilitation approach is generally well supported in the contemporary criminal justice system in Western societies, opponents to this approach do exist. This section reviews the literature relevant to the criminological debate about the effectiveness of rehabilitation in reducing offending behaviour.

The Process of Rehabilitation

Rehabilitation consists of planned interventions that are aimed at the dynamic areas of an offender's life, behaviour, attitudes and social environment which are identified as contributing to or causing criminal offending behaviour (Ward and Stewart 2003). These areas can be such things as drug or alcohol addiction, gambling, peer group, homelessness, poor educational level, unemployment, poor anger management skills or antisocial attitudes. Criminologists refer to these areas as being **criminogenic**. Offenders have a wide range of criminogenic needs and success in addressing them largely depends upon the thoroughness of the risk and needs assessment that is undertaken when the offender first enters the correctional justice system (Harper and Chitty 2005). Once an assessment has been undertaken, interventions can be targeted towards the criminogenic needs of the individual offender. The risk factors for criminal offending can be divided into two groups: dynamic and static risk factors. Dynamic risk factors such as accommodation, education level, unemployment, gambling and substance misuse are more easily influenced and changed whereas the static factors such as age, gender and previous criminal history cannot. The rehabilitative effort is targeted towards dynamic risk factors in addition to the offending behaviour itself (Andrews and Bonta 1998). Ward and Stewart (2003) agree that rehabilitation is important but criticise the Andrews and Bonta model. They argue that rehabilitation should not just be about addressing criminal offending behaviour but should take a holistic approach to enhancing the life and social skills of the individual. They also argue that the model fails to adequately explain the inter-relationships between the offenders' criminogenic needs (e.g. how vocational achievement relates to psychological components such as self-esteem or alienation).

The Key Assumptions of Rehabilitation

The body of evidence that supports the principles and assumptions behind offender rehabilitation is commonly referred to as the 'what works literature' (Andrews and Bonta 1998; Golias 2004). According to this evidence-based literature, the key assumptions that underpin offender rehabilitation programmes are that crime is caused by distinct patterns of psychosocial factors that increase the likelihood that the individual will offend and that targeting these factors will decrease offending rates. Furthermore, that individuals are different in their predisposition to commit crime; and treatment should be tailored to meet the individual and unique needs of the offender (Ward and Stewart 2003). Meta-analytical studies, which bring together the findings of a range of studies undertaken around the world, have found that rehabilitation programmes that target a range of problems are more effective in reducing reoffending than those that just focus on a single problem (Harper and Chitty 2005). McGuire (2000) presents a list of key factors that increase the effectiveness of offender rehabilitation programmes. These are: theoretical soundness; risk assessment; assessment of criminogenic needs; targeting criminogenic needs; **responsivity**; structure; methods; and programme integrity. There is considerable evidence to suggest that cognitive-behaviour programmes are particularly helpful approaches in changing attitudes, thinking and behaviour to reduce reoffending and these approaches are commonly adopted in offender rehabilitation programmes.

Does Rehabilitation Work?

There has been significant debate over the years as to whether rehabilitation actually works in reducing **recidivism**. For example, Martinson (1974) undertook 231 studies of prison rehabilitation programmes and concluded the treatment of offenders was largely ineffective. This led to a 'nothing works' perspective that argued against the investment of money and other resources into the rehabilitation of offenders. Interestingly, in 1979 Martinson attempted to overturn his original thesis (Martinson 1979), acknowledging several flaws in his studies;

however, by this time his original position had found a receptive audience among economic rationalists and conservative penalists. During this time, known as the 'nothing works era', there was a philosophical shift in corrections from rehabilitation to surveillance and control (Burnett and Roberts 2004).

Sarre (1984) highlighted the inherent flaws in Martinson's thesis and in particular that there was a lack of funding to support the programmes under review. He also pointed out the counteracting criminogenic effect of the prisons where the programmes Martinson and his colleagues evaluated were being conducted. Gendreau and Ross (1987) also challenged Martinson's original thesis with persuasive evidence that rehabilitation programmes did in fact work to reduce reoffending. Since then, many studies have been undertaken which show the effectiveness of offender rehabilitation. Lipsey (1995) conducted a meta-analysis of 400 treatment programmes and compared treatment groups to untreated (control) groups. The net outcome of this comparison showed a 10% reduction in recidivism noted in the treated groups. Similar findings have been obtained in other studies. Between 1985 and 2000 a total of 18 meta-analytical studies were conducted showing the net effect of rehabilitation to be between 5 and 10% reduction in recidivism (McGuire 2000). Some researchers have undertaken longitudinal studies to determine the long-term effectiveness of offender rehabilitation. Harper and Chitty (2005) assessed the effectiveness of rehabilitation by using reconviction rates and found that while the reconviction rates of offenders in the UK had been over 50% for several years, they began to drop following the introduction of rehabilitation programmes, suggesting that the rehabilitation programmes were working.

Types of Programmes and Interventions

Rehabilitation programmes are fundamentally guided by the 'risk' and 'needs' assessments. The 'risk principle' is an assessment of how likely a person is to reoffend and this principle determines that interventions are targeted according to the level of risk. For example, higher risk offenders receive the greatest level of intervention and lower risk offenders receive the lowest level of intervention (McGuire 1995). The 'need principle' refers to the offender's criminogenic needs which are assessed by the correctional services officer. It allows correctional services officers to target resources where they are most needed and in particular to address 'known predictors of crime and recidivism' (Layton-Mackenzie 2006:59). Criminogenic needs can be dynamic or static. Dynamic criminogenic needs include: antisocial/pro-criminal attitudes; criminal/negative associations; antisocial behaviour; poor intelligence; below average verbal and cognitive skills; poor educational achievement; impulsivity; poor socialisation; risk-taking behaviour; poor self-control; poor problem-solving skills and a lack of vocational skills that affects employability. These are referred to as dynamic needs because they are all areas that can be addressed in rehabilitation programmes. Static criminogenic needs are fixed characteristics such as race, gender and age. These factors can be highly correlated with certain types of offending (e.g. being male) but they cannot be changed through involvement in rehabilitation programmes (Layton-MacKenzie 2006).

Cognitive-behaviour Programmes

Rehabilitation programmes can be provided in prison or in the community. When programmes are provided in the community, offenders also receive supervision by the probation and parole officer. The types of programmes that are offered in corrections depend largely on whether they are provided in prison or in the community. For example, probation, parole, home detention and community service work are only offered in the community. Therapeutic programmes such as sex offender programmes, violent offender programmes, education and anger management can be offered in prison and also in the community. Rather than focusing on where the programmes are offered, of greater importance is how the programmes are run. Meta-analytical studies have shown that whether conducted in the prison or in the community, programmes containing cognitive-behavioural approaches are more likely to reduce recidivism (as measured by reconviction rates) than other methods employed (Burnett and Roberts 2004). In the UK, the prison and probation services have both invested heavily in cognitive-behavioural programmes for this reason. Wherever they are offered, it is important that programmes are guided by the 'what works principles' for correctional programmes.

The What Works Principles

In 1998, the probation service of England and Wales launched the *Effective Practice Initiative*, which utilised the 'what works principles'. The framework used is presented in Figure 6.1. This initiative demonstrated the importance of well-designed programmes in community corrections but additionally highlighted that the 'what works' approach is also concerned with systemic factors. This involves the staff having a sense of mission, purpose and shared responsibility with practice approaches that are guided by a consistent philosophy and informed by research and evaluation. Above all, the focus is 'on changing reasoning and thinking patterns [which] should be matched by a focus on environmental and social factors linked to offending' (Burnett and Roberts 2004:3).

- Practice based on evidence
- The use of design methods
- A commitment to learn and develop effective practices
- Aim for quality and consistency
- A commitment to evaluate programmes
- The use of cognitive and behavioural perspectives in programmes
- Engaging offenders in a change process
- Developing personal and social responsibility in offenders
- Working towards community integration of offenders
- Emphasising the personal impact on staff

◻ **Figure 6.1**   Effective practice principles (adapted from Burnett and Roberts 2004:15)

This suggests that collaboration of relevant institutions, the community and the offender is crucial to successful outcomes in community-based correctional programmes. Layton-MacKenzie (2006) has proposed five principles that should underpin rehabilitation programmes. These principles are: programme integrity; criminogenic needs; skill-oriented, behavioural/cognitive theoretical models; risk; and responsivity. This model has since been simplified to become known as the risk-need-responsivity model (Bonta and Andrews 2007).

The Risk Principle

The risk principle refers to the risk of reoffending. It is recommended that the greatest level of resources be targeted at the highest risk offenders. This principle is contrary to the early offending intervention model (Harris 1997) which has not gained broad acceptance in adult offender programme areas.

The Needs Principle

The needs principle refers to the requirement that programmes target the criminogenic needs of the offender. These are the dynamic factors in the offender's life that are directly related to the offending behaviour.

The Responsivity Principle

The responsivity principle refers to pitching the right intervention to the right level for the offender. It also refers to the ability of the offender to learn from the intervention and therefore the need to tailor the programme to the learning style, motivation, abilities and skills of the offender.

Summary

This section has discussed the literature relevant to the criminological debate regarding the effectiveness of rehabilitation to reduce offending behaviour, including the argument that rehabilitation does not work. The argument that rehabilitation does not work gained some ground in the 1970s and 1980s and continued to influence correctional policy into the 1990s. A flood of empirical studies undertaken during this time, however, showed that in fact the rehabilitation of offenders does work if it is grounded in the principles of the 'what works' approach. Moving forward, the contemporary approach to correctional administration reveals that rehabilitation is a cornerstone of sentence management because it not only deals with punishment but also addresses recidivism.

Restorative Justice

The actions taken by a society to address the harms and losses felt by victims and to meet their need for restitution, while also making the offenders accountable for putting right the consequences of their offending behaviour, is known as restorative justice (Zehr 2002). It is argued by Howard Zehr (2002) that restorative justice is a set of beliefs and principles that promotes respect for all, even those who are enemies. Restorative justice grew out of a belief that the criminal justice system was not sufficiently involving the community or victims in the criminal justice process (Seymour 2001). It is argued that as a result the criminal justice system has become a system of punishment, stigma and shame that is administered by public servants and which is inherently harmful to offenders with little likelihood of reducing the risk of reoffending. Ann Seymour (2001) outlines the principles of restorative justice, which she argues increases the likelihood of reducing offending over the long term by rehabilitating offenders (see Figure 6.2).

The community, schools, police and courts can hold restorative justice programmes such as reparation, victim–offender mediation and family group conferences. The more the family, victim and community are engaged in the restorative justice process, the more successful it is likely to be in reducing future offending behaviour.

Key Criminological Research Debates

Is rehabilitation more successful in community corrections or in prison?
There is ongoing debate within criminology about the most successful way to deal with criminals in society. Some, mainly conservative, theorists and researchers support a hard-line punitive approach which generally involves imprisonment even for low-key offenders. More liberal theorists and researchers advocate for rehabilitation within the community, arguing that prisons create more problems than they solve. For many years, specific criminological research has been undertaken to try to answer the question as to whether the imprisonment of offenders or punishment in the community is more successful in reducing recidivism in criminal offending. A related line of research seeks to show whether rehabilitation programmes implemented in the community actually work better than those that are conducted within prison. A number of studies have shown that programmes conducted in prison are more successful at reducing recidivism (Callan and Gardner 2007) while others suggest that programmes implemented in the community are more successful and that in fact prison may increase recidivism (Howells and Day 1999; Warren 2007). There are yet other studies that show that there is no difference in the recidivism rate for offenders who undertake programmes in prison or those who undertake programmes in the community, with a reduction in recidivism likely to occur with both forms of rehabilitative programmes (MacGregor 2008). There is also another line of thought that enters this debate which is that rehabilitation programmes are a waste of time and money because rehabilitation doesn't work (Martinson 1974). Research has been extensively undertaken to dispute this perspective, with much of it showing that offender rehabilitation does in fact work (Howells and Day 1999).

- Crime is an offence against human relationships;
- Victims and the community are central to justice processes;
- The first priority of justice should be to assist victims;
- The second priority of justice is to, as far as is possible, restore the community;
- The offender has personal responsibility to victims and to the community for the crimes committed;
- The offender will develop improved competency and understanding as a result of the restorative justice process;
- Stakeholders share responsibility for restorative justice;
- Victim needs are more comprehensively served by restorative justice.

Figure 6.2   Principles of restorative justice

Origins of Restorative Justice

The principles and some of the practices of restorative justice have their origins in Canadian, New Zealand and Australian Indigenous culture. The movement towards adopting restorative justice programmes based on the Indigenous principles of community and victim involvement and restitution began as a response to the consistently high proportion of Indigenous peoples in prisons around the world. The first victim–offender reconciliation programme, based on restorative justice principles, was held in Kitchener Ontario in the early 1970s and it commenced in the US in 1974 (Immarigeon and Daly 1997). These programmes were aimed at the First Nations People of Canada and the Native Americans of the US. New Zealand adopted restorative justice practices in the 1980s in order to address the high number of Maori people in in prison in that country. From the mid-1980s to early-1990s Australia, the UK and Scandinavian countries also began to use restorative justice programmes for juvenile offenders (Daly and Immarigeon 1998). As time went on Australia began to develop Indigenous-specific programmes such as circle sentencing (Lawlink 2009) and adult conferencing (Joudo Larsen 2014), in addition to the programmes of family conferencing being used with juveniles,

and has become a leading jurisdiction in the use of restorative justice.

Victim–Offender Mediation

Victim–offender mediation is a restorative justice programme and may be undertaken along with a police warning or caution. Mediation can occur without the victim and offender meeting face to face if either is unable to do that. This is referred to as 'indirect mediation'. Deferred prosecution can also be negotiated as part of the mediation process. This form of mediation is generally limited to the development of a reparation agreement between the victim and the offender. The mediator must be independent and impartial and is therefore usually employed by a private mediation service or a non-government welfare agency. Reparation may take the form of a financial payment; restorative work for the victim; work for a community cause (often selected by the victim); specific undertakings (e.g. to attend a counselling course); or a mixture of these (Marshall 1999:11).

 What positive outcomes do reparation actions offer to victims and offenders that punishment alone can't?

Criminal Justice-focused Approaches

Restorative justice is applied differently by different countries. Most countries adopt a model that focuses attention on the victim and the offender and bringing these two parties together. Other countries focus more on the criminal justice processes and ensuring the offender 'pays their debt to society' but without involving the community (Marshall 1999). These countries generally do not have an Indigenous population and therefore are not motivated or influenced by the cultural principles that have underpinned the programmes in countries such as Canada, America, Australia and New Zealand (see Figure 6.3). Restorative justice approaches that

UK strategy for restorative justice	
The British Home Office (Marshall 1999) has defined the UK government's strategy for restorative justice with juvenile offenders as being:	
Restoration	Offenders apologise to their victims and make amends for the harm they have caused.
Reintegration	Offenders pay their debt to society and re-join the law-abiding community.
Responsibility	Offenders, and their parents, face the consequences for the offending and take responsibility for the cessation of that behaviour.

▣ **Figure 6.3**   UK strategy for restorative justice

involve the victim, offender and the community are most effective in reducing the recidivism of young people, particularly young people from Indigenous backgrounds (van Wormer and Walker 2013).

Family Group Conferences

Restorative justice also includes the holding of family group conferences. These programmes involve the processes of negotiation, mediation, consensus building and peacemaking facilitated by a neutral but well-trained facilitator. Those accused of breaking the law meet with victims and listen as the victim expresses how the crime has impacted on them. The offender also has the opportunity to apologise to the victim and offer an explanation as to why they committed the offence. The people involved in the restorative justice programme may suggest ways in which the offender can make restitution to the victim and/or the community.

Summary

It is clear that in modern society victims of crime have a much greater involvement in the criminal justice processes than in previous points in time (Marsh et al. 2011). This is addressing the concern of victims that they are marginalised in the system and that their expectations are not necessarily met by the sentencing outcomes. By making the offender responsible for remedying the harm caused to victims in addition to punishing the offender, restorative justice seeks to address the offending behaviour. The involvement of community members and elders, especially for

Indigenous offenders, has been shown to be effective in reducing the numbers of Indigenous people in prisons. It also has the effect of increasing the trust that Indigenous communities have in the criminal justice system. Evaluations of restorative justice programmes are showing promising results and it is becoming a more popular approach to criminal justice worldwide.

 What benefits does restorative justice have for the victim, the community and the offender?

The Criminal Justice System Process

Fortunately most people do not commit crimes and are also not very likely to be a victim of an offence. As such, there may be limited public understanding of the process of the criminal justice system. The events that make up the process depend on specific laws that will vary depending on the jurisdiction. What we provide here is a general overview of some of the key events across the criminal justice system process. To supplement this information it is a good idea to look for details on government websites within your own jurisdiction. In order to give you a sense of the breadth of activities that may occur we divide the process into five stages – system entry, pre-trial, trial, sanctioning and post-trial, and note some of the key events that may occur at each of these stages (see Figure 6.4). It is important to

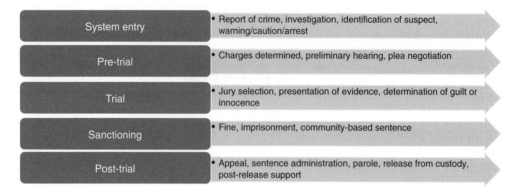

System entry	• Report of crime, investigation, identification of suspect, warning/caution/arrest
Pre-trial	• Charges determined, preliminary hearing, plea negotiation
Trial	• Jury selection, presentation of evidence, determination of guilt or innocence
Sanctioning	• Fine, imprisonment, community-based sentence
Post-trial	• Appeal, sentence administration, parole, release from custody, post-release support

▣ **Figure 6.4**   Stages in the criminal justice system process and example activities

remember that not all crimes will be solved and, even when a suspect is identified, that that person may not be found guilty of the offence they are charged with and may be acquitted. At each stage of the process there is the potential for people to 'drop out' and not continue through the entire process.

One factor that will influence the extent to which an alleged offender proceeds through the various stages of the criminal justice system, what charges they face and what if any punishment they receive if the offence is proven, is the concept of criminal responsibility. Criminal responsibility is defined in law and in many nations involves looking at the intention of the person who committed the act that the law defines as criminal as well as the age and mental capacity of that person at the time the offence was committed. If I hit someone that may be considered assault, but if I was defending myself against an attack from another person, and this can be proven, then it is unlikely that I will be charged with an offence. If I assault someone, but am suffering from a mental impairment at the time and did not know that what I was doing was wrong, the charges against me will likely be different than if I assaulted someone with the intention of causing them harm. Whether I am held criminally responsible will also depend on my age. In some countries, for example New Zealand and Australia, the minimum age of criminal responsibility is set in law but *doli incapax* also applies. Doli incapax is

a presumption that 'a child is incapable of crime', therefore children of certain ages (10–14 in New Zealand and Australia) can only be convicted if it can be proven that they understood their actions were wrong and constituted an offence. See Table 6.2 for an overview of the age of criminal responsibility in a sample of countries.

System Entry

In order for the criminal justice system process to commence a criminal offence needs to have been committed and identified (often by someone reporting the offence to the police). The investigation may or may not identify a person/persons who are suspected of responsibility for committing the offence or there may not be enough evidence to proceed. The police exercise their discretion when determining how to deal with a suspected offender. Depending on the severity of the crime the police may give the offender a warning, a caution or make an arrest. If arrested, the offender may be taken into police custody pending an application for bail.

Pre-trial

During the pre-trial stage the charges against the accused will be determined. The police will usually prepare a brief of evidence which states all the evidence against the accused person and the facts they have determined through their

⬛ Table 6.2 Age of criminal responsibility in selected countries

Country	Age of criminal liability	Legislation
England and Wales	10	Children and Young Persons Act 1933
Scotland	12 (cannot be prosecuted until 12 years of age), cannot be found guilty if under 8, an offence between 8 and 12 may be included in a criminal record	Criminal Procedure (Scotland) Act 1995
Northern Ireland	10	Criminal Justice (Children) (Northern Ireland) Order 1998
New Zealand	10 (although the law also specifies further limits for children aged 10–14)	Crimes Act 1961; Children, Young Persons and Their Families Act 1989
Australia	10 (all jurisdictions)	Each state and territory and the Commonwealth has its own legislation
Canada	12	Youth Criminal Justice Act 2002; Criminal Code 1985
US	Varies by state from a low of 7 in North Carolina to a high of 10 in Wisconsin	33 states set no minimum age, the remaining 17 states and the federal government have their own legislation

investigation. The prosecutors (who may be police prosecutors, specialist state/government lawyers, or in some jurisdictions private lawyers) will review the evidence and determine whether charges will be laid or the case dismissed. The charges that the accused will face will be based on the available evidence and consideration of the interests of the public in pursuing the case. Prosecutors must consider the likely outcome of the case if it goes to trial to ensure a public benefit in the cost of a trial. If, for example, a person is accused of a serious assault and there is sufficient evidence to pursue a charge it will likely be determined that going to court/trial is in the public interest. However, if a young person is suspected of stealing a chocolate bar from a grocery store it may be determined that another course of action is more appropriate. If the charges are serious enough there may also be a preliminary hearing (or in the US, a Grand Jury). During these sessions evidence is heard by a judge (or the Grand Jury) and a decision is made as to whether there is enough evidence to proceed to trial. The prosecution and the defence might also engage in plea

negotiation (also referred to as plea bargaining or plea agreements). Many cases are resolved through these negotiations rather than trials. In a plea negotiation the defendant will agree to plead guilty to one or more charges, usually in exchange for a reduced sentence, dismissal of additional charges or recommendations for leniency in sentencing.

Trial

A trial may be held before a judge (or magistrate) or a judge and a jury depending on the seriousness of the crime. Most trials do not involve a jury. The process of selecting a jury differs between jurisdictions. For example, in the US prospective jurors may be questioned by both the defence and the prosecution lawyers prior to being accepted, or not, to sit on the jury. Questioning may cover the jurors' attitudes and beliefs as well as general information about their occupation or family circumstances. In New South Wales in Australia, potential jurors are given a number; their personal details are not made available for consideration to be on the jury. Juror numbers are called randomly and if your number is called you become part of the jury. Under the adversarial system that operates in the UK, Canada, the US and Australia, the prosecution and the defence will present evidence at trial and examine witnesses. Once all of the evidence has been presented the judge will instruct the jury (if there is one) and the trial will be adjourned pending the decision. The judge (or the jury) will then consider whether the evidence presented established guilt beyond a reasonable doubt or not.

Sanctioning

Sanctioning the offender, by way of a fine, sentence of imprisonment or other order, occurs following a determination of guilt during a trial. There are many rules governing the types of sentences that can be given. In the UK the Sentencing Council prepares sentencing guidelines to help judges and magistrates decide on appropriate sentences. These guidelines help to ensure a sentence is proportionate to the crime committed. Sentencing principles are reflective of the purposes of punishment. The aim is to provide a specific deterrent to the offender so they will not commit future offences, a general deterrent to the public, an opportunity for rehabilitation, protection of the public and retribution.

Post-trial

Once a sentence has been imposed it is generally the responsibility of the department of corrections or corrective services to administer the sentence. This may mean supervising the offender in the community (on probation) or in prison. Often, when someone is given a community-based sentence the judge or magistrate may impose additional requirements, for example non-association orders that mean the offender is not allowed to have contact with specific people while under sentence.

Sectors Within the Criminal Justice System

It is useful to think of the criminal justice system in terms of its function and also the roles that each sector within it has to perform. At the front end of the criminal justice system are the police who respond directly to law breaking by cautioning or arresting the offenders; in the middle of the system are the lawyers and courts which deal with testing the allegations of law breaking, and at the end of the system are the correctional services which carry out the sentences of the courts.

Policing

One of the largest and most important sectors within the criminal justice system is the policing sector. Police are at the front line in terms of interacting with the public and dealing with law breaking. With a focus on community safety and security, police services (through the legitimate use of policing powers) enforce laws, provide support to victims, care for the welfare needs of the community and manage behaviour in public spaces. In order to have legitimacy the police rely not only on their legislative powers but also on what is called policing by consent. This consent comes from the public at large. The police rely on most people being observant of laws and believing that the institution of policing has a right to exist and a right to exercise its power.

 What would happen if most of the population decided to ignore or wilfully disobey the law?

Police Discretion

Police discretion is critical in the execution of powers and responsibilities. Properly applied, this discretion increases the police's legitimacy by making their decisions defensible and contributing to public confidence and trust. The principle behind discretionary power is that street-level police are able to make subjective decisions regarding an offence or offender depending on a particular situation or circumstance. This includes an officer's decision on whether to expend energy and resources on a certain person or situation, whether the offender poses a risk and whether or not an offender would benefit from a diversionary option. Take, for example, the police's role in the reduction of the supply of illicit drugs. When faced with a drug-affected person the police may exercise discretion when determining whether they will warn the person about their drug use, manage their behaviour to reduce potential harm, refer to treatment, issue a caution or make an arrest.

Approaches to Policing

Modern police forces use a range of approaches to prevent and detect crime (see, for example, the discussion of broken windows theory and the zero tolerance approach to crime prevention in Chapter 3). In this section we describe three of the most widely used approaches – community, intelligence-led and problem-oriented policing. Each approach (described further below) incorporates information gathering and problem solving; however, there are key differences in how problems are contextualised and thus in how problems are dealt with. Although these three approaches to policing differ in many ways, they may operate similarly at the point of service delivery. Facing specific problems, police may employ one or all approaches depending on the nature of the situation and the preferred style of the individual officer. Additionally, specific approaches may be adopted within specialist units of policing services; for example, an intelligence-led policing approach may be used by police drug squads in efforts to detect and reduce drug supply.

Community Policing

In modern society, police departments are enormous bureaucracies that are concerned with their own safety and security as well as the safety of the broader community. For this reason,

the structure can be complex and difficult for the general public to understand and filing a report or following up on an ongoing case can be difficult for the ordinary person who does not often come into contact with the police. Due to the bureaucracy of the department, the police can often seem distant and disconnected from the community. Community policing is about police being more accessible to the public and allowing the community to have more say in what the police do and how police services should be delivered to that community (Rogers et al. 2011). The genesis of this approach was identifying that the traditional policing model was not effective. Public trust in police was eroding and the community was becoming disengaged from police (Myhill 2009).

Community policing differs from other models of policing in that it is both a philosophy and an operational strategy. 'Community policing stresses policing *with* and *for* the community rather than policing *of* the community' (Tilley 2003:315, emphasis in the original). One of the potential benefits of this approach is increasing community confidence levels in policing through active engagement; however, it is the engagement process that is the most difficult aspect to fully implement. The desire within police organisations to fully engage with the public has led to the development of police–community partnerships and multi-agency collaborations. Community policing has become a vital approach in crime prevention (Rowe 2014) with intelligence gathered at the community level and responses to crime designed to promote collaboration with the community.

Intelligence-led Policing

Intelligence-led policing focuses on the traditional law enforcement role of police using modern methods and incorporating modern technology. At its heart this approach is about improving the efficiency of police. Tilley (2003) identifies that the core emphases of the model are: a focus on crime control, disruption and enforcement; reducing problems by understanding the ability of criminals to do their business; and using intelligence work to inform the best ways of enforcement. The intelligence-led policing model was first developed in the UK, by the Home Office Audit Commission and was first operationalised by the Chief Constable of the Kent Police Service (Ratcliffe 2016). Under this model police gather information from a number of sources and use the information to apply a targeted approach to crime control. A key strength of intelligence-led policing is its use of technology to identify crime hotspots and find links between incidents. One of the difficulties associated with an intelligence-led policing approach is the limitations that police have in terms of their impact on the overall level of crime in society. Police have minimal influence over many of the structural determinants of crime; however, building partnerships with other agencies can assist police to have greater influence over some of the causal factors of crime (Ratcliffe 2003).

Problem-oriented Policing

Problem-oriented policing holds yet another view of the role of policing. Under this approach the focus is on recurrent problems and finding long-term strategies to resolve them. Analysis of the underlying causes of the problem is essential. For this reason problem-oriented policing requires police to take a proactive approach and to understand crime problems and problematic individuals in local areas. In this approach, identifying the problem accurately is crucial and the tactics employed to disrupt crime depend on how the problem has been defined. This approach involves police, communities and local agencies working in partnership. The typical process of problem identification and analysis is called SARA which involves:

- *Scanning*: identifying problems using local knowledge and data from a range of sources;
- *Analysis*: using data to identify the problems caused;
- *Response*: devising solutions to the problem using situational and social approaches; and
- *Assessment*: looking back to see if the solution worked and what lessons can

be learned (see the Center for Problem-Oriented Policing at www.popcenter.org for more information).

 What benefits for the police and the community could come from these approaches to policing?

Problem-oriented policing (POP) is widely used around the world and provides a framework for police to be able to consider the various causations of crime and the influence of criminogenic factors. The models developed by various police agencies are unique to the jurisdiction but share the underlying principles of the POP framework.

Covert Policing

Covert policing involves investigating particular crimes under a veil of secrecy rather than out in the open. It is a strategy that is used in reactive and proactive investigations and involves gathering information about a particular person, group or activity. Covert police investigations use methods such as static surveillance, active surveillance, use of technology and working undercover (Rogers et al. 2011).

Static and Active Surveillance

Surveillance is the close monitoring and/or observation of a person or group of people accused of, or suspected of engaging in, criminal activity (McKay 2015). The surveillance activities of police are guided and constrained by legislation. The police are not allowed to put just anyone under surveillance, they must have reasonable suspicion that the person or people they want to monitor are engaging in criminal activity. The level of authority the police have in regard to surveillance changes from jurisdiction to jurisdiction depending on the legislation in place. Static surveillance involves watching, photographing and listening from a distance. Active surveillance involves the use of a team of operatives who customise a surveillance

Key Criminological Research Debates

Traffic infringements: Revenue raising or preventing traffic accidents?
One of the main roles of police in modern society is to monitor compliance with traffic laws and to issue infringement notices to drivers who fail to adhere to these laws. This is done by driving police vehicles, both marked and unmarked, within the flow of traffic; sitting stationary beside the road with radar equipment that detects the speed of passing motorists; and responding to incidents and accidents on the roads (McGrath 2011). Police also monitor the safe operation of motor vehicles such as the use of seatbelts, the illegal use of mobile phones and any other behaviour that may distract the driver from safe driving. Research is frequently undertaken by criminologists and government bureaucrats to evaluate the effectiveness of these policing strategies in terms of reducing the death toll on the roads. Research also focuses on whether in fact actions such as talking and texting on mobile phones does in fact contribute to car accidents (e.g. Johal et al. 2005). Research into the distracted brain while driving has increased as mobile phone usage has increased and some of the more recent research has looked at the impact of mobile phone use in comparison to driving under the influence of alcohol (Strayer, Drews and Crouch 2006). While this research is compelling in the amount of evidence to show that drivers are distracted by such activities as talking on the phone or texting, there is an opposing view that traffic infringements are not related to making the roads safer and are in fact just sources of revenue raising for governments and research has been undertaken to look at the impact that such perceptions have on driver behaviour (Watling and Leal 2012). Such research and the evaluation of such debates are important as they continue to provide support for, and critical analysis of, police actions in relation to the general public.

operation to suit the situation. This can require a lot of police resources.

Undercover Police Work
Undercover police work can be very dangerous but it allows police the opportunity to obtain high quality intelligence about the criminal activities of a particular group. The police officers involved must be careful not to be identified as a police officer, but at the same time they must also be careful not to actively initiate the criminal conduct themselves. They can engage in low-level offending, such as smoking marijuana, in order to maintain their cover but cannot engage in serious offending. Gary Marx (1981) argues that such methods of policing may constitute covert facilitation in that the police are ignoring some criminal activity in order to gain intelligence about other activities. He also describes some actions of undercover policing as being entrapment. Marx (1981)

suggests that entrapment is an illegal method of policing that undercover police sometimes engage in. It involves undercover police inciting a member of the public to commit an offence they would not otherwise have committed (see case study).

 Is it ethical for police to break the law, even at a low level, in order to catch someone else breaking the law?

Legal and Ethical Issues
Covert policing is an area of law enforcement that is fraught with legal and ethical issues. For example, should a confession gained when a police officer is working undercover, posing as a member of a drug syndicate, be able to be used in court? When does covert policing become entrapment? Is it ethical for police to form

Case Study

Undercover Police Blasted by Judge for 'Entrapment' After Setting up Sting to Deliberately Sell Stolen Cable to a Scrapyard Boss

In a recent case in the UK, a judge was very critical of undercover police for using entrapment to trick a scrapyard dealer into buying stolen railway cable from them. The scrapyard boss initially refused to buy the cable because he believed it to be stolen. The undercover police went away and returned with stripped-down cable. The scrapyard dealer checked the cable thoroughly with a forensic device and could not find anything amiss and believed the cable not to be stolen and so agreed to buy it. The scrapyard boss and a young employee were then arrested and charged for purchasing the cable that 'could have been stolen'. They underwent two years of anxiety and public shaming while awaiting trial. The judge condemned the police tactics as unscrupulous and accused the covert police of trampling on the human rights of the scrapyard boss and his employee.

Source: Dunn, J. 2015, 15 July. 'Undercover Police Blasted by Judge for "Entrapment" After Setting up Sting to Deliberately Sell Stolen Cable to a Scrapyard Boss' *Daily Mail.* Accessed online on 9 November 2016 at: http://www.dailymail.co.uk/news/article-3160454/Undercover-police-blasted-judge-after-setting-sting-to-deliberately-sell-stolen-cable-scrapyard-boss.html.

romantic relationships with the people they are investigating? In addition to these ethical questions, there is also the negative impact on the individual undercover police officer that must be taken into account. It is apparent that in order to be believable in their undercover role they must develop relationships with the people they are investigating. This can involve friendships and romantic relationships, where sometimes children are also involved (Evans and Lewis 2013). When the investigation is completed these officers are pulled out of their role and are expected to leave this life behind (see case study).

 Should the police be held accountable and take personal responsibility for their actions when engaging in covert investigations?

Case Study

United Kingdom: Undercover Surveillance of Environmental Groups

Throughout the 1980s and 1990s British police infiltrated environmental, social activist and animal rights groups and gathered intelligence on their activities. It is not unusual for police to go undercover to investigate criminal groups but what was unusual about this case is that the police became activists themselves and not only engaged in demonstrations and political activism, they also allegedly incited some of these activities. It is also possible some of them even engaged in serious criminal activities such as arson. What was also unusual about this case is that these officers developed relationships with female members of the groups they infiltrated and at least one even had children with the woman with whom he was involved. When they were 'pulled out' they never had any further contact with the women or the children involved; they just disappeared, and the undercover police relocated to other parts of the UK and even overseas. This case created a huge scandal in the UK when it was made public by the media. The main outrage of the public focused on the moral dilemmas this case threw up and also the huge costs to the taxpayer involved in having police officers undercover for so long when they were spending much of their time drinking alcohol and having sex with their targets. Most of the undercover police officers were married with children at the time they were undercover, which added another dimension to the moral outrage. It became apparent that the police unit involved operated largely independently of the police department and did not follow normal police protocols but questions were asked as to how that could occur.

Source: Evans, R. & Lewis, P. 2013. *Undercover: The True Story of Britain's Secret Police.* London UK: Guardian Books.

Policing and Duty of Care

Police have a duty of care to members of the community and the alleged offenders they take into custody. In this final section on policing we cover two situations that illustrate this duty of care – police custody and motor vehicle pursuits. Police custody is a very important role that police undertake. Depriving someone of their liberty is a serious matter and there are rules that govern this action. Police decision to pursue motor vehicles has ramifications beyond just the capturing of offenders. The safety of the general public, the offenders and the police themselves are put at risk every time this action is taken. There are many other aspects of police duty of care that could be covered but we will focus on these two because of their importance.

Police Custody

As soon as a member of the public is stopped by a police officer, and they are of the belief that they are unable to proceed freely unless the officer tells them they can go, they are legally in the custody of the police and the police have a duty of care to them. This can mean that they have been placed under arrest and are held in police holding cells awaiting interview or processing (formal custody), or it can be that they have simply been stopped for a roadside check such as a random breath test (informal custody). The police have a duty of care to ensure that when they stop someone in a public place, they do so in a safe manner being cognisant of the safety of the public while they are detained. Police custody is the exercising of the ultimate power of police to deprive a person of liberty in certain legally defined circumstances (Williams 2011). Police custody is governed by legislation and by rules of procedural fairness. Persons in custody must be read their rights and must be given access to the basic necessities such as water and toilet facilities. Some, if not all, aspects of police custody may be outsourced to private security agencies or corrective services

Key Criminological Research Debates

Are deaths in police custody racially biased?

Deaths in police custody are a sensitive topic for the police and for politicians but one that raises the emotions of the community very quickly, particularly when Indigenous people are involved. Indigenous people are particularly vulnerable when held in custody and care must be taken to ensure they remain safe. In Australia, an inquiry into Aboriginal deaths in custody was held in the late 1980s and was called the Royal Commission into Aboriginal Deaths in Custody (RCIADIC). This inquiry was in response to the high number of deaths of Aboriginal people held in police and corrective services custody and made several recommendations including that police should avoid arresting Indigenous people where possible and use alternative options to arrest. For example, avoiding arresting Aboriginal people for being drunk and instead taking them to their home or hospital if they are causing a disturbance or have fallen asleep in a public place (RCIADIC 1991). Ten years later, the Australian Institute of Criminology did an evaluation of the progress made and found that the deaths of Aboriginal people in custody decreased from 4.4 per 100,000 in the 1980–1988 decade to 3.8 deaths per 100,000 in the 1990–1999 decade (Williams 2001). In Canada, McAllister et al. (2012) point to the over-representation of Aboriginal Canadians in deaths in police custody figures with 60% of Aboriginal deaths in custody being in police custody. Furthermore, while Aboriginal Canadians make up only about 4% of the population, they represent 18% of the prison admissions and 21% of remandees. There does appear to be a race issue in terms of the numbers of Indigenous people incarcerated and also the high number that are represented in deaths in custody, and research seeks to understand the relationship between deaths in custody and race.

but police will still take charge of interviewing suspects (Skinns 2011). Being in custody is a very distressing time for many people, especially if they have not been involved with the criminal justice system before. They will be fearful and anxious about family members or employment responsibilities. Due to the distressing nature of police custody, extra care is taken to ensure the safety of detainees. Cameras are placed inside and outside the cells and detained people are physically sighted at regular intervals. Items of clothing and accessories such as belts and shoe laces are removed so that they cannot be used for the purpose of self-harming. If a person is under the influence of drugs or alcohol they can be seen by a health professional while in custody.

Motor Vehicle Pursuits

Police also have a duty of care when trying to apprehend offenders during motor vehicle pursuits. The decision as to whether to pursue needs to take into consideration the severity of the offence the person being pursued is suspected of, as well as the risks involved to the offender, the general public and the police themselves when initiating a high-speed motor vehicle pursuit. With advances in technology, much debate exists as to whether in fact there is any need for a pursuit when

Key Criminological Research Debates

Are high-speed police chases worth the risk to the public?
From time to time police can be involved in high-speed chases. This can occur when motorists fail to stop when police officers request them to do so or when they flee a situation where police have detained them, such as for a roadside breath test. High-speed police chases create controversy due to the danger they pose to other road users and to the general public. In the UK there have been 115 deaths resulting from high-speed police chases since 2004 (Casciani 2007). In the US it is claimed that there is a death a day from police chases and since 1979 there have been more than 5,000 deaths of bystanders and passengers due to police pursuits (Frank 2015). The same report claims that minor infractions trigger police chases with 89% being for vehicle code violations such as speeding, reckless driving and motor vehicle theft. Only 5% of pursuits involved chasing an offender wanted for a violent offence. Ironically, police pursuits require that in most cases the police themselves break the same traffic laws they are policing when undertaking such a chase. When the consequences of high-speed police chases are so severe, are police chases worth the risk? Police argue that restrictions on high-speed police pursuits should be lifted if they are to be effective in controlling crime. Steve Ashley (2004) of the Police Policy Studies Council argues for a measure of reasonableness to be applied to police pursuits rather than banning them completely. This would mean that a principle of proportionality would be applied where the amount of force used to apprehend an offender is proportional to the risk posed by the offender. This would include the risk posed to the community. There are moves in many jurisdictions, however, to abandon dangerous high-speed police chases as there is a belief that offenders can be located and apprehended without the need for high-speed chases. Some states in Australia have restricted the circumstances when police can engage in high-speed pursuits and/or the point at which such pursuits should be abandoned (Kerin and Herbert 2010). In the US there are also calls for police pursuits to be banned (Crockett 2015; Frank 2015). The debate regarding high-speed police chases is complex and the subject of much research.

the police can track the offenders from the air and intercept them at a point where is safe to do so.

Criminal Profiling and Forensics

Criminal profiling and crime scene analysis are areas of criminal justice activity that support police investigations and also provide evidence for criminal court cases. Many of these areas have gained attention due to television programmes such as *Crime Scene Investigation*. In reality the work in these areas is not as exciting as portrayed on television and is mostly conducted behind the scenes. It is nevertheless extremely important.

Criminal Profiling

Criminal profiling is an investigative tool that aims to assist police investigators to more accurately predict the likely characteristics and behaviour of particular criminal suspects. According to Holmes and Holmes (2008), there are three major aims of offender profiling which are:

1. to provide police with a social and psychological assessment of the offender;
2. to provide police with a psychological evaluation the offender's possessions (e.g. type of motor vehicle); and
3. to give suggestions and strategies for the interview process.

The main approaches used by police in offender profiling are:

The geographical approach: the crime scene is analysed to identify patterns of time and location as a means of identifying where the offender lives and works.

Investigative psychology: the offender's behaviour and characteristics of the offence are analysed and combined with psychological theories to categorise the offender.

The typological approach: characteristics of the crime scene are analysed and the offender categorised according to 'typical' characteristics displayed.

The clinical approach: psychiatry and clinical psychology are used to determine the existence of mental illness or psychological abnormality (Ainsworth 2001).

Each of these approaches has something unique to offer the investigative process and a profiler will frequently specialise in a particular approach or field of profiling and, with time and experience, will become known as an expert in that field.

Crime Scene Processing and Analysis

The crime scene is processed by the police and also by an array of various subsections within the criminal justice system. These sectors are predominantly scientific in nature. Their job is to analyse the scene of the crime and process the evidence. This means that the evidence is identified in situ with a marker and is photographed in situ before being placed in an evidence bag by a crime scene analyst who is wearing gloves. The personnel who are involved in analysing the crime scene must be sure that they do not contaminate the evidence. Table 6.3 shows the types of evidence that are collected from a crime scene.

■ **Table 6.3** Types of evidence collected from a crime scene (Reno et al. 2000)

Biological	blood, semen, hair, vomit, etc.
Latent prints	fingers, feet and palms
Impressions	motor vehicles and shoe treads
Electronic evidence	Computers, phones, GPS
Trace evidence	Fibres, soil, vegetation, etc.
Documentary evidence	Financial statements, letters
Chemical evidence	Drugs, flammable liquids, bomb-making chemicals
Weapons and tools	Guns, knives, house-breaking tools
Any other evidence deemed relevant to the case	Cars, carpet, furniture, photographs, films, clothing, etc.

The evidence must not be touched by anyone and so gloves and special tools are used to retrieve and capture the evidence which is placed into sealed bags and containers and is marked so as to clearly identify the case, the day and the time of collection and the person responsible for the collection.

Forensic Services

Forensic services refers to the services responsible for the gathering, preservation and analysis of crime scene evidence according to scientific principles. Forensic services are predominantly scientifically based services that may sit within the police department or may belong to an external organisation such as a private laboratory (Coleman 2013).

Rules of Evidence

The rules of evidence are necessary for ensuring justice for the offender in the criminal justice system. It is related to the offender's right to a fair trial. These principles are usually entrenched in law and determine what evidence can and cannot be introduced to a criminal court. They also establish rules for the handling of evidence before and during the trial. The 'chain of evidence' is an extremely important concept within the rules of evidence which are the legal principles that govern how evidence is handled.

> ❯ Why is it important to have rules in place as to how evidence should be collected, preserved and analysed?

In the UK the rules of evidence are contained within the *Police and Criminal Evidence Act 1984*. In Australia they are contained within the *Evidence Act 1995*. In New Zealand these principles are included within the *Evidence Act 2006* and in Canada within the *Evidence Act 1985*. Each of these legislations will have some differences but they all include principles and guidelines for the collection, preservation, processing and admissibility of evidence.

The Legal System

The legal system operating in English-speaking countries with criminal justice systems based on the British system is an adversarial system. Under an adversarial system the principal contest is between the accused and the state. The court processes and rules focus on ensuring the rights of the accused are protected so that the facts of the case can be determined. The process is not about finding the truth necessarily but is instead about presenting sufficient evidence to establish guilt, or if sufficient evidence beyond a reasonable doubt is not presented, then setting the accused free. Other legal systems, such as the inquisitorial system used in France, are more focused on establishing truth and are considered by some to be more neutral.

Lawyers

The criminal justice system includes lawyers that operate both for the prosecution and for the defence which may seem counter-intuitive given that these are opposing sides. The system is governed by rules, regulations and ethics that ensure that each part of the legal framework works in harmony together but operates independently of each other. An accused person is considered innocent until they are proven guilty in a court of law and it is the right of every accused person to have access to legal representation when they are required to defend charges in court. It is also the right of victims to be able to bring an accused person before a trial and to seek justice for the harm caused to them. This is known as the prosecution and it is the government that represents the victim in the prosecution. Each side will have a variety of legal personnel available to them such as barristers, Queen's Counsel, solicitors, researchers and legal assistants.

Public Prosecutions

The agency responsible for the prosecution role in Western societies goes by many different names such as the Crown Prosecution Service

(UK), Department for Public Prosecutions (Australia), Crown Attorney Office (Canada), Crown Solicitors (New Zealand) and District Attorneys (US). The function of the prosecution office is to collate evidence from the police investigation that suggests the guilt of the accused, and to present this evidence in court. The prosecutors are qualified lawyers who are paid by the public service to fulfil this role but they act independently of any government. In some jurisdictions private prosecutions can also occur. In these circumstances the prosecutor does not represent the state.

Defence

Defence lawyers are privately employed and have the role of defending the accused person against the charges. Defence lawyers are entitled to have access to all the evidence that the prosecution depends on to build their case against the accused person. This again goes back to the principle that the offender has the right to a fair trial. They have the right to defend themselves against the charges in court and they have the right to explain or refute any evidence presented by the prosecution.

Legal Aid

Legal aid is provided for people who are unable to afford a private defence lawyer. This again goes to the principle that every person is entitled to have a fair trial but it is a principle in its own right: that every person is entitled to have legal representation in court. It has recently been reported by Barrett (2014) that Britain has the largest legal aid budget in Europe as it currently spends £2 billion a year on legal aid. The average expenditure across Europe is estimated to be around £97 million. While some people are concerned about this expenditure, this commitment of resources is an indication of Britain's determination to ensure procedural fairness for all people who find themselves having to go to court to answer criminal charges. As most people do not have legal training they rely on lawyers to do this on their behalf; however, lawyers are very costly and many people cannot afford to hire one.

 Why is it important to have legal aid available to poor people who are accused of committing a crime?

Legal aid is a programme that allows people to access a lawyer who is either paid a minimal salary by the government or who provides their services for free (referred to as 'pro bono' in the US). This means that everyone can access a lawyer to assist them in defending themselves in court even if they cannot afford it.

Criminal Courts and Civil Tribunals

The courts are the institutions within the criminal justice system that administer justice and can be either criminal or civil. The hearing of trials (known as cases) are held in the court. In major urban centres, several court cases can be heard at the same time because there are usually several courtrooms available. During a trial, the prosecutors will put forward the evidence to argue for the guilt of the accused person and defence lawyers will present evidence to refute the accusations raised. In Western countries such as the UK, Canada, Australia and the US, the accused person is considered innocent until they are proven guilty in a court of law; however, court processes may differ between jurisdictions. The decisions of the court do not just impact on the case being heard but can also be used as a guide for how other courts might interpret the law and influence future court decisions through a process called precedence.

Plea Negotiation (Plea Bargaining/Plea Agreement)

The accused person (the defendant) must decide, in consultation with their legal representative, whether they will plead guilty or not guilty when they reach court. A decision to plead guilty may be a decision based on the actual guilt of the person and the amount of evidence against them. It can also be a strategic legal decision to plead guilty to a lesser charge in exchange for a lighter sentence in cases where the legal team believe it is unlikely the person will be found not guilty even when they are in fact not guilty (Marsh 2004). Before a plea is taken, plea negotiation may take place between the defence and the prosecution. Plea bargains save the court's time and money, but as it is a process that involves downgrading charges in exchange for a guilty plea it is often criticised for resulting in lighter sentences that do not reflect the gravity of the offences committed (see case study).

Appeals Court

In addition to a hierarchy of courts, each jurisdiction also has an appeals court in which a person who has been found guilty can appeal aspects of the verdict or the sentence. They will first appeal to the next highest court in the hierarchy which will hold an appeals court. In the UK there is an appeals court that is the second highest court in the country, the first being The House of Lords (Marsh 2004). Appeals courts do not hear new evidence but they can order a new trial. The appeals court will consider technical aspects of the case and reach a decision based on the transcripts and documents from the case rather than hearing witnesses.

Tribunals

Tribunals originate from the Romans who had tribunes whose job it was to mediate disputes. Tribunals are not courts, but have similar statutory authority to hear cases and make a decision on the outcome. They usually hear cases relating to questions about the administrative governance and the decisions of government entities and minor civil matters. They are set up according to specific areas of law. Tribunals allow swift hearing of these cases, are less costly and relieve pressure on the courts (Australian Law Reform Commission 2004). Judges sitting on tribunals usually wear normal dress rather than legal regalia. Tribunals can be administrative or civil but they do not consider criminal matters.

 What benefits do tribunals offer to ordinary people and especially those from lower socio-economic areas?

The Judiciary

The people who make the formal decisions in court are referred to as the judiciary and carry titles of judge, justice and magistrate. They have a law background and preside over the hearing of cases where people are accused of a crime and evidence to support their guilt or innocence is presented and argued. The judiciary direct the jury prior to them retiring to consider their verdict and they also have the statutory responsibility for making decisions about the sentence the convicted offender will receive.

Court Administration

The court administration is managed by the Registrar of the Court. This section is responsible for providing administrative support to the judiciary and to the courts and

---

Case Study

United States: 'Federal Guilty Pleas Soar as [Plea] Bargains Trump Trials'

The Wall Street Journal reported on 23 September 2012 that a man by the name of Kenneth Kassab was about to plead guilty to a charge of illegally transporting explosives even though he did not commit the crime. He was going to plead guilty in order to avoid risking being found guilty and having to serve a lengthy prison sentence. His decision to plead not guilty at the last minute was based on not wanting to tell a lie before God. He was acquitted by a federal jury a week later. The authors went on to describe a system in the US where 97% of federal cases were resolved by plea bargaining.

Source: Fields, G. & Emshwiller, J. R. 2012, 23 September. 'Federal Guilty Pleas Soar as Bargaining Trump Trials' *The Wall Street Journal*. Accessed online on 9 November 2016 at: http://www.wsj.com/articles/SB10000872396390443589304577637610097206808.

ensuring the smooth running of the courts. Any correspondence that is required to go to lawyers, offenders or witnesses is sent by the court administration. Correspondence to notify people they are required for jury service is also sent out by the court administration.

Witnesses

Witnesses may be called to give evidence in court and they will usually stand or sit in the witness box to give their evidence. Some courts will provide support for witnesses, especially if they are also victims. Expenses incurred due to giving evidence in court may be claimed back from court administration. Most employers will maintain salary while a person is required to be a witness. Child witnesses and witnesses who have to be protected can give evidence via a video link to the court. A witness protection programme exists in most jurisdictions but is rarely used. When it is used, witnesses are provided with a new identity and given assistance to 'disappear' in order to keep them safe.

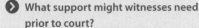

> What support might witnesses need prior to court?

The Jury

The jury is made up of 12 people who should be representative of the community in which the offence occurred. The impartiality of the jury is established prior to the commencement of the trial. They will listen to the evidence presented by the prosecution and the defence and will then be addressed by the judge before being required to reach a verdict of guilty or not guilty. The decision of the jury is accepted by the court and the judge is unable to interfere in that decision (Marsh 2004). Sometimes, especially when a case is complex or has a great deal of technical information to consider, the case will be heard by a judge alone and a jury will not be used. The defendant is allowed to make this decision in consultation with their legal representative.

Sentencing

Once the verdict regarding guilt is handed down by the judge or jury, the judge will issue a decision on sentencing. This can be done at the time or at a later date. The sentence is generally guided by legislation; however, the judge usually has a degree of discretion that allows them to choose a particular sentence option and a sentence period that falls between stated maximum and minimum limits within the legislation. The judge can also rule on points of law throughout the trial and, if the sentence is to include a period of imprisonment, the judge will set a non-parole period on the sentence. This is the period of time the offender must serve before he or she is eligible to apply for parole.

Court Security

All courts will have cells where they hold people who are awaiting trial. These cells must be supervised. This is sometimes done by a separate unit within the courts or can be outsourced to a private company. This section will also be responsible for providing security to the court and for escorting the accused person to and from the cells. Security is important in the court as emotions often run high and some cases can attract the attention of dangerous people.

Correctional Services

Correctional services is the sector within the criminal justice system that contains people who are accused of crimes and are awaiting trial, and also supervises sentenced offenders. Most people will be aware of the custodial areas of correctional services which include remand centres and prisons. There are also community-based services provided to offenders through correctional services.

History of Correctional Services

The earliest forms of corrections in most Western countries were prisons, and in countries such as Australia, Canada and the US these were combined with the punishment of transportation. Transportation was in use in Europe in the seventeenth century and possibly even earlier, and was used by many countries such as France, the Netherlands, Portugal, Italy and Denmark as a means of containing their prisoners (Welch 2004). When sentenced to transportation, the prisoners were sent to outlying settlements or islands away from the mainstream society to serve out their term of imprisonment. In the seventeenth century, transportation also involved poor people and criminals from Europe being sold to the captains of sailing ships which were bound for the colonies. These people were then sold on to landowners in America and Australia to become indentured servants (Stohr and Walsh 2012). These people were often used in agricultural roles in the new colonies.

> ▶ Was transportation proportional to the crime (as advocated by Beccaria) when many of these people have been charged with vagrancy or stealing food such as a loaf of bread?

Britain used transportation to the Australian colonies as a means to control and manage its orphans, poor and criminals and to help it to populate and build the new settlements (Clark 1993). Some of the colonies built at this time were renowned for their brutality and harsh conditions (see case study).

The modern prison system in Britain and its settlements arose from these early beginnings. As the prison system developed and a more humane approach to prisons was introduced, governments saw the need to build more appropriate accommodation and to introduce reforms in the way in which prisoners were managed. Modern prisons are expensive and predominantly funded by the government; however there has been some movement towards privatisation in some jurisdictions in an effort to reduce the costs to government.

Privatisation

It is true that most correctional services are provided by the government, but rising costs have seen the need for the privatisation of some corrective services such as prisons and electronic monitoring. The US has a high level of prison privatisation with around 8% of inmates being held in private prisons and this rises to 16% of inmates in federal prisons (Stohr and Walsh 2012). In the UK many prisons were privatised in

Case Study

Australia: Norfolk Island Penal Colony

A well-known Australian penal colony existed on Norfolk Island which is 1,609 kilometres (1,000 miles) off the coast of New South Wales. It was established in 1788 and the entire island was used as a prison. It received prisoners from England and Australia and was regarded as a brutal and cruel place. Prisoners were often poorly fed and clothed and the accommodation was basic, cold and austere. The treatment of prisoners was harsh and they were used as labour to construct the buildings the settlement needed to house the soldiers and island administrators. Alexander Maconochie is a historical figure in Australia who requested a placement to Norfolk Island (usually considered the worst place to be sent) in order to try out his ideas of prison reform. He was successful in changing the culture and practices of the convict settlement on Norfolk Island from the most brutal, chaotic and violent place in Australia to a penal colony that was organised, humane and productive. Maconochie believed that prisoners should be treated humanely and with respect and should be rewarded for good behaviour by a system of marks that were linked to privileges. On their release, the prisoners were called 'Maconochie's Gentleman' because of the way in which they behaved.

Source: Morris, N. 2002. *Maconochie's Gentleman: The Story of Norfolk Island and the Roots of Modern Prison Reform*. Oxford UK: Oxford University Press.

order to keep pace with the rapidly rising prison population. It was deemed to be the most cost-effective solution at the time (Prison Reform Trust 2016). Australia has also privatised some of its prisons and parts of correctional services such as prisoner transport (Harding 1998). Privatisation was seen as a cost-effective option by many jurisdictions but this has not always been the case. Regardless of the cost however, the convenience and the reduced bureaucracy, especially when building new prisons, has resulted in the continuation of privatisation in the US and elsewhere (Stohr and Walsh 2012).

> ❯ Is cost the only, or even the most important, consideration when contemplating the privatisation of prisons?

Community-based Corrections

The majority of sentences are served in the community in a sector of corrective services known as community-based corrections. The programmes offered by community-based corrections are alternatives to imprisonment and give the courts flexibility in sentencing. Community-based corrections involves government officials, predominantly probation and parole officers, supervising offenders in the community. Prisons are costly and there is a growing view that they should be reserved for very dangerous offenders and that it is counterproductive to place low-level and less dangerous offenders with hardened criminals because prison itself has a criminogenic effect (Stevenson 2011). Meanwhile community-based corrections is much more economical and provides better opportunities for rehabilitation. Most offenders coming through the criminal justice system will end up with a community-based order rather than a sentence of imprisonment. In New Zealand, for example, over 30,000 offenders are serving community-based sentences at any point in time compared to 9,000 offenders serving

terms of imprisonment (NZ Department of Corrections 2016) and the majority of these offenders are on probation.

Sections Within Community-based Corrections

Community-based corrections are made up of a range of service areas that differ in the level of surveillance and control the organisation has over the offender. The service areas include:

Probation: supervision of an offender in the community with or without conditions; this includes bail supervision;

Parole: supervision in the community of a released prisoner;

Home detention: supervision of an offender restricted to a specific location in the community, with or without permission to work and curfew arrangements;

Community service work: supervised work in the community, usually undertaken with gangs of workers;

Therapeutic programmes: the offender is required to participate in rehabilitation programmes in the community as a condition of their probation or parole.

The largest of these services is the probation and parole service. The community-based orders covering bail, probation and parole are very similar but have different starting points.

Bail

Bail is given to people accused of an offence but who have not been found guilty in a court. They can be remanded in custody or given bail. Bail is a supervision order and allows the accused person to continue living in the community which means they can continue with their employment, study or family responsibilities while they are awaiting trial. The bail order means that they are to be supervised by the probation area of community-based corrections. The conditions of their bail may include where they reside, a curfew to stipulate when they must be at home and places and people they are to avoid. If they reoffend while on bail they may be breached and placed on remand in custody. Police can issue bail or it can be issued by the court (UK Crown Prosecution Service 2016).

Parole

At a predetermined point in a prison sentence, inmates may become eligible to apply for **parole** which allows them to be released from prison to be supervised in the community (UK Parole Board 2016). Both probation and parole orders require the offender to be supervised in the community and may apply conditions such as not using alcohol or drugs, not associating with certain people, having to reside at a particular place and/or applying a curfew. Offenders may also have to attend therapeutic programmes, counselling or drug and alcohol rehabilitation. Sometimes they will also be required to wear an electronic monitoring device on their ankle.

While on parole, a person is referred to as a 'parolee' and is supervised by a 'parole officer'. A failure to comply with the conditions of a parole order may result in the parolee being sent back to prison to serve the remainder of their sentence of imprisonment behind bars. The parole officer has some discretion in regard to establishing whether the behaviour constitutes a breach of the order or not.

Probation

Probation orders are given to offenders to prevent them from having to go to prison whereas parole orders allow inmates to be released before their sentence finishes. Probation orders are similar to parole orders but exist on their own and are not related to release from prison. They combine punishment with rehabilitation. The punishment involved in a probation order is having freedoms curtailed rather than completely deprived, as with imprisonment, and this is achieved by being under the surveillance of a probation and parole officer and having to report regularly to this officer. The offender will also have conditions placed on them by the court that they must comply with. The rehabilitation aspect of probation is expected to occur as a result of the continued supervision

with a qualified probation officer and exposure to positive role modelling (Stohr and Walsh 2012). In addition, involvement in counselling and programmes provides offenders with an opportunity and the support to change their behaviour.

Community Service Work

Community service work orders are orders that require offenders to undertake a specific number of hours of work in the community. They have the dual objectives of **restitution** to the community and **public shaming**. In New Zealand offenders can be required to do between 20 and 200 hours of community work by the court (NZ Ministry of Justice 2016a) and this is a fairly standard range to be found in Western countries. In Germany and the Netherlands, the focus is on rehabilitation and alternatives to imprisonment are preferred by the courts (Subramanian and Shames 2013). In Germany in particular, community service work is used as an alternative to incarceration for fine defaulters (Dünkel and Snacken 2000). This reduces the risk that these low-level offenders will be exposed to more serious offenders and gives them the opportunity to 'pay back' to the community without having to actually pay money. Community work gangs are made up of offenders who have been given community work orders by the court and are supervised by one or more community corrections officers. The restitution objective is fulfilled by the offenders providing their labour to meet community needs. Some examples of community service work are: restoring and maintaining national parks, maintaining the grounds of public buildings, and establishing and maintaining community parks and playgrounds. Care is taken to ensure the offenders chosen for community service work are not a danger to the community (i.e. sex offenders will not be placed on a work gang that is maintaining playground or school areas).

Home Detention

Home detention is another community-based initiative that is an alternative to imprisonment. The offender is sentenced to imprisonment, but if the offence isn't too serious the court can order that this sentence be served at a particular address. This is usually their own address or the address of a relative. One reason why the court may order home detention is so that the offender can maintain their employment. In this case, the order will include particular times that the offender is expected to be at that address and the offender will generally wear an electronic ankle tag so that compliance with these conditions can be monitored by the community corrections officer. Sometimes home detention is provided as a transition to release for inmates who are coming to the end of their sentence. On home detention they can engage in some restricted activities under the supervision of community corrections officers (Henderson 2006). Home detention is a more restrictive community-based supervision programme than parole but is not as restrictive as prison.

Prisons

Prisons are sometimes referred to as the penal system and the study of prisons is sometimes referred to as penology. The scope of penology has been expanded beyond prisons to also include parole supervision, which is the supervision of offenders who have been released from prison into the community. Some form of incarceration in buildings resembling prisons has been used for centuries by law enforcement authorities around the world. Despite this option being available there was a preference up to as late as the eighteenth century in some cases for barbaric forms of punishment such as beheading, flogging, use of the wheel and rack, burning at the stake, and numerous other methods of torture which were often undertaken publicly for the entertainment of the masses (Marsh 2004). Bentham (1789/1982) attempted to reinvent the prison system in the 1790s by introducing a radical new prison design he called the 'panopticon' (see *Classicism* (Chapter 3) for more information about Jeremy Bentham). He tried to convince the government authorities that more humane approaches to punishment were needed and that prison could be a more humane option. He argued that the architectural design of the panopticon provided increased security with fewer guards needed to monitor and control prisoners. This was because it was based on a circular building design arranged around a central point at which every cell could be visible, providing prison guards with continuous surveillance of inmates. He also highlighted the need to keep inmates gainfully occupied while incarcerated and introduced the concept of paid employment of prisoners as a method of behavioural control. Bentham is acclaimed as introducing the concept of the modern prison that is still widely used today.

> Why is employment in prison important for offenders and for the security of the prison?

We cannot engage in an academic discussion about prisons without referring once again to the work of Michel Foucault who has written extensively on the relationship between power and social control, particularly in relation to prisons. In particular Foucault (1975) discusses the social control role that institutions such as prisons, hospitals and schools have in society and how each of these organisations operate similarly by strictly controlling the activities, time and space of the individuals within them. He points out that the modern prison had its origins in the sixteenth-century model of the Rasphuis of Amsterdam which was originally built as a workhouse to contain beggars and young troublemakers. It had the objective of educating inmates to become well-behaved citizens through the process of hard work. It wasn't long before work in prisons became obligatory and was driven more by economic imperatives than by reformation of the individual.

> In what ways can prison employment be corrupted and inmates exploited?

By the eighteenth century, American models of prison (known as the penitentiary) found their way to England with the building of one single penitentiary in Gloucester, England. A model of prison reform known as the Philadelphia Model became influential at this time and a well-known institution called Walnut Street Prison was established in 1773. These models of incarceration were greatly influenced by the Quakers who believed in an austere environment to provoke reflection and repentance as the means to address criminal behaviour (Foucault 1975). They were therefore harsh environments with no comforts and no formal rehabilitation of inmates.

 Is an austere environment conducive to rehabilitation?

The modern prison systems hold the welfare and rehabilitation of prisoners to be important goals of incarceration and are designed accordingly. Although single cells are the ideal, most prisons still house several prisoners to one cell due to economic imperatives. When this occurs it is referred to by prison officials as prisoners being doubled up. This is not ideal but is a pragmatic response to a sudden increase in the prison population.

Prison Security Ratings and Remand

Prisons are usually organised according to the classification of the prisoner which is determined by a) the type of offence they have committed; b) their behaviour; c) their history; and d) their needs (Department of Justice 2016). Some prisons are built just to hold people who are on remand. These inmates are referred to as 'detainees' or 'remandees' rather than prisoners because they are yet to be found guilty in court. Remand inmates must not be placed with sentenced inmates. In Canada and Australia facilities that hold people awaiting trial are called remand centres but some prisons also hold remand inmates in a separate section. In the UK and New Zealand all adults on remand are held in a separate section of a prison. In the US, remand facilities are referred to as jails and facilities that hold sentenced inmates are called prisons and people on remand are

not held in prisons (Stohr and Walsh 2012). Remand facilities are generally classified as high security because the inmate's behaviour and temperament are unknown and must be assessed. Once they have been sentenced by a court to a term of imprisonment, an inmate is sent to a prison. Maximum security prisons house the most dangerous inmates while low security prisons and pre-release centres tend to house inmates who are at the end of their sentence and who are awaiting release into the community. It is important that prison inmates are kept occupied as too much unstructured time can lead to unrest and to inmates engaging in illegal activity such as making shivs (home-made knives) and contraband (such as home-made alcohol). *See The Role of Punishment.*

 What are the benefits of ensuring that prisoners have a constructive day? What are the risks involved in large groups of prisoners becoming bored?

Prisoner Health Services

The World Health Organization stipulates that prisoners should receive health care that is equivalent to that in the community (World Health Organization 2007b). This means that prisoners should receive preventative health care as well as timely access to diagnostic services, treatment and rehabilitation. Prison health services can be provided by the government or can be privately run with the government providing the facilities within the prison from which the private company can operate. In Australia, prisoner health services are provided by state and territory governments (AIHW 2014) and in New Zealand these services are provided by the Department of Corrections (Wakem and McGee 2012). In the UK there is a *National Partnership Agreement for the Co-Commissioning and Delivery of Healthcare Services in Prisons in England* which came into effect in April 2013 (NHS England 2013). This is a partnership arrangement between the National Health Service (NHS), the National Offender Management Service (NOMS) and

Public Health England (PHE) for the provision of health services in prisons.

Special Populations in the Prison

There are specific groups within the prison that require special attention and management either due to their vulnerability or due to the security risk they pose. Vulnerable groups include young offenders, transgender inmates, elderly and infirm inmates, disabled inmates and inmates who have a background in the criminal justice system (i.e. police, prison officers, judges, lawyers, etc.). People who have a background in the criminal justice system will usually be housed in protective custody which involves them being kept in a protection wing away from the mainstream population (Barnes 2001). This is because they may be targets of assault and/or murder by other inmates due to their previous employment. Other groups held in protection include paedophiles and criminals who have given evidence against other criminals. Sometimes inmates are so high risk, due to their crimes or potential to escape, that special protection is needed (see case study).

Prison Employment and Education

It is exceptionally important that inmates have access to employment and education while they are imprisoned. Unemployment and incomplete education are criminogenic, which means that they are linked to offending. Addressing low skills and a lack of qualifications, numeracy and literacy are things that will directly improve the chances of rehabilitation. Prison employment and education also have benefits in regard to maintaining the good order of the prison.

Prisoners who are constructively occupied are less likely to engage in unlawful behaviour inside the prison. Prisoners get paid for the work they do, as well as having the opportunity to gain qualifications that will make them more employable when they are released. Being paid for the work on the inside allows prisoners to purchase limited items they need and want from the prison shop in a process known as 'buy-ups' (Williams et al. 2009). In addition to providing significant benefits to the inmates, prison employment also provides benefits to the organisation. With inmates doing the laundry, cooking and cleaning, the prison does not need to employ external people to undertake these jobs. Prison industries provide employment in areas such as textiles, printing, furniture manufacturing and agriculture, all of which provide goods and services back to the prison. In some areas prisoners are even building affordable housing to sell on and transportable cells to assist with the overcrowding problems experienced from time to time (NSW Corrective Services 2016). The organisation offsets the costs of housing prisoners and prisoners themselves gain qualifications and skills in these areas that help

---

Case Study

Australia: Long Bay Correctional Complex's Special Protection Unit

In an article in the *Daily Telegraph* on 3 August 2014, James Phelps reports on a story about six of the most serious offenders in New South Wales's criminal history (serious sadistic sex offenders/murderers and child killers), being held in a Special Protection Unit at Long Bay Correctional Complex. This is necessary because they are considered to be too high risk for normal protection. Their crimes are so heinous that these offenders have been marked for death within the prison. There is also an accusation that prison guards at the Complex had meted out jailhouse justice to some of the six inmates. The special protection unit is segregated from the mainstream prison population and from normal protection too. The security of this unit is exceptionally high.

Source: Phelps, J. 2014, 3 August. 'Protecting Society's Scum: Inside Long Bay Jail Special Protection Unit and the Criminals it had to Save from Other Inmates.' *Daily Telegraph*. Accessed online on 9 November 2016 at: www.dailytelegraph.com.au/news/nsw/protecting-societys-scum-inside-long-bay-jail-special-protection-unit-and-the-criminals-it-had-to-save-from-other-inmates/news-story/3680db9aa7fc17b4ad337cb4677a0f9b

them to find employment when they are released and to become contributing members of society.

 What are the benefits to the inmates and to society of the inmates contributing to the cost of their incarceration in this way?

Prison Programmes

Prison programmes include a range of therapeutic and psychosocial interventions and activities. Prison education is usually included in the basket of 'prison programmes' and is possibly the largest of the programmes run in the prison. In addition to education, therapeutic programmes are attached to the psychology unit and include programmes such as: sex offender treatment, anger management, violent offender treatment, domestic violence treatment, cognitive skills and a range of counselling, and crime-specific programmes (Heseltine et al. 2011). Some programmes have crossovers with the health services section of the prison, such as the substance abuse treatment programmes. Prison-based social work services provide an interface between the inmates and the outside world and assist them in maintaining contact with their family and establishing such things as housing and employment in preparation for release.

Pre-release

Preparation for release is sometimes referred to as 'pre-release', 'reintegration' or 're-entry' preparation. Some institutions will have a specific facility or section of a prison devoted to pre-release preparation. These areas combine a lower level of security with limited and controlled access to the wider community to give long-term inmates an opportunity to experience life outside while still having the support of the institution. The freedom provided to the inmate is curtailed if they breach the trust given to them. It is an opportunity for them to develop internal control and to need external control less in order to do the right thing. *See* **Rational Choice Theory** (Chapter 3).

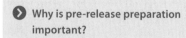 **Why is pre-release preparation important?**

The Parole Board

The parole system is administered by the Parole Board which is an independent statutory body. Even though parole boards are independent, they still come under the auspices of a government entity. In the UK the Parole Board comes under the auspices of the Ministry of Justice. In the US there is a Parole Commission that oversees parole boards and this comes under the auspices of the Department of Justice. In Australia each state has its own Parole Board which is usually attached to the State or Territory Department of Justice. Canada has a National Parole Board for federal prisoners under the auspices of Public Safety Canada but each province has its own parole board for offenders serving sentences of less than two years. New Zealand also has a national Parole Board. Regardless of the jurisdiction, the appropriate parole board determines whether a particular offender can be safely released into the community (UK Parole Board 2016). Parole is considered to be a privilege that is earned by the good behaviour of the prisoner and not a right. At the time of sentencing the court will set down a minimum term of incarceration before parole can be considered. An independent body such as a Parole Board will consider each case on its own merits, including the views of victims, when making its decision to grant or withhold parole.

Juvenile Justice

Young offenders, also referred to as juvenile offenders, are usually dealt with differently to adults and are processed by specially established sections within the criminal justice system, including having separate legislation and special youth/children's courts. Some jurisdictions have parts of the juvenile justice system, such as community supervision and detention, administered under the child welfare system.

Juveniles will come into the system in the same way as adults, via contact with the police, but they must have an adult present when they are interviewed. In most jurisdictions a juvenile criminal record will be sealed unless reoffending occurs in adulthood at which point the record will remain unsealed forever. Just as children and teens are dealt with in a separate system, juvenile matters are dealt with in a separate court to adult matters.

The Children's Court

The Children's Court (or Youth Court) is a separate court that is less formal than the adult court and deals with children between the ages of 10 and 17 for criminal matters and children under 18 for care and protection matters. There are no juries in the Children's Court and the magistrates/judges will often dispense with wearing legal regalia in order to make children feel more comfortable. The Children's Court deals with criminal matters, adoption, surrogacy, apprehended violence orders involving children, care and protection matters, and school attendance matters. All Children's Court matters are closed to the public. Sometimes a case will be transferred to the adult system if the criminal matter is of a serious nature. The Children's Court has a different benchmark to the adult court when deciding child protection matters. The adult court determines matters based on the standard of proof of 'beyond reasonable doubt', whereas when the Children's Court determines child protection matters the standard of proof is on the 'balance of probability' (NSW Department of Justice 2015). In both child protection and criminal matters the best interests of the child are paramount unless what is best for the child clashes with community safety and then the court will seek to do the least amount of harm to the child/teen by the decision made. The need to balance the welfare orientation of juvenile justice with the community safety goals of the criminal justice system more generally create many dilemmas for policy makers and practitioners working in and for the juvenile justice system.

 Are the best interests of the child, or the need for community safety, being given precedence when the decision is made to try a young offender as an adult?

Community Youth Supervision

When given community-based orders by the Youth/Children's Court, such as probation and community service work orders, young offenders are supervised by youth justice workers rather than probation and parole officers. The focus is on redirecting the child/teen from a criminal lifestyle. There is an underlying assumption that children and teens will sometimes pass through a phase of offending due to their immaturity and lack of impulse control and that they will most often pass through this phase without developing a lifetime criminal career (Barry 2010). The main focus of intervention with children and teens is therefore to seek to operate within the best interests of the child or teen and to seek to protect the welfare of the child/teen. These aspects are balanced with the need to protect the community and reduce recidivism. Community service work is frequently used as a sentence option for young offenders.

Juvenile Detention

In the adult system there are prisons and jails but in the juvenile justice system there are detention centres. Calling a facility a detention centre instead of a prison is aimed at making the child/young person feel less anxious. This is due to the assumption that youth offending is transient and with time and the correct support, the offending behaviour will naturally dissipate. It is viewed as the testing of boundaries as children move through a process of maturation (NZ Ministry of Justice 2002). It is important that children and teens have the appropriate behaviours modelled to them so that they can develop in the right way and be diverted from criminal offending. Children and young people will be given access to age-appropriate education while in detention. Retention in school has a positive effect in regard to preventing offending (Stephenson 2005). It is therefore very important that the causes of disrupted education are addressed and children and teens are reconnected with school.

Health services and art and recreation programmes are also made available to children and teens in detention. Maintaining contact with the family is very important so efforts are made by social workers within the detention centre to make contact with a young offender's family and assist them in maintaining contact. Where the family of origin is a bad influence or is abusive or neglectful, family therapy may be recommended in an effort to improve the family dynamics. It is not ideal for a child/young person to be released to a family environment that is criminogenic but, as **foster placements** for such children and especially for teens are

hard to find, it is often the only option available. *See **Pathways to Youth Offending** (Chapter 5) for more information.*

Strip Searching of Children and Teens

The strip searching of children is a contentious area of practice within the juvenile detention system because many of the children that are in detention are victims of childhood sexual abuse (Stewart et al. 2002; Sherman 2005) and strip searching can traumatise them. Teenagers also are often very self-conscious of their bodies and can be distressed by the experience of strip searching in front of strange adults. Despite these concerns, the security of the facility and the safety of staff and other detainees requires strip searches to be conducted to ensure the detainee does not have any contraband or weapon on their person. Strip searching of children and teens should, however,

---

Key Criminological Research Debates

Should children be tried and incarcerated as adults?
There is arguably nothing more controversial in the criminal justice system than to treat a child/teenager as an adult. Research shows that children and adolescents are developmentally incapable of understanding the consequences of their actions and controlling their impulses in the same way that adults can (Schiraldi 2016). Despite this, in the US alone, children as young as 13 years of age have been tried as adults and as a result, in 2014 there were almost 3,000 children in the US serving life sentences with no possibility of parole (Equal Justice Initiative 2014). In the UK, the law provides for children between 10 and 16 years to be tried as an adult for serious offences that would normally attract a sentence of between 14 years and life for an adult but children under 16 years are not held in adult facilities in the UK (Law Library of Congress 2015). In the US, in addition to trying children in court as adults, they are also held on remand in adult remand facilities and sentenced to serve terms of imprisonment in adult prisons. When incarcerated in adult facilities, children and juveniles are more likely to commit suicide and are exposed to greater risk of physical and sexual assault. They are also less likely to be able to continue their education or engage in age-appropriate rehabilitation, training and employment (Schiraldi 2016). The debate about whether children should be tried and incarcerated as adults is one that pitches liberal approaches to juvenile justice against conservative approaches. Liberal approaches favour a welfare model of justice whereas conservative approaches favour a control model of juvenile justice.

be strictly limited to only those that are absolutely necessary and the modesty and dignity of the detainee should be preserved. As with adults, strip searching should always be conducted by members of the same gender. Transgender children and teens are usually given a choice as to which gender should be present during a search.

Strip searching of children and teens should be avoided unless it is absolutely necessary.

 Why might a child or teen with history of childhood sexual abuse be traumatised by a strip search?

Summary

The criminal justice system is a massive bureaucracy that is devoted to the processing of, and intervention with, criminal offenders. This chapter has only been able to provide an overview of the system which has many variations in different jurisdictions. The intersection of principles and values associated with punishment, rehabilitation and restorative justice continue to influence how the system operates and what it tries to achieve. Some of the perspectives of criminal justice that are essential to understand have been presented along with some of the key debates that are important to be aware of.

Further Reading

Cohen, S. 1985. *Visions of Social Control*. Cambridge, UK: Polity Press.
    This book by Stanley Cohen looks at the shifts in thinking as to how society should deal with crime and delinquency in the US, Great Britain and Western Europe. It examines the historical roots of criminal justice reforms that were implemented in the 1960s and discusses the outcomes of these policy shifts. Cohen completes the book with a discussion of the policy implications that these changes have brought to the criminal justice system and the broader society.

Marsh, I. 2004. *Criminal Justice: An Introduction to Philosophies, Theories and Practice*. With Cochrane, J. & Melville, G. London: Routledge.
    This book provides a useful overview of punishment and the role of punishment in the criminal justice system. It has a chapter that looks at the history of the criminal justice system and provides a broad look at the various subsystems that make up the criminal justice system. It is a good introductory book for students of criminology. It has been specifically designed for students and tutors involved in the study of the criminal justice system.

Marsh, I. 2011. *Crime and Criminal Justice*. With Melville, G., Morgan, K., Norris, G. & Cochrane, J. Oxon: Routledge.
    This book by Ian Marsh and colleagues provide an overview of key criminological theories and the key issues of the criminal justice system, many of which have been covered in this chapter. They look at punishment, victimology and policing among other things. This is a good sourcebook for students of criminology and a good introduction to these issues.

Careers in Criminology

You have been learning about criminology and now have a better idea of what the criminal justice system does, but what exactly do criminologists do? What types of roles are they employed in within the criminal justice system and beyond? Regardless of your background, your studies and experiences as a criminology student will have opened you up to new ways of thinking about victims, offenders and the impact of crime on society. There are a variety of roles within the criminal justice system that can satisfy your particular interest. This chapter will present you with a range of career options within the criminal justice system and the qualifications and experience required to fill them.

Career Pathways

Criminology is a versatile qualification that opens up many opportunities in the criminal justice system and in other related fields. It is a diverse, interdisciplinary field and with that comes a broad choice of careers. Generally your options will fall within one of three areas: policy, practice and research, but there are a variety of opportunities as to where these positions are placed and what aspects of criminology a career path focuses on. For example, within the areas of research, policy and practice a variety of roles exist that range from direct frontline response to case management, team leadership and management roles. A first step is to decide whether you are seeking a direct practice role or a behind-the-scenes role. Do you want to work directly with people and if so is it with offenders or victims that you prefer to work? Are you wanting to learn more about crime and how crime impacts on individuals and communities? Are you wanting to develop

better ways in which crime can be managed and prevented? The way in which you answer these questions will help you to narrow down your employment search.

> **Let's Consider!**
>
> **The Differences Between Practice and Research/Policy**
> Your studies have given you a sense of the criminal justice system and the key actors across this system. Your studies have also developed your awareness of the personal and social aspects of crime and key issues and theories applied across the field of criminology. When considering your career options it may be useful to first think about those aspects of your studies that you found most interesting and the skills you excelled at. Are you interested in systems or people? Does informing policy appeal to you or would you like to work with victims or offenders? Did you enjoy researching and analysing information? *See* Table 7.1 *for more details on the differences between these roles.*

Remember that you are not limited to just working in the criminal justice system, as roles that utilise criminology qualifications can also be found across the welfare and health sectors and also in academia (see Table 7.2). In this chapter we provide general information about the qualifications that are needed but these need to be taken only as a guide. Different jurisdictions will have different requirements so it is best to check the job specifications provided by the employer to determine what qualifications they require.

◘ **Table 7.1** Comparing practice and research/policy

	Practice	Research/policy
Main focus	Direct frontline contact with either victims or offenders.	Behind-the-scenes work with little to no direct contact with victims or offenders.
Objective of the roles	Work with victims to respond to their immediate trauma and/or to help them to navigate the government systems. Work with offenders to take them out of society or to help them to change their behaviour. Work with communities to identify crime hotspots and develop crime prevention strategies.	Work with governments or local councils to develop crime response and prevention policies. Research different aspects of crime and work with government departments such as the police to improve crime response and prevention strategies. Enquire into new and emerging trends and issues to inform governments and communities about the likely causes and options for control.
Positioning in the system	Direct practice roles are usually in the criminal justice system but some roles can be found in the health and welfare systems.	Positioned in policy and research units within government departments and academic institutions.
Main tasks involved	Varied tasks. First responders to crime, managing offenders, working with victims and their families.	Research, analysis, writing, stakeholder consultations.

◘ **Table 7.2** Examples of careers in criminology across various sectors

Academic	Legal	Criminal justice	Health	Welfare	Other
University lecturer	Victim support officer	Police officer	Drug and alcohol counsellor	Child protection worker	Journalist
Criminal profiler	Witness liaison officer	Juvenile justice counsellor	Mental health worker	Youth worker	Ministerial advisor
Author	Court clerk	Probation / parole officer	Coordinator of offender programmes e.g. sex offenders	Victim support worker	Advisor to film and television producers
Academic researcher	Legal researcher	Data analyst, statistician	Health researcher or data analyst	Welfare researcher	Forensic specialists
Consultant/ Advisor	Legal policy officer	Criminal justice policy officer	Health policy officer	Welfare policy officer	
	Court registrar	Criminal profiler		Offender support worker	
		Prison officer		Domestic violence crisis worker	
		Crime prevention officer			

Academic and Policy Roles

We have grouped these career roles together because they share some similarities. At first glance policy development, teaching and research may appear to be quite boring, especially when compared to roles such as criminal profiler, crime scene analyst or forensic expert, and it is true that these are very different roles. Research, teaching and policy development can, however, be interesting and exciting in their own way. It all depends on the environment in which you are working and the topics you are dealing with.

Lecturer

Criminologists are often employed by universities and technical colleges where they teach students about criminology, crime and the criminal justice system. They also undertake research into specific areas relevant to the field of criminology and publish this research in academic journals and books. The areas in which you can teach are many and varied but include subjects such as criminology, criminal justice, crime, criminality, victimology, corrections, policing and penology.

Qualifications needed

In order to teach at tertiary level, you will need to have postgraduate qualifications in the field you intend to teach in and in most instances this will mean a PhD. Some academic institutions will also require you to have published in this field or to be willing to publish once you are employed as an academic.

Crime Researcher

Research roles can be found in academia but also in several government and non-government organisations. Some examples are the UK Home Office, Statistics Canada, the Australian Institute of Criminology and the Scottish Centre for Crime and Justice Research. As a researcher in these and other organisations like them, you may undertake programme evaluations, write literature reviews, analyse and report on data or conduct primary research. Researchers may also be involved in interviewing and observing offenders and writing up the results of these research activities in journal articles, books or reports. Criminologists are also employed as researchers and analysts in specific organisations that have a primary focus on tracking and researching crime such as the Australian Institute of Criminology, or the Home Office in the United Kingdom.

Qualifications needed

A degree in criminology or criminal justice and/or research qualifications. Some crime researchers use previous research experience gained on the job to demonstrate their abilities in undertaking research. Combined with the criminology or criminal justice degree, this is usually sufficient to qualify them for a crime research position.

Policy Development Officer

Policy development roles are typically found in government agencies but some are also available in the non-government sector such as in academic institutions. As a policy officer you will develop policy for specific areas within the criminal justice system such as the police or corrections. You may also develop policy for other government or non-government agencies that deal with the clientele of the criminal justice system, such as the mental health service or a victim support agency. These roles will generally involve a lot of writing, some project management, and stakeholder consultation. You may be involved in policy directly related to a sector within the criminal justice system, for example corrections policy, or for a particular programme, for example, an alcohol and drug rehabilitation programme.

Qualifications needed

Most policy development positions will require only subject-specific qualifications such as a degree in criminology or criminal justice but sometimes such jobs may also need you to have an additional qualification in policy development or project management.

> **What advantage would a department of health have in employing a criminologist to develop policies and procedures for the provision of health services to offenders in prison rather than just a generalist policy officer?**

Legal System Roles

While criminologists are not specifically trained in law, and cannot work as lawyers, they are employed in support roles such as legal advisors, researchers and court administrators. The courts also employ witness liaison and victim support officers who provide direct support to people required to attend court but who are not charged with an offence. It is often stressful for victims and other witnesses to appear in court to give evidence because the alleged offender and his/her family is often present. Having the support of the witness liaison and victim support officers makes this process substantially easier for these victims and witnesses.

Qualifications needed

A criminal justice or criminology degree is well regarded by law companies looking to employ people in support roles. A criminology degree can sometimes be combined with an additional degree in law, depending on what the job role requires.

Criminal Justice System Roles

Many criminologists work in direct practice areas, not all of which are exclusively related to criminology or crime and justice issues. Advertisements for these roles may specifically require a criminology 'or other relevant degree' or may be pitched at other disciplines such as social work, but will accept applications from candidates with 'other relevant degrees' such as criminology. The ubiquitous 'other relevant degree' is therefore something to watch out for to ensure you consider all your available options. Direct practice roles include law enforcement, corrections, youth justice workers, counselling and support workers. Given the diversity of roles you will need to think broadly when examining job advertisements as you are unlikely to come across anything as specific as 'Help wanted – criminologist', although many jobs will list criminology among the qualifications considered to be desirable or essential for the job being advertised.

Policing Roles

Police departments are always looking for good candidates, and applicants who have a criminology or criminal justice qualification are highly competitive for these jobs. Final acceptance into policing will of course be dependent on the candidate successfully passing the recruitment training process that includes physical fitness and aptitude testing. There are so many roles available within policing that we recommend you research your own police department to find out what is available. We only cover a small sample of them here.

General Duties Police

General duties police officers are the uniformed police officers you see on the street or driving around in police cars dealing with traffic infringements, domestic disputes and thefts (Rowe 2014). They are often the first responders to emergency incidents such as car crashes and to major crimes such as homicides. They secure a crime or crash scene in preparation for the specialist police services to process the area. General duties police have an interesting job that exposes them to a great deal of variety every day. Shift work is a necessary part of the job so you shouldn't consider policing as a career unless you are willing to accept this part of the job. Shift work has advantages and disadvantages for juggling social and family commitments. Entry into the police service is via general duties policing but unless you specifically choose to remain in that role there are many options for career advancement. These include moving up the hierarchy into management roles and moving sideways into specialist roles. Most specialist roles have a hierarchy that allows you to move up in rank as you gain experience and pass the appropriate tests. Choosing a speciality early in your policing career allows you to target the specific range of work experiences that will give you an advantage for acceptance into the specialist role of your choice.

Detectives

Detectives are usually sworn police officers who have applied for and been promoted to the role of detective (detective constable, detective sergeant, detective inspector, etc.). In the UK they can also be civilian staff who are employed for their qualifications and skills in conducting investigations with qualifications such as criminology, psychology and science who undertake roles that sworn police cannot undertake or can be freed up from having to do (Sheldon 2011). Detectives frequently work in special teams or units which operate according to guidelines specific to the type of crime they are responding to: for example, financial crime unit, cybercrime unit, sexual crime unit, homicide unit, drug crime unit, etc. Detectives usually wear plain clothes and may sometimes go under cover. *See Covert Policing* (Chapter 6).

Tactical Response Officers

The tactical response unit employs officers with exceptional levels of physical fitness and aptitude for handling weapons. They are highly trained officers who must respond to some of the most dangerous situations faced by police. They wear special clothing that is designed to protect them from shooting and stabbing injuries, but the risk of such injuries is still high. They are trained to shoot weapons from a distance and are also trained to work as a team. It is the tactical response section of the police that provides the officers you see responding to hostage and siege situations or dangerous incidents involving guns and knives. *See Terrorism* (Chapter 5).

Riot Police

Riot police are also specialist police officers. They need to be specially trained to deal with large and sometimes unruly crowds. They also need to respond to unpredictable and potentially dangerous situations. You will sometimes see them on television holding large plastic shields and moving in a long line to encourage a large crowd of people to move backwards to clear a road or other public area. They will also use tactics and weapons such as tear gas to break up and dissipate a large and volatile crowd to prevent the crowd from getting out of control. Riot police must be able to control their emotions and reactions and work with team to defuse incidents rather than escalate them. As with many of the police specialist roles, riot policing is dangerous and requires a willingness to work abnormal hours at short notice.

Police Air, Sea and Rescue Officers

Police air, sea and rescue units employ pilots, engineers and those in related fields who have also completed basic police training and the specialist training to gain entry to this unit. This is an exciting area of policing that attracts people who are interested in extreme sports and activities such as abseiling. There are various roles for police air, sea and rescue team members but all officers working in this unit have to be able to abseil from a hovering helicopter and must be able to lift heavy weights. This is because it is a requirement of the job that these officers are often required to lift people and objects into the helicopter from precarious places. If you are anxious about heights or find it uncomfortable to fly, you would not be suited to these roles. Rescuing people from cliffsides, from mountains, from the sea and from remote areas is a standard part of the job and can test the toughest nerves. If attracted to sea policing you need to be able to cope with being on the water and must be a strong swimmer. Many of the functions of general duties police are also carried out by sea police. Police divers must have the appropriate diving qualifications and will be called on to assist other units, such as homicide detectives or the drug squad, to locate people, bodies or smuggled illegal substances.

Dog Handler

Dog squad officers are assigned a dog which they will train and which they will take home and spend most of their leisure as well as all their work time with. The dog must 'become one' with the handler so both the dog and the handler have to know each other very well. A dog squad officer will also be trained in the specialist area that their dog is to be used for, whether drug detection, seeking out cadavers or tracking offenders. You must be interested in working with dogs and must like interacting with dogs in order to work in this role as most of your time is spent with dogs.

Mounted Police Officers

The mounted police are police officers who ride horses. They are usually present at public events and assist riot police with public gatherings that may get out of control. Mounted police can often go into public places where cars can't go and being atop a horse gives the officers a standpoint above the crowd so that they can see what is happening. If you wish to work as a mounted police officer you will need to have some experience with horses in addition to the general police recruitment training.

Criminal Profiler and Forensic Specialist Roles

Besides policing, the roles of criminal profiler and forensic specialist are possibly the most well known by people who do not work in the criminal

Qualifications needed
Most police departments will require applicants to have a qualification in a human service area such as social work, psychology, criminology or criminal justice. Applicants who hold criminology degrees have an obvious advantage because of the relevance of these degrees to the work of a police officer. They may also give applicants an advantage when applying for specialist policing roles. The qualification only gets you past the first stage of recruitment and each jurisdiction has a recruitment process with physical fitness and aptitude testing that must be passed in order to gain employment as a police officer.

justice system due to television programmes that sensationalise these roles.

Criminal Profiler

An experienced criminologist may work closely with the police as a criminal profiler, assisting the police to identify and catch possible offenders. This is interesting and sometimes exciting work and attracts a lot of people. What is not always known, however, is that a criminal profiler may also be involved in profiling specific demographic areas to estimate future crime trends and this may in fact be what they do most of the time. Despite the entertainment industry portraying the criminal profiler as having a pivotal role in a criminal investigation the reality can be quite different. These roles are often not as exciting as those portrayed on television and in most jurisdictions criminal profilers and forensic specialists do not do the investigative role – this is done by police. They will therefore rarely be authorised to carry and use guns and will have only a limited role in the investigation of crime. Sometimes these roles are located within the police department but frequently they are based in private companies. Criminal profilers may also hold another job such as an academic or clinical psychologist post.

Key Criminological Research Debates

Women police officers: Challenging stereotypes
Throughout the twentieth century police departments around the world began employing women. Prior to this, policing was a traditionally male profession. At first, roles of police women were restricted to dealing only with women and children. Although their numbers remained small until around the 1970s, women eventually made inroads into other areas of policing and today women range from 13% to 27% of sworn officers in most Western police forces and are engaged in many specialist areas in addition to general duties (Robinson 2013). Women in policing has been, and continues to be, a popular area of criminological study. One of the main research debates centres on why the numbers of women in policing remain low relative to men in the profession. One side of the debate suggests that structural and cultural barriers exist at recruitment that serve to limit the number of women entering the policing (Robinson 2015). An alternative view argues that it is women themselves who are choosing not to enter policing as a career choice due to their preference for focusing on family and childcare commitments. There is also a similar but slightly different perspective, that men are socialised to pursue masculine professions such as policing due to the nature of the job being physical and dangerous, and women are socialised to pursue more nurturing career options such as nursing and teaching. As society has changed over time, however, the role of the police has also changed and the modern police role is much less physical and more sedentary (Lonsway 2003). Women police have been found to be less aggressive when faced with dangerous situations and rely more frequently on their communication skills to diffuse conflict (Robinson 2015). The numbers of women entering the career of policing are growing but they still have a long way to go before they are representative of the general population. Research into the reasons why women are under-represented in policing will continue to occur while the numbers of women in the profession remain substantially lower.

Crime Scene Analyst

A crime scene analyst is also known as a **forensic** science investigator and forensic analyst, and is responsible for supporting criminal investigations conducted by the police, collecting and processing evidence that is later produced in court. Crime scene analysts will often work unusual hours because of the nature of the work and the deadlines that must be met. Overtime is often needed to keep the chain of custody intact in respect to the evidence. Forensic analysts may work in a laboratory, where they process the evidence collected.

Qualifications needed
The qualifications needed to be a criminal profiler will vary according to the type of profiling being undertaken. For example, general criminal profiling will usually require a degree in criminology but profiling that also involves detailed psychological analysis will require psychology qualifications. Often profilers will hold two qualifications such as criminology and psychology degrees.

Qualifications needed
Forensic analysts may have criminology or criminal justice degrees but in most cases will also be required to have a science degree. Some jurisdictions have these positions as specialist policing roles and will support the police officer to gain the necessary science degree.

How does a knowledge of criminology assist forensic analysts in processing a crime scene or evaluating the evidence?

Corrective Services Roles

Departments of corrective services and private correctional companies hire criminologists in various roles. These may be different according to the jurisdiction so it is worth checking with the correctional organisations near you to find out what roles are available.

Probation and Parole Officer

Probation and parole officers supervise offenders who are on a court or parole board supervision order. They meet regularly with offenders to discuss their offending behaviour and to ensure they are complying with the order. They will also do assessments of criminogenic needs and link offenders to appropriate services and programmes to address those needs. They will write pre-sentence reports to inform the court about the circumstances of offenders prior to them being sentenced. People employed in this role need to have good communication and conflict resolution skills. Specific job training is usually provided during the recruitment process.

Community Service Work Supervisor

Community service work gangs are supervised by community service work supervisors. These officers will generally be qualified and/ or experienced in the specific work areas that the gangs are required to work in. For example, horticulturalists will supervise gardening gangs; painters, painting gangs; carpenters, building projects, etc.. Depending on the size of the work gang there will often only be one or two supervisors per gang. Such a job therefore requires resilience and the ability to show initiative. It also requires good communication, interpersonal and conflict resolution skills as the supervisor works very closely with offenders.

Qualifications needed

A degree in a human service area such as social work, psychology, criminology or criminal justice and experience or qualifications in an industry which is required by the community service needs.

Prison Officer

As the name suggests, prison officers work in prisons and remand centres. Prison officers supervise and interact with prisoners and they also must display appropriate social behaviour to encourage prisoners to adopt better ways of behaving. Prison officers must undertake shift work and need to be able to work overtime when required. You will need to have good communication and conflict resolution skills and be able to cope with high levels of stress in order to be a prison officer.

Qualifications needed

Any behavioural science, social science or human service degree is generally acceptable for these roles; however, social work, psychology, criminology and criminal justice degrees are highly regarded.

Qualifications needed

Most jurisdictions are beginning to require prison officers to have tertiary-level qualifications, particularly qualifications that fall into the social and behavioural sciences areas such as social work, psychology, criminology and criminal justice degrees. Prison officers will also receive in-house training prior to commencing their job which will include psychometric testing and may also require fitness testing.

Programme Officer

Programme officers develop and implement programmes with offenders. They can be based in the community or in the prison system. The background of the person applying for these positions will depend on the types of programmes being offered. These can be interesting job roles but they can also be stressful and require a great deal of control to maintain the right level of professional distance and emotional involvement. Programme officers need to have good communication and groupwork skills.

See this chapter's case study for an example of the types of programmes run by a correctional services department.

Juvenile Justice Roles

Many of the positions available in juvenile justice are similar to those mentioned previously, but instead of working with adults you would be working with children and teenagers. To avoid repetition we will only cover the one position here that is not found in the adult criminal justice system because it is specific to juvenile justice.

Youth Worker

Youth workers are employed throughout the juvenile justice system. If you work as a youth worker in the juvenile justice system you will be specially trained in how to deal with young offenders. You will be employed in areas such as youth detention centres, programme units and community youth justice.

Qualifications needed

A degree in social work, psychology, criminology or criminal justice is needed to work as a youth worker in youth justice. You will also be given on-the-job training and in some cases in-house training prior to commencing in the role.

Qualifications needed

Programme officers will usually have social work or psychology degrees. Depending on the type of programmes to be implemented, degrees in criminology and criminal justice will also be considered and may even be preferred. Having prior experience in programme development will also assist in this type of employment.

Health and Welfare Roles

There are a great many job opportunities for criminologists within the criminal justice system but there are also many employment

---

Case Study

Western Australian Department of Corrective Services Rehabilitation Programmes

The Western Australian Department of Corrective Services provides a range of programmes for prisoners. These include:

- *Pathways Program* (an intensive 21-day programme focused on substance abuse and offending)
- *Drug-Free Units* (drug-free environment for prisoners

who have completed the Pathways Program)
- *Gender-Specific and Culturally Designed Substance Abuse Programs* for prisoners
- *Offence-Specific Treatment Programs* such as sex offending and violent offending programmes

- *Cognitive Skills Programmes* (focused on improving problem-solving and social interaction skills)
- *Building on Aboriginal Skills Programme* (designed for Aboriginal prisoners who want to connect with their land and culture)

Source: WA Corrective Services. 2013. 'Rehabilitation Programs'. Accessed online on 3 November 2016 at: www.correctiveservices.wa.gov.au/rehabilitation-services/rehab-programs.aspx

opportunities outside the criminal justice system too. It pays to be curious and keep your options open when considering areas of employment. Here we provide a small sample of such positions but keep in mind that we are unable to cover all jobs so we have just chosen the most common jobs that you will come across. You need to seek out positions specific to your own area.

Health and Welfare Programme Workers

There are many areas within the health and welfare sectors that employ criminologists to develop and implement offender programmes, especially in the areas of drug and alcohol programmes, domestic violence and mental health programmes. More frequently, criminologists working in these areas would run programmes with the victims of crime such as rape crisis support programmes, child abuse programmes and programmes for the victims of domestic violence. In health and welfare areas, criminologists may work within a multidisciplinary team or may work alone. Often they work jointly with a psychologist, psychiatric nurse or social worker to develop and run programmes. Research positions are also common.

Victim Advocate and Victims of Crime Support Officer

It is quite well known that many victim support officer jobs can be found in the criminal justice system but it is less well known that they can be found outside the criminal justice system too. Victim advocates tend to be located outside the criminal justice system in victim support agencies. The roles of victim support officers and victim advocates are both focused on the needs of victims and assisting them to negotiate the criminal justice system. Sometimes the advocacy and support roles are combined within the same position. A strong victim empathy and knowledge of the criminal justice system are necessary characteristics for someone wishing to gain employment as a victim advocate or a victim support worker.

Qualifications needed

A degree in social work, psychology, criminology or criminal justice is needed for victim advocacy and victim support positions.

Other Roles

The employment opportunities that arise from having a criminology degree are only limited by your imagination. When we were considering all the roles in which criminologists can be employed, we came across roles at the highest level of government, in media and even within the arts. Here are a small selection of some of the lesser-known and not so obvious roles.

Journalist/Crime Reporter

Journalists responsible for reporting on criminal matters will often hold criminology or related qualifications. Areas such as the police, prisons and community-based corrections employ people with criminology qualifications. In these roles, you will deal directly with offenders and will work within the criminal justice or juvenile justice systems. Increasingly, private organisations are moving into the law enforcement, security and corrections areas and will also seek to employ people with appropriate qualifications such as criminology.

Qualifications needed

Usually a degree in journalism or media studies and a second degree in a subject-specific area such as criminology or criminal justice. An arts degree with a journalism or media studies major and criminology, forensics or criminal justice second major/minor or equivalent will also be accepted.

Crime Prevention Officers

Criminologists work with or within local councils to profile specific localities and influence environmental design in order to prevent crime in specific urban spaces. These specialist roles are known as crime prevention officers. It is essential that crime prevention officers have knowledge of community stakeholder consultation methods as much of this work will require consulting with members of the community.

> **Qualifications needed**
> Criminology qualifications are most often required for crime prevention roles; however, additional qualifications in project management or environmental design are also useful.

Ministerial Advisor

Governments cannot operate effectively without appropriately qualified advisors to assist its ministers to develop policy and to help them to understand the issues involved in the social processes occurring at grass-roots level. Criminologists become advisors to the ministers responsible for the criminal justice portfolio of government. Much of the work in this role will be research, with some stakeholder consultation. A person working with those in a ministerial role will need to be adaptable with good communication skills as it requires being able to operate at macro, meso and micro levels. These roles are usually behind the scenes but may require more overt involvement at times when criminal justice becomes a central policy issue for the government.

How Do I Make Myself Marketable and Competitive?

From your own studies and the descriptions of courses contained in Chapter 2: *Studying Criminology*, it should be evident that as an

undergraduate in this field you are developing general knowledge about crime and justice issues and how to apply criminological thinking to a deeper understanding of those issues.

> — **Let's Consider!** —
>
> **Where to From Here?**
> As you approach finishing your degree you are likely to start thinking about the future. What will you do? What do you want? It's important to ask yourself what stage you are at. Do you want to pursue further study? Do you want to get a job right away? Do you want to take a year off? Are you completely unsure? You can consider these questions on your own or seek out some support and assistance from your university's careers centre or advisor. Most universities have career counsellors available who can assist you with employment decisions and with getting started on writing those very important initial applications.

It's important to reflect on the skills you have gained while completing your degree and what these skills will offer a future employer. Some of these skills are directly related to your programme of study while others are general skills that are transferable to a wide range of career options. The skills you will have acquired include:

- knowledge of the criminal justice system;
- knowledge of crime and justice issues;
- awareness of the key players across the criminal justice system;
- awareness of victim and offender needs;
- research and analytical skills;
- communication skills;
- interpersonal skills (including teamwork);
- ability to link theory and practice; and
- organisation skills.

After coming up with your own list of skills, you'll need to do some research so that you are informed, make use of available networks and are prepared for when you get an interview.

Be Informed

Since the administration of justice is different across countries, and between jurisdictions within the same country, you will need to explore the specific requirements for a job where you live. In the UK and particularly in Scotland, the probation field is still dominated by social work and it may be necessary to undertake further studies in this field or in another direct practice discipline in order to be competitive for a position. In Australia, most criminal justice jurisdictions require relevant tertiary education in criminology, criminal justice or a related field and will then provide additional vocational training at a Certificate III or IV level in the job area (for example, community corrections). Many employers are also looking for well-rounded employees. Your grades matter but so too does your engagement across the field. You may want to take opportunities to attend conferences or seminars, deliver presentations or volunteer in your community. Find out what criminal justice-related jobs are in your area and what is needed to be successful in applying for them.

Network

Build up a network of colleagues and associates in the criminal justice system. These days impartiality must apply to the recruitment process but it always helps to obtain some insider knowledge when going for a job. If you don't know anyone in the system then telephone the contact person to find out more information about the job. Use open questions such as 'What can you tell me about the job?' as this takes the focus off you and encourages the person on the other end to tell you about the job and what it entails. Find out who is on the interview panel and look them up on the internet. It is always wise to be prepared and to know whom you are meeting.

Be Prepared

You will often find quite senior people in the organisation such as a police superintendent or a senior manager chairing an interview panel. It always makes a good impression if you can show that you are familiar with who they are and what they do. Make a good first impression.

Presentation

Dress in smart business attire and ensure your hair is neat and tidy. We recommend you hide any tattoos and remove piercings. They certainly don't affect your abilities to do the job but unfortunately people form stereotypes in their minds and outward presentation may be the difference between them choosing you or someone else. It may seem unnecessary in today's world but remember that some areas within the criminal justice system, such as corrections and the police, have uniforms and a hierarchy which means that they will expect you to display a level of respect and to take some effort with your presentation.

Research

Preparation also entails researching the organisation and the job role. You need to know about the organisation and you need to be able to confidently answer questions related to the job. There is nothing worse than being in an interview and suddenly finding yourself unable to answer the questions. It pays to be proactive in researching the position prior to the interview. Seek out the organisation's website and find out who is going to be on the interview panel and their area of interest in the organisation. Look at the strategic objectives of the organisation and the organisation chart so you have an idea of how it is structured. Above all, ensure you have a good understanding of the role you're applying for and the knowledge you need for the role. Even if you think you know this very well, it is worth taking the time to refresh and update your knowledge. Go to the interview with examples from your own experience or real case examples from the media.

- Recruitment sites for information about current vacancies

    o Government department websites (for example: www.gov.uk/government/organisations/home-office or bulk graduate recruitment sites)

    o National government job search engines (for example: www.apsjobs.gov.au)

    o Social policy and research agency websites which may include links to other agencies you may not have even considered (for example: www.globalsocialjustice.eu/index.php/links)

- Notice boards in your criminology department

- Your university student liaison section or criminology department

- Your network of contacts and connections within the criminal justice system

- Volunteer association websites (volunteering in the criminal justice system is a good way to develop contacts and relevant experience)

Figure 7.1 Useful resources for planning your career

See Figure 7.1 for ideas on where to look to find useful resources to help you when researching for job opportunities.

Criminal History Checks

Almost all jobs in the criminal justice system will require you to undertake a criminal history check. The best way to address this is not to be involved in criminal behaviour so that your criminal history check comes back clear. If you do have a negative history recorded it is best to be forthcoming about that before the criminal history check goes in to be processed. This allows you the opportunity to explain the circumstances. A minor offending career will not necessarily prevent you from gaining employment in the criminal justice system. If you are a reformed offender with a serious offending history it is best to make an appointment with the appropriate contact person to speak to them about it. Whether you are then employed or not will depend very much on the role you are applying for. A main principle that the organisation will be mindful of is whether you are likely to have associates as clients within the system and whether you might be open to manipulation by those offenders.

Summary

This chapter has sought to give you an overview of the types of employment opportunities that are open to you once you complete your criminology/criminal justice degree. Each jurisdiction is different in terms of the types of jobs it will have available and the qualifications it will require so it is wise to check the organisations in your local area for specific details. Ultimately your degree will open the door but it is largely down to you, and how much effort you are willing to put in, as to whether you are successful in winning that perfect job or not.

Key Terms, Concepts and Definitions

There are many unfamiliar definitions, terms and concepts used in criminology and it is easy to get confused by this new language. In this chapter we will introduce you to the key definitions, terms and concepts that you will come across when studying this course. We have tried to steer away from reintroducing information we have included in earlier chapters but instead have taken a broader look at criminology and the criminal justice system in order to provide you with an understanding of the peripheral language and terminology used.

Quick Reference for Terms, Concepts and Definitions

The chapter has been structured alphabetically so that it can be used by the student much as a dictionary might be used. Where key terms and concepts are linked or inter-related we make reference to other entries you might wish to consult in trying to understand a particular definition, term or concept.

Actuarial Justice

Actuarial justice is a concept used to identify what was seen to be a shift in the primary orientation of criminal justice agencies towards the identification and management of risk; primarily through the classification of individuals against the behaviour of statistical groups. Four characteristics are commonly associated with actuarial justice:

- deviance is normal, crime is inevitable and efforts should go towards managing the impact rather than eliminating crime;
- individuals are risk objects and classified according to their risk profile;

- individual behaviour is managed according the level of risk presented and the goal of treatment is oriented towards risk reduction rather than transformative behaviour change; and
- the potential for future harm is given weight over actual past harm caused.

Administrative Criminology

Around the 1960s two distinct and opposing theoretical streams emerged in Britain: radical criminology and administrative criminology. Administrative criminology was said to have a narrow, empiricist and policy-oriented focus with a reliance on statistics. Radical criminology was considered to be more open and creative as it presented a view of crime causation as being rooted in class conflict and social inequality.

Anomie

Anomie is a condition of society where there is a breakdown of social bonding and cohesion so that some members are disenfranchised from the mainstream resulting in a rejection of that society's norms and regulations. Paradoxically, according to Durkheim, a society that is over-regulated with too little individual discretion can also produce a type of anomie.

Anthropological Criminology

Anthropological criminology (or criminal anthropology) is the study of humans and criminality. It is influenced by the positivist school of criminology. In contemporary criminal justice this field of criminology includes influences from the disciplines of psychology and biology and is expanded to include personality traits and psychological characteristics and behaviour. In the criminal justice system it is often referred to as criminal profiling.

Antisocial Behaviour

Another way of defining deviance is to refer to it as antisocial behaviour. This can include any behaviour that the majority of the community would find offensive or bothersome. It also includes criminal offending behaviour. Antisocial behaviour orders are available in Britain and other countries and are intended to help police to control the behaviour of individuals and groups where the behaviour escalates to criminal offending. There are criticisms that in actuality these orders are not used to stop criminal behaviour but are used to control the normal behaviour of adolescents who tend to congregate in groups in public places and often create a nuisance just because of their presence.

Atavism

Atavism is a term introduced by Charles Darwin that refers to a throwback to earlier stages of development. This conceptualisation appealed to Lombroso who applied it to the study of criminals. Lombroso (1876/1911) referred to criminality, which he believed was innate, as being a throwback to earlier, more primitive stages of human development. *See Cesare Lombroso (Chapter 3).*

Bail

Bail is used by the courts to make sure a person who has been charged with a crime appears in court on a particular day. A person who is charged with a crime and is held in custody may apply for bail. If the person agrees to appear in court on a certain day and agrees to abide by the conditions set by a court, that person can avoid custody and remain in the community. Once placed on a bail order the person must adhere to the conditions placed on them by the court. In many jurisdictions police can also issue police bail to offenders to avoid the need to remand them in custody until they can appear in court.

Biological Determinant

A biological determinant is a condition or trait that is thought to be inborn and therefore unable to be changed. Just as some theorists consider criminal behaviour to be biologically determined, some theorists also consider mental illness to be biologically determined.

Burden of Proof

Burden of proof is a term used in the criminal court and refers to the legal requirement for the prosecution to reach a legal threshold in order to prove the guilt of the accused person. For example, in criminal cases the burden of proof is *beyond reasonable doubt*. While the prosecution must carry the burden of proof, the defendant benefits from an assumption of innocence. The accused person, or the defendant, does not have to prove their innocence because it is assumed by the court; the burden of proof to show guilt beyond reasonable doubt rests with the prosecution.

Capitalism

Capitalism is a social, political and economic system in which the means of production, distribution and exchange (trade) is controlled privately and not by the state. Economic wealth and resources (including the country's natural resources) are owned and maintained by individuals and corporations within a capitalist system. This is known as a free market economy and the process of trade is called free enterprise.

Case Management

Case management is a service delivery framework that operates in a variety of contexts. Within the criminal justice system this framework is typically applied when working directly with offenders; for example, in prisons and community-based corrections. Case management involves a number of primary tasks frequently conducted in overlapping stages (see Taxman 2002; Kemshall et al. 2004; for a full account). These tasks include: preparation, assessment, planning, intervention and evaluation. Case records are generally kept in a file by the case manager which allows several professionals to be able to work with the offender without being in conflict with each other.

Chicago School

In the 1920s and 1930s, researchers in the Department of Sociology at the University of Chicago developed new methods of enquiry in urban sociology, pioneering an ecological approach to the understanding of society and crime. Although criticised for an over-reliance on environmental factors as the cause of crime and disorder, the Chicago School was influential in developing ethnographic approaches, crime mapping and the use of quantitative statistical analysis to the study of crime.

Circle Sentencing

Circle sentencing is an alternative court process for Indigenous offenders which involves Indigenous Elders and people from the Indigenous community in the sentencing process. The Circle has the full powers of a criminal court and empowers the Indigenous community to participate in deciding the appropriate sentence for the offender. Circle sentencing is having success in Australia in reducing the number of Indigenous people in prison.

Community Order

A community order is a sentence that is served in the community and does not involve imprisonment. A community order can include probation, parole, home detention, community service work or an order to attend a community-based programme. All community orders will generally have a component of supervision or monitoring attached to them and this role is fulfilled by a probation and parole officer or youth worker employed in the young offenders sector.

Community Policing

Community policing is an organisational strategy used by a police force to be more involved in, and responsive to, the community. This strategy seeks to obtain the views of community members and involve them in the crime prevention effort. This includes neighbourhood watch schemes, education programmes, crime prevention programmes, community safety strategies and partnerships with other community organisations or citizen groups.

Community Safety

The term community safety refers to a group of strategies aimed at reducing crime and improving resilience and safety within a community. It is also a term that is applied to the duty of care that members of the criminal justice system have in ensuring that the risk to the community is considered when decisions are made (such as the early release of a prisoner).

Corrections

A range of services and functions in society that are aimed at carrying out the punishments issued by the court are referred to as corrections. Most jurisdictions have organisations in place that have the sole purpose of carrying out these functions and are usually referred to as 'correctional services'. Correctional services include prisons and community-based corrections. *See Penology and Community-based Corrections (Chapter 6)*.

Crime Prevention

Community effort that is focused on lowering the crime rate and preventing crimes in a particular locality is known as crime prevention. A well-known crime prevention programme is the Neighbourhood Watch Programme. In more recent times crime prevention has also been applied to any measures taken by police to reduce crime and in particular to efforts aimed at improving physical security and reducing situational crime. Crime prevention strategies include: offender-centred strategies, victim-centred strategies, community-based strategies, integration strategies and environmental strategies.

Criminalisation

Criminalisation is the process by which crime is created and individuals are made into criminals. Criminalisation can occur as a result of the introduction of a new law, making a once lawful behaviour criminal. It can also occur as a result of judicial processes and decision making. The rule of law generally guards against once legal behaviour being retrospectively made criminal, but this can happen in some cases.

Criminal Career

Criminal career refers to both the life course of an individual's involvement in crime (from onset through desistance) and also a body of research focusing on both the frequency and specialisation of offending.

Criminogenic

Criminogenic refers to any factors that are linked to offending behaviour in the sense that they cause or significantly contribute to the person's offending behaviour. Criminogenic factors can be static (i.e. unable to be changed such as gender and age) or dynamic (able to be changed).

Criminological Research

Criminological research allows criminologists and others to make sense of criminal behaviour and crime occurrence that otherwise would appear random and senseless. It also allows social scientists and policy makers to put crime rates and the public's fear of crime into perspective with the reality.

Criminologist

Criminologists study criminal behaviour and examine the systems whereby people accused of crimes are brought to justice. They attempt to explain the reasons for criminal behaviour and may suggest ways in which law enforcement can better respond to crime in order to reduce the rate of crime.

Cultural Evolution

Cultural evolution is a term used to describe a process whereby societies change, or evolve, over time. According to cultural evolution theory, particular ethnic groups possess characteristic adaptations that have been passed on by heredity and social learning. Changes are socially acquired over time and are incorporated into the biological make-up of the group. The process of natural selection ensures only the most necessary and successful characteristics are maintained within an ethnic group.

Cybercrime

Cybercrime is conceptualised as crime involving information and communication technology either as the direct target of the offence or the tool to commit the offence. It is inherently difficult to define because it encompasses a range of offence behaviours and types. It involves language specific to the criminal activities involved that we might call the language of cybercrime.

Death Penalty

The most severe punishment that can be issued by a court is the death penalty. The death penalty is also referred to as capital punishment. The manner of execution differs in various jurisdictions but generally includes a manner such as lethal injection, hanging, shooting or the electric chair. In most Western countries, the death penalty has been abolished but in some states of America, and some Asian countries such as Malaysia and Indonesia, it is still in force.

Desistance

Desistance refers to both stopping and refraining from offending. Understood as a process, research examining desistance seeks to identify the role and impact of individual choice, social forces and societal practices on the decision to desist from crime. Linked in part to developmental criminology and criminal careers research, desistance draws on several theoretical frameworks including: maturation and ageing, rational choice and social learning theories. Key researchers in the field include John Laub, Richard Sampson, Maruana Shadd and Stephen Farrall.

Detention Centre

A detention centre is a facility used to contain offenders who belong to a special population (e.g. youth, immigration, remand). Detainees held in a detention centre are kept separate from the mainstream adult criminal population due to their age (youth detention) or due to the fact they have not yet been found guilty of an offence on court (people on remand). People in immigration detention are not always guilty of a criminal offence but have breached the immigration laws. See *Juvenile Justice* and *Prisons* (*Chapter 6*).

Determinism

Determinism is an approach to studying human phenomena that seeks to explain human behaviour by identifying factors beyond their control. An example of this approach is the Italian criminologist Lombroso (1876/1911) who sought to explain criminal behaviour by looking at genetic predisposition to criminal offending. Determinism assumes that people have innate tendencies towards criminal behaviour that are not within their control. This approach therefore focuses on early identification and containment of offenders rather than rehabilitation.

Deterrence

Deterrence refers to the belief that punishment should be severe enough to deter other people from committing the same types of crime in the future. By deterring people from committing crime, it is believed that the crime rate can be reduced. The arguments for the retention and/or reintroduction of capital punishment has centred on a belief in the deterrence value of such severe

punishments. There are two main components of deterrence. The first is that a punishment imposed on an individual offender is expected to deter that offender from future criminal offending and the second is that others will witness the punishment of an offender and be deterred, out of fear of punishment, from criminal offending themselves.

Differential Opportunity Theory

Everyone has access to both legitimate and illegitimate opportunity structures. An individual's access to legitimate opportunities will positively affect their adjustment problems, but when faced with limitations for legitimate opportunities will revise downwards to seek illegitimate opportunities. See *Opportunity Theory* (*Chapter 3*).

Distributive Justice

According to distributive justice, a socially just society is one that fairly distributes its goods and in which incidental inequality is absent. Utilitarian conceptions of distributive justice argue that rewards and punishments should be distributed according to merits and demerits. Distributive justice is often related to the welfare state and egalitarian conceptions of the fair distribution of goods, social conditions and political influence. Jeremy Bentham sought to apply it to his view of utilitarian jurisprudence by arguing that each person has the right to secure the conditions under which they can pursue their own conception of 'the good life'. See *Jeremy Bentham* (*Chapter 3*).

Double Deviance

There is a theory that female criminals are treated more harshly by the criminal justice system due to a process known as double deviance. According to this theory women are not just punished for the crime they commit but also for breaking the norms of society in regard to the acceptable behaviour of women and girls. Women who are convicted of serious crimes such as sexual crimes, other than prostitution, are said to be punished more harshly than their male counterparts owing to the role of double deviance. This contention is not supported by court statistics. *See Feminist Criminology (Chapter 3).*

Doubled Up

When a prison cell designed for one person is used to house two prisoners, it is referred to as being doubled up. Sometimes the doubling or tripling up of a cell designed for a single prisoner occurs because the prison population rises faster than the system can respond.

Drug Addiction

The physical and emotional dependence upon illicit drugs such as cannabis, opiates, narcotics and amphetamines is known as drug addiction. Drug dependence can also occur on legally prescribed medication. It is a medical, health and social problem and is difficult to control. Drug addiction is seen to be a criminogenic factor in crime and is therefore targeted for therapeutic intervention when it is identified in an offender's risk and needs assessment. An offender's involvement in drug offences such as distributing, trafficking and production of drugs has its roots in drug addiction. Drug addiction is also referred to as substance abuse.

Dualities of Crime

Jock Young is a British criminologist who emphasised the dualities of crime which are: offender and victim; actions and reactions; crime and control. He proposes that crime rates are generated by the social relationships between four elements: interaction between police and other institutions and agents of social control and the offender, the victim and the public. Young is a left realist theorist and his views are strongly influenced by this perspective.

Electronic Monitoring

The use of an electronic monitoring device, usually attached to the ankle of an offender, which sends signals via global positioning satellite (GPS) to a receiving device (such as a mobile phone), which is monitored by a community corrections officer. It is a means of ensuring that offenders on home detention remain within the restricted area designated by the court. It is also a means of ensuring offenders comply with a court ordered curfew. *See Community-based Corrections (Chapter 6).*

Empirical Evidence

Empirical evidence is a scientific term and refers to concrete and tangible sensory evidence that can be seen, touched, smelled or heard. It is not sufficient to be told something anecdotally or to assume that something is a certain way. For something to be considered real and proven, it must be supported by tangible evidence. *See Chapter 4:* Criminological Research.

Ethnicity

Ethnicity is the term used to refer to the culture of a geographically similar group of people. It is not the same as race, which is a genetically determined characteristic. It refers to the language, traditions, religion and customs of a group that also shares similarities in terms of the area in which they or their parents were raised. *See Race and Crime (Chapter 5).*

Evolutionary Psychology

Evolutionary psychology is a relatively new branch of psychology that is being applied to the study of crime. This theoretical perspective holds that people not only adapt physically to their changing environment but that they adapt psychologically as well. In essence human beings evolve physically and psychologically. This perspective also suggests that the process of natural selection applies to psychological evolution in much the same way as it applies to biological evolution. The 'survival of the fittest' process drives male behaviour in two ways: sexual jealousy and sexual rivalry. These are unconscious, rather than conscious, drivers.

Focus Group

A focus group is a group of participants who are brought together because they are part of a cohort the researcher is investigating. By interviewing the participants in a group the researcher saves time but can also gain more data as a result of observing the group dynamic. *See Qualitative Research (Chapter 4).*

Forensic

The word 'forensic' refers to the application of science to criminal law and criminality. It has been broadened over time to also include professional practice in the criminal justice field. It is a word that can be used to define various areas of work in the criminal justice system such as forensic science, forensic psychology and forensic social work. *See Forensic Services (Chapter 6).*

Foster Placements

Foster placements, or foster care refers to alternative family living arrangements for children who are unable to live with their family of origin. When a child is found to be neglected or abused and their family is either unable or unwilling to care for them, specially trained foster parents are found to look after them and the government financially supports this arrangement. *See Pathways to Youth Offending (Chapter 5).*

Hate Crime

Hate crimes are also known as bias-motivated crimes and refer to a range of crimes (usually involving violence) where a perpetrator targets a victim purely because of their perceived membership or association with a specific social group. The social groups most commonly victimised by hate crimes are characterised by gender, sexual orientation, ethnicity or disability.

Hegemonic

Hegemonic refers to the state of dominance or predominant influence in a particular setting, situation or group. For example, a political party could have hegemonic control of all or certain aspects of society or a particular gender could have hegemonic control of a workplace culture. Hegemony also denotes leadership or supremacy and can be applied to the process of a dominant and wealthy developed nation aggressively expanding their dominance and control over smaller and less developed nations.

Hidden Crime

The term 'hidden crime' refers to criminal activity that may not appear in the official statistics. These crimes are predominantly, but not always, in the domestic arena such as domestic violence, elder abuse and child abuse. Criminologists are aware that these crimes are largely under-reported and therefore much of the crime that occurs in these areas is hidden. Criminologists are also aware that due to this phenomenon official statistics cannot be relied on as a true indicator of the actual level of these crimes.

Human Rights

Human rights are universally accepted as being the inalienable and fundamental rights to which a person is entitled by virtue of being human. These are not something a person has to earn and they cannot be removed from a person. These basic inalienable rights are enshrined in the *United Nations Universal Declaration of Human Rights* (UNDHR). In the United Kingdom the *Human Rights Act 1998* received Royal Assent on 9 November 1998 and came into force on 2 October 2000.

Humane

Having the characteristics of compassion, mercy, kindness and benevolence towards people and animals. Acting with respect and in a way that causes the least amount of harm. What is considered humane practice and response within the juvenile justice and criminal justice systems is guided by legal apparatus such as legislation and the United Nations Declarations.

Hypothesis

A hypothesis is a statement of a proposed theory in a way that can be tested by research methodology. This statement predicts an outcome or a relationship between two or more variables and may or may not have a direction included within the statement. *See Quantitative Research* (*Chapter 4*).

Inductive Logic

Inductive analysis is a process by which all the individual facts are analysed without prior expectation. By looking closely at the individual elements that make up a larger picture, an overall conclusion, theory or principle can be formed. This is inductive logic. *See Qualitative Research* (*Chapter 4*).

Intelligence-led Policing

Intelligence-led policing focuses on the traditional law enforcement role using modern methods and incorporating modern technology. The police enforcement and disruption measures are aimed at reducing the problem of crime by understanding the ability of criminals to do their business, informed by intelligence work aimed at understanding this business and those involved in it. *See* (*Chapter 6*).

Jurisprudence

Jurisprudence is the study of the philosophy of law and legal theory. The term has also been applied to the analysis of the rule of law, judicial decision making and the fair and transparent processing of law within society. *See Cesare Beccaria* (*Chapter 3*).

Learned Helplessness

Learned helplessness is a process by which the victim, having been exposed to ongoing abuse over a period of time, becomes dependent on the abuser and loses self-confidence and self-esteem, making it difficult to leave the situation. *See Domestic Violence* (*Chapter 5*).

Macro, Meso and Micro Factors

Sociological commentators will often refer to macro, meso and micro factors involved in specific social phenomena. Macro factors are the big picture influences and national systems such as the socio-political system, the laws and economics. Meso factors are the influences at the local and community level. Micro is the individual level and includes the immediate family unit. *See Pathways to Youth Offending* (*Chapter 5*).

Managerialism

Managerialism, or the 'new public management' (Consadine and Painter 1997) is characterised by an orientation towards efficiency, productivity and accountability. From the 1980s, government, facing growing public perception that it had failed to produce results across the criminal justice and broader social welfare sector, moved towards private sector entrepreneurial management. This orientation has led to the outsourcing of key service and programme delivery to the non-government sector and to an emphasis on documenting efficiency and outcomes based on identified key performance indicators.

Moral Panics

Moral panics are one way in which crime can be socially constructed and the formal response to crime can be engineered by the media and interest groups. A moral panic occurs when a particular issue is exaggerated by the media or interest groups in a way that may not be related in fact to the real or potential harm or damage caused by the problem. This phenomenon was raised by Stanley Cohen (1972) in his book *Folk Devils and Moral Panics*, using such terms as 'social constructionism' and 'deviancy amplification' to explain moral panics. In his book, Cohen describes how moral panics are created and escalated by the mass media and are then reinforced by social commentators such as ministers of religion, accredited experts and politicians. These people, along with the editors of the media outlets, become the moral entrepreneurs of society. *See **Stanley Cohen** (Chapter 3)*.

Natural Justice

The term natural justice is a technical term used in British law for the rule against bias and the right to a fair trial (also known by the Latin term *audi alteram partem*). It refers generally to the duty to act fairly in administrative and legal processes. Natural justice embodies the concepts of:

- The right to be heard;
- The right to answer any accusations;
- Prior notice of a case to answer;
- The opportunity to present one's own case.

Any case that may affect the rights or interests of a person is subject to the requirements of natural justice. *See **The Function of the Criminal Justice System** (Chapter 6)*.

Net Widening

There is a concern among some people working within criminal justice system that some programmes aimed at rehabilitation, such as restorative justice programmes, may actually be extending the sphere of social control among people (especially youth) who may not have received a sanction if restorative justice were not available.

Null Hypothesis

A null hypothesis is a default position that is an opposite statement to that which a researcher considers to be the expected result. The null hypothesis does not assume a relationship between variables. It is the null hypothesis that the researcher will strive to disprove, nullify and reject. The null hypothesis is assumed to be true until proven otherwise. *See **Quantitative Research** (Chapter 4)*.

Offender Management

The primary offender management and rehabilitation model employed within corrections is the risk-need-responsivity model (RNR). The RNR model was developed in America and Canada in the 1980s in response to the stance against rehabilitation expressed throughout the 1970s and the move towards a risk management framework within the field of corrections. Conceptually the RNR model individually and psychometrically identifies risk. Risk factors are quantified with the potential risk posed by individuals predicted on the basis of the presence of accumulated factors associated with offending behaviour. These factors are derived from models generated from the demographic, social and offence history profiles of known offenders. Risk factors are commonly expressed as either static or dynamic. Static risk factors are those factors that cannot be changed and include previous offence history, poor history of compliance, sex and age at onset of offending. Dynamic risk factors may be either stable or acute. *See **Sentence Administration; Community-based Corrections** (Chapter 6)*.

Organised Crime

Organised crime is characterised by offenders acting in planned and synchronised collaboration with each other to engage in criminal activity on a large scale. The criminal organisations that are formed operate centralised enterprises that are focused predominantly on financial gain or ideological ends. The types of crime that tend to characterise organised criminal activity include: human trafficking; drug production, distribution and smuggling; child pornography; arms dealing; and terrorism. *See **Human Trafficking** (Chapter 5)*.

Panopticon

The panopticon is a specific design for prisons and detention centres created by Bentham (1789) who tried to convince the authorities that an architectural design based on a circular building arranged around a central point at which every cell could be visible provided continuous surveillance and therefore increased security. Bentham argued that this architectural design and operational approach would provide an answer to the human problems of incarceration including idleness, mental instability and poverty (Bentham 1789/1982). While there were two prisons built according to the theoretical propositions advocated by Bentham, one in France and one in the United States, his theories have largely remained unimplemented by modern correctional organisations. *See Jeremy Bentham (Chapter 3).*

Parole

Conditional early release of a prisoner to serve the remainder of their sentence in the community under the supervision of a parole officer. Strict conditions apply to their behaviour, associations and activities while they are on parole. *See Community-based Corrections (Chapter 6).*

Penology

Penology is the study of prisons, people who work in prisons, inmates, prison management, sentences of imprisonment and any punishment that includes custody or which occurs within a custodial setting. *See Prisons (Chapter 6).*

Problem-oriented Policing

Problem-oriented policing (POP) holds that the role of policing:

- focuses on real recurrent problems;
- attempts to work out why they have persisted;
- analyses their underlying sources;
- figures out what might be done to ameliorate or remove them on the basis of the analysis; and
- checks whether the strategy has had the intended outcome (Tilley 2010:183).

In this approach identifying the problem accurately is crucial and 'calls for the close specification of problems' (Tilley 2003). POP is therefore oriented towards dealing with underlying problems, patterns in offence types or offender/victim typologies, and the tactics employed are contingent upon how the problem has been defined. There is scope to involve the community and address root causes of crime as in community policing but the focus is on problem identification and analysis. *See Policing (Chapter 6).*

Public Shaming

Public shaming is a process by which people are publicly humiliated as a means of punishment or to enforce conformity to group norms. Through this process the individual is thought to experience emotionally pain brought about by the realisation that they have brought dishonour on themselves and their family. Public shaming is also a formal judicial process by which a convicted person is sentenced to public humiliation instead of imprisonment. An example of this is people caught stealing being forced to walk around with a sign around their neck reading 'I am a thief'. Few jurisdictions use this form of punishment. *See Republican Criminology (Chapter 6).*

Punishment

Many criminologists have advanced theories about the role of punishment in encouraging conformity to society's norms. Punishment can have the primary function of incapacitation, deterrence, retribution, restitution or reformation. Then main types of punishment used in modern Western society are: imprisonment, community-based supervision, fines, reparative actions and community service work. Some Western jurisdictions such as some American states still have the death penalty. Community-based sanctions are widely used and are a cost-effective means of punishment. Prisons allow the authorities to have systematic control over the time, space and behaviour of individuals who are confined to imprisonment. *See Jeremy Bentham (Chapter 6).*

Recidivism

Repeat offending, despite social sanctions applied to stop the offending behaviour, is referred to as 'recidivism'. Recidivism also refers to the continued offending of someone who has previously been involved with the criminal justice system and has been exposed to punishment and/or rehabilitative interventions aimed at extinguishing the behaviour. Recidivism is also referred to as relapse and there are specific programmes operating in the correctional system that are aimed at relapse prevention. Some categories of offenders are at higher risk of repeat offending than others such as sex offenders and domestic violence perpetrators.

Recidivism Redacted Data

Redacting data is the process by which sensitive or classified government information is removed from a document before it is released to the public. It is sometimes referred to as sanitising the document. In relation to other applications outside government, redaction can be applied to the removal of confidential information before it is released to another person. An example of this is the removal of personal addresses and phone numbers from a committee list before releasing it. *See Chapter 4*: Criminological Research.

Rehabilitation

The process by which criminal offenders are encouraged to change their attitudes and behaviours as a result of targeted intervention in the criminal justice system. Rehabilitation is the process by which people are restored or established anew in a non-offending lifestyle and mindset. *See Rehabilitation (Chapter 6)*.

Reintegration

Reintegration refers to an offender's transition from prison custody into the community. Also referred to as 're-entry' or 'resettlement', the focus is on establishing connections (through employment, family, services, etc.) to promote engagement in a productive, crime-free lifestyle. Ideally, the process of reintegration will begin upon reception to the custodial facility and will involve collaborative service delivery designed to support an individual during their entire period of incarceration and for a period of time post-release

(also referred to as aftercare). *See Rehabilitation and Restorative Justice (Chapter 6)*.

Reliable Versus Unreliable Websites

Unreliable websites are those where authorship is uncertain, that do not have publication dates or that have unsupported opinions about the criminal justice system. The reason for this is that you are unable to verify whether in fact the author has any authority in relation to discussing the topic and whether the information provided is accurate. Reliable websites, by contrast, are those that belong to registered organisations such as the government sites, or associations such as the Offenders Aid and Rehabilitation Service or the Victim Support Service. These associations have the authority to discuss topics related to the criminal justice system and are well-regarded stakeholders within the criminal justice system.

Responsivity

Responsivity is the extent to which the individual offender is responsive to the treatment programme and how responsive the programme is to the criminogenic and non-criminogenic needs of the individual. A programme is only effective if it targets the specific needs of the individual in a way the individual can respond to. *See Rehabilitation (Chapter 6)*.

Restitution

Restitution is the process of restoring to the rightful owner something that has been lost, stolen or damaged. In the criminal justice system, restitution means restoring the damage that criminal offending has caused and/or returning something that has been stolen. Restitution can be made to the victim and/or to the community and can be in the form of monetary compensation or actions aimed at repairing the harm done (for example, cleaning away graffiti from a public area). It is believed that by the act of making retribution to the community, the offender can also restore their own place within that community, increasing their chances of rehabilitation. *See Restorative Justice (Chapter 6)*.

Retribution

Retribution is also known as 'just deserts' and refers to an approach to punishment. Retribution aims to show the offender the anger, disappointment and disapproval of society towards the crimes that have been commitment. Retribution is not concerned with rehabilitation or deterrence because it is based on the need for society to seek revenge on the offender. A basic principle of punishment in the criminal justice system is that it should be proportional to the crime; however, retributive approaches are often disproportionate (for example mandatory sentencing of juveniles to detention for relatively minor offending in some jurisdictions).

Situational Crime Prevention

Situational crime prevention refers to approaches that are aimed at specific crimes. These approaches generally involve the manipulation and management of the local environment in order to reduce specific crime categories. An example of this is improved lighting in shopping centre car parks to reduce the risk of car thefts. The aim is to make it more difficult for offenders to successfully engage in criminal behaviour. *See Environmental Criminology (Chapter 3).*

Social Exclusion

Social exclusion is a term that describes the marginalisation of people within society due to a range of complex social problems including poverty, intergenerational unemployment, social disadvantage, poor housing, poor health outcomes, family breakdown and discrimination. *See Pathways to Youth Offending (Chapter 5);* Strain Theory *(Chapter 3).*

Socialisation

Informal social control occurs in a process called socialisation where members of a family, group or society are 'taught' what is acceptable and unacceptable. People who deviate from the accepted norms of the group are exposed to stigma and punishment thereby ensuring future compliance. Socialisation results in the internalisation of the group norms so that external formal social control is no longer required in order for the individual to conform.

Social Solidarity

Social solidarity is the degree to which a society is bonded together. Another name for social solidarity is social cohesion. It is a state of interdependence based on kinship and community ties. In simple terms, social solidarity refers to the invisible ties that bind individuals to society.

The Good Lives Model

The good lives model (GLM) is a strengths-based approach to offender rehabilitation. The model, oriented towards 'goods promotion' (see http://www.goodlivesmodel.com) acknowledges the need for a risk management focus but stresses the enhancement of positive capabilities and human agency. In essence the GLM suggests that by promoting human good, risks are reduced. As such it can be seen as a supplementary approach to the RNR model.

Theory of Group Conflict

American George Vold (1958) argued that groups, for the benefit of their own or other groups, carry out criminal activity. Sometimes the criminal activity is a result of the tension and conflict that builds up between groups. He argues, for example, that certain types of crimes stem from conflicts between workers and the owners of industrial production. These crimes are often seen in the context of 'social problems' rather than criminality. *See American Radicalism (Chapter 3).*

Typology of Crime

American radicalist Quinney (1977) published a groundbreaking book entitled *Class, State and Crime* in which he provided a typology of crime. This typology of crime included:

- crimes of domination;

— crimes of accommodation and resistance; and
— crimes of resistance.

Crimes of domination include crimes of control such as crimes committed by the police and governments and financial crimes committed by large corporations. Crimes of accommodation and resistance include predatory crimes such as burglary and theft and personal crimes such as sexual assault and homicide. Crimes of resistance include political crimes and terrorism. *See American Radicalism (Chapter 3)*.

Utilitarianism

Utilitarianism is the theory that the best course of action is that which maximises the utility or usage of a situation for the moral good while reducing human suffering and negative consequences for the majority. Put simply, utilitarianism means 'the greatest happiness for the greatest number'. It involves actions that should on balance be intended to produce good or at the very least reduce harm for many, even if this causes discomfort to one or two individuals.

Verdict

The decision of the court that is a pronouncement of the guilt or innocence of an accused person and is made by the judge or jury involved in a court case. *See The Legal System (Chapter 6)*.

Victim Precipitation

Victim precipitation is a term that was coined by theorist Benjamin Mendelsohn. It refers to the belief that the victim has encouraged, incited, provoked or otherwise attracted the criminal acts of the offender. *See Victims and the Justice System (Chapter 5)*.

Victimology

Victimology is a relatively new branch of criminology that focuses specifically on victims and victim issues. It covers a broad range of topics, including victim impact, victim response, victim representation, victim compensation and restorative justice. *See Victims and the Justice System (Chapter 5)*.

Violence

Violence refers to aggressive behaviour that is aimed at intimidating and/or harming another person or their property. It includes threats and intimidation. *See Violent Crime and Domestic Violence (Chapter 5)*.

Young Offender

A young offender is a person who is, or has been, engaged in criminal activity and who is under the age of 18 years. Young offenders are dealt with in a separate section of the criminal justice system known as the juvenile justice system. Work with young offenders is usually directed towards rehabilitation and diverting them from the adult criminal justice system. Some programmes that have shown promising results in this regard are family group conferencing and restorative justice. *See Pathways to Youth Offending (Chapter 5)*; *Juvenile Justice (Chapter 5)*.

Zero Tolerance

Zero tolerance is the idea that no crime should be ignored, even small crimes. If small crimes are ignored then more serious crimes will be committed.

References

Adler, F. 1975. *Sisters in Crime*. New York, USA: McGraw-Hill

Agnew, R. 1992. 'Foundations for a General Strain Theory of Crime and Delinquency' *Criminology* 30, 47–87.

Agnew, R. 2001. 'Building on the Foundation of General Strain Theory: Specifying the Types of Strain Most Likely to Lead to Crime and Delinquency' *Journal of Research in Crime and Delinquency* 38(4) November, 319–361.

AIHW (Australian Institute of Health and Welfare). 2014. 'Prisoner Health Services in Australia' *Bulletin* 123, August. Melbourne, Victoria: Australian Institute of Health and Welfare.

Ainsworth, P. B. 2001. *Offender Profiling and Crime Analysis*. Portland, USA: Willan Publishing.

Akers, R. L. 1985. *Deviant Behaviour: A Social Learning Approach* (3rd edition). Belmont, California: Wadsworth.

American Psychiatric Association. 2000. *Diagnostic and Statistical Manual of Mental Disorders Fourth Edition (DSM-IV)*. Washington: American Psychiatric Association.

Amnesty International. 2006, 28 March. 'UK: Rape: New Government Measures Welcomed, But Much More Needed' Press Release. Accessed online on 4 November 2016 at: www.amnesty.org.uk/press-releases/uk-rape-new-government-measures-welcomed-much-more-needed.

Andrews D. A. & Bonta, J. 1998. *Psychology of Criminal Conduct* (2nd edition). Cincinnati, USA: Anderson.

Andrews, D. A., Bonta, J. & Wormith, J. S. 2011. 'The Risk-Need-Responsivity (RNR) Model: Does Adding the Good Lives Model Contribute to Effective Crime Prevention?' *Criminal Justice and Behaviour* July 38(7), 735–755.

Ashley, S. 2004. 'Reducing the Risks of Police Pursuit' Police Policy Council. Accessed online on 27 November 2016 at: www.theppsc.org/Staff_Views/Ashley/reducing_the_risks_of_police_pursuit.htm.

Ashmore, Z. 2005. *Poor Educational Outcomes are Linked to Youth Offending*. London, UK: The British Psychological Society, Division of Forensic Psychology BPS Press Office.

Attorney General's Office. 2016. *Australia's Counter Terrorism Laws*. Information Pamphlet. Canberra: Australian Attorney General's Department.

Australian Bureau of Statistics. 2015. *Population Growth December Statistics 2013–2014*. Accessed online on 5 November 2016 at: www.abs.gov.au.

Australian Human Rights Commission. 2016. 'Agenda for Racial Equality 2012–2016' Accessed online on 31 October 2016 at: www.humanrights.gov.au/publications/agenda-racial-equality-2012-2016-agenda-racial-equality.

Australian Institute of Criminology. 2008. 'People Smuggling Versus Trafficking in Persons: What is the Difference?' *Transnational Crime Brief* 2. Canberra: Australian Institute of Criminology.

Australian Institute of Criminology. 2009. 'Key Issues in Domestic Violence' *Research in Practice Summary Paper* 7 December.

Australian Law Reform Commission. 2004. 'Tribunals in Australia: Their Roles and Responsibilities' *Reform* Autumn, 84.

Bagaric, M. & Alexander, T. 2014. 'A Rational Approach to Sentencing White-collar Offenders in Australia' *Adelaide Law Review* 34, 317–349.

Bandura, A. 1978. 'Social Learning Theory of Aggression' *Journal of Communication* 28(3), 12–28.

Bandura, A. 1986. *Social Foundations of Thought and Action: A Social Cognitive Theory*. Englewood Cliffs New Jersey, USA: Prentice-Hall.

Bandura, A. 2002. 'Social Cognitive Theory in Cultural Context' *Applied Psychology: An International Review* 51(2), 269–290.

Bandura, A. 2006. 'Toward a Psychology of Human Agency' *Perspectives of Psychological Science* 1(2), 164–180.

Banks, D., Davies, C., Gosling, J., Newman, J., Rice, M., Wadley, J. & Walvarens, F. 2008. *Environmental Crime: A Threat to Our Future*. London, UK: Environmental Investigation Agency.

Barnes, L. A. 2001. 'Protective Custody and Hardship in Prison' in Potas, I. (ed.) *An Analysis of New South Wales Sentencing Statistics and Related Issues*, Number 21 February. Sydney: Judicial Commission of NSW.

Barrett, D. 2014, 9 October. 'Britain Has Largest Legal Aid Budget in Europe, Says Report' *The Telegraph*. Accessed online on 30 November 2016 at: www.telegraph.co.uk/news/uknews/law-and-order/11149868/Britain-has-largest-legal-aid-budget-in-Europe-says-report.html.

Barry, M. 2010. 'Youth Transitions: From Offending to Desistance' *Journal of Youth Studies* 13(1), 121–136.

Batrinos, M. L. 2012. 'Testosterone and Aggressive Behaviour in Man' *International Journal of Endocrinology and Metabolism* 10(3), 563–568.

Beccaria, C. 1764/1819. *Essay on Crimes and Punishment* (2nd American edition). Philadelphia: Philip H Nicklin Publishers.

Becker, H. S. 1963. *Outsiders: Studies in the Sociology of Deviance*. New York: The Free Press.

Belknap, J. 2001. *The Invisible Woman: Gender, Crime and Justice*. Belmont USA: Wadsworth.

Bennet, T. & Holloway, K. 2005. *Understanding Drugs, Alcohol and Crime*. Maidenhead, UK: Open University Press McGraw-Hill House.

Bentham, J. 1789/1982. *A Fragment of Government and an Introduction to the Principles of Morals and Legislation*. London: Hafner Press.

Bernburg, J. G. & Krohn, M. 2003. 'Labeling, Life Chances, and Adult Crime: The Direct and Indirect Effects of Official Intervention in Adolescence on Crime in Early Adulthood' *Criminology* 41(4), 1287–1318.

Bernburg, J. G., Krohn, M. & Rivera, C. 2006. 'Official Labelling: Criminal Embeddedness and Subsequent Delinquency' *Journal of Research in Crime and Delinquency* 43(1) February, 67–88.

Berry-Dee, C, 2003, *Talking With Serial Killers*. London, UK: John Blake Publishing.

Bevier, L. 2015. 'The Meaning of Cultural Criminology: A Theoretical and Methodological Lineage' *Journal of Theoretical and Philosophical Criminology* 7(2), 34–48.

Bevilacqua, M. 2013, 29 March. 'Study: Urban Vegetation, When Well Maintained, Deters Crime' Next City. Accessed online on 30 November 2016 at: https://nextcity.org/daily/entry/study-urban-vegetation-when-well-maintained-deters-crime.

Blau, P. M. & Golden, R. M. 1986. 'Metropolitan Structure and Criminal Violence' *Sociological Quarterly* 27, 15–26.

Blumer, H. 1969. *Symbolic Interactionism: Perspective and Method*. Englewood Cliffs NJ: Prentice-Hall.

Blyth, M., Hayward, G. & Stephenson, M. 2004. 'Effective Educational Interventions With Young People Who Offend' in Burnett, R. & Roberts, C. (eds) *What Works in Probation and Youth Justice*, Devon Willan Publishing: London UK.

Boles, S. & Miotto, K. 2003. 'Substance Abuse and Violence: A Review of the Literature' *Aggression & Violent Behaviour* 8, 155–174.

Bonger, W. 1916. *Criminality and Economic Conditions*. Boston, USA: Little, Brown & Co.

Bonta, J. & Andrews, D. 2007. *Risk-Need-Responsivity Model for Offender Assessment and Rehabilitation 2007–06*. Ottawa, Canada: Public Safety Canada.

Box, S. 1987. *Recession, Crime and Punishment*. London, UK: Tavistock.

Bragg, H. L. 2003. *Child Protection in Families Experiencing Family Violence*. Washington DC: National Clearinghouse on Child Abuse and Neglect Information.

Braithwaite, J. 2011. 'The Irony of State Intervention' in Lilly, J. R., Cullen, F. T. & Ball, R. A. (eds) *Criminological Theory: Context and Consequences* (5th edition), 139–165. Thousand Oaks, California: Sage Publications.

Braithwaite, J. & Pettit, P. 1990. *Not Just Deserts: A Republican Theory of Criminal Justice*. New York, USA: Oxford University Press.

Braithwaite, J. & Pettit, P. 1994. 'Republican Criminology and Victim Advocacy' *Law and Society Review* 28(4), 765–776.

Brantingham, P. L. & Brantingham, P. J. 1993. 'Environment, Routine and Situation: Toward a Pattern Theory of Crime' in *From Routine Activity and Rational Choice: Advances in Criminological Theory* Volume 5, 259–294. New Jersey, USA: Rutgers.

Brennan, S. 2011. *Police-reported Crime Statistics in Canada 2011*. Ottawa: Statistics Canada.

Bricknell, S. 2008. 'Trends in Violent Crime' *Trends & Issues in Crime and Criminal Justice* 359. Canberra: Australian Institute of Criminology.

Broidy, L. & Agnew, R. 2004. 'Gender and Crime: A General Strain Theory Perspective' in Chesney-Lind, M. & Pasko, L. (eds) *Girls, Women and Crime*. Thousand Oaks, California: Sage.

Brown, S., Esbensen, F. A. & Geis, G. 2015. *Criminology: Explaining Crime and Its Context*. New York, NY: Routledge.

Bucy, P. H., Formby, E. P., Raspanti, M. S. & Rooney, K. E. 2012. 'Why Do They Do It? The Motives, Mores, and Character of White Collar Criminals' *St Johns Law Review* 82 (2)Spring, 401–572.

Bune, K. L. 2007, 5 March. 'Understanding the Dynamics of Domestic Violence' Officer.com. Accessed online on 31 October 2016 at: www.officer.com/article/10250106/understanding-the-dynamics-of-domestic-violence.

Burnett, R. & Roberts, C. 2004. *What Works in Probation and Youth Justice: Developing Evidence-based Practice*. Devon, UK: Willan Publishing.

Bush, G.W. 20 September 2001. 'Address to the Joint Session of the 107th Congress'. Selected Speeches of President George W. Bush 2001–2008, Whitehouse Archives. Accessed online at: http://georgewbush-whitehouse.archives.gov/infocus/bushrecord/documents/Selected_Speeches_George_W_Bush.pdf

Callan, V. & Gardner, J. 2007. 'The Role of VET in Recidivism in Australia' in Dawe, S. (ed.) *Vocational Education and Training for Adult Prisoners and Offenders in Australia: Research Readings*, 27–36. Adelaide: NCVER.

Campbell-Culver, M. 2006. *A Passion for Trees: The Legacy of John Evelyn*. London: Transworld Publishers.

Canadian Government. 2009. 'Children and Youth as Victims of Violent Crime' National Victims of Crime Awareness Week. Accessed online on 31 October 2016 at: www.victimsweek.gc.ca/res/r56.html.

Canberra Domestic Violence Crisis Service. 2016. 'What is Domestic Violence, Family Violence and Intimate Partner Violence?' Accessed online on 31 October 2016 at: http://dvcs.org.au/.

Caspi, A., McClay, J., Moffitt, T. E., Mill, J., Martin, J. Craig, I. W., Taylor, A. & Poulton, R. 2005. 'Role of Genotype in the Cycle of Violence in Maltreated Children: Fears of the Future in Children and Young People' *Journal for Sociology of Education and Socialization* 25(2) 133–145.

Carlen, P. 1983. *Women's Imprisonment*. London, UK: Routledge & Kegan Paul.

Carlen, P, 2002. *Women and Punishment: The Struggle for Justice*. Portland Oregon, USA: Willan Publishing.

Carrington, K. 1993 *Offending Girls*. St Leonards, Australia: Allen & Unwin.

Casciani, D. 2007, 18 September. 'Needless Risks in Police Chases' *BBC News*. Accessed online on 27 November 2016 at: http://news.bbc.co.uk/2/hi/uk_news/7000318.stm.

Cattarello, A. 2000. 'Community-level Influences on Individual's Social Bonds, Peer Associations, and Delinquency: A Multilevel Analysis' *Justice Quarterly* 17, 33–60.

Caulfield, L. & Hill, J. 2014. *Criminological Research for Beginners: A Student's Guide*. New York: Routledge.

Centre for Innovative Justice. 2014. *Innovative Justice Responses to Sexual Offending: Pathways to Better Outcomes for Victims, Offenders and the Community*. Melbourne: RMIT University.

CEOPC. 2015. 'CEOP Command' National Crime Agency Webpage. Accessed online on 31 October 2016 at: www.ceop.police.uk/ About-Us/.

Chambliss, W. 1964. 'A Sociological Analysis of the Law of Vagrancy' *Social Problems* 12(1), 67–77.

Chambliss, W. 1975. 'Towards a Political Economy of Crime' *Theory and Society* 2(2), 149–170.

Chambliss, W. 1978. *On the Take: From Petty Crooks to Presidents*. Bloomington: Indiana University Press

Chesney-Lind, M. 1997. *The Female Offender: Girls, Women and Crime*. Thousand Oaks, California: Sage Publications.

Chesney-Lind, M. & Pasko, L. 2004. *Girls, Women and Crime*. Thousand Oaks, California: Sage.

Chulov, M. 2014, 11 December. 'Isis: The Inside Story' *The Guardian*. Accessed online on 8 November 2016 at: www.theguardian. com/world/2014/dec/11/-sp-isis-the-inside-story.

Clark, M. 1993. *History of Australia* (abridged by Michael Cathcart). Melbourne: Melbourne University Press.

Clarke, A. 2008. *E-Learning Skills* (2nd edition). Basingstoke, UK: Palgrave Macmillan.

Clarke, R. V. 2011. 'Seven Misconceptions of Situational Crime Prevention' in Tilley N (ed.) *Handbook of Crime Prevention and Community Safety*, Chapter 3, 39–70. London: Routledge.

Cliff, G. & Desilets, C. 2014. 'White Collar Crime: What It Is and Where It's Going' *Notre Dame Journal of Law, Ethics & Public Policy* 28(2), 523.

Cloward, R, & Ohlin, L. 1960. *Delinquency and Opportunity*. New York, USA: Free Press.

Cohen, A. 1955. *Delinquent Boys*. New York, USA: The Free Press.

Cohen, L. & Felson, M. 1979. 'Social Change and Crime Rate Trends: A Routine Activity Approach' *American Sociological Review* 44(4), 588–608.

Cohen, S. 1972/2002. *Folk Devils and Moral Panics* (3rd edition). London, UK: Routledge.

Cohen, S. 1985. *Visions of Social Control*. Cambridge, UK: Polity Press.

Coleman, J. 2013. *Handbook of Forensic Services*. Quantico, Virginia: Federal Bureau of Investigation.

Colgan, P. 2015, 24 September. 'These New Stats Reveal the Horrifying Scale of Domestic Violence in Australia' *Business Insider*. Accessed online on 25 November 2016 at: www.Businessinsider.com.au/these-new-stats-reveal-the-horrifying-scale-of-domestic-violence-in-australia-2015-9.

Collier, R. 1998. *Masculinities, Crime and Criminology*. London, UK: Sage Publications.

Collins, J. & Spencer, D. 2002. 'Linkage of Domestic Violence and Substance Abuse Services' *Research in Brief Executive Summary* US Department of Justice.

Comte, A. 1844/1903. *Discourse on the Positive Spirit* (translated by E Beesley). London: W Reeves.

Comte, A. 1848/1880. *A General View of Positivism* (translated by J. Bridges). London: Trübuer & Co.

Comte, A. 1856. *Religion of Humanity: Subjective Synthesis, or Universal system of the Conceptions Adapted to the Normal State of Humanity*. London: Routledge.

Commission of the European Communities. 2007. *Towards a General Policy on the Fight Against Cybercrime*, COM {SEC (2007) 641} final of 22.5.2007. Accessed online on 25 November 2016 at: http://www.sicurezzacibernetica.it/db/[2007]%20COM%20 267%20-%20Towards%20a%20general%20policy%20on%20the%20fight%20against%20cyber%20crime.pdf.

Connor, S. 1995, 12 February. 'Do Your Genes Make You a Criminal?' *The Independent*. Accessed online on 4 November 2016 at: www.independent.co.uk/news/uk/do-your-genes-make-you-a-criminal-1572714.html.

Consadine, M. & Painter, M. (eds). 1997. *Managerialism: The Great Debate*. Melbourne, Australia: Melbourne University Press.

Conte, A. 2010. *Human Rights in the Prevention and Punishment of Terrorism: Commonwealth Approaches: The United Kingdom, Canada, Australia and New Zealand*. Berlin: Springer.

Corby, B. 1997. 'Mistreatment of Young People' in Roche, J. & Tucker, S. (eds) *Youth and Society*. London, UK: Sage Publications.

Cornish, D. & Clarke, R. V. 1986. 'Introduction' in Cornish, D. & Clarke, R. (eds) *The Reasoning Criminal: Rational Choice Perspectives on Offending*, 1–16. New York, USA: Springer-Verlag.

Cortoni, F., Hanson, R. K. & Coach, M. E. 2010. 'The Recidivism Rate of Female Sexual Offenders are Low: A Meta-analysis' *Sexual Abuse* December 22(4), 387–401.

Cottrell, S. 2013. *Study Skills Handbook* (4th edition). Basingstoke, UK: Palgrave Macmillan.

Cottrell, S: 2017. Critical Thinking Skills: Effective Analysis, Argument and Reflection (3rd edition). London, UK: Palgrave.

Council of Europe. 2015. 'Responding to Cybercrime' CETS 185 Treaty Office. Accessed online on 8 November 2016 at: http:// conventions.coe.int/Treaty/EN/Treaties/html/185.htm.

Cowell, A., Broner, N. & Dupont, R. 2004. 'The Cost-effectiveness of Criminal Justice Diversion Programs for People With Serious Mental Illness Co-occurring With Substance Abuse' *Journal of Contemporary Criminal Justice* 20(3), 292–315.

Craddock, N. 2011. 'Horses for Courses: The Need for Pragmatism and Realism as Well as Balance and Caution: A Commentary on Angel' *Social Science and Medicine* 73, 636–638.

Creative Spirits. 2016. 'Aboriginal Prison Rates' Law & Justice. Accessed online on 31 October 2016 at: www.creativespirits.info/aboriginalculture/law/aboriginal-prison-rates.

Crime and Misconduct Commission. 2005. *Policing Domestic Violence in Queensland: Meeting the Challenges Report*. Brisbane, Qld: Crime and Misconduct Commission.

Crockett, Z. 2015, 22 July. 'The Case for Banning High-speed Police Chases' Priceonomics. Accessed online on 31 October 2016 at: https://priceonomics.com/the-case-for-banning-high-speed-police-chases/.

Cunneen, C. 2002. *NSW Aboriginal Justice Plan Discussion Paper*. Sydney Australia: Aboriginal Justice Advisory Council, University of Sydney.

Dahrendorf, R. 1959. *Class and Class Conflict in Industrial Society*. Stanford, USA: Standford University Press.

Daily Mail. 2015, 12 July. 'Cities Across the Country Report a 'Scary' Rise in Violent Crime: Shootings Rise by up to 18 Per Cent After Months of Anti-cop Anger' Accessed online on 7 November 2016 at: www.dailymail.co.uk/news/article-3158139/Cities-country-report-scary-rise-violent-crime-Shootings-rise-18-cent-anti-cop-anger.html.

Daily Mail. 2016, 20 October. 'Boy, 12, Appears in Court Charged with Rape of Six Year Old Girl in the School Toilets' Accessed online on 7 November 2016 at: http://www.dailymail.co.uk/news/article-3854024/Boy-12-appears-court-charged-rape-six-year-old-girl-school-toilets.html.

Dalton, K. 1961. 'Menstruation and Crime' *British Medical Journal* 2(5269) December, 30, 78–86.

Daly, K. & Immarigeon, R. 1998. 'The Past, Present, and Future of Restorative Justice: Some Critical Reflections' *The Contemporary Justice Review* 1(1), 21–45.

Das Gupta, R. & Guest, J. 2002. 'Annual Cost of Bipolar Disorder to UK Society' *British Journal of Psychiatry* 180, 227–233.

Davies, P., Francis, P. & Greer, C. 2007. *Victims, Crime & Society*. London, UK: Sage Publications.

Davies, P., Francis, P. & Jupp, V. 2011. *Doing Criminological Research*. London, UK: Sage Publications.

Davey, M. 2014, 2 November. 'Luke Batty: Killed by a Father No One Truly Knew' *The Guardian*. Accessed online on 7 November 2016 at: www.theguardian.com/australia-news/2014/nov/02/-sp-luke-batty-killed-by-a-father-no-one-truly-knew.

Day, A. & Wanganeen, R. 2003. *The Needs of Young Indigenous People in Secure Care in South Australia*. Adelaide, Australia: University of South Australia and the Sacred Healing Centre.

Day, E. 2015, 19 July. '#Blacklivesmatter: The Birth of a New Civil Rights Movement' *The Guardian*. Accessed online on 7 November 2016 at: www.theguardian.com/world/2015/jul/19/blacklivesmatter-birth-civil-rights-movement.

Department of Justice. 2016. 'Security Ratings' Corrections Victoria 10 October. Accessed online on 19 January 2017 at: http://www.corrections.vic.gov.au/home/prison/going+to+prison/prisoner+placement/.

Dhami, M. K. 2007. 'White-collar Prisoners' Perceptions of Audience Reaction' *Deviant Behaviour* 28, 57–77.

Domestic Abuse Project. 2016. 'Domestic Violence is Complex' Accessed online on 31 October 2016 at: www.domesticabuseproject.com/get-educated/dynamics-of-domestic-abuse/.

Donnerstein, E. & Linz, D. 1995. 'The Media' in Wilson, J. Q. & Petersilia, J. (eds) *Crime*, 237–266. San Francisco, USA: Institute for Contemporary Studies Press.

Draine, J., Salzer, M., Culhane, D. & Hadley, T. 2002. 'Role of Social Disadvantage in Crime, Joblessness, and Homelessness Among Persons With Serious Mental Illness' *Psychiatric Services* May 53(5), 565–573.

Dünkel, F. & Snacken, S. 2000. *Crime and Criminal Justice in Europe*. Berlin, Germany: Council of Europe.

Dunn, J. 2015, 15 July. 'Undercover Police Blasted by Judge for "Entrapment" After Setting up Sting to Deliberately Sell Stolen Cable to a Scrapyard Boss' *Daily Mail*. Accessed online on 9 November 2016 at: www.dailymail.co.uk/news/article-3160454/Undercover-police-blasted-judge-after-setting-sting-to-deliberately-sell-stolen-cable-scrapyard-boss.html.

Durkheim, E. 1893/1964. *The Division of Labour in Society* (translated by W. D. Hallis). New York: Free Press.

Edelhertz, H. 1970. *The Nature Impact and Prosecution of White Collar Crime*. Washington, USA: US Department of Justice.

Edwards, M. 2015. 'Identity Theft: More Than 770,000 Australian Victims in Past Year' Australian Broadcasting Corporation. Accessed online on 8 November 2016 at: www.abc.net.au/news/2015-04-14/identity-theft-hits-australians-veda/6390570.

Elliyatt, H. 2013, 14 August. 'Why White-collar Financial Crime Is Here to Stay' CNBC Europe News. Accessed online on 31 October 2016 at: www.cnbc.com/id/100961639.

Engels, F. 1845/1969, *The Condition of the Working Class in England*, Moscow: Leipzig.

Equal Justice Initiative. 2014. 'Children in Prison' Accessed online on 31 October 2016 at: www.eji.org/childrenprison.

Evans, M. 2016, 14 January. 'How Male Victims of Domestic Abuse Often End up Getting Arrested Themselves' *The Telegraph*. Accessed online on 31 October 2016 at: www.telegraph.co.uk/news/uknews/crime/12061547/How-male-victims-of-domestic-abuse-often-end-up-getting-arrested-themselves.html.

Evans, R. & Lewis, P. 2013. *Undercover: The True Story of Britain's Secret Police*. London, UK: Guardian Books.

Fakhoury, W. & Priebe, S. 2007. 'Deinstitutionalisation and Reinstitutionalisation: Major Changes in the Provision of Mental Healthcare' *Psychiatry* 6(8), 313–316.

Fazel, S. & Danesh, J. 2002, 16 February. 'Serious Mental Disorder in 23,000 Prisoners: A Systematic Review of 62 Surveys' *The Lancet* 359, 545–550.

Fazel, S, & Grann, M. 2006. 'The Population Impact of Severe Mental Illness on Violent Crime' *American Journal of Psychiatry* 163(8) August, 1397–1403.

Fazel, S., Långström, N., Hjern, A., Grann, M. & Lichtenstein, P. 2009. 'Schizophrenia, Substance Abuse, and Violent Crime' *Journal of the American Medical Association* (JAMA) 20 May 301(19), 2016–2013.

Felson, M. 1998. *Crime and Everyday Life* (2nd edition). Thousand Oaks, California: Sage Publications.

Felson, M. & Clarke, R. V. 1998. *Opportunity Makes the Thief: Practical Theory for Crime Prevention*. London, UK: Home Office, Policing and Reducing Crime Unit.

Felson, R. B. 2009. 'Violence, Crime and Violent Crime' *International Journal of Conflict and Violence* 3(1), 23–39.

Ferrell, J., Hayward, K. & Young, J. 2008. *Cultural Criminology: An Invitation*. London, UK: Sage Publications.

Fields, G. & Emshwiller, J. R. 2012, 23 September. 'Federal Guilty Pleas Soar as Bargaining Trump Trials' *The Wall Street Journal*. Accessed online on 9 November 2016 at: www.wsj.com/articles/SB10000872396390443589304577637610097206808.

Fileborn, B. 2011. 'Sexual Assault Laws in Australia' *ACSSA Resources Sheet*. Melbourne: Australian Centre for the Study of Sexual Assault, Australian Institute of Family Studies.

Filloux, J. 1993. 'Émile Durkheim 1858–1917' *Prospects: The Quarterly Review of Comparative Education* 23(1/2), 303–320.

Finan, V. 2016, 13 March. Police Investigated Five-Year-Old Boy for Rape as New Figures Show 70 Sex Attacks Were Committed by Children Under 10 Last Year. *Daily Mail*. Accessed online on 31 October 2016 at: www.dailymail.co.uk/news/article-3489961/Police-investigate-five-year-old-boy-rape-new-figures-70-sex-attacks-committed-children-10-year.html.

Foucault, M. 1975. *Discipline and Punish: The Birth of the Prison*. London: Penguin Books.

Frank, T. 2015, 30 July. 'High-speed Police Chases Have Killed Thousands of Innocent Bystanders' *USA Today*. Accessed online on 31 October 2016 at: www.usatoday.com/story/news/2015/07/30/police-pursuits-fatal-injuries/30187827/.

Fransham, M. & Johnston, V. 2003. 'Drugs, Young People and Service Provision: Findings on Needs and Services' *Research Briefing 6*. London, UK: NACRO Research and Evaluation.

Friedrichs, D. O. 2010. *Trusted Criminals: White Collar Crime in Contemporary Society*. Belmont, CA, USA: Wadsworth.

Fuller Torrey, E., Kennard, A., Eslinger, D., Lamb, R. & Pavle, J. 2010. *More Mentally Ill Persons Are In Jails and Prisons Than In Hospitals: A Survey of the State Report*. Virginia, USA: National Sheriffs Association and Treatment Advocacy Centre.

Gaylord, M. S. & Galliher, J. F. 1988. *The Criminology of Edwin Sutherland*. New Brunswick, NJ. USA: Rutgers.

Gendreau, P. & Ross, R. 1987. 'Revivification of Rehabilitation: Evidence from the 1980s' *Justice Quarterly* 4(3), 349–407.

Gendreau, P., Goggin, C. & Cullen, F. 1999. *The Effects of Prison Sentences on Recidivism*: A Report to the Corrections Research and Development and Aboriginal Policy Branch. Ottawa, Canada: Department of the Solicitor General.

Gilmore, J. 2015, 30 April. 'The 'One in Three' Claim about Male Domestic Violence Victims is a Myth', *The Sydney Morning Herald*. Accessed online on 25 November 2016 at: www.smh.com.au/lifestyle/news-and-views/opinion/the-one-in-three-claim-about-male-domestic-violence-victims-is-a-myth-20150429-1mw3bs.html

Glaser, B. G. & Strauss, A. L. 1967. *The Discovery of Grounded Theory: Strategies for Qualitative Research*. Hawthorne, NY: Aldine de Gruyter.

Godfrey, J. 2014. *Reading and Making Notes* (2nd edition). Basingstoke, UK: Palgrave Macmillan.

Golias, P. 2004. *Offender Management Framework: Prisons and Community Correctional Services*. Melbourne, Victoria: Victorian Corrections.

Gonzales, A., Schofield, R. & Schmitt, G. 2005. *Co-offending and Patterns of Juvenile Crime*. Washington DC, USA: US Department of Justice Programs.

Grubb, B. & Massola, J. 2014, 6 August. 'What Is "Metadata" and Should You Worry If Yours Is Stored by Law?' *The Sydney Morning Herald*. Accessed online on 31 October 2016 at: www.smh.com.au/digital-life/digital-life-news/what-is-metadata-and-should-you-worry-if-yours-is-stored-by-law-20140806-100zae.html.

Gruner, R. S. 2005. *Corporate Criminal Liability and Prevention*. New York, USA: Law Journal Press.

Harding, R. 1998. 'Private Prisons in Australia: The Second Phase' *Trends & Issues in Crime and Criminal Justice* 84 April. Canberra: Australian Institute of Criminology.

Harper, G. & Chitty, C. 2005. *The Impact of Corrections on Reoffending: A Review of 'What Works'* (3rd edition). Home Office Research Study 291. London: Home Office.

Harris, R. 1997. *Early Intervention Prevention*. Paper Presented at the Paedophilia: Policy and Prevention Conference 14–15 April. Sydney, Canberra: Australian Institute of Criminology.

Hart, K. & Kritsonis, W. 2006. 'Critical Analysis of an Original Writing on Social Learning Theory: Imitation of Film-mediated Aggressive Models by: Albert Bandura, Dorothea Ross and Sheila A Ross' *National Forum of Applied Educational Research Journal* 20(3), 1–7.

Hartwell, S. 2004. 'Triple Stigma: Persons With Mental Illness and Substance Abuse Problems in the Criminal Justice System' *Criminal Justice Policy Review* 15(1), March, 84–99.

Hayward, K. J. & Young, J. 2004. 'Cultural Criminology: Some Notes on the Script' *Theoretical Criminology* 8(3), 259–273.

Healy, A. 1998. 'Illicit Drugs and Crime: Chicken and Egg?' *Mental Health Research Review* 5 May, 11–13.

Heidensohn, F. 1968. 'The Deviance of Women: A Critique and an Enquiry' *The British Journal of Sociology* 19(2), 160–175.

Heidensohn, F. 1996. *Women and Crime* (2nd edition). Basingstoke, UK: Macmillan.

Heidensohn, F. 2006. 'New Perspectives and Established Views' in Heidensohn, F. (ed.) *Gender and Justice: New Concepts and Approaches*, 1–10. Oxon, UK: Routledge.

Henderson, M. 2006. *Benchmarking Study of Home Detention Programs in Australia and New Zealand*. Melbourne: National Corrections Advisory Group.

Hepburn, S. & Simon, R. 2013. *Human Trafficking Around the World: Hidden in Plain Sight*. New York: Columbia University Press.

Herrnstein, R. & Murray, C. 1994. *The Bell Curve: Intelligence and Class Structure in American Life*. New York, USA: The Free Press.

Heseltine, K., Day, A. & Sarre, R. 2011. 'Prison-based Correctional Offender Rehabilitation Programs: The 2009 National Picture in Australia' *Research and Public Policy Series* 112. Canberra: Australian Institute of Criminology.

Hilton, A. & MacDonald, K. 2008, 9 December. 'Race as a Social Construct? No – and Yes!' *The Occidental Observer*. Accessed on 27 November 2016 at: www.theoccidentalobserver.net/2008/12/race-as-a-social-construct-no-%E2%80%94-and-yes/.

Hirschi, T. 1969. *Causes of Delinquency*. Berkley: University of California Press.

History on the Net. 2014. *Medieval Life – Crime and Punishment*. Accessed online on 8 November 2016 at: www.historyonthenet.com/medieval_life/crimeandpunishment.htm.

Hodgins, S. 1992. 'Mental Disorder, Intellectual Deficiency and Crime: Evidence from a Birth Cohort' *Archives of General Psychiatry* 49, 476–483.

Hogg, S. M. 2011. *The Level of Service Inventory (Ontario Revision) Scale Validation for Gender and Ethnicity: Addressing Reliability and Predictive Validity*. Thesis College of Graduate Studies and Research. Saskatoon, Canada: University of Saskatchewan.

Hollis-Peel, M. E., Reynald, D. M., van Bavel, M., Eiffers, H. & Welsh, B. C. 2011. 'Guardianship for Crime Prevention: A Critical Review of the Literature' *Crime, Law and Social Change* 56(1), 53–70.

Holmes, R. M. & Holmes, S. T. 2008. *Profiling Violent Crimes: An Investigative Tool* (4th edition). Thousand Oaks, California: Sage Publications Inc.

Home Office. 2013. 'Focus on: Violent Crime and Sexual Offences, 2011/12' Statistical Bulletin, Office for National Statistics. Accessed online on 31 October 2016 at: www.ons.gov.uk/ons/dcp171778_298904.pdf.

House of Commons. 2001. 'Elderly People – Fear and Risk of Crime' *Social and General Statistics* 16 May. London: House of Commons.

The Howard League. 2011. *Response to Breaking the Cycle: Effective Punishment, Rehabilitation and Sentencing of Offenders*. London, UK: The Howard League for Penal Reform.

Howells, K. & Day, A. 1999. 'The Rehabilitation of Offenders: International Perspectives Applied to Australian Correctional Systems' *Trends & Issues in Crime and Criminal Justice* 112 May. Canberra: Australian Institute of Criminology.

Hoyle, A. 2013, 5 December. 'Why Are So Many MEN Becoming Victims of Domestic Violence?' *Daily Mail*. Accessed online on 31 October 2016 at: www.dailymail.co.uk/femail/article-2518434/Why–Men-victims-domestic-violence-its-Britains-remaining-taboos-abuse-men-home-rise-html.

Hsieh, C. & Pugh, M. D. 1993. 'Poverty, Income, Inequality and Violent Crime: A Meta-analysis of Recent Aggregate Data Studies' *Criminal Justice Review* 18(2), Autumn, 182–202.

Huesmann, L. R. & Miller, L. S. 1994. 'Long-term Effects of Repeated Exposure to Media Violence in Childhood' in Huesmann, L. R. (ed.) *Aggressive Behaviour: Current Perspectives*, 153–186, New York, USA: Plenum Press.

Hull, L. 2013, 5 July. 'Fury as Venables Gets FOURTH New Identity as He Is Set for Early Release From Child Porn Sentence' *Daily Mail*. Accessed online on 7 November 2016 at: www.dailymail.co.uk/news/article-2356231/Jon-Venables-gets-FOURTH-new-identity-set-early-release-child-porn-sentence.html.

Hume, D. 1739/1958. *The Treatise of Human Nature* Selby-Bigge, L. A. (ed.) Oxford, UK: Oxford University Press.

IEP (Institute for Economics and Peace). 2012. 'US Peace Index 2012' Accessed online on 31 October 2016 at: http://economicsandpeace.org/wp-content/uploads/2015/06/2012-United-States-Peace-Index-Report_1.pdf.

IEP (Institute for Economics and Peace). 2013. 'UK Peace Index 2013' Accessed online on 31 October 2016 at: http://economicsandpeace.org/wp-content/uploads/2015/06/UK_Peace_Index_report_2013_0.pdf.

Illinois Department of Corrections. 2014. 'Stateville Correctional Center' Accessed online on 3 November 2016 at: https://www.illinois.gov/idoc/news/2016/Pages/StatevilleCorrectionalCenter'sFHouseofficiallyclosed.aspx.

Immarigeon, R. & Daly, K.1997. 'Restorative Justice: Origins, Practices, Contexts and Challenges' *Journal on Community Corrections* 8(2) August, 13–30.

Jansson, K. 2006. *British Crime Survey: Measuring Crime for 25 Years*. London: Home Office.

Johal, S., Napier, F., Britt-Compton, J. & Marshall, T. 2005. 'Mobile Phones and Driving' *Journal of Public Health* 27(1), 112–113.

Johnstone, J. W. C. 1983. 'Recruitment to a Youth Gang' *Youth and Society* 14, 281–300.

Jones, R., Masters, M., Griffiths, A. & Moulday, N. 2002. 'Culturally Relevant Assessment for Indigenous Offenders: A Literature Review' *Australian Psychologist* 37, 187–197.

Jorde, L. B. & Wooding, S. P. 2004. 'Genetic Variation, Classification and "Race"' *Nature Genetics* 36, 528–533.

Joudo Larsen, J. 2014. 'Restorative Justice in the Australian Criminal Justice' *System Research and Public Policy Series* 127. Canberra: Australian Institute of Criminology.

Kelling, G. L. 2015, 11 August. 'Don't Blame My Broken Windows Theory for Poor Policing' *Politico Magazine*. Accessed online on 31 October 2016 at: www.politico.com/magazine/story/2015/08/broken-windows-theory-poor-policing-ferguson-kelling-121268.

Kelling, G. L. & Coles, C. 1997. *Fixing Broken Windows: Restoring Order and Reducing Crime in Our Communities*. New York, USA: Touchstone.

Kelling, G. L. & Wilson, J. (1982). 'Broken Windows: The Police and Neighbourhood Safety' *Atlantic Monthly* March, 249(3), 29–38.

Kemshall, H., Holt, P., Baily, R. and Boswell G. 2004. 'Beyond Programmes: Organisational and cultural Issues of What Works' in G. Mair (ed). What Works and What Matters. Cullhompten: Willan.

Kenny, D., Seidler, K., Keogh, T. & Blaszczynski, A. 1999. *Clinical Characteristics of Australian Juvenile Offenders: Implications for Treatment*. Sydney, Australia: NSW Department for Juvenile Justice.

Kerin, L. & Herbert, B. 2010. 'Banning Police Pursuits Not the Answer' Australian Broadcasting Corporation. Accessed online on 31 October 2016 at: www.abc.net.au/news/2010-03-22/banning-police-pursuits-not-the-answer/375414.

Kessler, R. K., Burgess, A. W. & Douglas, J. E. 1992. *Sexual Homicide Patterns and Motives*. New York, USA: The Free Press.

Kitsuse, J. 1969. 'Societal Reactions to Deviant Behaviour: Problems of Theory and Method' *Social Problems* 17, 247–256.

Kitsuse, J. I. & Cicourel, A. V. 1963. A Note on the Uses of Official Statistics *Social Problems* 11 (2)Autumn, 131–139.

Korn, N. 2004. *Life Behind Bars: Conversations with Australian Male Inmates*. Sydney, Australia: New Holland Publishers.

Kostic, M. 2010. 'Victimology: A Contemporary Approach to Crime and Its Victims' *Law & Politics* 8(1), 65–78.

Krienert, J. L. 2003. 'Masculinity and Crime: A Quantitative Exploration of Messerschmidt's Hypothesis' *Electronic Journal of Sociology*. Accessed online on 30 November 2016 at: www.soc.iastate.edu/sapp/Masculinity2.Pdf.

Kuo, F. E. & Sullivan, W. C. 2001. 'Environment and Crime in the Inner City: Does Vegetation Reduce Crime?' *Environment & Behaviour* 33(3) May, 343–367.

Laccino, L. 2014, 29 January. 'Top 5 Countries With the Highest Rate of Rape' *International Business Times*. Accessed online on 31 October 2016 at: www.ibtimes.co.uk/top-5-countries-highest-rates-rape-1434355.

Laczko, F. 2002. 'Human Trafficking: The Need for Better Data' *The Online Journal of Migration and Policy*, 1 November. Accessed online on 25 November 2016 at: www.migrationpolicy.org/article/human-trafficking-need-better-data.

LaFree, G. & Dugan, L. 2004. 'How Does Studying Terrorism Compare to Studying Crime?' *Terrorism and Counter-terrorism: Criminological Perspectives Sociology of Crime, Law and Deviance* 5, 53–74.

LaFree, G., Dugan, L. & Miller, E. 2015. *Putting Terrorism in Context: Lessons From the Global Terrorism Database (Contemporary Terrorism Studies)*. New York, USA: Routledge Publishing.

Laming, W. H. 2003. *Victoria Climbié Inquiry Report*. Norwich, UK: HMSO Crown Publisher.

Law Library of Congress. 2015. 'Children's Rights: United Kingdom (England and Wales)' Accessed online on 31 October 2016 at: www.loc.gov/law/help/child-rights/uk.php.

Lawlink. 2009. 'Aboriginal Programs: Circle Sentencing' *Fact Sheet*. NSW Lawlink. Paramatta, Sydney: NSW Department of Justice and Attorney General.

Layton-MacKenzie, D. 2006. *What Works in Corrections: Reducing the Criminal Activities of Offenders and Delinquents*. Cambridge, UK: Cambridge University Press.

Lea, J. & Young, J. 1984. *What Is to Be Done About Law and Order?* Harmondsworth, UK: Penguin.

Ledwith, M. 2013, 13 December. 'Three Out of Four Benefit Cheats Are Not Prosecuted and Another 2,500 Are Spared Jail – Despite Taking More Than £10,000 Each' *Daily Mail*. Accessed online on 31 October 2016 at: www.dailymail.co.uk/news/article-2522979/Three-benefit-cheats-prosecuted.html.

Leins, C. 2015, 9 October. 'Sobering Stats for Domestic Violence Awareness Month' *US News*. Accessed online on 31 October 2016 at: www.usnews.com/news/blogs/data-mine/2015/10/09/sobering-stats-for-domestic-violence-awareness-month.

Levitt, M. 2013. 'Perceptions of Nature, Nurture and Behaviour' *Life, Sciences, Society and Politics* 9(13), 1–11.

Lincenberg, G. S. & Neuman, A. A. 2016, 25 August. 'United States: White-collar Crime Defence' *Global Investigations Review*. Accessed online on 31 October 2016 at: www.globalinvestigationsreview.com/insight/the-investigations-review-of-the-americas-2016/1024345/united-white-collar-crime-defence.

Lindesay, J. 1996. 'Elderly People and Crime' *Reviews in Clinical Gerontology* 6(2), 199–204.

Lipman, V. 2013, 25 April. 'The Disturbing Link Between Psychopathy and Leadership' *Forbes Magazine*. Accessed online on 31 October 2016 at: www.forbes.com/sites/victorlipman/2013/04/25/the-disturbing-link-between-psychopathy-and-leadership/.

Lipsey, M. W. 1995. 'What Do We Learn From 400 Research Studies on the Effectiveness of Treatment With Juvenile Delinquents?' in McGuire, J. (ed.) *What Works? Reducing Reoffending*, 63–78. New York, USA: John Wiley.

Lloyd, C., Mair, G. & Hough, M. 1994. 'Explaining Reconviction Rates: A Critical Analysis' *Home Office Statistical Bulletin* 6/97. London: Home Office.

Lombroso, C. 1876/1911. *Criminal Man* (5th edition) (translated by G. Ferrero). New York, USA: GP Putnam.

Lombroso, C. & Ferrero, G. 1895. *The Female Offender*. New York, USA: D Appleton & Company.

Lonsway, K. 2003. 'Tearing Down the Wall: Problems with Consistency, Validity and Adverse Impact of Agility Testing in Police Selection' *Police Quarterly* 6, 237–277.

Lovell-Hancox, R. 2013, 8 July. 'Worst Cases of Child Abuse' *The Telegraph*. Accessed online on 27 November 2016 at: www.telegraph.co.uk/news/uknews/baby-p/7527795/Ryan-Lovell-Hancox-worst-cases-of-child-abuse.html.

MacGregor, S. 2008. 'Sex Offender Treatment Programs: Effectiveness of Prison and Community Based Programs in Australia and New Zealand' *Research Brief* April. Indigenous Justice Clearinghouse, Sydney, NSW: NSW Attorney General's Department.

Machery, E. & Faucher, L. 2005. Social Construction and the Concept of Race *Philosophy of Science* 72 December, 1208–1219.

MacPhail, A. & Verdun-Jones, S. 2013. *Mental Illness and the Criminal Justice System*. Vancouver Canada: International Centre for Criminal Law Reform and Criminal Justice Policy.

Mallicoat, S.L. & Ireland, C. E. 2014. *Women and Crime: The Essentials*. Thousand Oaks, California: Sage Publications.

Mangalore, R. & Knapp, M. 2007. 'Cost of Schizophrenia in England' *The Journal of Mental Health Policy and Economics* 109, 23–41.

Marriott, L. 2016. 'Courts More Lenient on White Collar Criminals' Victoria University of Wellington. Accessed online on 31 October 2016 at: www.victoria.ac.nz/research/expertise/business-commerce/fraud-sentencing.

Marron, D. 2008. '"Alter Reality": Governing the Risk of Identity Theft' *British Journal of Criminology* 48, 20–38.

Marsh, I. 2004. *Criminal Justice: An Introduction to Philosophies Theories and Practice*. New York, NY, USA: Routledge.

Marsh, I., Melville, G., Morgan, K., Norris, G. & Cochrane, J. 2011. *Crime and Criminal Justice*. Oxon, UK: Routledge.

Marshall, T. 1999. *Restorative Justice: An Overview*. London, UK: Home Office Research Development and Statistics Directorate.

Martinson, R. 1974. 'What Works? – Questions and Answers About Prison Reform' *The Public Interest* 35 Spring, 22–54.

Martinson, R, 1979, 'New Findings, New Views: A Note of Caution Regarding the Sentencing Reform' *Hofstra Law Review* 7, 243–258.

Marx, G. 1981. 'Ironies of Social Control: Authorities as Contributors to Deviance Through Escalation, Non Enforcement and Covert Facilitation' *Social Problems* 28(3)February, 221–247.

Marx, K. 1857/1976. *A Contribution to the Critique of Political Economy*. Peking: Foreign Languages Press.

Marx, K. 1848/1977. 'The Communist Manifesto' in McLellan, D. (ed.) *Karl Marx Selected Writings* Oxford, UK: Oxford University Press.

Matthews, R. 2014. *Realist Criminology*. Basingstoke, Hampshire: Palgrave, Macmillan.

Matthews, R. & Young, J. (eds) 1986. *Confronting Crime*. London, UK: Sage.

Matthews, R. & Young, J. (eds) 1992. *Rethinking Criminology: The Realist Debate*. London, UK: Sage Publications.

Matza, D. 1964. *Delinquency and Drift*. New York, USA: John Wiley.

Maudsley, H. 1876. *Responsibility in Mental Disease*. London, UK: King & Co.

McAfee. 2014. 'Net Losses: Estimating the Global Cost of Cybercrime' Santa Clara, California: McAfee Intel Security. Accessed online on 31 October 2016 at: www.mcafee.com/uk/resources/reports/rp-economic-impact-cybercrime2.pdf.

McAllister, D., Holmes, R., Jones, G., Kara, F., Marin, A., Slarks, H., Wadham, J. & Wood, D. 2012. *Police-involved Deaths: The Need for Reform*. Vancouver, Canada: B C Civil Liberties Association.

McCreadie, S., Harland, K. & Beattie, K. 2006. 'Violent Victims? Young Men as Perpetrators and Victims of Violent Crime' *Centre for Young Men's Studies Research Update* No 1 January, 1–4.

McGrath, R. 2011. 'The RPU Officer, ANPR Operator, Road Death/Collision Investigator and AFO' in Pepper, I. K. (ed.) *Working in Policing*, 108–130. Exeter, UK: Learning Matters.

McGuire, J. 1995. *What Works: Reducing Reoffending: Guidelines for Research and Practice*. London: John Wiley & Sons.

McGuire, J. 2000. Can the Criminal Law Ever Be Therapeutic? *Behavioural Sciences and the Law* 18, 413–426.

McGuire, M. R. 2012. *Technology, Crime and Justice: The Question Concerning Technomia*. Abingdon, Oxon, UK: Routledge.

McGuire, M. R. & Dowling, S. 2013. 'Cybercrime: A Review of the Evidence' *Research Report* 75, October. London: Home Office.

McKay, S. 2015. *Covert Policing*. Oxford, UK: Oxford University Press.

Mead, G. H. 1934. *Mind, Self and Society*. Chicago, USA: University of Chicago Press.

Melamed, Y. 2010. 'Mentally Ill Persons Who Commit Crimes: Punishment or Treatment?' *The Journal of the American Academy of Psychiatry and the Law* 38, 100–103.

Mendelsohn, B. 1956. 'Une Novelle Branch de la Science Biopsycho-social: La Victimology' *Review International de Droit Penal et de Criminologie et de Police Technique 2*.

Merrick, J., Brady, B. & Youde, K. 2012, 8 January. 'Race in Britain 2012: Has Life Changed for Ethnic Minorities?' *The Independent*. Accessed online on 31 October at: www.independent.co.uk/news/uk/home-news/race-in-britain-2012-has-life-changed-for-ethnic-minorities-6286786.html.

Merton, R. K. 1938. 'Social Structure and Anomie' *American Sociological Review* 3(5) October, 672–682.

Merton, R. K. 1957. *Social Theory and Social Structure* (2nd edition). New York: The Free Press.

Messerschmidt, J. 1986. *Capitalism, Patriarchy and Crime: Towards a Socialist Feminist Criminology*. Totowa, USA: Rowman & Littlefield.

Messerschmidt, J. 1993. *Masculinities and Crime: Critique and Reconceptualisation of Theory*. Lanham, MD: Rowman & Littlefield.

Messerschmidt, J. 2000. 'Becoming "Real Men": Adolescent Masculinities Challenges and Sexual Violence' *Men & Masculinities* 2(3) January, 286–307.

Michael, S. E. & Hull, R. 1994 *Effects of Vegetation on Crime in Urban Parks*. Blacksburg, Virginia, USA: Virginia Polytechnic Institute and State University.

Michael, S. E., Hull, R. & Zahm, D. 2001. 'Environmental Factors Influencing Auto Burglary: A Case Study' *Environment and Behaviour* 33(3), 368–388.

Michaelsen, C. 2006. 'Balancing Civil Liberties Against National Security? A Critique of Counterterrorism Rhetoric' *University of New South Wales Law Journal* 29(2), 1–21.

Mitchell, A. 2014, 21 October. 'Australian 'Paradise' for White-collar Criminals, says ASIC Chairman Greg Medcraft' *Sydney Morning Herald*. Accessed online on 31 October 2016 at: www.smh.com.au/business/australia-paradise-for-whitecollar-criminals-says-asic-chairman-greg-medcraft-20141021-119d99.html.

Moffitt, T. E. 1993. 'Adolescence-limited and Life-course-persistent Antisocial Behaviour: A Developmental Taxonomy' *Psychological Review* 100, 674–701.

Monahan, J. & Steadman, H. 1983. 'Crime and Mental Illness: An Epidemiological Approach' in Morris, N. & Tonry, M. (eds) *Crime and Justice Vol 4*. Chicago, USA: University of Chicago Press.

Monahan, J. & Steadman, H. 1994. *Violence and Mental Disorder: Developments in Risk Assessment*. Chicago, USA: University of Chicago Press.

Monash University. 2016. 'Maintenance and Reliability Engineering: What are Academic Sources?' Accessed online on 31 October 2016 at: http://guides.lib.monash.edu/c.php?g=219722&p=1453814.

Morreale. August 19 2015. 'Hiding in Plain Sight: the Spiralling Cost of White-collar Crime' Comprehensive Financial Investigation Solution, Virginia, USA. Accessed online on 31 October 2016 at: www.aitcfis.com/2015/08/19/hiding-in-plain-sight-the-spiraling-cost-of-white-collar-crime/.

Mouzos, J. 1999. Mental Disorder & Homicide in Australia *Trends & Issues in Crime and Criminal Justice* 133 November, 1–6.

Murray, C. 1990. *The Emerging British Underclass*. London, UK: IEA Health and Welfare Unit.

Mutingh, L. 2005. 'Offender Rehabilitation and Reintegration: Taking the White Paper on Corrections Moving Forward' *Research Paper* No 10. Cape Town, South Africa: Civil Society Prison Reform Initiative.

Myhill, A. 2009. 'Community Engagement' in Fleming, J. & Wakefield, A. (eds) *The Sage Dictionary of Policing*, 26–27. Los Angeles, CA: Sage.

NAACP (National Association for the Advancement of Coloured People). 2016. 'Criminal Justice Fact Sheet' Accessed online on 31 October 2016 at: www.naacp.org/pages/criminal-justice-fact-sheet.

Nedim, U. 2014. 'How do Penalties for White Collar Crime and Security Fraud Compare?' Sydney Criminal Lawyers. Accessed online on 31 October 2016 at: www.sydneycriminallawyers.com.au/blog/how-do-penalties-for-white-collar-crime-and-social-security-fraud-compare/.

Newsday. 1991, 16 June. 'Successful PMS Defence in Virginia Case Revives Debate' Accessed online on 5 November 2016 at: http://articles.baltimoresun.com/1991-06-16/news/1991167033_1_pms-richter-defense.

NHS England. 2013. 'National Partnership Agreement for the Co-commissioning and Delivery of Healthcare Services in Prisons in England' National Health Service News. Accessed online on 31 October 2016 at: www.england.nhs.uk/2013/10/partner-prisons/.

NSPCC. 2013. 'Child Protection Registers Statistics – UK' *NSPCC Inform: The Online Child Protection Resource*. Accessed online on 27 November 2016 at: www.nspcc.org.uk/globalassets/documents/statistics-and-information/child-protection-register-statistics-england.pdf

NSPCC. 2016. 'Child Sexual Exploitation' Research and Resources. Accessed online on 31 October 2016 at: www.nspcc.org.uk/preventing-abuse/child-abuse-and-neglect/child-sexual-exploitation/research-and-resources/.

NSW Corrective Services. 2016. 'Explore the Opportunities' Corrective Services Industries (CSI). Accessed online on 31 October 2016 at: www.csi.nsw.gov.au/.

NSW Department of Justice. 2015. 'Care and Protection Cases' Children's Court website. Accessed online on 31 October 2016 at: www.childrenscourt.justice.nsw.gov.au/Pages/typesofcase/care_protection/care_protection.aspx.

NZ Department of Corrections. 2016. 'In the Community', 'Working with Offenders' Auckland, NZ. Accessed online on 31 October 2016 at: www.corrections.govt.nz/working_with_offenders/community_sentences.html.

NZ Ministry of Justice. 2002. *Youth Offending Strategy: Preventing and Reducing Offending and Re-offending by Children and Young People*. Wellington, NZ: Ministry of Justice and Ministry of Social Development.

NZ Ministry of Justice. 2008. *Conviction and Sentencing of Offenders in New Zealand: 1997 to 2006*. Wellington: New Zealand Ministry of Justice.

NZ Ministry of Justice. 2016a. 'Community Service' Accessed online on 27 November at: www.justice.govt.nz/assets/Documents/Publications/sentencing-1999.pdf

NZ Ministry of Justice. 2016b. 'Over Representation of Maori in Prison' Accessed online on 27 November 2016 at: www.hrc.co.nz/files/6314/3130/4434/HRC_submission_to_CAT_Final.pdf

O'Brien, M. 2005. 'What is Cultural about Cultural Criminology?' *British Journal of Criminology* 45(4), 599–612.

Office of the Correctional Investigator. 2013. 'Aboriginal Offenders – A Critical Situation' Accessed online on 31 October 2016 at: www.oci-bec.gc.ca/cnt/rpt/oth-aut/oth-aut20121022info-eng.aspx.

Office of the United Nations High Commissioner for Human Rights. n.d. 'Human Rights, Terrorism and Counter-terrorism, Fact Sheet no. 32' Geneva: OHCHR. Accessed online on 31 October 2016 at: www.ohchr.org/Documents/Publications/Factsheet32EN.pdf.

One in Three. 2015. 'Family Violence – Australia Says No!' One in Three Campaign. Accessed online on 31 October 2016 at: www.oneinthree.com.au/.

Packer, H. 1968. *The Limits of the Criminal Sanction*. Stanford: Stanford University Press.

Paul, J. 2003. *When Kids Kill*. London, UK: Virgin Books, Thames Wharf Studios.

Payne, B. K. 2012. *White-collar Crime: The Essentials*. Thousand Oaks, California: Sage Publications.

Peachy, P. 2015, 28 October. 'Human Trafficking: How a Charity Is Rescuing the Victims the Authorities Knew Nothing About' *The Independent*. Accessed online on 25 November 2016 at: www.independent.co.uk/news/uk/home-news/human-trafficking-how-a-charity-is-rescuing-the-victims-the-authorities-knew-nothing-about-a6712661.html.

Peck, J. & Coyle, M. 2005. *The Student's Guide to Writing, Spelling, Punctuation and Grammar* (2nd edition). Basingstoke, UK: Palgrave Macmillan.

Pepper, I. K. 2011. *Working in Policing*. Exeter, UK: Learning Matters Ltd.

Phelps, J. 2014, 2 August. 'Protecting Society's Scum: Inside Long Bay Jail Special Protection Unit and the Criminals It had to Save From Other Inmates' *Daily Telegraph*. Accessed online on 9 November 2016 at: www.dailytelegraph.com.au/news/nsw/protecting-societys-scum-inside-long-bay-jail-special-protection-unit-and-the-criminals-it-had-to-save-from-other-inmates/news-story/3680db9aa7fc17b4ad337cb4677a0f9b.

Phillips, C. & Bowling, B. 2003. 'Racism, Ethnicity and Criminology: Developing Minority Perspectives' *British Journal of Criminology* 43(2), 269–290.

Pollak, O. 1950. *The Criminality of Women*. Philadelphia, USA: University of Pennsylvania Press.

Potter, G. 2010. 'What is Green Criminology?' Accessed online on 27 November 2016 at: www.greencriminology.org/monthly/WhatIsGreenCriminology.pdf.

Prenzler, T. 2011. 'Welfare Fraud in Australia: Dimensions and Issues' *Trends & Issues in Crime and Criminal Justice* 421 June, 1–6.

Price, M. & Norris, D. M. 2009. 'White-collar Crime: Corporate Fraud and Securities and Commodities Fraud' *The Journal of the American Academy of Psychiatry and the Law* 37, 538–544.

Prichard, J. & Payne, J. 2005. 'Key Findings From the Drug Use Career of Juvenile Offenders Study' *Trends & Issues in Criminal Justice* 304 October. Canberra, Australia: Australian Institute of Criminology.

Prison Reform Trust. 2016. 'Private Sector Prisons' Projects and Research. Accessed online on 31 October 2016 at: http://www.prisonreformtrust.org.uk/projectsresearch/privatesectorprisons

Pritchard-Hughes, K. 1998. *Contemporary Australian Feminism 2*. Melbourne, Australia: Addison-Wesley Longman Pty Ltd.

Qualtieri, S. & Robinson, S. 2012. 'Social Investment in Children: Comparing the Benefits of Child Protection Early Intervention and Prevention Programs in Canada, Australia and the United Kingdom' *Canadian Social Work* 14(1), 27–52.

Quinney, R. 1970. *The Social Reality of Crime*. Boston, USA: Little Brown.

Quinney, R. 1977. *Class, State and Crime*. New York, USA: Longman.

Rafter, N. 2009. *The Origins of Criminology. A Reader*. New York, USA: Routledge.

Ramesh, R. 2010, 6 September. 'Substance Abuse, Not Mental Illness, Causes Violent Crime' *The Guardian*. Accessed online on 31 October 2016 at: www.theguardian.com/society/2010/sep/06/substance-abuse-mental-illness-crimes.

Ratcliffe, J. H. 2003. 'Intelligence-led Policing' *Trends & Issues in Crime and Criminal Justice* 248. Canberra: Australian Institute of Criminology.

Ratcliffe, J. H. 2016. *Intelligence-led Policing* (2nd edition). Oxon, UK: Routledge.

RCIADIC. 1991. *Royal Commission Into Aboriginal Deaths in Custody National Report: Overview and Recommendations*. Commissioner Elliott Johnson. Canberra, ACT: Australian Government Printing Services.

Reno, J., Marcus, D., Robinson, L., Brennan, N. & Travis, J. 2000. *Crime Scene Investigation: A Guide for Law Enforcement*. Washington DC: US Department of Justice Office of Justice Programs.

Richardson, N. 2005. 'Social Costs of Child Maltreatment' *Resources Sheet* Number 9, March. Melbourne, Australia: Australian Institute of Family Studies, National Child Protection Clearing House.

Roach Anleu, S. 1995. *Deviance, Conformity and Control* (2nd edition). Sydney, Australia: Longman Publishing.

Robinson, S. 1998. 'From Victim to Offender: Female Offenders of Child Sexual Abuse' *European Journal of Criminal Policy and Research* 6(1), 59–73.

Robinson, S. 2013. 'Promotional and Non-stereotypical Policing Roles: Are Women Opting Out?' *Salus Journal* 1(3), 1–12.

Robinson, S. 2015. 'Rethinking Recruitment in Policing in Australia: Can the Continued Use of Masculinised Tests and Pass Standards that Limit the Number of Women be Justified?' *Salus Journal* 3(2), 34–56.

Rogers, C., Lewis, R., John, T. & Read, T. 2011. *Police Work: Principles and Practice*. Abingdon, Oxon, UK: Routledge.

Rollings, K. & Taylor, N. 2008. Measuring Police Performance in Domestic Violence and Family Violence *Trends & Issues in Crime and Criminal Justice* 367. Canberra: Australian Institute of Criminology.

Ronken, C. & Johnston, H. 2012. *Child Sexual Assault: Facts and Statistics* December. Arundel, Queensland: Bravehearts.

Rosenfeld, R. 2004. 'Terrorism and Criminology' in Deflem, M. (ed.) *Terrorism and Counter-terrorism: Criminological Perspectives*, 19–32. Oxford, UK: Elsevier Ltd.

Roush, D. 1996. 'Desktop Guide to Good Juvenile Detention Practice' *Research Report* October. National Juvenile Detention Association. Michigan, USA: Centre for Research and Professional Development Michigan State University.

Rowe, M. 2014. *Introduction to Policing* (2nd edition). London, UK: Sage Publications.

Ruane, J. 2005. *Essentials of Research Methods: A Guide to Social Science Research*. Malden, MA: Blackwell Publishing.

Ruggiero, V. & South, N. 2010. 'Green Criminology and Dirty Collar Crime' *Critical Criminology* 18, 251–262.

Ruggiero, V. & South, N. 2013. 'Toxic State-corporate Crimes, Neo-liberalism and Green Criminology: The Hazards and Legacies of the Oil, Chemical and Mineral Industries' *International Journal for Crime Justice and Social Democracy* 2(2), 12–26.

Saar, M.S., Epstein, R., Rosenthal, L., & Vafa, Y. 2015. The Sexual Abuse to Prison Pipeline: The Girl's Story. Washington, D.C.: Georgetown University Law Centre.

Safer Society. 2007. *Do Children Sexually Abuse Other Children?: Preventing Sexual Abuse Among Children and Youth*. Brandon, VT, USA: The Safer Society Press.

Sampson, R. J. & Laub, J. H. 1993. *Crime in the Making: Pathways and Turning Points Through Life*. Cambridge, Massachusetts: Harvard University Press.

Sampson, R. J. & Laub, J. H. 2005. 'A Life-course View of the Development of Crime' *Annals of the American Academy of Political and Social Sciences* 602, 12–45.

Sampson R.J. & Wilson, W.J. 1995. 'Toward a Theory of Race, Crime and Urban Inequality', in Hagan, J. & Peterson, J. (eds). Crime and Inequality. Stanford: Stanford University Press.

Saraga, E. 2011. 'Dangerous Places: The Family as a Site of Crime' in Muncie, J. & McLaughlin, E. (eds) *The Problem of Crime* Chapter 5, 190–237. London, UK: Sage Publications.

Sarantankos, S. 2012. *Social Research* (4th edition). Basingstoke: Palgrave Macmillan.

Sarre, R. 1984. 'The Orwellian Connection: A Comment on Recent Correctional Reform Literature' *Canadian Criminology Forum* 6(2), 177–188.

Savage, J. 2004. 'Does Viewing Violent Media Really Cause Criminal Violence? A Methodological Review' *Aggression and Violent Behaviour* 35, 1123–1136.

Scheffler, R., Wallace, N., Hu, The-Wei., Bloom, J. & Garrett, B. 1998. 'The Effects of Decentralisation on Mental Health Service Costs in California' *Mental Health Research Review* 5 May, 31–32.

Schroeder, H. W. & Anderson, L. M. 1984. Perception of Personal Safety in Urban Recreation Sites *Journal of Leisure Research* 16, 178–194.

Schur, E. 1971. *Labelling Deviant Behaviour*. New York, USA: Harper & Row.

Seymour, A. 2001. 'Restorative Justice/Community Justice' in *National Victim Assistance Academy Textbook*. Washington DC, USA: National Victim Assistance Academy.

Shaw, C. R. & McKay, H. D. 1942. *Juvenile Delinquency in Urban Areas*. Chicago, Illinois: University of Chicago Press.

Shaw, J., Hunt, I., Flynn, S., Meehan, J., Robinson, J., Bickley, H., Parsons, R., McCann, K., Burns, J., Amos, T., Kapur, N. & Appleby, L. 2006. 'Rates of Mental Disorder in People Convicted of Homicide' *British Journal of Psychiatry* 188, 137–147.

Sheldon, B. 2011. 'The Investigation Evolves' in Pepper, I. (ed.) *Working in Policing* Chapter 4. Exeter, UK: Learning Matters Ltd.

Sherman, T. 2005 *Pathways to Juvenile Detention Reform: Detention Reform and Girls: Challenges and Solutions*. Baltimore, USA: Annie E Casey Foundation.

Sheth, H, C, 2009, 'Deinstitutionalisation or Disowning Responsibility' *International Journal of Psychosocial Rehabilitation* 13(2), 11–20.

Schiraldi, V. 2016, 26 February. 'How to Reduce Crime: Stop Charging Children as Adults' *New York Times*. Accessed online on 31 October 2016 at: www.nytimes.com/2016/02/26/opinion/how-to-reduce-crime-stop-charging-children-as-adults. html?_r=0

Siegel, L. 2006. *Criminology* (10th edition). Lowell, USA: Thomson Wadsworth.

Silmalis, L. 2014, 15 February. 'How Luke Batty's Father Descended Into a Deadly Madness' *Herald Sun*. Accessed online on 7 November 2016 at: www.heraldsun.com.au/news/law-order/how-luke-battys-father-descended-into-a-deadly-madness/story-fni0ffnk-1226828297392.

Simon, R. 1975. *The Contemporary Woman and Crime*. Washington DC, USA: Government Printing Office.

Skinner, B. F. 1963. 'Operant Behaviour' *American Psychologist* 18(8), 503–515.

Skinns, L. 2011. *Police Custody: Governance, Legitimacy and Reform in the Criminal Justice System*. Oxon, UK: Willan Publishing.

Smart, C. 1976. *Women, Crime and Criminology: A Feminist Critique*. London, UK: Routledge & Kegan Paul.

Smith, C. & Allen, J. 2004. *Violent Crime in England and Wales*. Home Office Online Report 18/04. London, UK: Home Office Research, Development and Statistics Directorate.

Spector, M. & Kitsuse, J. I. 1977. *Constructing Social Problems*. Menlo Park, California: Cummings.

Spencer, H. 1857. 'Progress: Its Law and Causes' *The Westminster Review* 67 April, 445–465.

Spivakovsky, C. 2013. *Racialized Correctional Governance: The Mutual Constructions of Race and Criminal Justice*. Surrey: Ashgate.

Stark, R. 1987. 'Deviant Places: A Theory of the Ecology of Crime' *Criminology* 25(4), 893–909.

Stathopoulos, M. 2014. 'The Exception That Proves the Rule: Female Sex Offending and the Gendered Nature of Sexual Violence' *ACSSA Summary*. Melbourne: Australian Centre for the Study of Sexual Assault, Australian Institute of Family Studies.

Steadman, H. & Naples, M. 2005. 'Assessing the Effectiveness of Jail Diversion Programs for Persons With Serious Mental Illness and Co-occurring Substance Use Disorders' *Behavioural Sciences and the Law* 23, 163–170.

Steffensmeier, D. 2003. 'Gender and Crime: Toward a Gendered Theory of Female Offending' *Annual Review of Sociology* 22(1), 459–487.

Stephenson, M. 2005. *Unlocking Learning, Rethinking Crime and Punishment* February. London, UK: Esmée Fairbairn Foundation.

Stern, J. & Berger, J. M. 2015. *ISIS: The State of Terror*. London, UK: William Collins.

Sternberg, R. J., Grigorenko, E. L. & Kidd, K. K. 2005. 'Intelligence, Race and Genetics' *American Psychologist* 60(1), 46–59.

Stevenson, B. 2011. *Drug Policy, Criminal Justice and Mass Imprisonment* Working Paper prepared for the First Meeting of the Commission Geneva 24–25 January. Washington DC: Global Commission on Drug Policies.

Stewart, A., Dennison, S. & Waterson, E. 2002. 'Pathways From Child Maltreatment to Juvenile Offending' *Trends & Issues in Crime and Criminal Justice* 241 October, 1–6.

Stohr, M. & Walsh, A. 2012. *Corrections: The Essentials*. Thousand Oaks, California: Sage Publications.

Stolzenberg, L., Eitle, D. & D'Alessio, S. J. 2006. 'Race, Economic Inequality and Violent Crime' *Journal of Criminal Justice* 34, 303–316.

Stout, B., Yates, J. & Williams, B. 2008. *Applied Criminology*. London, UK: Sage.

Strayer, D. L., Drews, F. A. & Crouch, D. J. 2006. 'A Comparison of the Cell Phone Driver and the Drunk Driver' *Human Factors* 48(2) Summer, 381–391.

Stroud, B. 1977. *Hume: The Arguments of the Philosophers* (edited by Ted Honderich). London, UK: Routledge & Kegan Paul Ltd.

Stuart, H. 2003. 'Violence and Mental Illness: An Overview' *Mental Health Policy Paper* June. Ontario, Canada: Department of Community Health and Epidemiology.

Subramanian, R. & Shames, A. 2013. *Sentencing and Prison Practices in Germany and the Netherlands: Implications for the United States*. New York: VERA Institute of Justice.

Sutherland, E. 1939. *Principles of Criminology*. Chicago, Philadelphia: J.B. Lippincott Company.

Sutherland, E. 1940. 'White Collar Criminality' *American Sociological Review* (1), 1–12.

Sykes, G. & Matza, D. 1957. 'Techniques of Neutralisation: A Theory of Delinquency' *American Sociological Review* 22, 664–670.

Talbat, J. & Kaplan, R. 1984. 'Needs and Fears: The Response to Trees and Nature in the Inner City' *Journal of Arboriculture* 10, 222–228.

Tannenbaum, F. 1938. *Crime and Community*. London & New York: Columbia University Press.

Taxman, F. 2002. 'Supervision - Exploring the Dimensions of Effectiveness'. Federal Probation, 66(2), 14–27.

Taylor, I., Walton, P. & Young, J. 1973. *New Criminology: For a Social Theory of Deviance*. London, UK: Routledge & Kegan Paul.

Taylor, S. 2016. *Crime and Criminality: A Multidisciplinary Approach*. Oxon, UK: Routledge.

Thornberry, E. 2014. 'Labour's Britain: Ending White Collar Crime' Fabian Society 29 September. Accessed online on 31 October 2016 at: www.fabians.org.uk/labours-britain-ending-white-collar-crime/.

Tierney, J. 1996. *Criminology: Theory and Context*. London, UK: Harvester Wheatsheaf.

Tilley, N. 2003. 'Community Policing, Problem-oriented Policing and Intelligence-led Policing, in Newburn, T. (ed.) *Handbook of Policing* 311–339. Devon: Willan Publishing.

Tilley, N. 2010. 'Whither Problem-oriented Policing' *Criminology & Public Policy* 9, 183–195.

Torrey, E. 1994. 'Violent Behaviour by Individuals with Serious Mental Illness' *Hospital and Community Psychiatry* 45, 653–662.

Travis, A. 2015, 12 February. '1.4 Million Women Suffered Domestic Abuse Last Year, ONS Figures' *The Guardian*. Accessed online on 27 November 2016 at: www.theguardian.com/society/2015/feb/12/14-million-women-suffered-domestic-abuse-last-year-ons-figures-show.

Troy, A., Morgan Grove, J. & O'Neill-Dunne, J. 2012. 'The Relationship between Tree Canopy and Crime Rates Across an Urban-rural Gradient in the Greater Baltimore Region' *Landscape and Urban Planning* 106(3) June, 262–270.

Turk, A. 1969. *Criminality and Legal Order*. Chicago, USA: Rand McNally.

UK Crown Prosecution Service. 2016. 'Bail' Legal Guidance. Accessed online on 31 October 2016 at: www.cps.gov.uk/legal/a_to_c/bail/.

UK Parole Board. 2016. 'Getting Parole' Accessed online on 31 October 2016 at: www.gov.uk/getting-parole.

UK Social Exclusion Unit. 2004. *Tackling Social Exclusion: Taking Stock and Looking to the Future*. London, UK: Office of the Deputy Prime Minister.

United Nations. 1985. *Declaration of Basic Principles of Justice for Victims of Crime and Abuse of Power. Annex A 1 & 2*. Accessed online on 7 November 2016 at: www.un.org/documents/ga/res/40/a40r034.htm.

United Nations. 1993. 'Declaration on the Elimination of Violence Against Women' December. Accessed online on 31 October 2016 at: www.un.org/documents/ga/res/48/a48r104.htm.

United Nations. 2000. 'Protocol to Prevent, Suppress and Punish Trafficking in Persons' Accessed online on 31 October 2016 at: www.osce.org/odihr/19223?download=true.

United Nations. 2015. 'Facts and Figures: Ending Violence against Women. Various Forms of Violence' United Nations Women. Accessed online on 31 October 2016 at: www.unwomen.org/en/what-we-do/ending-violence-against-women/facts-and-figures.

University of Illinois. 2016. 'Evaluating Internet Sources' University Library. Accessed online on 31 October 2016 at: www.library.illinois.edu/ugl/howdoi/webeval.html.

US Department of Health & Human Services, April 18 1979, The Belmont Report, The National Commission for the Protection of Human Subjects of Biomedical and Behavioral Research. Accessed online on 17 January 2017 at: https://www.hhs.gov/ohrp/regulations-and-policy/belmont-report/

University of Melbourne. 2016. 'What About Violence Against Men?' Melbourne Research Alliance to End Violence Against Women and Their Children. Accessed online at: http://maeve.unimelb.edu.au/research/what-about-violence-against-men

Vandiver, D. M. & Walker, J. T. 2002. 'Female Sex Offenders: An Overview and Analysis of 40 Cases' Criminal Justice Review 27, 284–300.

van Wormer, K. & Walker, L. 2013. Restorative Justice Today: Practical Applications. Thousand Oaks, California: Sage Publications.

Victim Support. 2013. 'About Us. Accessed online on 31 October 2016 at: www.victimsupport.org.uk/about-us.

Victim Support & Make Justice Work. 2012. Out in the Open: What Victims Really Think About Community Sentencing September. London, UK: Victim Support & Make Justice Work.

Vold, G. 1958. Theoretical Criminology. New York, USA: Oxford University Press.

Wakem, B. & McGee, D. 2012. Investigation of the Department of Corrections in Relation to the Provision, Access and Availability of Prisoner Health Services. Wellington, New Zealand: Ombudsman Service.

Walklate, S. 2001. Gender, Crime and Criminal Justice. Cullompton, Devon, UK: Willan Publishing.

Wall, D. 2001. Crime and the Internet. London, UK: Routledge.

Walsh, E., Moran, P., Scott, C., McKenzie, K., Burns, T., Creed, F., Tyrer, P., Murray, R. & Fahy, T. 2003. 'Prevalence of Violent Victimisation in Severe Mental Illness' The British Journal of Psychiatry 183, 233–238.

Walshe, S. 2012, 27 April. 'Probation and Parole: A Study in Criminal Justice Dysfunction' The Guardian. Accessed online on 31 October 2016 at: www.theguardian.com/commentisfree/cifamerica/2012/apr/26/probation-parole-study-dysfunction.

Ward, T. & Stewart, C. 2003. 'Criminogenic Needs and Human Needs: A Theoretical Critique' Psychology, Crime & Law 9(2), 125–143.

Warren, R. K. 2007. Evidence-based Practice to Reduce Recidivism: Implications for State Judiciaries. Washington DC: U.S. Department of Justice, National Institute of Corrections.

Wathen, N. 2012. Health Impacts of Violent Victimisation on Women and Their Children. Ottawa, Canada: Department of Justice Canada, Research and Statistics Division.

Watling, C. N. & Leal, N. L. 2012. Exploring Perceived Legitimacy of Traffic Law Enforcement Paper presented at the ACRS National Conference 9–10 August. Menzies Sydney Hotel, Sydney, NSW.

WCSAP (Washington Coalition of Sexual Assault Programs). 2016. 'Understanding Sexual Assault: How Often does it Happen?' Accessed online on 31 October 2016 at: www.wcsap.org/how-often-does-it-happen.

Webber, C. 2007. 'Background, Foreground, Foresight: The Third Dimension of Cultural Criminology?' Crime, Media, Culture 3(2), 139–157.

Weber, M. 1905/2002. The Protestant Ethic and the Spirit of Capitalism (translated and edited by Peter Baehr & Gordon Wells). New York: Penguin Books.

Welch, 2004. Corrections: A Critical Approach (2nd edition). Boston: McGraw-Hill.

White, R. 2002. 'Understanding Youth Gangs' Trends & Issues in Crime and Criminal Justice 237 August, 1–6. Canberra, Australia: Australian Institute of Criminology.

White, R. 2007. Environmental Harm, Ecological Justice and Crime Prevention: The Challenge to Criminology. Paper presented to the Improving Community Safety: Lessons from the Country and the City Conference at the Jupiters Hotel, Townsville, Queensland, Australia 18–19 October. Canberra: Australian Institute of Criminology.

White, R. 2008. 'Environmental Harm and Crime Prevention' Trends & Issues in Crime and Criminal Justice 360 June. Canberra: Australian Institute of Criminology.

White, R. & Graham, H. 2015. 'Greening Justice: Examining the Interfaces of Criminal, Social and Ecological Justice' British Journal of Criminology 3 February, 1–21.

WHO (World Health Organization). 2007a. 'The International Classification of Diseases Version 10' Accessed online on 31 October at: www.who.int/classifications/apps/icd/icd10online/

WHO (World Health Organization). 2007b. Health in Prisons: A WHO Guide to Essentials in Prison Health. Copenhagen: WHO Europe.

WHO (World Health Organization). 2016. 'Violence Against Women: Intimate Partner and Sexual Violence Against Women' Fact Sheet No 239 January. Accessed online on 31 October at: www.who.int/mediacentre/factsheets/fs239/en/.

Wilkinson, P. 2006. 'Terrorism' in Gill, M. (ed.) The Handbook of Security. Basingstoke, UK: Palgrave Macmillan.

Williams, P. 2001. 'Deaths in Custody: 10 Years on From the Royal Commission' *Trends & Issues in Crime and Criminal Justice* 203 April, 1–6.

Williams, P. 2011. 'The Custody Suite' in Pepper, I. K. (ed.) *Working in Policing*, 131–150. Exeter: Learning Matters Ltd.

Williams, P., Walton, K. & Hannan-Jones, M. T. 2009. 'Prison Foodservice in Australia: Systems, Menus and Inmate Attitudes' *Journal of Foodservice* 20(4), 167–180.

Wilson, J. Q. & Herrnstein, R. 1985. *Crime and Human Nature*. New York, USA: Simon and Schuster.

Wincup, E., Buckland, G. & Bayliss, R. 2003. 'Youth Homelessness and Substance Abuse: Report to the Drugs and Alcohol Research Unit' *Home Office Research Study* 258. London, UK: Development and Statistics Directorate Home Office.

Wolfe, K. L. 2010. 'Crime and Fear: A Literature Review' in *Green Cities: Good Health*. Washington: College of the Environment, Washington University.

Wolfe, M. & Mennis, J. 2012. 'Does Vegetation Encourage or Suppress Urban Crime? Evidence from Philadelphia, PA' *Landscape and Urban Planning* November–December 108(2), 112–122.

Wordes, M. & Nunez, M. 2002. *Our Vulnerable Teenagers: Their Victimization, Its Consequences, and Directions for Prevention and Intervention*. May Oakland, California: National Council on Crime and Delinquency.

Wortley, S. 1999. 'A Northern Taboo: Research on Race, Crime, and Criminal Justice in Canada' *Canadian Journal of Criminology* 41, 261–274.

Wright, M. 2008. *Making Good: Prisons, Punishment and Beyond*. Hampshire, UK: Waterside Press.

Wroe, D. 2015, 29 March. '2500 Metadata 'Cops' to Search Phone and Internet Records' *The Sydney Morning Herald*. Accessed online on 31 October at: www.smh.com.au/federal-politics/political-news/2500-metadata-cops-to-search-phone-and-internet-records-20150327/-1m9e0a.html.

Wyatt, T., Beirne, P. & South, N. 2014. 'Green Criminology Matters' *International Journal for Crime, Justice and Social Democracy* 3(2), 1–4.

Yale Center for Teaching and Learning. 2015. 'Scholarly vs Popular Sources' Accessed online on 31 October 2016 at: http://ctl.yale.edu/writing/using-sources/scholarly-vs-popular-sources.

Young, J. 1988. 'Radical Criminology in Britain' *British Journal of Criminology* 28, 159–183.

Young, J. 2003. 'Merton With Energy; Katz With Structure: The Sociology of Vindictiveness and the Criminology of Transgression' *Theoretical Criminology* 7(3), 389–414.

Zehr, H. 2002. *The Little Book of Restorative Justice*. Intercourse, PA: Good Books.

Zimbardo, P. 2007. *The Lucifer Effect: Understanding How Good People Turn Evil*. New York: Random House.

Index